FAILING JUSTICE

Charles Evans Whittaker
on the Supreme Court

FAILING JUSTICE

Charles Evans Whittaker on the Supreme Court

CRAIG ALAN SMITH

McFarland & Company, Inc., Publishers

Jefferson, North Carolina, and London

What a shame it would be to fail, but how much
more the shame to fail even earnestly to try.
—Charles Evans Whittaker

LIBRARY OF CONGRESS CATALOGUING-IN-PUBLICATION DATA

Smith, Craig Alan, 1964–
  Failing justice : Charles Evans Whittaker on the Supreme Court /
Craig Alan Smith.
    p.   cm.
  Includes bibliographical references and indexes.

  ISBN 0-7864-2197-5 (softcover : 50# alkaline paper) ∞

  1. Whittaker, Charles Evans, 1901–1973.   2. Judges—United
States—Biography.   3. United States. Supreme Court—Biography.
I. Title.
KF8745.W53S63   2005
347.73'2634—dc22   2005012769

British Library cataloguing data are available

On the cover: Charles Evans Whittaker
(photograph courtesy Kent Whittaker)

Manufactured in the United States of America

McFarland & Company, Inc., Publishers
  Box 611, Jefferson, North Carolina 28640
  www.mcfarlandpub.com

Acknowledgments

This book would not have been possible without the generous assistance of certain individuals who agreed to be interviewed and who provided valuable written and photographic resources. I am especially grateful to members of Charles Whittaker's family who shared their recollections and their homes with me, including his sons Dr. C. Keith Whittaker and Gary Whittaker, and his sisters Dorothy Kiehnhoff and Hazel Ruhnke. Charles Whittaker's personal papers are in the possession of his son, Kent E. Whittaker, an attorney in Kansas City, Missouri, who made his office available to me for study. I wish to extend a personal note of gratitude to Kent for making those papers available, for sharing his recollections, and for reading parts of the manuscript and offering useful suggestions.

I am grateful to members of Charles Whittaker's former law firm who provided both interviews and documentation, including John Foard, Colvin Peterson, Vincent Rawson, and Charles Thompson. I also wish to thank other former associates who shared their recollections with me, including Russell Baker, Celia Barrett, Darrell Havener, Robert Donnellan, James Duncan, George Haydon, and Louis Poplinger. Particularly helpful were interviews with U. S. District Court Judge Joseph E. Stevens, Jr., and Mabel Gunn, two long-time friends of Charles and Winifred Whittaker. Other useful interviews were conducted with Charles Whittaker's niece, Norma Jean Parrot, U. S. District Court Judge Thomas Vanbebber, and Ilus Davis. In addition, useful materials were offered by Don Harter, Darrel Stufflebeam, and Professor Patrick Kelly (University of Missouri-Kansas City).

Since Charles Whittaker's personal papers included no materials from his federal court service, I relied upon the recollections of his former law clerks. I wish to extend my gratitude to Clyde Rayburn, Jr., who provided useful information on Whittaker's district and appeals court service. For valuable information on Whittaker's Supreme Court service, I wish to thank James Adler, U. S. Circuit Court Judge William Canby, Professor Kenneth Dam (University of Chicago), Heywood Davis, James Edwards, Alan Kohn, Jerome Libin, and Patrick McCartan. I also wish to thank other former Supreme Court law clerks who served during Whittaker's terms for sharing their recollections, including William Allen, U. S. Circuit Court Judge Richard Arnold, Paul Bender, Murry Bring, U. S. Circuit Court Judge Guido Calebresi, Jerome Cohen, Peter Ehrenhaft, John French, Professor Charles Fried (Harvard), Roderick Hills, Professor Bernard Jacob (Hofstra), Thomas Klitgaard, Jim Knox, Nathan Lewin, Dennis Lyons, Professor John McNulty (University of California), Charles Miller, U. S. Circuit Court Judge John Newman, William Powell, Dan Rezneck, Henry Sailer, and Professor Terrance Sandalow (University of Michigan). Several of these gentlemen agreed to interviews on the condition that their words received no attribution. Respecting their wishes, at times references are made simply to "clerk, interview" or "clerk, correspondence."

I wish to acknowledge the assistance of those institutions that aided materially in my research, including the Kansas State Historical Society, the Lawyers Association of Kansas City, the Leon E. Bloch Law Library at the University of Missouri-Kansas City, the Missouri Bar, the Missouri Valley Special Collections of the Kansas City Public Library, the National Archives, the Supreme Court Historical Society, the Tarlton Law Library at the University of Texas at Austin, the United States Supreme Court, and the University of Missouri-Kansas City Archives.

Finally, I am grateful to members of the faculty at the University of Missouri-Kansas City who encouraged and sustained me through the writing of this book. Professors Lawrence Larsen and David Atkinson were the chief advocates for this project and provided continuous support throughout its completion. Professors Dale Neuman, William Worley, and Louis Potts all read the text and offered beneficial suggestions. Of course, any errors of fact or interpretation are mine alone.

Contents

Preface

In the first two hundred years' history of the Supreme Court, Charles Evans Whittaker merited three distinctions. First, he was the only Missourian and the first native Kansan appointed to the Court; second, he was one of only two justices to serve at both the federal district and appeals court levels before ascending to the Supreme Court; and third, Court historians routinely rated him a "failure" as a justice. These distinctions were compelling enough in the summer of 1995 to convince me to pursue Charles Whittaker as a subject of study. I first encountered the name Charles Whittaker as I browsed through a book by Kansas City historian George Green entitled *A Condensed History of Kansas City Area: Its Mayors and Some VIPs*. Inserted toward the end of the book just after a brief mention of Missouri's notable president, Harry S Truman, was Charles Whittaker, associate justice of the Supreme Court. What followed was an overview of Whittaker's career path to the Supreme Court and his associations with various legal and community groups in Kansas City. Interested to learn more about this relatively obscure local VIP, I discovered quickly that a new federal courthouse for Kansas City had recently been named in his honor (at the time there was just a great hole in the ground of the building site). Otherwise, there was a dearth of substantive information about him, and what little had been written was so harsh in its criticism, so unforgiving in its assessment of his performance, that Whittaker as a justice seemed perpetually cast aside as one of the worst mistakes in Supreme Court history.

Certainly Charles Whittaker appears as an entry in any historical reference work on Supreme Court members, but because of his short tenure (1957–1962) he should rightfully be considered what David Atkinson termed

1

a "minor" justice. Not that his role on the Court was any less significant than
other members, but he had the misfortune of serving on the Court when it
did not produce many lasting changes in American constitutional law. Whittaker was not assigned any landmark decisions to write, nor did he write separately often, and at the time of his appointment he did not exceed any
member of the Court in repute or public recognition. That does not necessarily make him an unsuitable subject for study, however, for as Atkinson has
noted, "Anyone who sits on the Court has achieved a distinction far beyond
the grasp of most people."[1] The study of "minor" Supreme Court justices,
Atkinson has argued, can give us different insights into the Court as an institution and can offer new perspectives on the lives of its "major" justices.

The harshness of critiques against Whittaker's judicial service offers
another compelling reason for examining his work. Beginning with Leon
Friedman's biographical sketch in a collection of historical essays about the
lives of the justices, subsequent authors seemed determined to discredit anything associated with Whittaker. Friedman found that Whittaker "was not
fitted intellectually or physically for the job."[2] Bernard Schwartz considered
Whittaker "the worst justice of the century" and also "the dumbest Justice
ever appointed."[3] Relying on Friedman and Schwartz, Victoria Woeste then
concluded, "Whittaker was in every way unsuited for his exalted position."[4]
Once criticism of Whittaker as a justice was let loose, it seemed there was no
turning back. His reputation was forever heaped with scorn and ridicule.
What was missing from these accounts, though, was any kind of balance—
a fair assessment of his abilities or a recognition of the disabling condition
that led to his difficulties.

In order to find some balance that could place Whittaker's Court service in a more realistic light, I sought out primary sources that Whittaker's
critics had neglected. Instead of reading the handful of decisions that other
authors mentioned as notable or relying on Henry Abraham's preposterous
assertion that Whittaker authored only eight majority opinions,[5] I read all
of his Supreme Court and lower court opinions and found that some of those
overlooked by others still continue to serve as worthwhile precedents. I spoke
with members of his old law firm and local lawyers and judges who knew
him personally before and after he went to the Supreme Court. I interviewed
dozens of former law clerks who worked for Whittaker or other justices during the time he served. Most significant, though, I spent considerable time
speaking with his family and had unrestricted access to his private papers.
With this wealth of new information I realized that earlier bitter condem-
nations of Whittaker's judicial service actually gave a distorted, incomplete
view of his abilities, his difficulties, and his performance. I also noticed that
in different accounts certain episodes of his story became grossly inaccurate.
Finding accuracy within Whittaker's tale became one of my primary objec-
tives.

Just a few examples of the kinds of falsehoods promulgated about Whittaker should suffice. Following his nomination to the Supreme Court, *Time* magazine reported that Whittaker quit attending high school in Troy, Kansas, before graduating "because the six-mile trip on horseback was too long" and that he attended law school for "five hectic years."[6] Whittaker actually quit school because he fell into a deep depression over his mother's death, and he attended the Kansas City School of Law the required four years. In their appraisal of Supreme Court greatness, Professors Albert Blaustein and Roy Mersky claimed that Whittaker was an "ex–Kansas City politician" and "attorney of little note."[7] The evidence shows, however, that Whittaker never ran for elective office (save in the Missouri Bar, a professional association which hardly had a popular constituency), and he was one of the most successful, well-known and respected lawyers in the state. The *Kansas City Star* newspaper reported at the time of Whittaker's district court appointment that he had tried cases before the United States Supreme Court. Nearly fifty years later author Richard Miller unquestioningly relied on the *Star's* account.[8] In truth, Whittaker applied for admission to the Supreme Court bar as the quickest route to get a case heard before the California Court of Appeals. No one at his old law firm remembered him going to Washington except to pay the twenty-five dollar fee.[9] Two final examples include author Henry Abraham, who claimed that Whittaker became a district judge for the U. S. District Court for Kansas, and author Robert Steamer, who asserted that Whittaker retired from the Supreme Court after serving there for only three years.[10] Such patently false statements were all the more shocking because public records made them easily verifiable. Whittaker was a district judge for the Western District of Missouri, and he served on the Supreme Court exactly five years. Considering these relatively minor details were mistakenly reported, my suspicions grew about the reasonableness of his "failure" rating and the severity of his critics' claims. As I gathered and weighed my material, I discovered that Whittaker was not as awful on the Court as he had been portrayed, and that he suffered difficulties few of his critics realized.

Finally, I feel compelled to comment upon the work of three authors who merit special recognition because their writing focused exclusively on Whittaker as a subject. First, one of Whittaker's own law clerks, Alan Kohn, has written two fine short pieces about Whittaker that offer more balance than other references due to Kohn's personal association with the justice. In our interview together, Mr. Kohn was somewhat more forthright in his recollections than in his later "Reminiscence," although his published account offered many more details.[11] Second, a graduate student, Judith Cole, has written a comprehensive master's thesis detailing Whittaker's advancement through the three levels of the federal judiciary. Her work, while notable because she had the opportunity to interview Whittaker personally for it, was deficient as a biography for two reasons: first, since Whittaker was still living few of the other participants in the study were willing to speak on-the-record about their experiences, so too much relevant information was left out; and, second, Cole overlooked some available published sources and committed minor factual errors.[12]

The third author I wish to address, Richard Miller, has written what passes as a biography of Charles Whittaker when really it serves more as a polemic from which Miller can express his own political views. Relying on those authors who initially were so unforgiving in their appraisals, Miller presented a portrait of the justice that more than justified what critics had said all along. Instead of looking for balance or examining the context within which events occurred, Miller lambasted Whittaker with such unbridled shrillness that Whittaker was denigrated into a kind of caricature. As a result, Miller unwittingly presented an embarrassingly large number of material errors in his account. Much more damaging to Miller's professional reputation, though, than a perceived personal vendetta against Whittaker was Miller's over-reliance on my original source materials. Rather than conduct his own original research, Miller freely introduced into his text (at times without giving proper credit for their source) materials found exclusively in my work.[13] The resulting work, in my opinion, hardly bore up to a level of acceptable scholarship.

The present work began then as an inquiry into an obscure subject who presumably deserved closer scrutiny because of the high rank he achieved within the legal community. As I read and reviewed all of the then extant literature dealing even marginally with Whittaker, I discovered that as a justice he was held in the lowest esteem. If he was mentioned at all in historical accounts, it was usually with derision. The two previous attempts at a biographical story proved deficient and for different reasons were somewhat skewed. Cole's account, while not written explicitly as a biography, suffered from the propriety of discretion while writing about a subject still living, and Miller's version had a decidedly cynical stamp to it. The details of Whittaker's accomplishments, depending upon the source, were often inconsistent or plainly at odds with more reliable archival records. I soon realized that a complete, accurate portrait and a fair assessment of Whittaker's difficulties as well as his achievements was warranted. Far from being a "failure," Charles Whittaker was a victim of his own success. Suffering intense personal feelings of loss, inferiority, and self-doubt, he still persevered to rise to the top of the federal judiciary. Any denigration of his performance as a justice should be tempered with a fair amount of sympathy for what he endured.

1

Leaving the Farm

Born on George Washington's birthday, February 22, 1901, in a rustic Kansas farmhouse partly built of logs, Charles Whittaker never could completely turn his back on his modest, rural origins no matter how he tried. He was a Midwesterner who grew up on a farm at the beginning of the twentieth century, and, like most young men who sought their opportunities amid the noise and commotion of America's larger cities, Whittaker left his father's farm as soon as he was old enough and able, returning occasionally only to impress his family with his new success. Whittaker's dream, developed in his youth, was to become a great trial lawyer. Working on his father's farm, he learned the virtues of persistence, determination, and sacrifice. He took those attributes with him to law school where he excelled in the art of oratory. Fearless and undaunted, Whittaker possessed a love of language and a knack for speaking in front of other people. The law school he attended, however, was not as highly regarded as other more prestigious schools in the Midwest. Whittaker had no choice but to attend a part-time "night" law school because he failed to qualify for the minimum entrance requirements of any full-time "day" school. Therefore, his legal education, like his humble Kansas upbringing, carried the potential for embarrassment if he ever ventured beyond the comfortable confines of the Midwest.

Doniphan County, Kansas, where Whittaker spent his youth, was first settled in 1837 by white Presbyterian missionaries from Pennsylvania. They came to minister to the Native Americans who were relocated there from the east. When seventeen years later Whittaker's grandfather, John H. Whittaker, emigrated from Pennsylvania with his family to the same area, family lore told of him purchasing the original family settlement from the Native

5

Americans living there.[1] More likely, though, he arrived in 1854 when the Native Americans by treaty relinquished their claims on the land so it could become part of Kansas Territory. Situated in the northeast corner of the state bordering Nebraska and Missouri, Doniphan County is surrounded on its northern and eastern sides by the Missouri River. Still one of the smallest counties in the state, Doniphan contains rolling prairie in the west where corn, wheat, and oats are grown, but the eastern portion along the Missouri River is rougher, made of more hills and bluffs where once heavy bodies of timber grew. One of the original counties organized by the first territorial legislature in 1855, Doniphan was named in honor of General Alexander W. Doniphan, a Missourian who led an expedition of forces from Missouri to New Mexico during the war with Mexico. By the start of the twentieth century, Doniphan County had three different rail lines crossing it, the Rock Island, Burlington, and Union Pacific, making it a main trade route. The county seat, Troy, where the Whittaker family purchased supplies, achieved some wealth early in the twentieth century by cultivating apple orchards. A large apple-packing cooperative thrived there, about 10,000 acres, until the start of World War II when a sudden, drastic change in temperature destroyed the industry. Located six miles north of the Whittaker's farm, Troy, Kansas, saw the Pony Express ride past in April 1860 and heard in December 1859 Abraham Lincoln speak on the day before John Brown was hanged at Harpers Ferry, Virginia.[2]

Whittaker's father, Charles Edward, came to possess the family farm when he purchased from his six siblings the inheritance left by their father. When Whittaker's grandfather, John, who acquired the land at the opening of Kansas Territory, died in 1877, he left 240 acres to his wife, Mary, and their seven children. By 1900, following Mary's death, the youngest of the seven heirs, Charles Edward, had borrowed $6,100 to buy from his brothers and sisters the remainder of their father's property, plus another $500 to purchase an additional forty acres for use as school property.[3] Brush Creek School, where Charles Whittaker received his formal education, was situated on his father's land about a quarter of a mile west of their home. This one-room schoolhouse contained anywhere from thirty-five to fifty children annually ranging in age between five and twenty years old. Whittaker's father served as the treasurer of the school, which employed a different female teacher each year that Whittaker attended. County records indicated that the school remained segregated (there was a separate school in nearby Troy for "colored" children), and the school year lasted from early January until late June.[4] Whittaker's first teacher, Mary O'Brien (Willmeth), who boarded with the Whittaker family the year she taught, later recalled that Whittaker had been a bright and alert pupil. She also made sure that he and his brother, Samuel, did not dally on the way to school, following close behind them as they trekked the quarter mile together from farmhouse to schoolhouse.[5]

In April 1895 Whittaker's father married Ida Eve Miller, a schoolteacher originally from Hagerstown, Maryland. Their first child together, a girl named Nely Bly, died at the age of five of scarlet fever. Their next two children, both boys, grew up working on the farm together. The oldest, Samuel, followed in his father's footsteps and continued to farm the family property as an adult. The second son, christened Charles Edgar Whittaker,[6] later changed his middle name to Evans and left farming behind to become a lawyer. Whittaker also had two younger sisters. The first, Dorothy, has remembered how her two older brothers pulled her along between them on their way to school together. The youngest, Hazel, arrived much later, beginning school about the time her two older brothers were starting their own lives. Just before Hazel was born, Whittaker's father replaced the original farmhouse with a new two-story home, the first in the county to have electricity or plumbing.[7]

Even before Charles Whittaker realized he wanted to become a lawyer, he was developing those skills that made him such a formidable opponent in the courtroom. Possessing some natural talent and little inhibition, Whittaker gained a reputation as a public speaker, reciting humorous monologues during local Saturday evening literary society programs and acting as auctioneer at frequent box suppers. Since Brush Creek School served as both church and community center, Whittaker's performances were known to most of the folks in the area. The probate and county judge in Troy, William Strahan, recalled that Whittaker had "the most remarkable memory of anyone I ever knew and a natural gift for oratory."[8] When he was not at school, working at the chores on his father's farm occupied most of Whittaker's waking hours—there was just no end to the labor—preventing him from taking a more active interest in schoolwork. According to his sister, Dorothy, Whittaker and his brother, Samuel, "used walking cultivators and plowed corn when they were so young one couldn't see their heads above the corn." That did not stop Whittaker from developing his speaking skills, though. Dorothy also has remembered, "We had a horse and a mule, Mike and Molly, and Charley talked to them in the field, practicing projecting his voice."[9] His brother, Samuel, who worked alongside Whittaker, recalled how Whittaker stood on the plow and spoke to the horses as they made their endless passes across the fields of corn, wheat, and lespedeza. Becoming a farmer like the rest of his family, however, was never in Whittaker's plans, and one day while shocking oats with his brother Whittaker wiped his perspiring forehead and said he would find another way to earn a living.

Whittaker's interest in the law initially began during trips with his father to Troy where his father purchased supplies and Whittaker visited the district court. A murder trial in St. Joseph, Missouri, a town fourteen miles to the east, when he was fifteen years old then prompted Whittaker to want to become a lawyer. Oscar D. McDaniel, the Buchanan county prosecutor, was

accused of murdering his wife, Harriett, after he returned home one night
and found her fatally beaten. The local press thoroughly covered the trial,
which lasted seventeen days, and in the end, although he was acquitted, the
sensation of the trial cost McDaniel his bid for re-election. "I never forgot
that case," Whittaker later remarked, "From that time on, I knew I was going
to be a lawyer. My mind was made up. I started reading everything I could
find about great trials and famous lawyers."[10]

Before Whittaker could consider law school, though, his ambitions
endured several obstacles and one serious setback. His father, a director at
the First National Bank in Troy, did not want him to study law. He preferred
that his sons worked at farming or banking, and he was prepared to assist
them in those endeavors. Once Whittaker's older brother, Samuel, finished
high school their parents planned to move the family into Troy, leaving
Samuel in charge of farming their property. Whittaker might have had the
same opportunity, and for a time he did consider going into farming with
his brother; once he made up his mind to become a lawyer, though, nothing
could shake his determination. He had to save his own money for law school
because his father was either unwilling or unable to support that interest,
and the most practical means of making money was trapping small animals
and selling their pelts. "They brought me about three dollars each," Whittaker once said of the skunks he caught in his trap line, "but they didn't
improve my popularity at school. Teachers sent me home several times to
change my clothes."[11]

In order to gain acceptance at even a part-time law school, Whittaker
needed the equivalent of a high school education, so after nine grades at
Brush Creek School he began attending the segregated high school in Troy,
riding a pony the six miles there and back. After only one and a half years,
though, Whittaker quit high school. His mother, who had suffered kidney
problems, died unexpectedly on his sixteenth birthday.[12] Her death devastated him, and he sank into a deep depression, unable to return to school
and unconcerned for his own future. For the next three years Whittaker lived
at the family farm with Samuel and his new wife, working steadily. His father
moved to Troy with his two younger sisters; Dorothy, being ten years older,
then became like a mother to Hazel. Eventually Whittaker's father moved to
St. Joseph to be nearer to his new companion, Emma Brock, who owned a
boarding house there, but they never married. After that, Whittaker stopped
visiting his family altogether.[13] He worked tirelessly, doing odd jobs when
not in the fields, intent on one purpose—to leave farming and go to law
school. When he had $700 saved he left home for good and moved to Kansas
City.

Kansas City, Missouri, was a bustling town of almost 325,000 people
when Charles Whittaker arrived there in the summer of 1920, and it was
about as far away from his family's farm as he could afford to go—financially

or emotionally. Intent on becoming a lawyer, he enrolled in classes at the Kansas City (K. C.) School of Law, a part-time or "night" law school that rented rooms on the fifth floor of the Nonquitt building at 1013 Grand Avenue in downtown Kansas City. With no high school diploma or college credit, it was impossible for Whittaker to attend any of the regular, full-time law schools in the area, so necessity alone determined his choice of a part-time law school.[14] Lacking even the minimum year of high school English course work required for admission, Whittaker's acceptance at the K. C. School of Law was contingent on him attending high school classes at the same time. He must have made a persuasive appeal and a favorable impression, pleading his case directly to Oliver Dean, president of the school, for admission. "My admission was agreed to on my assurance I would complete my final two years of high school," Whittaker later explained, "I enrolled in a part-time course at Manual High School at the same time I started to law school."[15]

To earn the money needed for law school—and to be closer to lawyers—Whittaker went to work full-time as an office boy in the law offices of Watson, Gage and Ess, located one block to the north of the law school in the Temple building on Grand Avenue. He was also able to supplement his income from collecting on unpaid medical accounts left to him from a family relative, Dr. Hugh Miller, who practiced in Kansas City. His schedule left little time for other interests or activities. Six days a week from eight in the morning until he left for school Whittaker worked in the Watson law offices; three of those days he attended law school from four in the afternoon until ten at night, and the other three days from three until six he took classes at Manual High School. Whittaker must have completed his studies late into the night or under the tutelage of Watson associates (one of them was an instructor at the law school), being able to withstand the rigors of such an active schedule.[16]

By the time Whittaker enrolled, the K. C. School of Law had been in operation for a quarter of a century. Prior to its founding, there were only two other law schools operating in Missouri, Washington University in St. Louis and the University of Missouri in Columbia, both full-time, three-year programs. The founding of the K. C. School of Law was part of a larger drive across the country during the 1890s to open more part-time law schools once the main barrier to their expansion—a college affiliation—was overcome.[17] Three law students, Everett Ellison, Elmer Powell, and William Boreland, became the catalyst for the K. C. School of Law when they organized in 1893 a law students club, attracting about a dozen members. Each of these students was studying law in the office of an experienced lawyer, still the only way of preparing for the bar exam in cities without a law school program, but they felt the need for a more systematic and regular course of study. Although previous attempts at founding a law school in Kansas City had failed, in 1895 the Jackson County Circuit Court chartered the K. C. School of Law as a non-profit corporation under the eleemosynary laws of the state of Missouri. A two-year program was established leading to an LL.B. degree, and the only requirement for admission was the equivalent of a high school English course. Twelve lawyers, all active in the legal profession, constituted the first faculty. Except for those who attended to the management of the school, none of the faculty initially received compensation. Operating on a shoestring budget, tuition started at fifty dollars a year. The first class, beginning with fifty-seven students, graduated twenty-seven, including the first woman graduate.[18]

During the four years that Whittaker attended (1920–1924), the K. C. School of Law underwent several significant changes. Seven years after its establishment, the law school expanded its program of study from two to three years. Then in Whittaker's freshman year the program of study increased to four years, making the K. C. School of Law the only part-time school in the state to require four years of study. The students who enrolled one year ahead of Whittaker were the last to complete their degrees in three years, resulting in no graduating class of 1923. During their junior year, Whittaker and his classmates enjoyed the status of being the only upperclassmen, putting together the school yearbook two years in a row. Not until a decade after Whittaker graduated did the Missouri legislature require that all part-time law schools provide at least four years of study.

One result of lengthening the program of study was that new courses had to be added and several others modified. For example, courses in Roman Law, Damages, Guaranty and Suretyship, Workmen's Compensation, Mines and Mining (covering oil and gas), Conflict of Laws, International Law, and Federal Jurisdiction and Procedure were all added to the curriculum; Sales, Bailments and Carriers was divided into two subjects, and Insurance was extended from four to fifteen weeks.[19] To some extent these changes in the school's curriculum reflected the shifting emphasis in American law to address the needs of a more regulatory state. Expanding the program of study to four years also put the K. C. School of Law on a more equal footing with the state's full-time law schools, but the kind of instruction used at each still remained disparate. While Missouri's full-time law schools developed a system of instruction based on the casebook method, part-time law schools continued to follow the textbook method of instruction. Using Socratic-like questioning, the casebook method discovered principles of law by examining appellate court decisions. The textbook method, on the other hand, relied principally on lectures and rote memorization of legal principles. This was how Charles Whittaker first understood the law, as a closed, reliable, and rigid system to be learned, repeated, and followed.

Another significant change taking place at the K. C. School of Law during Whittaker's attendance there was the dramatic increase in the numbers of students and faculty. In the decade following World War I the school went through a period of substantial growth. Attendance figures showed over a seven-year period enrollment increases of over 400 percent, and by 1928 attendance at the K. C. School of Law exceeded the combined totals of all three of Missouri's full-time law schools.[20] In fact, there were so many freshmen enrolled the year Whittaker graduated—a record 367—that the class had to be divided into two groups for lectures. Normally a large number of Freshmen dropped out of the program due to financial or academic difficulties, but that year 155 quit after so much confusion was created during the first three lectures. Thereafter the school took greater care selecting students to limit the number enrolling each year. These enrollment increases necessitated the hiring of more instructors, and with increases in tuition the school could afford to start paying its faculty.[21]

To meet the needs of its growing student enrollment, the K. C. School of Law had to expand its classroom facilities. During Whittaker's freshman year the school occupied the entire fifth floor of the Nonquitt building on a five year lease. Before the five years was up, though, the school was cramped for space, so in 1925 school officials made a down payment on a building of their own at 913 Baltimore Avenue.[22] Part of the expansion process was to make room for the school's newly acquired library holdings. Unlike students at other part-time law schools, the students at the K. C. School of Law always had available to them a vast number of law books, even before the school came by its own collection. They used the Kansas City Law Library, incorporated in 1871, which contained between twelve and fifteen thousand volumes by the turn of the century. Then in 1919 the president of the K.C. School of Law, Oliver Dean, contributed a set of *Missouri Reports* for the school to start its own library. That same year the school also received donations of books from Wash Adams, a Kansas City judge, and from the family of the late federal District Judge John Finis Philips, who contributed their entire law collections. In order to hold its new library the graduating class of 1919 built bookcases in the school's quiz room. Just three years later the Kansas City Bar made its library available to law students every evening and Saturday afternoons.[23] Compared to other part-time law schools, the K. C. School of Law possessed considerable resources and offered as comprehensive a course of study as any full-time program.

All of the changes taking place at the K. C. School of Law in such a short period of time, the new curriculum, increased enrollments, and changing facilities, must have been a heady experience for Charles Whittaker. These changes also distinguished the K. C. School of Law among other part-time law schools in the region. Taking the lead, the K. C. School of Law went to a four-year program of study at a time when Missouri law did not require a minimum period of study for law students.[24] When Missouri finally did make two years of college course work a requirement for admission to full-time law schools in 1934, the K. C. School of Law became the only part-time law

The Kansas City School of Law at 913 Baltimore Avenue. Later incorporated first
by the University of Kansas City and then by the University of Missouri–Kansas
City, the Kansas City School of Law at the time of Whittaker's attendance had
more students and required more study than any of the full-time law schools in
the state. As a forerunner of part-time legal education, the school was nevertheless subjected to harsh scrutiny by eastern law elites. (Photograph courtesy of
Kansas City Public Library Special Collections)

school in the state to make the same requirement. Within a few years a small
day program started at the school, and the American Bar Association (ABA)
gave it a provisional first-class rating. The school finally gained a college connection in 1938, merging with the new University of Kansas City and becoming that university's first professional school. Then in 1963 the University of
Kansas City merged with the University of Missouri, and the law school
became part of the state university system.

Although the K. C. School of Law was on an equal footing in many
respects with some of the full-time law schools in the region, during Whittaker's attendance the fact remained that it was still a part-time law school,
meaning it was despised by much of the legal community outside of Kansas
City. Despite the claims of its supporters that the school was actually in the
forefront of legal education in America, those who taught in full-time law

schools and elite members of the bar considered part-time law schools an aberration. According to Lawrence Larsen, the K. C. School of Law appeared "an ugly duckling" compared to other urban law schools in Missouri because it lacked a full-time faculty and other attributes usually associated with comprehensive universities. Its students were older than the national average for law schools; most of them were businessmen or well-known citizens of Kansas City who were not intent on pursuing a career in law.[25] Elite members of the legal community called into question the reputation of anyone who attended a part-time law school and doubted whether a part-time education adequately prepared someone like Whittaker for the practice of law. To make matters worse, the four years Whittaker spent at law school coincided with the ABA's efforts to bring part-time legal education into such disrepute that the existence of part-time law schools was threatened.

The debate over the desirability of part-time legal education had its antecedents in the decades before Charles Whittaker enrolled at the K. C. School of Law, when part-time law schools first started competing with full-time schools for students. By the beginning of the twentieth century the number of law schools in America had increased dramatically, led by substantial increases in part-time law schools. By the time Whittaker enrolled in the K. C. School of Law, part-time law schools were nearly as numerous as full-time ones, but they contained substantially more students.[26] The reason for this lay in their relatively inexpensive tuition compared to full-time schools. Members of the ABA and Association of American Law Schools (AALS), representing elite members of the bar and full-time law schools, looked on this with suspicion. Full-time law schools were no longer confident they could compete with the lower tuition of part-time schools without lowering their own standards. With their pre-eminence threatened, many law professors and elite members of the bar began to openly criticize part-time legal education, sparking an internal debate over the utility of part-time schools.[27]

Raging in the pages of law reviews during the first three decades of the twentieth century, the debate over the quality of part-time legal education had both its detractors and its defenders. Critics claimed that part-time law schools, because they lacked a college affiliation, could not offer resources comparable to full-time schools, notably regular faculty members and adequate facilities, especially law libraries. Rather than academics, part-time law schools employed working lawyers and judges as temporary lecturers. Critics also believed that students who attended part-time schools would be too weary to sufficiently complete their studies because they worked during the day, making them inferior to full-time students who had the requisite leisure time for their studies. The alleged deficiencies of part-time, or "night" law schools were so widely circulated in American law reviews around the time that Whittaker attended law school that defenders of part-time legal education made a concerted effort to legitimize it.[28] The critics persisted, however, and about the time that Whittaker arrived in Kansas City a new effort was underway to eliminate part-time law schools for good.

In 1921 the ABA and AALS directed a national effort to impose unity on all law schools, thereby halting the proliferation of part-time schools. The ABA requested that the Carnegie Foundation conduct a study of all law schools in the hope of closing down part-time schools.[29] That study, conducted by Alfred Z. Reed, *Training for the Public Profession of Law* (1921), catapulted part-time legal education into the national spotlight. No longer was the sufficiency of part-time law schools debated; at issue was their survival.

The Reed Report, as it come to be known, sounded the clarion call for the abolition of part-time law schools; at least, that was what the leaders of the ABA heard. Reed found in his study that part-time law schools were "merely cheapened copies of the regular full-time model," and they had done "more harm than good to legal education." Because of the competition for students, full-time schools suffered by lowering their own standards, and, worse still, part-time law schools damaged lawyers' reputations by allowing less-qualified applicants to pass bar examinations.[30] Although it did not lead to the wholesale closings of part-time law schools, the Reed Report gave the ABA and AALS justification to publicly denounce part-time legal education in their drive to impose uniform standards on all law schools. The debate over the value of part-time legal education continued unabated another decade as part-time law schools attempted to vindicate themselves by raising their standards. The damage had been done, though. The Reed Report forever cast a suspicious eye on the quality of part-time law schools. The continuing debate over the sufficiency of part-time legal education lent credence to the belief that those trained in part-time law schools were not as well qualified to join the ranks of practicing lawyers. It was during the apex of this controversy over the quality of part-time legal education that Charles Whittaker passed through the K. C. School of Law. Even if he had possessed the means to afford a full-time education, Whittaker had no choice but to attend a part-time law school because of his deficient high school preparation. It mattered little that promoters of the K. C. School of Law considered it in the forefront of legal education; Charles Whittaker carried the stigma of an inferior, part-time legal education for the rest of his life.

The first two years he went to law school Whittaker lived at the Young Men's Christian Association (YMCA) in downtown Kansas City, located at the corner of Tenth and Oak Streets. This was actually the second YMCA building in Kansas City; the first one, located one block to the north at Ninth and Locust was destroyed before the turn of the century. Built on the site of the original YMCA is the new federal courthouse in Kansas City, named in honor of Charles Evans Whittaker.[31] Ironically, it was when Whittaker applied to law school that he first started using the name Charles "Evans" Whittaker.

Since no one in Kansas City had any reason to doubt he knew his own name, his new identity stuck. Years later, Whittaker's children teased him about the name change, claiming it had never been legal. When asked about the name change, his son, Kent, explained, "Charles Evans Hughes had been on the Supreme Court—at least was well-known. He just liked the way it sounded."[32] Undoubtedly Whittaker sought to give every appearance of becoming a great lawyer—even his name had to sound like one.

To more fully immerse himself in the life of the law, after his second year at law school Whittaker moved out of the YMCA building and spent his last two years living at the Phi Alpha Delta law fraternity. There he met Russell Gunn, who became Whittaker's life-long friend, and although they shared similar backgrounds growing up on farms the two of them seldom discussed plowing corn. "On winter nights, we often sat before the wood burning fireplace in the living room," Gunn later recalled, "sometimes talking about the law, sometimes quoting verses of poetry such as 'Man Without a Country' ... and sometimes [Thomas] Gray's 'Elegy Written in a Country Churchyard.'"[33] Serving as the law fraternity's treasurer for two years, Whittaker assumed a position of authority within that organization. During their senior year together, Whittaker and Gunn conspired to keep a freshman student named Harry S Truman from joining their fraternity. Truman, then thirty-nine years old, had become dissatisfied serving as a Jackson County court judge, so his friend, future District and then Appeals Court Judge Albert Ridge, another law student one year behind Whittaker, convinced Truman to go to law school. Prevented from joining the law fraternity, Truman attended the K. C. School of Law just two years without graduating.[34]

Whittaker did all that he could in law school to immerse himself in the study of law; in fact, it seemed to others that he did little else. One of his former classmates, William McAdams, remembered how Whittaker "never had any fun.... As a matter of fact when we were going to school the average student ... kicked the gong around pretty good but while everyone else was having fun, Charlie was studying law.... He was serious, very serious."[35] With his heavy schedule—working at the law offices, taking high school classes, and going to law school in the evenings—Whittaker had little time left for more sociable activities. Not that he desired recreation; from his youth he had learned the values of hard work and perseverance, and at law school he had to devote considerable time and energy just to keep up with his studies. Although he passed the Missouri bar examination in the fall of his senior year, Whittaker graduated with eighty other law students without receiving any special academic or extracurricular recognition. He was not among the five honored graduates in the class of 1924. An average student, Whittaker worked harder than most just to get through four years of part-time legal instruction.[36] He loved it, though, the pace, the work, the opportunity to become part of a legal fraternity, and he loved to discuss it. Garrulous by nature and uninhibited in conversation, Whittaker discussed (or debated) fine legal points with his friend, Russell Gunn, long after their fraternity brothers left the dinner table. The topic of these duologues usually involved some matter Whittaker had encountered that day at the law office. Whenever Whittaker tried to dominate the conversation around the dinner table, as he often did later in life, other members of the fraternity became impatient with his obsession for legal minutia. "There were those among the members," Gunn later recalled, "who would level sly barbs at the justice for bringing problems home from the office."[37]

The textbook method of training used at most part-time law schools required students to use rote memorization to learn legal principles, which were then applied in simulations during mock trials held at school. Whittaker was fascinated with the logical discourse of these legal principles, and he preferred to discuss them over more practical topics. While others may have enjoyed a respite from their studies to discuss world events, national politics, or the latest pastime, Whittaker lost himself in the language of law. It became his passion and only form of expression. This obsession with the language of law led Whittaker to memorize long passages from legal opinions just as he memorized legal principles at school. Fascinated with words, their meaning, their sound, their arrangement, Whittaker loved to recite these passages, especially ones he considered full of emotional or intellectual force. "He was interested in fine legal logic and reasoning," a contemporary wrote, "and equally interested in seeing such fine legal logic and reasoning expressed in beautiful language."[38] One of the cases Whittaker memorized as a young man, *Meredith v. Krauthoff*, involved the custody of a young boy whose parents had divorced. The mother made it difficult for the father to visit, and, when the mother tried to prejudice the boy against the father, he sued for custody. Whittaker became intrigued not so much by the plight of the parties involved or by the ruling in the case (the father was awarded custody), but by the language used in the opinion. A passage from the opening paragraph of the opinion offers a good example of the kind of language Whittaker recited "with fine oratorical effect and considerable emotion."

>...It is an unwelcome task, fraught with heavy responsibility. In its performance, however careful and sympathetic we may be, we must walk with heavy tread into the very sanctum sanctorum of parental affection, and, laying hands upon the jewel there enshrined, make such disposition of it as, in our finite wisdom, its best interest may seem to require. It is a painful duty, from which every well-regulated mind must shrink, since its performance has to do, not only with the tender relations of parent and child, but involves the future course of a human life, and perhaps may have influence upon the destiny of an immortal soul. One thought, however, affords some slight comfort, and that is that we are in no way responsible for the causes which have unhappily brought about the situation with which we are con-

fronted. We are called upon to act, the heavy obligation is laid upon us, and we have no choice but to meet it. Let those whose hearts are wrung remember this when, in their pain and tears, they realize the effect of this decree.

Despite his rural upbringing, his lack of high school preparation, or his tendency to dominate the conversation, Whittaker achieved a certain popularity at law school because of his public speaking skills. Each year the editors of the school's yearbook regularly mentioned the one activity most often associated with Whittaker at law school—making speeches. During his freshman year when he was still relatively unknown Whittaker campaigned for class officer, and, even though he lost in the election, his presentation left an impression on the upperclassmen who heard it. Subtly mocking his modest background, they wrote, "Fresh from K. U., Whittaker reeled off a line of flowered campaign talk that would do justice to an angel." That same year Whittaker's position as an office boy at the law firm of Watson, Gage and Ess received an ironic gibe as the editors penned next to his picture in the yearbook, "Of the firm of Whittaker, Watson, Gage and Ess."[39] Whittaker would, in fact, join the Watson firm as an associate soon after graduating law school, and while his name would never precede Watson's in the firm's title it did in time follow Ess's as Whittaker climbed the ranks of one of the largest, most successful law firms in Kansas City.

The opportunities for Whittaker to participate in public speaking at law school ranged from intramural debates to classroom presentations, and even though he approached the lectern with earnestness, his classmates found mirth in his unrestrained flamboyance. During Whittaker's sophomore year there was a revival of debating between the classes. These debates became so popular among the students, in fact, that by the time Whittaker graduated the school's dean, Edward Ellison, noted approvingly, "The students evidenced a great deal of interest in this work and in my opinion we should make a special point of debating."[40] To choose the members of their debate teams, each class held open auditions, allowing students to speak extemporaneously on a chosen topic. Certain of his own prospects for selection, Whittaker entertained the judges by delivering "an impromptu talk on himself—a worthy subject to be sure," and, according to the yearbook, he "would doubtless have been successful, had the listeners stifled their convulsions."[41]

On other occasions Whittaker argued cases in front of his peers during mock trials where he had an opportunity to role-play his ideal of a courtroom advocate. Of course, even in a routine injury case Whittaker argued so forcefully that his classmates chaffed at his bravado. One contemporary recorded in the school yearbook a parody of how different students might address a jury based on the positions they assumed when reciting in class. Whittaker, the author continued, "rests his left hand upon the desk, raises his right hand as if to begin, 'Friends, Romans, Countrymen!' knots his brow, clears his throat, and replies: '*Usque ad orcum, usque ad caelum, damnum adsque injuria*' [As far below as the eternal regions, as far above as the sky, damage without wrong]."[42] Despite the good-natured ribbing he received from his classmates, Whittaker's passion for public speaking earned him the title "class orator" next to his picture in the yearbook.

A popular student at law school, Whittaker was often the object of harmless teasing by his classmates who found his singular devotion to studying and his grandiose speech-making a bit overboard. Not content to eke out his living on a clerk's salary, Whittaker intended to make his name—and his fortune—as a lawyer. Having earned every dollar for law school on his own, Whittaker was proud of his self-sufficiency and determined to climb past his own place in the social order. Attending a part-time, "night" law school did not quell his ambition to become part of the class of legal elites. At law school, though, he was still just an office boy working in a moderate-sized law firm, and his classmates took aim at his aspirations by placing an advertisement in the school yearbook reading, "Wanted by Whittaker: Lessons on having my prospective clients of 1960 laying the green to the line."[43] Little could his classmates have guessed that in 1960 Justice Whittaker no longer had clients, although he did serve at one time some of the wealthiest in Kansas City. No less could his classmates have guessed that his penchant for spirited oratory would bring him success as a trial lawyer and national renown following his retirement from the Supreme Court. Instead, in 1923 Whittaker's fraternity brothers awarded him the dubious distinction of "Honorary Shoveler." This recognition, initiated in 1920—the same year Whittaker arrived in Kansas City—has been preserved under glass at the law school on a large shovel engraved, "Ancient Order of the Bovine Scoop."

During Whittaker's senior year his popularity as a speaker became evident when he was selected to deliver the keynote address at the school's annual Washington's Birthday Banquet, started in 1905 and held at the Hotel Muehlebach in downtown Kansas City. As the featured speaker, Whittaker must have felt tremendous conceit; he had arrived in Kansas City just four years earlier without a high school diploma but now had a license to practice law. It was his twenty-third birthday when he made his speech, entitled "Along the Paths of Glory,"[44] and in a few months he would graduate law school and go to work as an associate lawyer in the same law firm where he had just spent the last four years as an office boy.

When Charles Whittaker left the K. C. School of Law in the spring of 1924 he took his license to practice and his law degree to his new job as an associate lawyer. He also took the experience of the last four years when he earned the admiration (and some teasing) of his classmates at law school. He still had his fondness for public speaking, and his popularity as a speaker had only improved. The fact that he had attended a part-time, "night" law school should not have affected him adversely. The K. C. School of Law was the only part-time law school in the area to offer a four-year course of instruction. It had a substantial library and experienced lawyers as lecturers. During Whittaker's attendance there, the school's enrollment exceeded its own capacity, requiring it either to limit student enrollments or expand its facilities. From the moment he arrived in Kansas City, Whittaker had only one objective—to become a lawyer. Once that was achieved, no other occupation, interest, or diversion could attract him. Practicing law became the driving force in his life, and for the next thirty years he devoted himself to it completely. As long as he remained in Kansas City where his Alma Mater thrived, his legal training would never again be called into question.

2

Thirty Years at the Bar

When Charles Whittaker joined the law firm of Watson, Gage and Ess, large law firms were just beginning to take over the legal landscape as the dominant form of representation. Large firms such as Watson were not as numerous as partnerships or sole practitioners, but in the first quarter of the twentieth century they redefined the stature of successful lawyers. No longer were lawyers called upon as able advocates possessing strong speaking skills, rather they became corporate advisors. They moved out of the courtroom and into the boardroom. This transformation of the American lawyer in the first half of the twentieth century had a profound impact on Charles Whittaker. He had grown up reading about great trials and famous lawyers, and he went to law school hoping to become like those men about whom he had read, leading courtroom advocates like Daniel Webster and Rufus Choate. The demands of the firm, which were paramount to the desires of the individual, though, forced Whittaker to move more into the area of corporate counseling where he still achieved high levels of financial and professional success. Despite this success, Whittaker continued to find more satisfaction from the interplay of competing forces at trial, and after thirty years serving one of the most successful firms in Kansas City he desired to return to his first love—the immediacy of the courtroom.

Specializing in trial work, Whittaker initially defended streetcar companies against accident claims, but he enjoyed more defending insurance companies. Associates at his former law firm have described one anecdotal story about Whittaker and another associate, Carl Enggas, when they went to trial in a series of twenty-six cases in twenty-six weeks without losing a single case. "That's the way litigation was," an associate remarked, "There were no depositions, no preparations. You just went into court and tried the cases. [Enggas] and Whittaker would alternate. One of them would be in waiting for a jury to come in while the other one was going in and handling the jury [on the next case]. Then when one jury came in, whichever one of those two it was, would come over and help with the trial of the other case, and they just did this week in and week out."[1] Once when a former associate was having trouble with a case, Whittaker, by then a senior partner at the firm, looked over the case file and then proceeded to argue the case himself without any additional preparation. "His speech was perfection," remembered Whittaker's colleague, "He was proud of his writing.... A brilliant trial lawyer, wonderful speaker."[2] Rather than specialize in a particular field of law, Whittaker was what one of his colleagues described as "one of the last of the all-time generalists." This colleague has remarked, "One day he would be estate planning, the next it would be a corporation case, and the next he would be in trial."[3]

By the end of the nineteenth century the legal profession in America began to experience a transformation as lawyers moved into specialized fields of law. This move from courtroom advocate to corporate counselor was in response mostly to demands from the business world. Banks, railroads, and industry, all anxious for specialized legal services, increasingly hired lawyers away from the courtroom.[4] Many lawyers in America, however, were reluctant about making the move to specialization and the costs involved to their professional status. One contemporary considered the move toward specialized fields of law the "intellectual decadence" of the bar. By this he meant that lawyers no longer relied on their persuasive skills of presentation but more so on the fashioning of technical minutiae. The search for principle became subordinate to an investigation of precedent. Oratory and eloquence disappeared to be replaced by the practical, crisp, utterance of the legal brief, and American lawyers were transformed from professional men to businessmen.[5] This new business lawyer, according to one contemporary, lacked the literary culture of the earlier court lawyer: "He never draws a pleading, nor prepares a case for trial, nor tries a case, nor argues an appeal, and, quite likely, is never seen inside a courtroom."[6]

Initially, Charles Whittaker, like so many other lawyers trained to appreciate the art of courtroom presentation, was reluctant to move into more specialized fields of law if that meant leaving the courtroom. Throughout his career Whittaker enjoyed the interplay of courtroom trials, but inevitably he found his practice devoted more and more to corporate negotiations. When Whittaker's popularity as a defense lawyer increased, the senior partners at his law firm suggested he concentrate instead on corporate consultations and business cases. The reasons were obvious: the firm's partners wanted their best lawyers making the most money for the firm, which meant leaving the courtroom. When the senior partners at Watson, Gage and Ess recommended that Whittaker move into corporate consultations, he took their advice and gave his pending insurance cases to junior associates at the firm. The move was as much a personal promotion as it was strategically beneficial to the firm. Up until that time many urban lawyers charged their clients somewhat informally. Only the largest law firms used detailed billing methods—charging a set fee based on the amount of time involved.[7] As the Watson corporate client base grew, the firm adopted more stringent billing methods, and the best lawyers became business counselors. One of Whittaker's former colleagues, in fact, believed it was best for the firm to move Whittaker out of defending insurance companies because of the way he charged them based on his personal sense of fairness. In one such case, Whittaker successfully defended an insurance company against a claim, and the company settled the claim by paying only forty dollars. Whittaker told his junior associate assigned to the case to charge the insurance company half the cost of the settlement. To the associate this amount seemed too meager based on the amount of work put into the case. "An ethical fee would have been one based on the amount of work involved," this associate has claimed, "That case involved a forty dollar claim but took seven hundred dollars worth of work!"[8]

The move from trial lawyer to business lawyer taking place in the American bar early in the twentieth century ran parallel to the development of large law firms. Both were the product of American industrialization. Charles Whittaker played a major role in the transformation of his moderate-sized firm in Kansas City to one of the leading firms in the Midwest. After World War I, industrial corporations required the expertise of large law firms and lawyers who specialized in corporate finance, encouraging the creation of the "factory system" first pioneered by Paul Cravath in New York. This new mode of organization, the law "factory" where new associates were given a highly specialized task to complete, came to dominate the profession.[9] The Watson firm, though, was far less departmentalized than others in Kansas City, and associates at Watson considered their chief rival, Stinson, Mag, Thomson, McEvers and Fizzell, more of a "factory" where lawyers specialized than Watson. According to one associate, Watson lawyers were expected to be able to handle any legal matter rather than specialize in a particular field.[10]

When Charles Whittaker first joined Watson, Gage and Ess in 1924, it began its ascension to large firm status. With five members, Watson was one of the top ten largest firms in Kansas City at the time.[11] Although Watson as a firm had been in practice for thirty-seven years, having started in 1887, its appellation as Watson, Gage and Ess had been in use for only the last five years. Like most of its contemporaries, Watson continually underwent changing partnership arrangements, which necessitated name changes for the firm. Most often, these name changes lasted for less than a decade.[12] In fact, the longest period of time (forty years) that Watson continued under the same

The Temple building at Ninth and Grand. Located one block north of his law school, this was where Whittaker worked as an office boy and later became an associate member of the Watson, Gage and Ess law firm. Specializing in trial work, Whittaker initially defended streetcar companies. About the time he joined the firm, it began its ascension to one of the top firms in Kansas City. (Photograph courtesy of Kansas City Public Library Special Collections)

title was *after* Charles Whittaker left the firm in 1954. Unlike other Kansas City firms that could trace their origins to a particular founder, Watson had the distinction of having been in practice for over one hundred years under one enduring name.

Isaac Newton Watson, namesake of the Watson firm, was already sixty-five years old when Charles Whittaker joined the firm, and he soon ceased in the active practice of law. Watson's greatest legacy and what associates at the firm have remembered most about him was his active role in bringing indictments against the Pendergast organization and helping to end Democratic "machine rule" in Kansas City. Watson was not generally credited with the role he played in helping to bring down the Pendergast organization, yet it was the investigation that he alone initiated that gave the government the evidence it needed to begin issuing indictments.[13] It was not until after Pendergast lost his hold on Kansas City politics that members of the firm realized the extent of Watson's involvement. "We were an anti–Pendergast firm," one of Whittaker's former colleagues has remarked, "so was the *Kansas City Star*. So were all the major law firms. Kansas City was supposed to be so 'wide open' under Pendergast, but the actual working of the city was in the hands of, was connected to, the large law firms."[14] Following the fall of Pendergast, reformers attempted to "clean up" Kansas City politics in 1940 by electing John B. Gage as mayor. Gage, who had a reputation as one of the best trial lawyers in Kansas City especially representing railroads and newspapers, became so popular as the "Clean Up Mayor" that he served three terms in office from 1940 to 1946.

A prominent member of the Watson firm (1915–1932), Gage was also an alumni of the Kansas City School of Law, having graduated in 1909. Unlike Charles Whittaker, though, Gage received a university education, graduating from the University of Kansas before he went to work in his father's law firm where he worked for two years while attending law classes at night. In 1915 Gage joined Isaac Watson and his son, Raymond, in practice. Gage began teaching classes at his Alma Mater in 1911 on the condition that he got a different course every year so he could still learn while he taught.[15] Charles Whittaker became a member of the Watson firm, in part, because of his close association with Gage at law school. In his first year of law school Whittaker learned "Sales" from Gage; the following year it was "Bailments." By the time Whittaker graduated Gage had also taught him "Wills and Administration of Estate" and "Insurance." For over a decade Gage was Whittaker's mentor, first at law school and then in law practice. In 1932 Gage stopped teaching at the law school and left the firm, taking with him several important clients like the Kansas City Livestock Exchange and Traders National Bank to found his own firm, Gage, Hillix, Moore and Park.

Twenty years after his departure from the Watson firm, Gage went to trial in a comparatively mundane case serving as defense counsel for the National

Livestock Company of Kansas City, a commission company that sold cattle for slaughter, in what became one of the most memorable cases for members of the Watson firm. The two opposing lawyers were John Gage, three-term mayor of Kansas City and former associate, and Charles Whittaker, then the second highest ranking member of the firm and Gage's former law school student. It would have been unusual at that point in his career for Whittaker to represent the Oklahoma Hereford farmer who brought suit against the National Livestock Company; Whittaker no longer represented individual plaintiffs at trial unless the case involved one of the firm's most important corporate clients. Whittaker wanted this case for himself, though, for two reasons: it gave him a chance to best his former mentor, and it dealt with a topic personally dear to him—cattle. Five stolen purebred Heifers had been sold to the National Livestock Company for slaughter. In one of his last courtroom appearances as a lawyer, Whittaker argued to the jury that the company should have known from the animals' markings that they were registered purebreds and not for slaughter. Defending the company, Gage argued that the company had a duty to sell the cattle consigned to it. According to a former colleague who witnessed the trial, Whittaker's presentation before the jury as much as the strength of his arguments won the case for him: "Charles Whittaker spoke like a minister at the pulpit when he was at trial."[16]

The departure of Gage from the Watson firm brought several significant changes, not the least of which was Gage's name was dropped from the firm and Whittaker's name was added. The firm Watson, Ess, Groner, Barnett and Whittaker continued without further name changes for another fourteen years—the longest period of time at that point in the firm's history. Probably the most significant change, though, was that Henry Ess became the leading partner at the firm. Ess continued to dominate the firm, always having the final word in any decision, for another thirty years. He was what associates at the firm called a "business-getter" because he controlled key clients like Dierks Lumber, Sutherland Lumber, Safeway Stores, and the *Kansas City Star* newspaper.[17] Although there was little reason to retain the "Watson" name after Isaac Watson died in 1945, Henry Ess insisted that its founder's name continue to identify the firm. This was not so much out of respect for the Watson legacy as it was selfish promotion. Since law firms could not then advertise for clients, Ess worried that if people *heard* the name, "Ess, Whittaker, Marshall and Enggas," they might believe the senior partner was "S. Whittaker." Therefore, from 1949 to 1954 while Whittaker was *second* in command at the firm his name got *third* billing. Whittaker tried to make light of this by telling his family that if he ever practiced law again with a dead partner it would be with Abraham Lincoln.[18]

As the recognized leader of the Watson law firm, Henry Ess wielded considerable influence over the other members, and he insisted on the perfectionist approach. "In this competitive world," he told young lawyers, "there is no demand for just ordinary effort."[19] An impatient man, Ess was the only partner who regularly refused to attend the annual office Christmas party. A heavy drinker and chain smoker, Ess weaved from side to side when he walked, and associates were always cautious when sharing the same hallway with him. Ess held such tight control at the firm that he did not even permit an associate's name to be printed on office letterhead until they had been there for a few years. Ess's influence also meant that associates at the firm were generally anti–Semitic. Once when the partners interviewed a candidate who looked Middle Eastern for a position at the firm, Ess asked one of the associates to check the applicant's law school records to see if he was Jewish.[20]

None of the partners at the Watson firm were great friends with each other, but Charles Whittaker was particularly close to Henry Ess. When Ess took over leadership of the firm after the death of Isaac Watson, jockeying occurred among the other partners to see who would become second in command—most notably between Whittaker and Carl Enggas. Whittaker got the position, but Enggas persisted in challenging the existing hierarchy. Thereafter associates at the firm worked either on Whittaker's team or on the side of Enggas. The rivalry between the two men became so persistent that by the time Whittaker left the firm it was unlikely he would ever return to it. In fact, when Whittaker quit the Supreme Court in 1962, many of his former colleagues hoped he would return to the firm, but his rivalry with Enggas prevented it.[21]

When Charles Whittaker left the Watson firm in 1954 to become a district court judge, he had become disillusioned by the "politics" of the law firm partnership. Others soon followed. One former associate has described a "general exodus" from the firm about 1959 because of how the partners handled the distribution of profits. One of the partners, Powell Groner, president of the Kansas City Public Service Company who "showed up at the firm only to collect his check," left in 1945 because he was disappointed with his compensation. The problem was not that the firm failed to generate substantial profits but that Henry Ess kept too much of the profits for himself. He controlled key clients because of his close associations with men like William Rockhill Nelson and later Roy Roberts at the *Kansas City Star* and R. Crosby Kemper at City National Bank (now United Missouri Bank). Associates at the firm, envious of Ess's influence, often joked about how Ess received half of the firm's clients by winning them at poker. The large share of the firm's profits that he kept for himself was no laughing matter, though, and when one of the younger associates questioned Whittaker about it, he replied, "Be patient, Ess won't be around forever."[22]

Another prominent partner at the Watson firm at the time Whittaker joined it was Raymond Watson, who began to practice with his father in 1911 when the firm moved into the Grand Avenue Temple Building. Raymond became recognized in Kansas City as one of the best trial lawyers representing the Union Pacific Railroad, one of Watson's first clients. In the summer of 1930 Raymond was tragically killed in an airplane accident with four other men, prominent Kansas City businessmen and lawyers, on a fishing trip in Texas.[23] The loss of his son had a devastating effect on Isaac Watson and brought about major shifts in the positions and personnel within the firm. After the firm lost both Raymond and then Isaac Watson as principal litigators, it hired two new partners, Powell Groner and Paul Barnett, who brought a substantial number of new clients with them.[24] Most significant, though, for Charles Whittaker was that he received Raymond Watson's pending trial cases, making him a partner at the firm. Although he had become a "junior" partner just four years out of law school, it was not until he made "senior" partner two years later that Whittaker could claim some of the firm's profits for himself.

Becoming a partner at the Watson law firm, according to former associates, was always a simple matter. If an associate could leave the firm and take significant numbers of clients with them, then they could expect to become a partner. After enough years with the same firm most associates could take clients with them. Therefore, every associate, if they waited long enough, could expect to make partner. If, however, after a certain number of years an associate had not crossed the line to partner, then arrangements were made to find them another position, possibly at another law firm. There was no such rank as "permanent" associate. "If the partners felt at the annual review that an associate was not partner material, then they would assist you in finding other options," one former associate has said, "You would be judged if you had the necessary legal skills and could manage younger lawyers. Everyone hired was assumed would become a partner." When the time came to promote an associate to partner status, the decision was made without much fuss or fanfare. According to another former associate, "To become a partner, they snuffled the air, looked at you twice, met in the hall, then asked each other, 'What do you think of him?' There was no partnership meeting. The firm was characterized by a high degree of informality, which was probably the most informal in Kansas City. Of course, no one outside the firm knew that."[25]

Although not a law "factory," the Watson firm was neither a sociable place to work, and the distinction between associate members and partners was kept clear. All associates worked from 8:45 in the morning until 5:15 in the evening, Monday through Friday. On Saturdays, the associates worked from 9:00 until 3:00, but the partners left at 1:00 to have lunch at the University Club and did not return to the office. Relationships between associates and partners remained cordial, but one got the sense that there was always a line separating the two. Former associates have remembered how upset a partner became if an associate on their "team" completed work for another partner, or how they could be silenced with a look from a partner if they dared to correct or interrupt a partner who was speaking to a client. Antagonism existed between the partners because each one had their own "team" of associates, those they tutored informally, yet an associate could be called upon to do work by any one of the partners. "You worked for the partners," a former associate has said, "At first you had no clients of your own. Later you would be given more responsibility. There was not an emphasis on bringing in clients. The partners felt we had enough." Another associate has remembered how "a partner could call on anyone; there was little specialization, no departmentalization."[26]

The Watson law offices may have operated less formally than others in Kansas City, but unlike other law firms that did more socializing the Watson firm was all business. No associate ever worked overtime unless it was needed. They filled out their time sheets by hand, and the billing was done from the time sheets. All business done at the firm belonged to the firm; no personal business was allowed. "The work atmosphere was strict, formal," a former associate has remarked, "There was a certain decorum. We socialized only once a year at Christmas."[27] The annual Christmas parties held in the firm's library included much revelry and mixing, but the highlight of the festivities occurred when the intercom called an associate to Mr. Ess's office to collect their Christmas "bonus." According to former associates, nearly a third of their annual salary came from this "bonus," offered once a year and then only after the partners had divided their share of the firm's profits. The only other social event anyone at the firm remembered attending was the wedding of one of the senior partners' daughter. The partners felt that since the members of the firm did so much business together there was no reason to relax together.[28]

Success in the world of corporate law meant more than winning at trial (or avoiding trial altogether), it meant social prestige and a sizable income. Whittaker gained veneration from his professional colleagues due to his success at trial, and he received a comfortable six-figure income by the time he left the firm. He did not, however, achieve the kind of social prestige that other members of his firm enjoyed because of his lack of a university degree. His law degree did not entitle him to membership in the University Club of Kansas City where the most influential of Kansas City's legal elite socialized. Only after an associate was promoted to partner status were they invited to join the University Club, and, as one former associate has said, "If you were a university graduate, you knew you had arrived at the firm when you joined the University Club."[29] Whittaker never received even honorary membership in the club despite his standing as a senior partner in one of the largest, most successful law firms in Kansas City, and it must have been disconcerting to his self-image that he never did belong. All of the other partners at the firm, even those who joined the firm after Whittaker, were entitled to membership at the University Club. Without that, Whittaker was always reminded that, even though he possessed the position and income of the aristocratic set, some-how he just never "measured up." As a result, Whittaker became indifferent toward joining other clubs that offered membership to him, claiming that his only interest in joining any social clubs was to conduct business. "My parents weren't very social," his son, Keith, has remembered, "They didn't belong to many clubs. In fact, they had a prejudice against them."[30] Whittaker's lack of civic involvement, though, may have served another purpose. As a lawyer he could not assume a role with the public that might offend a present or future client.[31]

Attending the regular Saturday lunches at the University Club with the other partners as a "guest" rather than as a "member" was not the only distinction between Whittaker and the other partners at the firm. By the time his name became part of the firm's masthead in 1932 Whittaker actually had more in common with most of the associate members. He was at least a decade younger than all of the partners at that time, even younger than some of the associates.[32] While the other partners all had membership in the Kansas City Bar, the Missouri Bar, and the American Bar Association, Whittaker held membership only in the local association. A decade later he belonged to all three professional associations, but that was part of the socialization process taking place at the firm as it began paying for all of the members' association dues. The most striking difference between Whittaker and the other partners was his lack of university training prior to attending law school. Three other members of the firm in 1932, like Whittaker, had attended the Kansas City School of Law, but only one of those, Charles Garnett, lacked some kind of college preparatory education. By the time Whittaker left the firm in 1954, every member had a university degree but him, and only one other member, John Moberly, who joined the firm in 1931, had a law degree from a part-time law school.[33] Whittaker's upbringing, education, and law preparation certainly made him seem "out of his league," even among the members of his own firm.

Although not the largest law firm in Kansas City when Whittaker joined it in 1924, the Watson firm was still considered "large" for that era. During Whittaker's first decade with the firm the number of its corporate clients more than tripled as new partners brought more business with them. By the 1930s the Watson firm had doubled in size to become one of the three largest in Kansas City, and for the next two decades it dominated the region. Acting mainly as defense counsel for railroads (one of its earliest clients was the Union Pacific) and streetcar companies, during the 1920s and 1930s Watson lawyers defended clients against personal injury claims. During the 1940s the firm's client base expanded to include the lumber and insurance industries. Initially, Charles Whittaker handled a wide variety of legal topics for clients, including corporation, insurance, railroad, bankruptcy, and probate work. As the Watson firm grew, however, his work became more business-oriented, involving leases, contracts, taxes, mergers, and incorporation. The impressions of former associates as to the kind of work performed by Watson lawyers varied widely depending on when they started work at the firm. For example, a contemporary of Whittaker's who started there in 1929 remembered, "We didn't have near the complicated laws that we have pertaining to every field, and we didn't have any policy at that time in our firm respecting securities law, antitrust law; that developed for a period of time. Mergers and litigation was probably the main forte when I first came to the firm."[34] Another former associate who went to work at the firm thirty years later has remembered it this way: "We represented corporations on transactions like tax, security, labor, creditor's rights, or litigation, which was nearly always civil litigation. We did no criminal work except for established clients, and that was white-collar crime."[35]

The most significant field of law that Watson lawyers practiced involved defending corporations in antitrust litigation. One of the most important antitrust cases that Watson lawyers handled was the defense of the *Kansas City Star* newspaper. Considered by lawyers within the firm to be a "gift" from President Harry Truman because the *Star* had opposed his presidency, the charges against the *Star* came only days before Truman left office. Since the Watson offices had represented the *Star* for the past four decades (Isaac Watson himself had appeared before the Supreme Court in defense of the *Star*)[36] it was natural for Watson lawyers to once again aid in defending the *Star* even as its president and general manager, Roy Roberts, sought to place Charles Whittaker on the district court bench in Kansas City. In a two-month trial lasting from January to February 1955, the government persuaded a jury that the *Star* had engaged in monopolistic practices in violation of the Sherman Act, such as prohibiting newsstand distributors of the *Star* from selling competing newspapers and penalizing advertisers for placing notices in other journals. The jury found the *Star* guilty of both counts of the indictment, and Chief Judge Richard Duncan fined the *Star* $5,000 and ordered it to divest itself of its radio and television station, WDAF.[37] Two years later Watson lawyers appealed, but the Eighth Circuit Court of Appeals affirmed the earlier decision, ruling that the question of guilt should be left to the jury. The Supreme Court later that same year extinguished the last hope of the *Star* when it declined to hear the case.[38] Ironically, through some unusual twists of fate, Charles Whittaker, first as a district and then appeals court judge and later Supreme Court justice, followed the *Kansas City Star* case in its upward climb through the federal courts, being present at each level of trial and appeals but unable to participate in judgment.[39]

Knowing the kind of services members of the Watson firm—including Charles Whittaker—performed has been elusive because one of their largest and longest-served clients, the *Kansas City Star*, steadfastly refused to print stories about the firm. Watson lawyers defended the *Star* in liable litigation for years; in fact, the Watson offices gained a national reputation as experts in liable law, yet, according to one former associate, the *Star* would not mention the firm in a news story even if the *Star* was not involved in the case.[40] Another associate who joined the firm in 1959 has said, "As far as the work of the firm, you would never know from the papers who did the work."[41] The most reliable source of information about the work of the firm has been the recollections of former members. Two of Whittaker's colleagues who participated in taped interviews in 1987 about the firm's earlier work complained about the *Star's* treatment of the firm. Other Kansas City law firms received press coverage in the *Star* but not Watson. Former associate Vern Kassebaum told the interviewer, "When we represented the *Star* and we were in some of their big cases and even cases where we represented them and were victorious, our name was never mentioned or anything at all in the paper about they won the lawsuit. It was never mentioned." The interviewer then remarked that when he contacted the *Star* for stories about the Watson firm, a reporter from the *Star* quipped, "You say these people represented us?"[42]

Although the work of the firm—the big cases, the victories—cannot be found apart from the internal correspondence and collective recollection of former members, the size and importance of the firm during its "heyday" (1930s to 1960s) can be easily demonstrated. During these thirty years the numbers of clients and lawyers at Watson more than doubled, making it one of the most prominent—and prosperous—firms in Kansas City. One of the benefits of its success was that Watson lawyers were richly compensated for their efforts. A contemporary of Whittaker's, Vern Kassebaum, claimed that when he joined the firm in 1929 he was offered $25 a month salary and one-third of the business he brought to the firm. According to Charles Thompson, one of Whittaker's former associates, offering a young lawyer a salary at that time was rare; typically new associates received only one-third to one-half of the business they brought to the firm. Two decades later new associates were being offered $250 a month in salary, and by the time Charles Whittaker left the firm they could expect $357 a month to start.[43] Of course, partners at the firm took home the lion's share of the profits, and when Whittaker became a senior partner in 1930 he bragged to the rest of his family that he earned twelve thousand dollars a year. As the firm grew, so, too, did its profits. One former associate has remembered overhearing Whittaker in the 1940s telling other lawyers at the firm that there was enough money in the bank to run the overhead for another three years, and then he asked, "Doesn't that make you feel good?" By 1956, according to another former associate's estimate, the firm was making over a million dollars a year and paying twenty-five percent in overhead.[44] The remainder was divided between the partners, who found mirth in the small income associates made before becoming partners. As an associate, Whittaker took affront to this and, according to his close friend from law school, Russell Gunn, "He let them know in no uncertain terms that he considered his services worth much more. And he let them know when he got his raises, as well as letting them know several times after he got the raises."[45]

Charles Whittaker enjoyed his prosperity as much as he did his profession, and his office, relocated in 1930 to the Dierks building at Tenth and Grand in downtown Kansas City, became a showcase for his éclat. When a new associate at the firm in 1948 first spied Whittaker's office, he was struck by its rich furnishings, including a fireplace and patterned wood floor. Another associate with the firm during this same period has described how the Dierks building was horseshoe-shaped, with a light well facing north on Tenth Street. Henry Ess had an office in the northeast corner of the building, and Whittaker had his office in the southeast corner. "Whittaker's office had a fireplace, mantle, and paneled walls," this former associate has recalled, "It was impressive. Ess had more light, but Whittaker had better furnishings."[46] By the late 1940s Watson became one of the most prestigious law firms in Kansas City, leading other lawyers to refer to it as the "silk stocking" firm, an epithet derived as much because Watson represented wealthy clients as because its members were active in supporting the arts.[47]

By 1934 Whittaker was making enough money that he could afford to move his wife and infant son to Kansas City's more prosperous south side, and he purchased a two-story house at 1019 West Sixty-ninth Street just off of Ward Parkway. Not content merely to possess the usual trappings of a highly paid corporate lawyer, in 1941 Whittaker also purchased 240 acres of farmland twenty miles north of Kansas City just outside of Trimble, Missouri.[48] By 1954 the *Kansas City Star* reported that Whittaker's farmland had grown to 500 acres. Whittaker really had no interest himself in becoming a farmer; in fact, his younger sister and her husband, Hazel and Norman Ruhnke, lived there and operated the farm, which was stocked with Hereford cattle.[49] Instead, Whittaker used his farm as a means to demonstrate his wealth in the most manifest, personal way he knew—and as a place to fish. Whittaker had a lake installed nearby, and lawyers from his office have remembered being invited up to his farm to fish with him. For Whittaker, owning the farm was what mattered, working it he left to others, but, according to Whittaker's older sister, Dorothy, "Norman Ruhnke was no more of a farmer than Charley."[50]

Whittaker may have sought to become part of the moneyed class, but he also possessed an inherent generosity—especially for clients and family members. Having his sister and brother-in-law live on and operate his farm involved more than family fidelity. Whittaker felt sorry for them, and he wanted to help them financially. "They were very poor," his son, Keith, has explained, "My dad even offered to support them. I'm sure that was hard for them to accept."[51] Whittaker supported his wife's two younger sisters, Irene and Norine Pugh, who both earned just enough at clerical positions to take care

The Dierks building at Tenth and Grand. Occupying the fifteenth floor, by the late 1940s the Watson law offices had become one of the most prestigious in Kansas City. Although he was younger than the other partners and denied membership in the University Club, as the second in command Whittaker demonstrated his personal wealth through his elaborate office furnishings. (Photograph courtesy of Kansas City Public Library Special Collections)

of their immediate needs. Since neither of them ever married, Whittaker supported them financially throughout their adult lives.[52] Whittaker's generosity extended to preferred clients as well. Once Whittaker asked one of the younger associates at the firm, Darrell Havener, to go to the municipal court in Topeka, Kansas, to defend in a criminal prosecution the relative of the owner of one of the railway companies that Watson represented. Involved in the defense was a local lawyer from Topeka who represented another party in the case. Havener met with the local lawyer in the hallway outside the courtroom, which was crowded with lawyers looking for their clients or other lawyers. The local lawyer had met with his client already and impressed him with the jail time he would serve if convicted. Having received fifteen hundred dollars in advance for his services, the local lawyer then remarked to Havener, "You have to take advantage of your opportunities." When Havener returned to Kansas City and reported the outcome of the case to Whittaker, including his conversation with the Topeka lawyer, Whittaker expressed disgust, saying, "We don't take advantage of others like that. That railroad is a client of ours. In fact, they deserve a discount—charge them fifty dollars."[53]

Whittaker met his future wife, Winifred Regina Pugh, while taking law classes at night. His sister, Dorothy, has remembered that Winifred was attending a night secretarial school nearby at the same time.[54] Their courtship lasted several years, and on July 7, 1928, they married at Assumption Catholic Church in Kansas City, Missouri.[55] Since Winifred was a devout Catholic their wedding was a Catholic ceremony. Whittaker, on the other hand, was not strongly religious; in fact, most members of his family, including Charles, did not attend religious services of any kind. Charles and Winifred, or "Winnie," as he called her, had three sons together, and Winifred raised all of them Catholic.[56] The boys attended Catholic schools in Kansas City and accompanied their mother to services every Sunday while Charles stayed home and prepared breakfast. Not until much later in life did Whittaker become actively involved with the congregation of the Central Methodist Church of Kansas City, and even then he infrequently attended services. His involvement came as a result of his friendship with Russell and Mable Gunn, who attended services there, rather than any newfound religious devotion.[57] Religious observance was important to Winifred, though, and she often invited Charles to attend services with her. Since he refused, she asked the Gunns to invite Charles to join their church. "She knew he would not convert or join the Catholic Church," Mabel Gunn has said, "and it was important to her that he belong to one."[58]

Although he never converted, Whittaker respected the Catholic faith, and he supported his family's participation in it. Moreover, Whittaker made sizable contributions to both faiths, Catholic and Methodist. He became especially piqued in 1964 when Catholics withdrew from inter- or non-denominational educational associations in order to form a Catholic segregated group. Whittaker wrote to the president of Avila College in Kansas City, Sister Olive Louise, who had decried the withdrawal of Catholics, to express his delight that a prominent Catholic would make such a statement. "Those of us who were reared in another church," Whittaker wrote, "and for paternal, sentimental, and other reasons are quite satisfied to remain in the church of our fathers, yet would like to be friendly and helpful to, and cooperative with, our Catholic brethren, have frequently felt spurned and rejected by the repetitive voicing of 'the ghetto complex peculiar to the Catholic.'"[59]

Religious differences never diminished the commitment between Charles and Winifred; they remained devoted partners for over forty-five years. Their relationship has been described as typical of the era. They were close, but not demonstrative. Always candid with each other, there was no separatism.[60] Family trips every Sunday to visit Whittaker's relatives in St. Joseph, Missouri, though, caused tension between them. Their children have remembered how Winifred never much enjoyed making the weekly visitations to St. Joseph. After Whittaker purchased the farm near Trimble, Missouri, family gatherings took place there. Whittaker always enjoyed making these trips because it gave him the chance to discuss the law and boast about his accomplishments. Winifred, on the other hand, a fiercely independent woman, preferred to discuss clothing and fashion, which only irritated Charles. Sometimes they would have arguments about making these family trips, and Winifred instead visited her sisters.[61] Charles enjoyed these family gatherings because he became the center of attention. Since his days at law school he had been a popular speaker, and visits with his family gave him a chance again to monopolize the conversation. Family members have remembered clearly how he could spend hours arguing over the meaning of just one word.[62] A born advocate, Whittaker loved to argue, whether it was at family gatherings or during informal conversations with colleagues. One former Kansas City lawyer remembered whenever he took legal problems to Whittaker seeking support for his views, Whittaker invariably took the opposite point of view, cleverly pointing out weaknesses in the other lawyer's arguments. "Of course, he was more helpful to me in taking that attitude," this lawyer wrote, "but it shows his disposition and quick and fertile mind."[63]

Whittaker ate lunch regularly at the same downtown restaurant in Kansas City where he entertained other patrons at what became known as the "lawyer's table." Whether it was at the Williams Restaurant, located in the Gloyd Building, or later in the Tiffan Room at Wolfermans Restaurant, Whittaker could be found leading the discussion of world problems or legal situations surrounded by other lawyers and personal friends.[64] Some of the most influential men in Kansas City, bank presidents and other prominent business leaders, gathered to hear Whittaker orate on the issues of the day. These lunch time discussions became so popular, in fact, that future U. S. District Court Judge Elmo Hunter remembered how lawyers paid as much

as thirty-five or forty cents for lunch just to have the opportunity to participate. "Whittaker was always there and he was always one of the talkers,"
Hunter said, "He was one of the reasons that table was so very popular."[65]
In time these gatherings grew to such an extent that Whittaker had to fend
off other visitors to save space for his regular companions.[66] One of those
companions, a good friend by the name of Randolph, was a successful businessman who had lost his license to practice law. Despite his business success, other lawyers still recognized Randolph as the "disbarred lawyer." One
of Whittaker's former associates has remembered how out of place this disbarred lawyer seemed at Whittaker's table surrounded by some of the most
highly regarded lawyers of the time: "The presidents of some of the biggest
banks in Kansas City, some of the most socially influential people all sat
together at this table with the 'disbarred lawyer' [because] Whittaker would
not treat his friend any other way."[67]

A slim man, short of stature, Whittaker stood five feet nine inches tall
and weighed at most 150 pounds. His first law clerk at the Supreme Court,
Alan Kohn, remembered how in 1957 Whittaker seemed much too small for
his office or his desk.[68] Associates who worked with him have universally agreed
that he was a dignified man. A proper yet modest dresser, at the office Whittaker always wore a black or dark gray suit. In the summer he preferred a
light-colored, three-piece wool suit as casual attire. Even at home while till-
ing his garden his children have remembered him dressing in a starched shirt,
necktie, and straw hat. Planted during World War II in the vacant lot next
to their home, their "victory garden" yielded a large harvest. During the war
the Whittakers enjoyed more provisions than most of their neighbors since
they owned a farm that supplied them with meat and entitled them to more
war stamps for fuel.[69] Whittaker liked to maintain a rustic disposition, and
associates at his office considered him the epitome of the "country lawyer,"
but he was not what one associate called a "pat-on-the-back kind of charmer."
He preferred a certain formality, or distance, during social intercourse. An
affable man, Whittaker was always pleasant when addressing others, but
beneath his restrained demeanor lay an intensity of purpose.

His one passion in life was the law, and Whittaker exerted tremendous
energy as he struggled to excel at the study of law. After working seven days
a week, half a day on Sunday, which was common for lawyers then, Whittaker brought more work home with him to study after dinner. Considered
a "workaholic" by his children, Whittaker sat up late every night reading law
books, sometimes into the early morning. "He worked harder than two or
three people," his son, Keith, has said, "I doubt if he was ever surprised by
anything in the law." Furthermore, he rarely took time off from work for a
vacation. Arrangements were made every year in June to go hunting and
fishing at a clear water lake in Minnesota with a small group of his friends,
but Whittaker was not there every year as planned. Normally his family did

not journey with him, although a few times he took his boys fishing or on a long train ride with him. His son, Kent, wondered if Whittaker enjoyed his work too much to take vacations more often. One year Kent remembered coming home from school for two weeks at Christmas and hardly seeing his father at all. The only other pastimes that Whittaker took time to enjoy were a weekly bridge game with friends and baseball. Considered a good ballplayer himself, Whittaker sat on the porch of his home in the evenings listening to the games on the radio with his children. More often, though, he would pace the length of the porch reciting the details of his most recent case as he practiced his oral argument. Described as an "out-loud thinker," his words were not directed at anyone in particular. "None of us knew what he was talking about," Kent has said, "but it helped him to frame the issues."[70]

Whittaker may have struggled tirelessly to excel at the study of law to his own detriment. Certainly the long hours of endless study without diversion led to a remarkably successful law career with all the kudos that came with that success, but it also took its toll on him. Whittaker's physical health and mental well being at times suffered because of his relentless efforts to succeed. His complete devotion to his work became his undoing. The first indication that Whittaker had pushed himself too far—at least, his colleagues recognized that he was harming himself—came sometime around 1937. Whittaker's oldest son, Keith, who was still too young at the time to fully grasp all the implications, has remembered how Isaac Watson "forced" Whittaker to take a vacation in Arizona for nearly a month. Clearly Whittaker had been on the verge of a nervous breakdown and had become so disabled at the office that Watson "prescribed" what was then thought the best remedy for overwork. Undoubtedly Whittaker objected to such a treatment, preferring instead to rely on his own stubborn determination to overcome his difficulties, but Watson gave him no choice but to leave. When Whittaker returned to Kansas City, Keith has remembered, "He was tanned and feeling much better, but I think I understood why he was sent."[71] This was not the last time in his professional career that Whittaker suffered from nervous anxiety to the point where he had difficulty fulfilling his professional duties. Ever since the death of his mother when he was a teenager, Whittaker was prone to bouts of recurrent, severe depression.

The intensity with which Whittaker strove to master the intricacies of the law became manifest in his mannerisms and personality. Described by one associate as "intense, self-disciplined, and exacting," Whittaker's energy caused him to speak fast and walk fast. He also had what colleagues called a "nervous movement" about his mouth that made it appear as though he were chewing gum.[72] Always an impatient man, visitors to his downtown Kansas City office were hastily dealt with and dismissed as he nervously rearranged the corncob pipes he had arrayed on his desktop.[73] Whittaker did not smoke the pipes on display in his office, though, preferring instead cigarettes, which he began smoking just out of law school. A heavy smoker for nearly forty years, this habit began at the Watson law offices where smoking was part of the social milieu. Associates at the time have remembered few people in the office who did not smoke; in fact, all of the senior partners had spittoons displayed in their offices.[74] Unlike other partners at the firm, though, Whittaker rarely drank alcohol of any kind, even socially.[75] He was far too preoccupied with the details of his latest case to give in to distractions, even pleasant diversions. His work remained paramount, and Whittaker tended to shut everything else out. According to Whittaker's children, whichever case he happened to be working on at the time became the most important case of his career. "He was absorbed with himself," a former associate has recalled, "He would talk only about himself. He spoke to us about 'his' cases, going over 'his' arguments." Tireless and tenacious, Whittaker's confidence in his own abilities grew commensurate with his growing popularity, so much so that associates at his office often heard him say, "That's the law, sure as little green apples."[76]

Whittaker's success at trial gained him a reputation as a "lawyer's lawyer," and he willingly took on any legal matter for a client, more often winning than not. According to his son, Kent, Whittaker won disproportionately more cases than he lost. Because of his success at trial, he acquired a large following of devoted clients. One of Whittaker's largest clients in 1954, Robinson Shoes, in fact, left the firm at the same time Whittaker did rather than rely on another lawyer there.[77] According to one of his former associates, Douglas Stripp, jury members who heard Whittaker at trial were so impressed with his performance that they later called him for advice. Even opposing counsel who lost to Whittaker, Stripp said, called on him the next time they needed representation.[78] So popular was Whittaker's reputation as a successful litigator that one of his former associates has bluntly stated, "Other lawyers feared Whittaker."[79]

Long after he stopped actively litigating Whittaker could be overly modest as he reminisced with law association audiences about his days at trial. He remembered with "pains of inadequacy" his efforts to compete with the "giants of the bar," saying, "I was almost constantly plagued with doubts about how best to cope with the arts and wiles of opposing counsel." One lawyer in particular, James Reed, the mayor of Kansas City from 1900 to 1903 and a nationally recognized orator, prosecutor, and senator from Missouri, Whittaker remembered with reverence. What Reed said at trial was not as impressive as how he said it, which, Whittaker noted, "as every trial lawyer knows, makes quite a difference with a jury."[80] These depreciatory remarks belied the fact that Whittaker honestly thought of himself as an excellent lawyer. He had the wins, the clients, and the income to prove it. According to his son, Kent, a loss at trial devastated him; it was not in his nature to lose. "He may have worried about oral arguments," Kent has said, "but he was not inferior to opposing counsel. He could go up against the best of them."[81]

Even on the Supreme Court, praise ran high for Whittaker's skill as a lawyer. One of the last clerks to serve with him, James Adler, thought that Whittaker underestimated himself on the Court. "When I was there, he was probably the best lawyer on the Court," Adler has said, "If you needed a lawyer and your choices were the nine justices, he was the best."[82]

In time Whittaker's father came more to appreciate his son's chosen profession, although he never saw Whittaker elevated to the role of judge. Charles Edward had wanted his son to go into farming or banking, but whenever Whittaker went to trial in St. Joseph, Missouri, at the Buchanan County court, his father was a regular spectator. "He not only became my most consistent booster," Whittaker said, "but also the most enthusiastic. If I won a particularly tough case he was the proudest man in town."[83] Whittaker's father could afford to be proud of him; not only had Whittaker succeeded remarkably well at his chosen profession, considering his background and training, but he earned the admiration and praises of his professional colleagues. In 1948 the Missouri Bar elected Whittaker to its Board of Governors, where he continued to serve until his appointment to the district court. Then in 1951 Whittaker became the secretary of the Missouri Bar and one year later its vice president. His skill as a lawyer and prestige within the profession no doubt played a part in these elections, but there was also an element of campaigning. To be elected an officer of the state bar association, a lawyer had to be well liked. According to Ilus Davis, former mayor of Kansas City, "Charles Whittaker was highly regarded as a trial lawyer. He was active in Missouri Bar activities and had a personality everyone could appreciate."[84] Whittaker's father died in March 1952, and Whittaker later regretted that his parents never saw the honors bestowed on him. The following year the Missouri Bar chose Whittaker to be its next president. Upon assuming leadership of the state association on September 24, 1953, Whittaker proudly declared, "Working for my law firm is the only job I've ever had besides plowing and doing other work on my dad's farm."[85]

Public approbation for Whittaker's trial work came generally after his elevation to the federal courts, but these tributes still offer a sense of the high regard with which he was held by those in the legal profession. When presenting Whittaker with the Kansas City Bar Association's Man-of-the-Year Award in 1962, for example, Lowell Knipmeyer, former president of the K.C. Bar, reminded his audience of the success—and delight—Whittaker enjoyed as a lawyer. "There was an extra sparkle in his eye and an extra spring in his step when he was trying a lawsuit," Knipmeyer said, "His terrific capacity for work and his unswerving loyalty and devotion to the cause of his clients led to a tremendous clientele.... His keen analysis of factual and legal situations and the thoroughness of his preparation led to very successful trial results."[86] During the memorial service for Whittaker in 1975, Whittaker's one-time rival for control of the Watson firm, Carl Enggas, reflected on Whittaker's exceptional qualities as a lawyer, stating, "The difference between Charles and other good, even excellent lawyers, [was] that he did superlatively well everything that a lawyer is called upon to do. Some are able advocates, others write outstanding briefs and opinions, still others are wise counselors. Charles had it all."[87]

Not everyone who worked with Whittaker, though, held his writing abilities in such high regard. There were those who worked in his law office who thought he was a poor writer, especially on memoranda; one of his law clerks from the Supreme Court even described his writing style as "terrible." Although his non-legal correspondence generally showed no signs of long-windedness, his sentences on memoranda were unbelievably long, so long, in fact, that the reader lost track of the subject before finding the predicate. Whittaker's difficulty writing stemmed from his propensity to overanalyze the meaning of every word he used. For Whittaker, every word had an exact, unalterable meaning, and he struggled to discover the essential meaning in his own writing. He thought that if he found just the right word, then his point would be plain. In his judicial opinions he made frequent references to the meanings of "plain words," and he resented it if others failed to grasp his exact meaning. "He was very proud of his work and wanted to show it off," one of his former associates has said, "It disturbed him that his opinions were checked by someone at the Court. He objected so if others misinterpreted his work that he would go right back and change it until they saw precisely his meaning."[88]

In a similar fashion, Whittaker tended to overanalyze the words of others, whether they were written in a letter or a legal brief. He expected others to use only essential words, and he became hypercritical if there was any ambiguity. This led to his idiosyncrasy of underlining words in books and documents. He did not highlight significant passages with one lengthy underline, or simply mark noteworthy words for emphasis, rather he <u>underlined</u> <u>every</u> <u>word</u> <u>separately</u> in a sentence, paragraph, or document. As a former associate noted during Whittaker's memorial service, "He never underlined a sentence or a paragraph in a law book. His underlines were single lines under each word that he thought was important.... He studied and weighted each separate word."[89] Whittaker's difficulty, though, was that he thought *every* word was important, so he underlined them all. In the library at his law firm he had no compunction about marking up the law books with his underlines and then writing "Imp" in the margin of the page if he wanted to stress the "importance" of that particular passage. "It was a little disconcerting for us neophytes to conduct research using those cases with the underlined portion," wrote a Watson associate who joined the firm after Whittaker became a federal judge. "We felt that if Mr. Justice Whittaker thought that that was the important point of the case, who were we to decide that there might be other important points."[90]

Everything Whittaker did seemed bigger and busier than the other lawyers at his firm. He worked with an intensity that intimidated others. Considered a "lone wolf" by his associates, Whittaker preferred to work at his own frenzied pace without the interference of co-workers. Whenever the secretaries at the firm compared notes on the pleasurability of working for different lawyers, Whittaker's secretary, Celia Barrett, remembered how none of the secretaries wanted to work for him because he could be so demanding. Working for Whittaker required Barrett to put aside everything in her life, including Sunday school services, to work seven days a week. "It was hard to know he had a family," she has said, "although, of course, I knew he did." Barrett's father, George, had been a classmate of Whittaker's at law school, and they were still close friends. On Celia's first day of work for Whittaker she greeted him, "Good morning, Uncle Charley." Her familiarity was met with stony silence. After that he was always "Mr. Whittaker." "I didn't mind," she said, "I remember after he was elevated to the judgeship everyone in Kansas City wanted to go to work for him. I was lucky to keep my job."[91] Whittaker demanded no more of his support staff than he expected of himself, which meant a complete devotion to the service of his clients. The atmosphere in his office has been described as formal, even strict—and quiet. That is, unless Whittaker was working on an important argument. Associates who worked closest to his office always knew when he was dictating memoranda for a case at trial. Russell Baker, an associate whose office was down the hall, has remarked, "You could always tell when Charley was getting closer to the end of a brief he was working on because his voice got louder, and the general clatter of his office increased."[92]

Whittaker's passion at trial, his intensity of feeling, made him a formidable opponent for less experienced lawyers. His passionate oratory at times, though, landed him in trouble. Once when arguing a case in California on behalf of Pickering Lumber, a colleague of his has remembered how Whittaker's intensity during oral arguments made such a bad impression that the appeals judges ruled against him. Whittaker's team of lawyers had taken the train to the West Coast for the trial, taking their families with them, and the decision was rendered so quickly that it arrived back in Kansas City before their train did.[93] Another time Whittaker's intensity led to embarrassment. At the State Circuit Court more experienced lawyers usually arrived ahead of less experienced ones to argue motions on Fridays. One time a younger associate of Whittaker's, Darrell Havener, was waiting much further behind Whittaker to appear before a judge, so Havener took the opportunity to learn from observing Whittaker. While speaking before the judge, who was familiar to Whittaker from previous encounters, Whittaker became so worked up that the color showed in his face. Then in his enthusiasm, at the height of his appeal, Whittaker exclaimed, "Well, dammit, Paul!" Stopping suddenly and realizing the extent of his error, Whittaker immediately apologized and humbly proceeded. Whittaker was not typically profane, and Havener was shocked, to say the least, at what he had heard. Somewhat amused, Havener declared, "I, for one, was glad to see someone of his stature goof."[94] On a different occasion an anti–Semitic remark caused Whittaker to lose a case when the Missouri Court of Appeals reversed the trial court decision, in part, because Whittaker made mention of "the Jews' well-known love of money" during the trial.[95]

Those who worked closest to Whittaker, his research assistants, law firm associates, and court clerks, generally agreed that his greatest difficulty as a lawyer and later as a judge was his inability or reluctance to assign more work to his subordinates. He tended to rely too much on himself to do his own work, and when the work piled up he refused to yield to the assistance of others. This may, in turn, have caused the quality of his work to suffer. His health was certainly affected as his physical and mental well being strained under the pressure. Other partners at the firm, men like Elton Marshall and Carl Enggas, routinely assigned research to less experienced associates both as a way for the associates to gain needed experience and to give the partners time to concentrate on more substantial matters, but Whittaker did not. Either out of suspicion that it would not be done thoroughly enough or out of an overblown confidence in his own capabilities, Whittaker persisted in doing work others typically assigned to subordinates. This included both the tiresome and time-consuming task of doing his own research as well as simple clerical duties. Future U. S. District Court Judge Joseph Stevens, who worked as a research assistant for Whittaker in the summer of 1952, remembered how Whittaker mailed his own letters instead of letting his secretary put postage on them for him. One time after Whittaker asked Stevens to look up the facts of a case for him in the firm's library, Stevens could not find any of the books he needed. "It was an ordinary case," Stevens has said, "I asked him if he wanted them right away, and he said next week would be soon enough. The next day when I could not find the books I needed, one of the other assistants asked me if I had looked in Whittaker's office for them. Sure enough, there they were. He had looked for himself for the facts he had assigned me to look up the day before."[96]

This may have seemed like a harmless initiation for a novice, but Whittaker was not trying to "teach a lesson" here. He had little patience or toleration for the work of subordinates. As his former associate, Bruce Forrester, described him, Whittaker was like a country banker who had to shake the vault door himself to be sure it was secure. "I mean by this that he found it hard to delegate," Forrester said, "If he had himself done the work, he knew it was right."[97] This insistence on doing his own research rather than relying on his assistants caused Whittaker to expend far more time and energy than was necessary on a case. It also made him a great lawyer. Even after an associate prepared a memorandum summarizing the details of a case for him,

Whittaker still read every case related to it.[98] While other partners relied on the talents of their subordinates, Whittaker had what one associate called a "solo practice" at the firm. The one time Whittaker assigned research to Colvin Peterson, another associate at the firm, Peterson recalled the curious ritual that took place next: "As soon as I finished with a book, he picked it up. We took turns. First I looked in a book, then he did. I wondered why he had assigned me the case. He insisted on doing things himself."[99]

Even though he treated them as though he had little use for their services, the younger associates at Watson came to appreciate Whittaker for his guidance. As associates worked late in the afternoon to complete research in the firm's library, partners at the firm might stop by to speak informally with them. Whittaker, in particular, was prone to do this. He enjoyed the opportunity to surround himself with attentive listeners so he could expatiate upon the law. For those who paid attention, these dialogues were both beneficial and informative. "We talked about ethics, philosophy, finances, the profession," one former associate has said, "You could learn more in one week with Whittaker than you could after years with someone else. He was very gregarious."[100] Another former associate remembered how Whittaker dominated these discussions with the details from his latest case, but even then his command of language made the conversation engaging.[101] Whittaker enjoyed these late afternoon discussions so much that even as a Supreme Court justice, whenever he returned to Kansas City for a visit he could be found in the firm's library on a Saturday afternoon. Leaning his chair back with his feet on a table, he explained how the Court operated to the members of the firm. Sometimes he might ask them their opinions on a particular issue without revealing the specifics of a case pending before the Court. These conversations involved only those lawyers who knew Whittaker before he left for the Court, but even the newer associates could listen, and, as one of them put it, "to a newly graduated law student, this was very impressive."[102]

Typically these late afternoon discussions turned towards questions of professional ethics, or how lawyers *should* behave, with Whittaker enthusiastically expounding his own code of conduct. Whittaker fervently believed in a high moral character for lawyers, and he wanted to impart this belief to his younger associates. Expressions about integrity and honor were not mere maxims, for Whittaker these words embodied his moral code just as much as hard work and perseverance. Considered "out of touch" by some, Whittaker genuinely believed that those in his profession should abide by these virtues. During one late afternoon discussion a younger associate asked Whittaker an ethical question related to a case where an associate had gone to trial to discover that the opposing counsel was not present. The opposing counsel, Whittaker was assured, was aware of the time and day of the hearing, but chose not to appear. Whittaker's young associate then asked Whittaker should he have immediately asked for a ruling in his favor or attempted to find the absent lawyer? Whittaker considered this, then told the associate, "The fact that you had a question in your own mind gave you the answer you were looking for. You had to find him."[103]

After Whittaker was elected president of the Missouri Bar in 1954, he took his message of professional integrity to a much larger audience. Speaking before a crowd of 300 at the third annual law day of the University of Kansas City School of Law, Whittaker reminded his audience, "It is the responsibility of lawyers to police themselves and enforce their canons of ethics. One foul or misdeed by a lawyer brings down the public wrath. Even though that is not fair, it nevertheless happens."[104] A lawyer's professional conduct by itself was for Whittaker only half of the equation. A lawyer's personal life, as well, had to be above reproach if the profession was to gain any stature with the public. At the Missouri Judicial Conference in Kansas City, Whittaker told his audience, "The bar associations can speak for us, but they can't act for us…. We lawyers are practicing public relations—good or bad— in every act of our waking life, private or professional. Good manners are good public relations and the responsibility for good public relations at the grass roots is yours and mine."[105] For younger audiences, though, Whittaker had more practical advice. During a speech to the Young Lawyers Group, an outgrowth of the Lawyers Association of Kansas City of which Whittaker was a founding member, Whittaker instructed his audience, "I would keep my clothes neatly pressed, my hair trimmed, and my shoes shined."[106]

Through his own initiative, self-sacrifice, and sheer doggedness, Charles Whittaker realized his boyhood dream of becoming a great lawyer. First as a trial lawyer and later as corporate counselor, he successfully represented an increasingly large following of clients. For thirty years he strove to master wide-ranging, divergent fields of law. As second in command of one of the leading law firms in the Midwest, he amassed impressive personal wealth and earned the respect and admiration of his professional colleagues. At age fifty-two, he could have continued for many more years to enjoy the prosperity he had worked so hard to achieve and to which he had grown accustomed. He was not, however, completely satisfied with how far he had strayed from his favorite venue, the trial courtroom. He had also become disillusioned by the power struggles and growing bureaucracy involved in operating one of the largest law firms in Kansas City. Wanting to become more involved in the intimacy and personal interplay of the trial courtroom, the struggle of competing claims, Whittaker considered becoming a judge. He doubted, though, whether he had the requisite qualifications. One day while driving one of his associates home from work, Whittaker remarked, "I will never be a judge because I don't have the education for it."[107]

On his own, Whittaker might not have succeeded in making the transition from lawyer to judge. What he needed was a sponsor, someone with enough influence and connections to the right people in power to get him appointed. Whittaker knew many influential people in Kansas City. He had represented some of them as counsel, had even entertained them during lunchtime conversations. As he considered his options, he spoke informally with his best friend, Russell Gunn, about his plans for the future. Whittaker had thought about pursuing either a position as general counsel for a large transportation system or appointment as a federal judge. Gunn found the federal judgeship more attractive because, he later said, "That same [transportation] system had some years prior to this killed one of my horses and never paid for it. [Whittaker] expressed merriment at this disclosure and told me I should have sued them."[108]

3

The Lower Courts

Charles Evans Whittaker was one of only two justices in Supreme Court history to serve as both a federal district court and later appeals court judge before ascending to the high bench.[1] Certainly, serving on lower courts was never a prerequisite for justices of the Supreme Court; many justices, though, acquired their judicial competence initially serving on either lower federal or state courts. Whittaker has the distinction of having served on all three levels of the federal judiciary, but his rapid advancement made that distinction all the more remarkable. His tenure on the District Court for the Western District of Missouri was just two years, and his service on the Eighth Circuit Court of Appeals lasted only nine months, making his total lower court experience less than three years. Because of his short term of service legal historians generally have overlooked Whittaker's decisions as a lower court judge.[2] Apart from his promotion to the Supreme Court Whittaker's success as a lower court judge can be measured from the lasting impact of some of his decisions. Of the sixty-three lower court opinions he authored, few were appealed to a higher court, and none of those were reversed. More significant, some of Whittaker's lower court opinions influenced the direction of later appeals court decisions and altered the Federal Rules of Criminal Procedure. Despite his short service there, Charles Whittaker performed admirably on the lower federal courts.

The criteria established by the Eisenhower administration for the selection of federal judges was necessary for Whittaker's advancement through all three levels of the federal judiciary. This criteria, while it made Whittaker's appointment to the district court possible, also ensured that Whittaker's advancement to the court of appeals and then to the Supreme Court was more than possible, but probable. One of the first hurdles a prospective judicial candidate had to overcome was party affiliation. When President Dwight Eisenhower took the oath of office in January 1953, over eighty percent of all active federal judges had been appointed during Democratic administrations. This led to a political imbalance on the federal courts. Both Presidents Franklin Roosevelt and Harry Truman had made partisan appointments, making four out of every five federal judges Democrats.[3] During his first term as president, Eisenhower hoped to achieve a better balance, which meant filling vacancies with Republican judges.[4] Although Eisenhower wrote after his presidency that he had not used federal judgeships as "matters of political patronage," instead seeking out only "individuals of the highest possible standing," by the end of his second term he had effectively restored numerical parity between the two parties.[5] According to his deputy attorney general at the time, William Rogers, Eisenhower planned to practice bipartisanship only when the ratio of federal judges got closer to fifty-fifty. "In short," Rogers said, "getting the best men meant for all practical purposes getting the best Republicans."[6] Partisan considerations had, in fact, prompted Chief Judge Albert Reeves to retire from the District Court for the Western District of Missouri. Reeves, who was then eighty years old, had served on the court for thirty-one years and was waiting to retire until a Republican administration could replace him with a Republican judge.[7] When Eisenhower chose Whittaker to replace Reeves, it became the first judicial appointment to the Western District of Missouri by a Republican administration in twenty years.

Since Whittaker had never held public office before, Justice Department officials had to contact members of his law firm to verify that he was, indeed, a Republican. The only political partisanship his colleagues could point to was a two hundred dollar contribution Whittaker made to the Republican Party in 1952, and that, apparently, satisfied the Justice Department.[8] Whittaker later admitted, "Never in my life ... [was I] active in partisan politics, so, as a result, I stay[ed] aloof. I have always been a registered Republican and made small contributions to the party annually."[9] Only once in his life when he was still a young man did Whittaker campaign actively for the Republican Party. It was not an event that gained much notice. As Whittaker related the story, the Republican State Committee had asked him to go to the nearly one hundred percent Democratic community of Fulton, Missouri, to make a political speech. Whittaker began his trip at the bus station in Columbia, Missouri, and once he found the bus bound for Fulton he took a seat on it five rows from the front. Fulton, Whittaker liked to remind his audiences, was "also well remembered as the home of Missouri's asylum for the feeble minded." His situation became ludicrous when, Whittaker continued, "There came a group of marching men followed by one in uniform. These men filed into and took seats on the bus, whereupon the uniformed one closed the door and, pointing with his finger, counted, '1, 2, 3, 4,' and then coming to me he asked, 'Young man, what's your name; where are you going; and what for?' I calmly answered, 'My name is Whittaker; I am going to Fulton to make a Republican political speech,' whereupon he instantly continued '5, 6, 7.'"[10]

President Eisenhower developed several criteria for the selection of federal judges that became a fairly rigid framework from which potential nominees had to pass muster. According to then Attorney General Herbert Brownell, this set of criteria evolved over time and was communicated piecemeal to Brownell as Eisenhower gained more experience with judicial selections.[11] Eisenhower and Brownell, as well as others in the Justice Department, have readily disclosed the criteria used for judicial selections during Eisenhower's administration, which included the age and health of the candidate (not to exceed 62 years); recommendations from the local bar association as to the candidate's reputation in the community; a favorable background check by the Federal Bureau of Investigation (FBI) to determine the candidate's effectiveness as a judge; and finally, the endorsement of the American Bar Association's (ABA) Standing Committee on the Federal Judiciary.[12] According to then Deputy Attorney General William Rogers, Eisenhower placed considerable weight on the recognition of the ABA, and it was during Eisenhower's administration that the Standing Committee on the Federal Judiciary came to play an institutionalized role in the selection process of all federal court nominees. As long as Eisenhower nominated only individuals "enthusiastically recommended" by the ABA, it no longer suggested names of candidates in advance of being asked for a recommendation. Starting in 1956, then, the ABA rating of each judicial nominee was included in the attorney general's formal recommendation to the president.[13] In addition to these formal criteria, Eisenhower also told Brownell that he "placed great value on solid common sense—a quality hard to define but well understood by most—and that [he] would exclude from any lists of prospects candidates known to hold extreme legal or philosophic views."[14]

Eisenhower developed this framework for the selection of federal judges along with his attorney general, Herbert Brownell, but it was Brownell who ultimately bore the responsibility for following through with Eisenhower's mandate. Although Brownell noted in his memoirs that Eisenhower took an "unusual personal interest" in judicial appointments, it has become clear that Eisenhower's interest was only in the abstract principles outlined in a set of criteria; the job of finding men to fit that criteria belonged to Brownell. According to Brownell, Eisenhower did not rely on the White House staff to screen potential judicial nominees but instead made Brownell his chief advisor.[15] This fit Eisenhower's military style of leadership, which was to outline his expectations and then rely on others to execute his commands. Eisenhower knew so little about the functioning of the federal courts that he instead relied on "experts" to guide his decision-making. This often left Eisenhower "out of the decision-making loop," but he was more content to have judicial selections go through the *process* laid out by the Justice Department than be *involved* in that process himself. It was important for Eisenhower that potential candidates for federal judgeships go through the proper channels (i.e. the Justice Department) rather than seeking personal patronage. Even members of Congress had to deal with the Justice Department for judicial appointments; the White House was off-limits.[16]

In order to fill judicial vacancies, Justice Department officials, at the direction of the attorney general, filtered through all potential candidates to see which one most closely matched Eisenhower's carefully designed criteria.[17] This criteria-driven search was pursued so aggressively that, at times, the Justice Department recommended to the president candidates who, though highly qualified, might be objectionable to Republican senators. Eisenhower, though, deferred to the judgment of his attorney general. When Eisenhower finally did receive the recommendation, it was only "to give his imprimatur to whatever his Attorney General was recommending."[18] So while Eisenhower could claim by 1956 to have taken judicial nominations "under his own eye," it was his attorney general that vigorously pursued qualified candidates based on the rigid guidelines that Eisenhower had laid out over the course of his first term.

In order to become a federal judge, then, one needed to pass each of the various criteria set forth by Eisenhower and Brownell, and, presumably, the candidate with the highest overall ratings got the position. First, though, one had to get the attention of the Justice Department to be placed under consideration, and that meant obtaining a political backer. Campaigning for a district court appointment usually involved finding a member of Congress who was willing to support a candidate's name before the administration. Candidates for judicial appointments never publicly admitted they were campaigning, but, according to Joel Grossman, that was precisely what they did. While there may have been exceptions to this, namely, "a few well-known lawyers or political figures who may literally be 'chosen' by the recruiting agents," this rarely happened. More often there was concerted jockeying among political backers to place their candidate in a more favorable position, and, Grossman noted, "The candidate who does not make at least a minimum effort in his own behalf is likely to remain a private citizen."[19]

When Judge Albert Reeves announced his retirement from the District Court for the Western District of Missouri, effective February 2, 1954, the *Kansas City Star* reported that there was a "heated scramble among Republican lawyers for the court vacancy." Among those actively seeking the post was Marion Bennett, a commissioner on the Court of Claims in Kansas City and former Missouri member of the House of Representatives. Backing Bennett was Representative Dewey Short, the senior Republican from Missouri, who, the paper reported, never wavered in his demands for Bennett. Launching an active campaign for the post, Short and Bennett put heavy pressure on both the Justice Department and the White House, attracting the attention of Sherman Adams, assistant to Eisenhower and former colleague of Bennett's in the House. It seemed, by this account, that Bennett was the front-runner.[20]

Charles Whittaker, among other Republican lawyers in Missouri, sought the district judgeship in Kansas City, in part, because he had grown tired of the office bureaucracy managing one of the largest law firms in Kansas City. He also longed to return to the intimacy of the trial courtroom. As a district court judge, Whittaker would be able to enjoy again the competitive legal sparring between opposing counsel—this time without the risk of losing his case. He would be in control of his own courtroom, without interference, able to exact judgment according to his understanding of the law (he could remember losing cases as a lawyer because of judges' mishandling of the trial, for example, by liberally commenting on the evidence).[21] A district judgeship, however, did not make one rich. Whittaker's wife, Winifred, was understandably concerned about their financial well being. With two sons in college and another not far behind, Whittaker would also have to give up a six-figure income as a lawyer to accept the $15,000 a year of a district judge.[22] What appealed to Whittaker, though, was the security a federal judgeship offered; he figured that at age fifty-three he could not earn or save enough money as a lawyer to receive the same kind of lifetime annuity that a judicial appointment would provide for his retirement.[23] After considering his options and weighing the financial and personal benefits of a district appointment, Whittaker decided he wanted the position. He needed to find a political backer, though, someone with enough influence that Whittaker could modestly seem to be above the fray without losing his chances of being nominated. Whittaker made only one call, and that was all he needed to do. The man he called, Roy Roberts, was someone who could ask the president for a favor.

Roy Allison Roberts, the sixty-seven-year-old self-proclaimed "kingmaker," had been president and general manager of the *Kansas City Star* since 1947. A large, jowly man whose weight ranged anywhere from 200 to 300 pounds, Roberts was the very image of a ward politician. Smoking a dozen Corona-Coronas a day against his doctor's orders (he was allowed six), Roberts was an exuberant good fellow who delighted in backslapping and handshaking. Starting in 1908 as a political correspondent for the *Star*, Roberts maintained the same office there that he had used since he became its managing editor in 1928. Recently, though, Roberts had encountered personal hardships. His first wife, Barbara, died in 1952, and the following year Roberts nearly died himself after he was hospitalized with a stomach ulcer. After losing ninety pounds Roberts stopped drinking, but his fervor for work (and cigars) did not diminish. As the force behind a powerful Republican newspaper Roberts had tried, and failed, three times to secure the presidency for his choice of candidates. In 1936 Roberts was the prime mover in obtaining the Republican nomination of Alf Landon, governor of Kansas, and he admitted later to being one of the insiders on the nominations of Wendell Willkie and Thomas Dewey.[24] His appellation as "king-maker," though, came from the role he played from 1948 to 1952 in the nomination and election of Dwight Eisenhower.

By his own account Eisenhower considered Roberts to be one of his "trusted political advisors."[25] Back in 1948 when both parties were still courting Eisenhower's candidacy, it was Roberts who spent an entire night talking privately with Eisenhower; he then returned to Kansas City and reported Eisenhower was a "good Kansas Republican." When Eisenhower declined to campaign at that time, Roberts wrote it was "the statement of a patriot." Eisenhower's confidence in Roberts's political acumen was apparent in the letter Eisenhower wrote to him a few days later. "Frankly, during the days that I was trying to decide whether or not it was wise to make an additional public statement," Eisenhower wrote, "I felt a great desire to confer with you. In all our talks, on every subject, you have always shown to me such a broad and common sense attitude toward intricate problems that I should have liked very much to have had the benefit of your counsel."[26] Starting in 1950, Roberts became one of the first among prominent Kansas Republicans to crusade for Eisenhower's candidacy. Writing stories as trial balloons for public sentiment, Roberts importuned Eisenhower in 1952 to become a candidate and then cheered his decision to run for president. Once Eisenhower was in the White House, Roberts became a frequent visitor (usually off-the-record), and Eisenhower continued to consult him on a variety of issues.[27] Although no documentation has yet been discovered to confirm that Roberts simply asked Eisenhower to make Whittaker a federal judge, that is most likely what happened.

It would have been inconceivable for Eisenhower to interfer with the efforts of the Justice Department to fill a lower court vacancy because of the solicitations of any congressman or party leader, but Eisenhower was a realist who recognized political obligations even if they made him uncomfortable. In his first appointment to the Supreme Court, Eisenhower named Earl Warren, governor of California, to be chief justice to fulfill a promise made to Warren for the first Court vacancy. In his second appointment, Eisenhower yielded to the importunity of his attorney general, Herbert Brownell, to name Brownell's good friend, John Marshall Harlan, without giving serious consideration to any other candidates.[28] For district court appointments, however, Eisenhower relied entirely on the work of Justice Department officials and recommendations from his attorney general. Ordinarily when a district court vacancy arose a state's two senators, if they belonged to the president's party, solicited the Justice Department with potential nominees. Since both of Missouri's senators, Stuart Symington and Thomas Hennings, were Democrats, though, there was an opportunity for prominent Missouri Republicans to influence the nomination.[29] The key to Whittaker's nomination was the tremendous personal influence Roy Roberts had with Eisenhower. It was Roberts who made a personal request for the district appointment, and Eisenhower then initiated Whittaker's selection, which, as Sheldon Goldman noted, was an atypical example of the usual selection process used during the Eisenhower administration.[30]

While Whittaker obtained the support of Republican Party officials, notably Senator Frank Carlson of Kansas, the only backing he needed for the district court appointment was that of Roy Roberts and his *Kansas City Star*. Whittaker later acknowledged in an interview that he had spoken to Roberts about obtaining the judgeship: "I let it be known that I was available and would like to have it. That's the only time I had anything to say, whether I did or did not want the job."[31] Whittaker may have been circumspect about Robert's influence in this interview, because he had earlier admitted to his clerk at the district court, Clyde Rayburn, that Roberts secured his appointment.[32] The *Kansas City Star*, when announcing Whittaker's nomination, claimed that Whittaker "was not an active candidate for the judgeship," but that he "nonetheless was receptive to the efforts of Kansas City and outstate lawyers to obtain his appointment."[33] Certainly the *Star* was being too discreet. Whittaker may not have been as "active" as Bennett and his supporters, but he had the full support of Roberts and the *Star*, which was all he needed.

According to one contemporary, Whittaker *owed* his district appointment to having been a lawyer for the *Star*: "He was quite a factor in legal circles. He represented the *Star*, and he represented it well. He had quite an 'in' down there, and the *Star* was a big booster of his."[34] Whittaker certainly benefited from the support of former Kansas Senator Harry Darby, but he did not owe his nomination to Darby, who brazenly took full credit for it. "I was a close friend to Herbert Brownell and to President Eisenhower," Darby later claimed, "[Whittaker] received close attention because of my close association with Herbert Brownell and President Eisenhower."[35] Other Republican activists in Kansas City have discounted Darby's influence. Darby, among other Republican officials, "were for [Whittaker] and that was all fine," said William Orr, "but he needed somebody with a direct line to the White House and that was Roy Roberts."[36] Another gentleman, who wished to remain anonymous, admitted to being friends with Darby, but, he said, "If it hadn't been for Roy Roberts, Charles Whittaker would never have been a judge."[37]

Once Eisenhower initiated Whittaker's name as the top choice, based on Roberts's personal request, then it was up to Brownell and his team at the Justice Department to insure that Whittaker, indeed, met all of Eisenhower's criteria. Had Whittaker failed to receive the recommendations of local, state, and national bar associations, had he been too old or not succeeded in passing the FBI's character check, then chances were Eisenhower would have balked at the nomination, so emphatic was he that his criteria be controlling. In his letter to Eisenhower recommending Whittaker for the district court appointment, Brownell reported, "Mr. Whittaker bears an excellent reputation as to character and integrity, has judicial temperament, and is eminently qualified, I believe, to be a United States District Judge."[38]

During the interim between his nomination and confirmation Whittaker busied himself preparing for his new duties. Associates at his law firm have remembered seeing him in the office's library reading the Federal Rules of Criminal Procedure during this time. Whittaker had had little experience in that field of law in his thirty years at the bar, and he knew that as a federal judge he would have to be conversant in it.[39] On July 6, 1954, the Senate Judiciary Committee reported favorably on Whittaker, and the following day the full Senate unanimously approved his appointment. On Monday, July 19, retired District Judge Albert Reeves, the man who he replaced, read the judicial oath to Whittaker. Alongside Whittaker at his swearing-in ceremony were his two new colleagues on the district court, Judges Richard Duncan and Albert Ridge. Following his oath, Whittaker addressed the crowd of more than four hundred people who gathered to witness, saying, "I now say farewell to the practice of law I have loved so well…. With God's help, upon whom I have often leaned, a fair measure of justice can be expected in these halls."[40]

Whittaker moved into his new office on the fourth floor of the old federal courthouse[41] in downtown Kansas City with a relatively small staff: he brought his secretary, Celia Barrett, with him from his law firm, and a retired Kansas City police officer, Elmer Doane, served as his bailiff. Not until October did Whittaker acquire a law clerk to assist him. The man he hired, Clyde Rayburn, remained his only clerk throughout his short tenure on both the district and appeals courts. Rayburn had recently graduated from the law school at the University of Kansas City, the same law school Whittaker attended before it merged with the university, and, despite the large number of applicants for his position, Rayburn has maintained that Whittaker hired him because of their association with the same law school.[42]

The other two judges who shared duties with Whittaker on the district court, Duncan and Ridge, were a study in contrasts. Duncan, who became chief judge at Reeves's retirement, had been on the court for eleven years. He has been described as a "Democratic wheelhorse" whose main interest was politics. Prone to volatile mood changes, Duncan could be homespun and humorous on the bench. He kept things moving in his courtroom, gaining a reputation among lawyers for making it clear which side he favored during a proceeding. By comparison, Judge Ridge, who had attended the Kansas City School of Law at the same time as Whittaker, was a dignified, often stern, somber man. Having served on the district court for nine years, Ridge seldom took vacations. His only hobby seemed to be his courtroom. On the bench he was all business, displaying cool, impersonal dignity.[43] Of the two, Whittaker's judicial style most closely resembled Ridge's. Whittaker continued his habit of working long hours, six days a week without vacations. His reputation as a "lawyer's lawyer" gave way easily to being a "lawyer's judge." Hoping to serve as fairly and righteously on the bench as he had at the bar, Whittaker said at the reception following his judicial oath, "If you have liked me as a lawyer then you should like me as a judge. For I shall not change."[44]

Inside of Whittaker's courtroom there was never any doubt who was in charge. Before his retirement Judge Reeves had fallen behind in his cases, which were rotated randomly among the three judges, and Whittaker worked with zeal to clear the congested docket. Notifying lawyers that this was now *his* court and they would be on *his* schedule, Whittaker wanted cases tried within six months of their filing. One month before the date of trial, Whittaker met with the two opposing lawyers for a pretrial conference where he tried to induce them to come to an agreement rather than go to trial. After one such meeting a lawyer left saying, "I had to fight in there just to keep from getting a judgment against me." If a lawyer stalled during a trial or failed to appear, Whittaker dismissed the case for lack of prosecution. Wanting juries selected speedily, Whittaker interrupted lawyers who made lengthy arguments out of their questions for jurors. His clerk at the court has remembered, "A lot of lawyers got somewhat battered and bruised in all his zeal."[45]

In order to speed up jury deliberations, Whittaker asked the jury if they wanted to dispose of the case that day or come back the next. Usually the case was disposed that day. Once while riding circuit to Joplin, Missouri, Whittaker had the jury stay late to finish a case. The jury had to ride the elevator to the floor above the courtroom to complete their deliberations, but when it became too late in the evening the elevator operator went home, leaving them stranded. As his clerk related the story, "In court Whittaker demanded, 'Where is that son-of-a-bitch? I'll throw him in jail!' When Whittaker wanted to finish a proceeding, he wanted to finish *now*."[46] Careful not to comment on the evidence in a trial, Whittaker instructed the jury about the applicable laws in a case from memory, which was impressive considering the wide-ranging fields of law involved in federal litigation. "As a district judge, Whittaker was wonderful," remarked one of his former colleagues, "He could talk to a jury in ways that would make them ecstatic. His charges to the jury were memorable."[47]

Whittaker's approach to the task of judging was fairly simple: he studied the facts of a case to determine the controlling principle of law and then applied that principle to render judgment. A product of the early twentieth century school of thought known as Legal Formalism, Whittaker viewed law as a closed logical system. As Daniel Kornstein described this system, "The judicial function had nothing to do with adapting legal rules to changing conditions; it was restricted to discovering what the true rules of law were and always have been. The truth, once arrived at, is immutable and eternal. Adherence to precedent became the most important value."[48] Just as he believed that every word had only one recognized meaning, Whittaker thought there could be only one resolution to any legal controversy, and it was his responsibility to find it. That meant reading every case even remotely related to the case at hand. Resolution of legal disputes did not involve fashioning rules, but finding them. One just had to keep reading.

Evidence of Whittaker's philosophy of judging can be found in his tribute to Justice Louis Brandeis, who served on the Supreme Court from 1916 to 1939. "His paramount dedication was to simple truth—the uncolored facts," Whittaker wrote, "He used his great powers of concentration in accurately ascertaining, marshaling, and orderly stating the facts of the case, to which he then applied, but always quite succinctly, his view of the controlling law."[49] Whittaker admired Brandeis's devotion to the "uncolored facts," and he strove in his own writing to achieve Brandeis's "simple, straight-forward,

United States District Judge Charles E. Whittaker. Calling it "a perfect delight," Whittaker considered his two years as a district court judge the most satisfying of his federal court service. Unfortunately for him, supporters in Kansas City were not satisfied with leaving him at the district court level, and within three years he was on the Supreme Court. (Photograph courtesy of Kent Whittaker)

and lucid style, without rhetorical flourish."[50] At the Supreme Court he explained to his clerks how analysis of a case was built like a foundation— brick by brick. His judicial opinions were based on a complete understanding of the facts of a case. Once he had mastered all of the facts of a case, Whittaker thought the prevailing principle of law governing those facts was easily discerned. He believed, in fact, that justice would be better served if more fidelity were paid to the facts. "Legal questions do not arise in a vacuum," he once observed, "They arise only in relation to particular or concrete facts, and slight differences in the facts often make wide differences in results."[51]

The key to understanding Whittaker's judicial thinking was his devotion to the principle of *stare decisis*, which meant that once a court laid down a principle of law applicable to certain facts, then in future cases if the facts

were substantially the same, courts should apply that same principle. The problem, of course, was that in no two cases were the facts presented *identical*, so judges used their discretion to determine to what *degree* the facts presented approximated a prior decision in order to find the controlling principle of law. For Whittaker, this was an arduous, demanding task, much like scientific inquiry, involving long hours of research to find precisely that precedent to fit the case at hand. Whittaker gave great deference to the legislative process, and he would not substitute his judgment for what he understood to be the views of elected officials. Neither would he ignore long-standing legal precedents, however contrary they might be to his personal predilections. At the occasion of Judge John Sanborn's retirement from the Eighth Circuit Court of Appeals, Whittaker revealed his own propensities in his tribute to his former colleague: "Nor has he thought it to be the business of the court to arouse the conscious [*sic*] of the people or seek to cause them to alter their institutions. Rather, he has thought it to be his duty to observe the rule of *stare decisis*, to respect the legislative process, and rigidly to follow and enforce the law whether he thought it to be wise or not."[52] Whittaker admired Sanborn's "unassuming modesty," his "plain and unsophisticated ways." To Whittaker, judges were not supposed to be colorful—or charismatic; he venerated Sanborn's "disdain of display, particularly of erudition." Whittaker approached his task of judging with a determined modesty, cautious of coloring his opinions, or the jury's for that matter, with pretentiousness. His sentiment regarding Judge Sanborn was equally true of Whittaker: "In his judicial work, [Sanborn] has feared but one thing—that in a moment of abstraction, or of human weakness, he might commit some error and thus wield judicial power to the serious prejudice of a fellowman."[53]

Whittaker's work on the district court, his conscientiousness, earned him the esteem of the legal community. Lawyers especially recognized his efforts on their behalf. He was one of their own, and he conducted his trials and wrote his opinions ever cognizant of his principal audience—the lawyers. "He knew what the lawyer expected from the judge in presiding at trials and in writing opinions," Marlin Volz observed, "He understood the functions of the written judicial opinion from the lawyer's standpoint, which, among others, are clearly to decide and dispose of the case, state the facts and the issues precisely, answer where misinterpretation is possible, and through strong and convincing reasoning arrive at conclusions which gain a reasoned and general acceptance. On the bench he would be a lawyer's judge."[54] Whittaker had a clear concept of his role as a judge, and he relished the part. One year after his appointment to the district bench, at a dinner honoring him by the Phi Alpha Delta alumni chapter, he remarked, "The law has been my life. I wish every man who devotes his life to it could love it as I do."[55] This passion for his work, heartfelt and genuine, drove him to excel at his new job despite any misgivings he might have had about his legal training. Just as he had done as a lawyer, Whittaker overcompensated for any perceived inadequacies as a judge by working longer hours, without rest, to the exclusion of other activities. His dedication did not go unnoticed. Following his appointment to the Supreme Court, Volz praised Whittaker's efforts as a district court judge, writing, "He has a phenomenal knowledge of law and grasp of the fundamentals, both of substance and procedure. Above all he knows how to dig deeply in researching a problem, to use effectively legal authorities and to state a proposition logically, clearly and precisely."[56]

Cases coming before the district court could either be civil or criminal, and Whittaker enjoyed the civil cases more. This was due, in part, because of Whittaker's unease about pronouncing sentence on criminal defendants and because in civil trials, usually with no jury to render judgment, Whittaker could control the outcome of the case, demonstrating his comprehensive reading of the law in his written opinions. His favorite cases involved economic matters, something in which he had considerable experience, especially tax law. He did not enjoy patent law, though, because he thought it involved too much science and engineering. He often said to his clerk at the court, "If a patent lawyer has a question of law [for a judge], then he needs a lawyer." Since there was then little plea bargaining in criminal cases, most criminal defendants pleaded guilty, and Whittaker was obligated to pronounce sentence. This usually involved limited jail time; the majority of criminal cases to come before Whittaker involved such matters as the interstate transportation of women (for immoral purposes) or stolen vehicles and forged securities.[57] There was one criminal case, though, that Whittaker presided over that was not run-of-the-mill. The trial of Arthur Ross Brown, a thirty-year-old crane operator from California, made front-page news in Kansas City and gave Whittaker his one opportunity as a district judge to sentence another man to die. This case had a profound impact on Whittaker personally, contributing to his later difficulty at the Supreme Court making decisions when another person's life hung in the balance.[58]

Arthur Ross Brown arrived in Kansas City by train late Wednesday evening, August 3, 1955, with a .38 caliber Smith and Wesson. He had been to Kansas City once before, in mid–July, to help his estranged wife, Jean, move into an apartment following their separation. This time Brown had his suitcase with him, and he spent the night in the apartment at Thirty-second and Jefferson with his wife and eleven-month-old daughter. The next day Brown journeyed south, he later said, "to find a wealthy person to rob." He loitered in the fashionable Brookside area for over an hour—less than one mile from Whittaker's own home—when he spied Wilma Allen getting into her new 1955 blue and white Chevrolet convertible. He then made up his mind to hold her up.[59]

Wilma Allen, the stylish, thirty-four-year-old wife of William Allen, Jr., president of the Allen Chevrolet Company in Kansas City, had left her North

Kansas City home earlier that day to run some errands. An attractive brunette who devoted most of her time to her family, Allen had plans to meet her husband for dinner that evening at the Kansas City Club with some friends. She had already arranged a baby-sitter for her two boys, Bobby, age seven, and Bill, age nine. Ordinarily Wilma Allen scheduled her weekly hair appointments for Fridays, an arrangement she had kept for several years, but she had recently changed her appointments to Thursdays to be with her sons during their swimming lessons. Rather than return to her usual Friday appointment after the swimming lessons ended, Allen stopped at the Shears n' Tears Beauty Shop on this day, Thursday, August 4, without an appointment. She said she wanted to look nice for her dinner engagement that evening. Since there had been a cancellation, her hairdresser told her she could stay. As she left the Beauty Shop, a light, misty rain began to fall. It was only a short distance to her car, so she declined a magazine to hold over her head. As she started her car, Arthur Brown slipped into the passenger seat beside her.[60]

F.B.I. photograph of Wilma Allen. Her disappearance and murder in the summer of 1955 caused a media frenzy in Kansas City and became the most notorious criminal case Whittaker judged at the district court. (Photograph courtesy of National Archives, Central Plains Region)

William Allen, Jr., waited until late that evening to notify police of his wife's disappearance. Earlier when Wilma did not arrive for their dinner date he sent salesmen from his car company to search for her car. It was not until early Friday morning, fourteen hours after her disappearance, that police officers found the car. It had been abandoned in a small vacant lot beneath the Broadway viaduct between Twenty-first and Twenty-second Streets in Kansas City, Missouri. The car had been backed into a parking space, the convertible top was raised, and the car was locked. There was evidence that blood had been wiped from the chrome strip beneath the driver's side door and along the back bumper. Once inside the car, police discovered a blood covered washcloth behind the rear seat cushion, which had been pulled out about five inches and was splattered with blood, and the rear floor behind the driver's seat was blood-soaked. Inside the trunk of the car they found Wilma Allen's clothing, all splattered with blood, including her white blouse, torn at the shoulder, which was particularly blood stained. Concluding she was dead, city police, county sheriffs, and the Missouri highway patrol immediately began an intensive search for Allen's body.[61]

Half an inch of rain fell Friday night as more than fifty law officers from four counties in Missouri and Kansas searched for evidence of Allen's whereabouts. Authorities focused their search efforts on finding those items missing from Allen's car, like her scarf and purse, hoping these would lead them to her body. Late in the afternoon on Saturday, a farmer living near Stanley, Kansas, a sparsely populated section of Johnson County, found Allen's purse along the side of U. S. Highway 69. Authorities then turned their attention to that part of Johnson County, Kansas, but a rain downpour halted their efforts until Sunday at daybreak. Early Sunday morning 150 airmen from the Grandview air base in Missouri arrived in Stanley to join the search. After a pair of women's stockings was found near the Blue River, two miles south of Stanley, efforts were underway to drag the river bottom when news arrived that Allen's body had been found. In a field seven miles southwest of Stanley, a farmer and his son had been searching for their stray cow when they discovered Allen's body lying face up near a thick hedgerow lining the field. Her hands were tied behind her with her scarf, and the cuts and scratches on her hands indicated she had fought an attacker. Although her body had suffered considerable decomposition, two areas of bruising were visible on her right arm. The autopsy showed that two bullet wounds to the back of her head had killed her, but it was impossible to determine if she had been raped.[62]

The moment Wilma Allen's body was discovered in Johnson County, Kansas, federal jurisdiction became an issue. The federal kidnapping statute, or Lindbergh law as it was called, applied if a person were kidnapped and transported across state lines. Immediately the FBI joined the investigation, believing it had enough evidence to determine jurisdiction. On Monday, August 8, Whittaker impaneled a new federal grand jury, and U. S. District Attorney Edward Scheufler told reporters, "If there is federal jurisdiction, the matter will be handled with dispatch. The matter is being thoroughly investigated with an eye to federal jurisdiction."[63]

For the next three months investigators searched in vain for evidence leading to Allen's murderer. The local press continued its coverage of the investigation, beseeching its readers to call with any information, but after a few weeks leads in the case had dwindled to nothing. The Kansas City Crime Commission offered a $10,000 reward for information leading to the capture of the killer, and the FBI pursued leads from Chicago to Omaha; but no one collected the money, and none of the leads yielded any useful information. Frustrated but undaunted by the paucity of evidence in the case, investigators met again on Wednesday, November 9, to review the murder. That same day, Jean Brown was kidnapped in Kansas City and held at gunpoint for three hours by her husband, Arthur, who alternately threatened to kill her or commit suicide, pleading with her for a reunion. Jean Brown escaped the encounter, which was not the first time her husband had threatened her, and remained under police protection. Described as a stocky, sturdy man with ruddy, weathered skin and strong features betrayed only by a weak chin, Arthur Brown was wanted by federal and state authorities even before he abducted his wife in Kansas City.[64] He faced charges of rape and burglary of a San Jose, California, woman and the wounding of a sheriff in Sheridan, Wyoming. The sheriff had sought to question Brown about the theft of a yellow Bel Air sedan stolen from Omaha, Nebraska, the same vehicle Brown used to kidnap his wife in Kansas City, when Brown shot him three times in the abdomen. Brown faced federal charges of flight to avoid prosecution in the Wyoming incident and possibly federal kidnapping charges for the abduction of his wife in Kansas City.[65] Ironically, though, at no time was Brown considered a suspect in the murder of Wilma Allen.

Local and federal authorities finally apprehended Brown in San Francisco at three in the morning on Monday, November 14, as he slept inside of a locked yellow Bel Air sedan, a fully loaded .38 caliber Smith and Wesson on the floor. Following his arraignment on the charge of driving a stolen car over state lines, federal agents questioned Brown about other crimes in which he had been implicated. During their questioning, Brown interrupted the agents and stated, "I'm really wanted in Kansas City." Following his unsolicited confession to the murder of Wilma Allen, his bond was raised from $20,000 to $100,000, and agents in Kansas City frantically tried to prove or disprove his claims. Once Brown's palm prints were confirmed on the door of Allen's car, plans were made to return him to Kansas City. When he arrived on Wednesday, November 16, agents had Brown retrace the route he had taken with Wilma Allen to show how the murder took place.[66]

In his signed confession for authorities, Brown admitted that his purpose for kidnapping Wilma Allen had been to rob her. He had directed her to drive her car south out of Kansas City to find an isolated spot but then made up his mind to kill her in order to avoid identification. The farther they drove south along U. S. Highway 69, Brown realized he was running out of time. Turning off of the highway they found a field with the gate left open. Once parked, Brown tied Wilma's hands behind her back with her scarf and had her move to the back seat of the car. There he undressed her and made her lie face down on the floor behind the front seat. When she asked what he would do, he said he would tie her up and leave her there, but she became hysterical. Brown raped her and then climbed into the driver's seat and rolled up the windows to muffle the noise. After fifteen minutes of hysterical crying, Wilma Allen quieted down. Holding the gun in his left hand, Brown reached

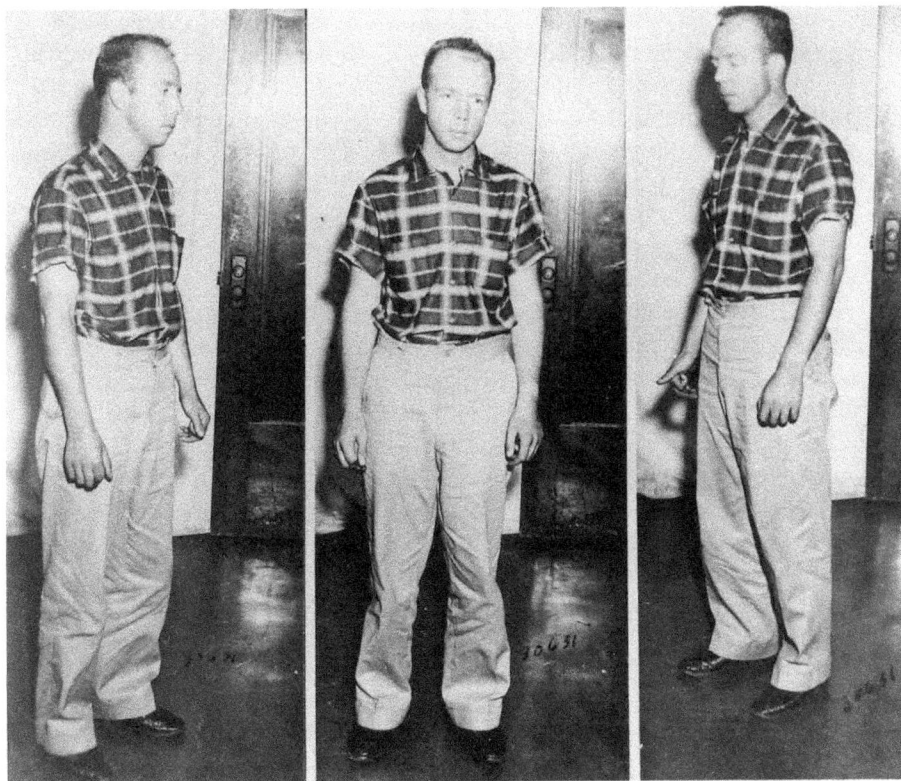

Arthur Ross Brown on the date of his arrest. For over three months local investigators had no leads in the murder of Wilma Allen. Brown was apprehended in San Francisco on unrelated charges, and were it not for his confession Allen's murder might have gone unsolved. Brown was the only person Whittaker ever sentenced to die by execution. (Photograph courtesy of National Archives, Central Plains Region)

over the front seat and shot her once in the head. He then dragged her body from the car and threw it toward the hedgerow. As he drove out of the field, he thought he saw Wilma's eyes moving, so he parked the car, walked back to her body, and shot her a second time.[67]

Once he abandoned Wilma Allen's car under the Broadway viaduct, Brown did not immediately flee Kansas City. He returned to his wife's apartment, hoping to arrive before she got home from work, with a small toy he had purchased for his daughter. Giving no indication of what he had done, Brown had dinner with his family, but when his wife saw he had a gun she told him he had to leave. After spending the night in St. Joseph, Missouri, Brown returned to Kansas City the next day in a stolen car to eliminate any fingerprints left on Wilma Allen's car, but by then the police had already discovered it. So he drove out to the field where her body laid to recover her purse, which he had discarded out the car window the day before. Brown deposited the contents of the purse into a culvert but then decided that the purse's rough material would distort his fingerprints so he threw it out the window a second time. Brown then abandoned the stolen car in Kansas City and took a train west. For the next three months, Brown crisscrossed the country in a series of armed liquor store robberies, stopping occasionally to call his wife in Kansas City on the telephone to plead for reconciliation or to threaten to kill her.[68]

Following Brown's signed confession federal kidnapping charges were filed against him. Conviction meant either life in prison or death by execution. U. S. District Attorney Scheufler then asked Whittaker to recall the grand jury, and on November 28 the grand jury handed Whittaker the one count indictment six hours after the start of testimony. Brown pleaded guilty and was held without bond. Three days later Whittaker appointed two prominent lawyers from the Lawyers Association and the Kansas City Bar to defend Brown. At the urging of defense council, Whittaker then had a team of three psychiatrists examine Brown to determine if he was mentally competent to stand trial. They unanimously agreed that Brown was sane, and on Monday, January 23, 1956, his trial began.[69] Once impaneled, the only decision for the jury was sentencing. "The question of guilt will not be an issue in this case," Whittaker explained to the jury, "I have not heard the evidence, you have not heard the evidence. I have many doubts, many qualms as to what punishment shall be assessed and therefore you have been summoned to hear the evidence along with me."[70] As a result of the pre-trial strikes made by the prosecution, no person on the all-male jury had any compunction about imposing the death penalty. "We have no hesitancy whatever in demanding the death penalty for this crime," said Scheufler, "the horribleness of which reeks to high heaven."[71]

Over the next two days Scheufler presented for the jury detailed evidence describing the aggravated nature of Brown's crime, and, so there would be no hesitancy about executing Brown, Scheufler also recounted Brown's criminal past as well as his disturbing sexual fetish. It was revealed at his trial that Brown had been on parole after serving five years at San Quentin prison for arson and that he had already served time for nineteen different burglaries in California. More aberrant, however, was Brown's motive behind the burglaries. Obsessed since an early age with touching women's undergarments, Brown would gratify himself at his victim's homes by masturbating with their clothing.[72] Considered a psychopath and sexual deviant, it took the jury only fifteen minutes to sentence Brown to die. As Whittaker read the verdict, Brown was not visibly affected. Considered suicidal, Brown seemed ready for punishment. Whittaker allowed the defense team ten days to file a motion for a new trial, but they never did. A few minutes after midnight on Friday, February 24,

Brown died in the gas chamber at the Missouri State Penitentiary in Jefferson City. On hand to witness the execution was Whittaker's bailiff, Elmer Doane. Although there were over one hundred other requests to witness Brown's death, none came from Wilma Allen's family.[73]

Considering the heinous nature of Arthur Brown's offenses, it seemed unusual for Whittaker to have had misgivings about sentencing him to die. Pronouncing death, however, even for one so malicious as Brown, gave Whittaker pause. After thanking the lawyers for their dispassionate handling of the case, Whittaker turned to the jury and said, "It was not an easy thing to do. This is my first experience in sentencing a man to death, and I hope never to have it again. But it seems as if there was no other verdict commensurate with justice."[74] Back in his office following the execution, Whittaker became noticeably morose. "When the man was executed you could tell it bothered Judge Whittaker," his clerk later explained, "He was different in the office after that."[75]

Arthur Brown's sentencing was the most difficult—though legally uncomplicated—criminal case Whittaker decided as a district court judge. Of the civil cases he judged, Whittaker left behind forty-eight written opinions, each explicating the rationale of his judgment. Of those forty-eight written opinions, one, in particular, has received more than its share of undue attention. The high profile case of Horace Bancroft Davis, an associate professor in the department of Economics at the University of Kansas City, has been noted repeatedly as criticism of Whittaker's performance as a district court judge and was even offered in evidence during the Senate Judiciary Committee's hearings to demonstrate his unfitness for the Supreme Court. For all of the attention it has received, though, *Davis v. University of Kansas City*, a case that has had no lasting significance on either the law or the parties involved, was a simple matter to adjudicate.

The impetus for the *Davis* case occurred, ironically enough, the day before Judge Albert Reeves, who Whittaker replaced on the district bench, asked President Eisenhower to accept his retirement from active service. On that day, December 17, 1953, a tribunal consisting of the president of the University of Kansas City, the President's Advisory Council, and members of its Board of Trustees unanimously recommended Davis's dismissal as a faculty member there, but the case had its antecedents long before that. After joining the university in 1947, Davis was not eligible for tenure status until 1949, and during that time university officials gave Davis's request for tenure protracted consideration because he had made statements in and out of the classroom that they considered sympathetic to Communism. According to a report prepared by the Special Committee on Academic Freedom and Tenure for the American Association of University Professors, once Davis received tenure his administrative superiors "subsequently developed doubts as to the wisdom of the determination that had been made."[76] Characterized by students who attended the university as a "disciple of Communism," Davis and a colleague, Ralph W. Spitzer, associate professor of Chemistry at the university, were both subpoenaed in June 1953 to appear in Chicago before the Senate Internal Security subcommittee, commonly called the "Jenner committee" for its chairman Republican Senator William Jenner of Indiana. Subcommittee members questioned Davis about his possible membership in or support of the Communist Party, and, invoking the Fifth Amendment, Davis refused to answer their questions. Following his appearance before the Jenner committee, Davis told the press, "As a teacher of the social sciences, I am acutely aware of the baneful effect which the current hysteria has on education and the free expression of opinion. The Jenner committee has contributed to that hysteria."[77]

The controversy between Davis and the University of Kansas City, a private institution, arose soon after university officials learned of Davis's testimony, or lack of, before the Jenner committee. The President's Advisory Council at the university, consisting of three deans and five elected faculty members, unanimously recommended that the Board of Trustees investigate Davis's possible Communist affiliation; so the Board invited Davis to an informal meeting, explaining to him that, while no formal charges had been filed, his refusal to testify before the Senate subcommittee could not be ignored. Then the Board asked Davis questions similar to those asked by the Jenner committee. Davis again refused to answer, this time claiming the Board had *no right to ask* him those questions. In his statement for the Board, Davis did say, "I do not carry on propaganda in my classroom. My philosophy of education would preclude such a thing. My students are encouraged to think for themselves. Discussion in my classes is free and disagreement is not penalized."[78] The Special Committee on Academic Freedom and Tenure, in its own investigation of the university's actions, found, however, that in light of his testimony before the Senate subcommittee, the university "had the right, if not the obligation" to reexamine Davis's qualifications. Furthermore, the questions asked of Davis "*were appropriate* to such an inquiry," and "it was *the obligation* of Dr. Davis to answer."[79]

In August 1953 the university presented Davis with formal charges related to his termination, and four months later he was dismissed due to "commitments" that rendered him "unfit to continue in a position of educational trust," meaning he had refused to communicate openly with members of the Board of Trustees.[80] Considering, among other factors, that no member of the university tribunal recommending Davis's dismissal ever indicated any disagreement with the final judgment and that Davis did not object to the composition of the tribunal, the Special Committee on Academic Freedom and Tenure found that at no time in its consideration of Davis's dismissal did the university deprive him of procedural due process.[81] The day after Davis's dismissal, a *Kansas City Times* editorial commended the university's action:

Before his own colleagues and the governing body of the university Dr. Davis was given every opportunity to deny that he was a Communist and he refused. That was the crux of the case. Such refusal was very different from taking refuge in the Fifth Amendment before a Senate subcommittee. Here he was saying in effect that the university had no right to know whether it was employing a Communist teacher—an arrogant and impossible proposition.... The university has proceeded with full regard for its obligations to the teachers, the students, and the public. Its handling of the Davis case is an excellent example of responsibility.[82]

The case of *Davis v. University of Kansas City* that arrived in Whittaker's courtroom in mid–March 1955 was an easy case for Whittaker to judge because Davis's presentation of his own case as plaintiff was so poor. In his complaint against the university, the only *legal* argument that Davis raised was a charge of "conspiracy" between the university, the Jenner committee, and the *Kansas City Star* for its coverage of the Senate subcommittee hearings and subsequent university investigation. Although the Special Committee on Academic Freedom and Tenure found that there was no instance of inflammatory journalism on the part of the *Kansas City Star* or a demand for his removal, Davis claimed that the *Star's* coverage of events had inflamed public opinion against him, prompting his dismissal. For support, Davis pointed to the fact that a member of the *Star's* editorial staff had recently been made a member of the Board of Trustees of the university.[83] Not only was his conspiracy claim unsubstantiated in Davis's complaint, but, as the university's defense council argued in its brief, a conspiracy allegation was a tort action, and as a non-profit charitable institution the university was exempt from tort actions. Whittaker noted in the margin of the university's brief that this was "important."[84] This explained Whittaker's ruling that Davis had failed to state a claim upon which relief could be granted. The conspiracy statute on which Davis relied made it a federal crime for two or more persons to conspire to injure or oppress anyone in the free exercise of any right secured to them by the Constitution or laws of the United States.[85] Not only was the university exempt from tort actions, Davis failed to indicate how his constitutional rights had been violated. Nowhere in his complaint did Davis raise a Fifth Amendment issue; the only right he claimed was his tenured position at the university, which was certainly not secured by the Constitution or laws of the United States. Furthermore, Davis failed to indicate the amount of damages he sought from the university in case Whittaker decided not to enjoin the university from dismissing Davis, which, at that time, would have been required for federal jurisdiction.[86] The remainder of Davis's brief amounted to no more than a chronology of events that had transpired between himself and university officials with a plea for "decency and fairness" and a request that he be reinstated. Most damaging for Davis's case, however, was that he did not rely on a single legal precedent to support his contentions.

Certainly, Whittaker would not have ruled in favor of a plaintiff who lacked supporting authority for his arguments.

Davis's poor presentation of his case was compounded by his reliance on a Nashville lawyer, Fyke Farmer, to represent him. Throughout the proceedings, Davis represented himself as plaintiff *pro se* but listed Farmer as his counsel, even though Farmer was not a member of the Missouri Bar and was therefore ineligible to practice law in Missouri. Even before lawyers for the university could respond to Davis's initial complaint, Farmer sent to the court several motions on Davis's behalf requesting the production of certain university documents, which the clerk of the court returned unfiled because Farmer was not qualified to file them. Lawyers for the university turned this to their advantage, noting that Farmer had petitioned for the production of university documents even before the university had sought a dismissal of the case. Such disregard for proper procedure would not have gone unnoticed by Whittaker. Then, after Whittaker sustained the university's motion to dismiss Davis's complaint on the grounds that it failed to state a claim upon which relief could be granted, a kind of "comedy of errors" ensued. First, Davis filed a motion for rehearing because, he claimed, the clerk had made an error by not filing Farmer's motions in the first place. Those documents were necessary for Davis's "defense" (in other words, they could have substantiated his conspiracy charge), but, because Whittaker's final ruling had come too quickly, there was no time to make another filing for the production of documents. Of course, as plaintiff, once he had filed his initial complaint there was no need for Davis to "defend" himself; his complaint either substantiated a conspiracy charge or it did not. Davis further requested that Farmer be allowed to serve as his lawyer *without actually enrolling* with the Missouri Bar so that Farmer's original motion for the production of documents could be honored.[87] These unconventional legal maneuverings by Davis and Farmer were illustrative of the inadequacy of their preparation and did not make a favorable impression on Whittaker.

The University of Kansas City, on the other hand, represented by the largest law firm in Kansas City at the time, Stinson, Mag, Thomson, McEvers, and Fizzell, employed in its legal briefs the rules of law. Cogent arguments supported by numerous legal precedents were abundant in the university's briefs, and an examination of those briefs has revealed that Whittaker gave much greater weight to arguments relying on legal precedents for support than to Davis's appeal for "decency and fairness." In its brief to dismiss Davis's complaint, the university argued forcefully that Davis may have had a constitutional right not to incriminate himself by refusing to answer the Board's questions, but he had "no constitutional right to be a *public* school teacher."[88] The university's brief relied for legal authority on *Faxon v. School Committee of Boston*, a ruling of the Supreme Judicial Court of Massachusetts, which gave notice to the famous aphorism by Judge Oliver

Wendell Holmes, Jr., that "petitioner may have a constitutional right to talk politics, but he has no constitutional right to be a policeman."[89] On his copy of the university's brief Whittaker twice indicated that this was "important," and it was likely that the phrase "*public* school teacher" found its way into Whittaker's opinion because he found the university's arguments controlling. Whittaker certainly knew that the university was a private institution, but, as Daniel Kornstein observed, when compelling arguments have been put forth in legal briefs often judges will accept those arguments verbatim and incorporate them into their written opinions.[90] The university's brief then concluded by urging that Davis's dismissal was not wrongful but both "highly necessary and desirable," another sentiment that in strong language also found its way into Whittaker's opinion.

The ruling that Whittaker made in the *Davis* case seemed easy enough at the time since it had the support of both reason and law. An editorial in the *Kansas City Star* following Whittaker's ruling called it a "common-sense opinion that anyone could understand."[91] Whittaker dismissed Davis's complaint against the university because Davis had sought relief in equity by asking to be reinstated without proving, in fact, that the university had somehow injured him. Had he wanted to, Whittaker could have dismissed the case for lack of federal jurisdiction. Diversity did not exist, meaning both parties were from the same state, and Whittaker found Davis's one statutory contention questionable. Since the university did not raise a jurisdictional argument, though, Whittaker let it go.[92] Especially significant to Whittaker's ruling on the merits was the fact that Davis admitted his tenure was not undefeatable; it was subject to a covenant in his contract that provided his services could be terminated for "adequate cause," and it was clearly within the university's discretion to determine what constituted "adequate cause."[93] Although the Special Committee on Academic Freedom and Tenure disagreed that Davis's refusal to answer the Board's questions, taken alone, constituted "adequate cause," it did find that his refusal "raised serious doubts about him," and, "the decision to dismiss him cannot be unqualifiedly condemned." The Special Committee then concluded, "It is to the credit of the University Administration that at no time did it take the position that invocation of the Fifth Amendment by a faculty member could in itself be a ground of dismissal."[94]

Davis, however, never raised an argument based on the Fifth Amendment in his original complaint against the university. The first time in his many appearances before Whittaker that Davis presented a Fifth Amendment claim was when he filed an affidavit of bias against Whittaker following Whittaker's original ruling. Davis charged in his affidavit that Whittaker had a personal bias or prejudice either against him or in favor of the university and that Whittaker had not been faithful to his oath to uphold the Constitution when he disregarded Davis's exercise of a "constitutional right."[95] Whittaker dismissed this, among other supplementary motions, noting that it was "based entirely on the adversity to the plaintiff of the ruling already made," and, besides, "such rulings are reviewable otherwise."[96] In another appearance, this time in response to the university's motion to dismiss Davis's request for a new trial, Davis offered further support for his Fifth Amendment claim, but it proved to be immaterial to his original complaint against the university. Relying on the Missouri Supreme Court's interpretation of the Missouri Constitution, which found that freedom of speech included a correlative right to remain silent, Davis contended that the university Trustees "could not without violating the [Missouri] constitution *require* plaintiff to answer questions of the nature which he was asked." Whittaker agreed with such an obvious prohibition, as he noted in the margin of Davis's brief, but, he wryly observed, "They didn't have to *keep* him."[97]

Had Whittaker ruled simply to dismiss Davis's complaint, this case, much like Whittaker's other district court opinions, might have escaped notice. Whittaker did not confine his ruling to dismissing Davis's complaint, though, and, as a result, *Davis v. University of Kansas City* has been commented upon more often than any other Whittaker decision as a district judge.[98] What has been commented upon, however, has not been Whittaker's ruling *per se*, but the *dicta* in the opinion. In other words, Whittaker's personal views were expressed in the opinion but were not necessarily involved in the case or essential to its resolution. These views, specifically his indictment of Communism, have attracted so much commentary that they deserve extensive quotation. When asking whether Davis's failure to answer the questions asked of him by university officials constituted "adequate cause" for his dismissal, Whittaker answered,

> I believe it does. Plaintiff had a lawful right, under the Fifth Amendment to the Constitution, to refuse to answer, and no inference of criminality can be drawn from his failure to answer. But he did not have a constitutional right to remain a public school teacher. And the refusal of a teacher—in a most intimate position to mold the minds of the youth of the country—to answer to the responsible officials of the school, whether he is a member of a found and declared conspiracy by a godless group to overthrow our government by force, constitutes "adequate cause" for the dismissal of such a teacher. The public will not stand, and they ought not to stand, for such reticence or refusals to answer by the teachers in their schools. And the university officials would have been derelict in their duties had they not asked plaintiff—in the light of his refusal to answer the Senate subcommittee's questions as to whether he was a Communist—whether he was or ever had been a member of the Communist Party, and, having asked him those questions, and he having refused to answer them, would have been derelict of their duties, and would have destroyed the university, had they not dismissed him.

Clearly Whittaker found it necessary to offer far more rationale for this decision than was required to dispose of Davis's complaint. As Professors

David Atkinson and Lawrence Larsen pointed out, there was a great deal of supposition in the opinion; for example, there was no evidence that Davis's retention "would have destroyed the university."[99] Whittaker's invective against Communism expressed his deeply felt suspicion of it, which was reflected in the attitudes of many Americans at the time. So strong were his convictions that in his own handwriting Whittaker inserted the words, "by a godless group" into his original order.[100] This excursion into personal prejudice, while tangential, Whittaker believed was requisite in order to shore up his decision against possible, likely, attacks from civil libertarians who would mistakenly assume the case raised constitutional issues when, in fact, it did not.[101] The inordinate amount of *dicta* in *Davis* has served to detract from its actual holding and has raised serious questions regarding its value as a legal precedent.

Although the dismissal of a tenured college professor for alleged Communistic leanings resembled other anti–Communist cases of the 1950s, *Davis* did not raise the kinds of constitutional questions some have claimed. Leon Friedman, for example, in his criticism of Whittaker's decision, asserted that the Supreme Court in *Slochower v. Board of Education* later overruled Whittaker's interpretation "when it held that invoking the Fifth Amendment was not grounds for dismissing a public school teacher." Friedman also relied on *Shelton v. Tucker* where "the Court concluded that a state could not require a teacher to supply information on membership in political or other organizations for five years prior to appointment."[102] First, when the Supreme Court invalidated the New York City Charter that led to Slochower's dismissal because he invoked the Fifth Amendment to avoid answering questions before a legislative committee, it relied on the Due Process Clause of the Fourteenth Amendment, which the New York Board of Higher Education violated when it failed to accord Slochower proper notice, hearing, and appeal—a situation that did not occur in *Davis*. In fact, Justice Tom Clark, in his majority opinion, supported some of Whittaker's interpretation in *Davis*, writing, "This is not to say that Slochower has a constitutional right to be an associate professor of German at Brooklyn College. The State has broad powers in the selection and discharge of its employees...."[103]

Friedman's description of *Shelton*, while much closer to the kind of inquiry that occurred in *Davis*, again failed to account for one important distinction—in *Shelton* the Supreme Court invalidated a state law that exceeded the legitimate interests of the state, relying again on the Due Process Clause of the Fourteenth Amendment. At no time did Davis raise a Fourteenth Amendment argument. Ironically, Friedman criticized Whittaker's failure to recognize Davis as a private school teacher but then chose to compare *Davis* to holdings affecting public school teachers. More important, though, Friedman, among others, confused the precise issue that led to Davis's dismissal, assuming it was his invocation of the Fifth Amendment before the

Jenner Committee.[104] That was what prompted university officials to *investigate* him, not what compelled them to *dismiss* him. His dismissal followed his refusal to respond to similar questions asked by the Board of Trustees of the university. A fine point, to be sure, but one that could have made a material difference in Davis's complaint. Atkinson and Larsen likewise concluded that the university dismissed Davis because he "violated an educational trust by not answering the questions asked *by the Jenner Committee*," and that "the precise issue before the court … was whether a refusal to testify before *a congressional committee* to prior lawful activities constituted 'adequate cause.'"[105] The precise issue in *Davis* related not so much to an exercise of a constitutional right as it did to whether a private university exercised proper discretion when it determined what constituted "adequate cause" for dismissal.

Considering the issues presented by Davis's complaint, Whittaker's ruling to dismiss it seemed warranted. Davis relied on a questionable and unsubstantiated "conspiracy" charge to establish federal jurisdiction, but the right he claimed had been violated, namely, the "right to teach," was not covered under the Constitution or laws of the United States. Since the "right to teach" was the only right asserted, Whittaker met that contention by relying on those cases cited in the university's brief that bore directly on the issue. In four out of the five cases cited, a teacher had failed to comply with the request of the school's administrative authority and, as a result, was discharged. In each of those cases the teachers were asked about possible Communist associations. Although the tide of public opinion would turn against such intrusions, the law was certainly on Whittaker's side. As he later remarked about the case, "I declared no new law. I followed the adjudicated cases. They are clear. No judge loyal to his oath as a judge and acting as befits a judge could rule otherwise than I did."[106] From a legal standpoint, *Davis* was not a complicated question. Had Whittaker spared his opinion of its personal pique, he might also have spared his reputation from so much criticism.

While none of Whittaker's other district court opinions received the kind of headline coverage as the *Davis* lawsuit or the trial of Arthur Ross Brown, several of his opinions were subsequently relied upon by other federal district and appeals courts for their value as legal precedents. This was due in no small part to Whittaker's comprehensive analysis of the question presented, leading to a clearly stated, convincing result. As a district court judge, then, Whittaker should be regarded as a skilled opinion writer proficient in developing sound legal reasoning to support his judgments. Nothing in his work as a district court judge suggested he was doubtful or indecisive, and he certainly did not feel overwhelmed in his new position. Remarking on Whittaker's self-assured style, Marlin Volz wrote, "His opinions give the impression of a judge who is very sure of himself and who has a strong conviction as to the correctness of his decisions."[107] Most all of

Whittaker's district court opinions were rulings on motions and were therefore of little practical interest to anyone but the parties involved. This has not, however, diminished their importance as legal precedents. Whittaker's five decisions as a district court judge that were later appealed either to the Eighth Circuit Court of Appeals or to the Supreme Court all became accepted final rulings once they were affirmed.[108] More impressive, though, nearly a dozen of his district court opinions later influenced the rulings in other district courts or courts of appeals on similar issues (one such issue Whittaker himself resolved while at the Supreme Court), and one of his district court opinions led to changes in the Federal Rules of Criminal Procedure. Few authors have commended Whittaker's lower court opinions, and none have treated them beyond their actual holdings to appreciate their lasting significance.[109] Therefore, Whittaker's short service on the district court has been overlooked as merely a stop-over on his way to the Supreme Court when, in fact, some of his best judicial work was done there. Considering his earnestness and complete satisfaction with the position, Whittaker's district court service and the decisions he rendered there deserve greater recognition.

One of the more remarkable precedents Whittaker established as a district court judge was a question of venue that he himself got to affirm five years later as a member of the Supreme Court. In *General Electric v. Central Transit Warehouse* the defendants requested a transfer of the case to another district court for the convenience of the parties and witnesses. Whittaker ruled against their motion because his understanding of the statute in question did not permit him to exercise his discretion in determining which district provided the most convenient forum. He found the controlling phrase of the statute was where the case "might have been brought,"[110] meaning where the parties conducted their business, regardless of any waiver or consent by the defendants. Since the requested district was not where the case "might have been brought" as an original suit, Whittaker ruled it could not be transferred there. His justification highlighted his concern for the precise meaning of words and their use in a statute:

> We recognize, of course, that venue can be waived. So can jurisdiction over the person be waived. But does such a waiver of either or both—made *after* an action has been "commenced" (by the mere filing of a complaint with the clerk *in any district* ...)—establish that the action "might have been brought" there.... If it does, what, if any, meaning is left to the phrase "where it might have been brought," as adopted by Congress and used in the statute? Would not such construction be to read that phrase entirely out of the statute? Would not such construction permit transfer of the action *to any district desired by the moving defendants*, though they, or some of them, could not have been served with process there, and no statutory venue existed there, and the action could not have been *maintained* there, without their intentional waiver of venue and entry of general appearance?[111]

Following Whittaker's decision in *General Electric*, the District Court for the Western District of Pennsylvania applied his standard, as did the Seventh Circuit Court of Appeals, which remarked, "In our view, the opinion by Judge Whittaker is sound. His reasoning and logic is unassailable and we think he reached the correct result."[112] This latter decision was then appealed to the Supreme Court where Whittaker received the assignment to write the majority opinion. Ironically, as a Supreme Court justice Whittaker had the opportunity to buttress his own previous position as a district court judge. While the chain of events leading to *Hoffman v. Blaski* were somewhat convoluted, Whittaker's position on matters of venue was clear: "We do not think 'where it might have been brought' can be interpreted to mean 'where it may now be rebrought, with defendant's consent.'"[113] As Justice Felix Frankfurter noted in his dissent, twenty-eight district courts had previously applied differing interpretations to the phrase "where it might have been brought," and, while he disagreed with the Court's narrow interpretation of that phrase, he agreed that a uniform application of it was needed.[114] Since the time of Whittaker's original decision as a district court judge, the Supreme Court in forty-five years has yet to reexamine his ruling in *Hoffman*, Congress has yet to change any statutory language related to the issue presented, and as late as 1986 circuit courts continued to apply his interpretation in questions of venue.

Certainly Whittaker's reputation as a district court judge was enhanced because none of his forty-eight decisions were ever overruled, but those events occurred while he was still a member of the federal judiciary. The particular factual settings of most district court decisions made them less applicable to the development of broader legal doctrine, especially over time. Therefore, the true testament of Whittaker's prestige as a district court judge can be found in those decisions that exerted their influence long after he left the federal judiciary. In one such case, *Wright v. Steele*, the First Circuit Court of Appeals determined in 1981 that since Whittaker's decision every federal court that considered the same question reached the same conclusion as he did twenty-seven years earlier.[115] Whittaker's concern in *Wright* was the holding in custody of a mentally incompetent defendant until considered competent to stand trial. The defendant, accused of a Dyer Act charge for transporting stolen vehicles, had been in the custody of the U. S. Medical Center at Springfield, Missouri, for one and a half years. Pushing aside concern for the defendant's well being following his release, Whittaker declared, "[T]he humanitarian factor is not for my determination, but, rather, the question before me is whether petitioner is being unlawfully deprived of his liberty."[116] Whittaker then ordered the defendant released, believing that one and a half years was a reasonable time to determine his competency. "[C]are must be taken," he concluded, "to see that the period consumed in determining his competency or incompetency to stand trial upon those charges does not approximate, and certainly does not exceed, the probable sentence—less 'good' time—he would have received and served had he pleaded, or been found, guilty as charged, for that would be to turn the statutory shield into a sword."[117] The Eighth Circuit Court of Appeals later venerated Whittaker's position in *Wright*, quoting extensively from it, and the Supreme Court subsequently affirmed the Eighth Circuit's opinion.[118]

Whittaker's most significant district court decision, though, for its longlasting influence, was *United States v. Smith*, which has been cited as *the* controlling precedent regarding the disclosure of bills of particulars and was even presented as the exemplum behind an amendment to the Federal Rules of Criminal Procedure.[119] The defendant in the case, Aloe Smith, was charged with the illegal sale of narcotics, and after pleading not guilty he requested a bill of particulars describing the government's contentions regarding when, where, and to whom the alleged sale took place. At issue in the case were the competing claims of the defendant's right to a fair trial if he was unable to prepare a proper defense and the government's ability to present evidentiary proof of the crime. Whittaker's interpretation of Rule 7 (f) of the Federal Rules of Criminal Procedure led him to conclude that Smith was entitled to the information requested "as of right," and that the government's contention that Smith already knew what he had done and did not need the information "could be valid only if the defendant be *presumed to be guilty*." To Whittaker, the result seemed inescapable: "For only if he is presumed guilty could he know the facts and details of the crime. Instead of being presumed guilty, he is presumed to be innocent. Being presumed innocent, it must be assumed 'that he is ignorant of the facts on which the pleader founds his charges.'"[120] In three subsequent cases, all decided by the District Court for the Southern District of New York, Whittaker's explanation for granting the defendant's request for a bill of particulars was cited as persuasive and controlling, despite a long line of cases holding otherwise.[121] This then led to an amendment to Rule 7 (f) in 1966 to eliminate the requirement on defendants to show cause and "to encourage a more liberal attitude by the courts toward bills of particulars." The Advisory Committee recommending the amendment cited with approval Whittaker's opinion in *Smith* and recommended it as a "wise use of this discretion."[122] The next year the Eighth Circuit Court of Appeals, sitting *en banc*, applauded Whittaker's role in setting the new standard, remarking, "The excellent opinion of Judge (later Justice) Whittaker in *U. S. v. Smith* ... establishes the general principles in this regard," and in 1972 the District Court for the Northern District of Georgia credited Whittaker for his part in bringing about the amendment that brought more uniform application to the rule.[123]

Brief though it was, just two years, Whittaker's service on the District Court for the Western District of Missouri contributed far more to the development of American law than has been recognized. An examination of his district court decisions has shown that he strove to state accurately the facts of each case, exhaustively examined relevant statutes and legal precedents, and rationalized his final decision in the most direct, unequivocal terms. Following his appointment to the Supreme Court, *Time* magazine praised Whittaker's work on the district bench, noting how he helped to clear the lagging docket and how his "closely reasoned, clearly stated opinions" earned recognition at the Justice Department.[124] Whittaker felt most comfortable at the district court because of the close interaction he had with the people he understood best—the lawyers. Being a lawyer, Whittaker believed, was a noble calling, one that brought esteem and recognition to the individual, but also one upon which ultimately depended the search for truth in legal controversies. It was a heavy burden, especially if one's liberty or property were at stake, and Whittaker often undertook that burden himself if a lawyer arguing in his court was not up to the task. At times Whittaker had to restrain his natural impulse to argue the case for the lawyers before him. Striving to remain impartial, Whittaker sought to construct his judicial opinions using the same deliberate, inductive style he had employed in his legal briefs. He wanted the lawyers who relied upon his decisions to understand precisely their holdings. Through his written opinions, Whittaker hoped to instruct lawyers on the law. "His opinions are pleasing to the lawyer," Marlin Volz observed, "because they state the facts orderly and concisely, set forth the issue before the court with exactness, deal with each meritorious contention of counsel, reason convincingly to the conclusion, and announce the holding of the Court with unmistakable definiteness."[125]

To accomplish what he did in such a short time, Whittaker had to exert tremendous energy to keep up the pace he set for himself. At times that pace took its toll, particularly because he relied little on his subordinates to do his work. While Judges Duncan and Ridge allowed their clerks to draft opinions for them, Whittaker's clerk has remembered drafting only one opinion in three years, and Whittaker rewrote it entirely. "My duties were to look up particular points of law," his clerk has observed, "Sometimes these involved abstract question of law. If I had no facts on the case I would have to ask Judge Whittaker for the case file to learn the facts."[126] Even then, Whittaker might become impatient with his clerk if the information he sought were not on his desk immediately, and, replaying a scene that occurred countless times at his old law firm, Whittaker would be in the library looking through the same books as his clerk, each taking turns. The tension of his duties took its toll on Whittaker physically by causing him headaches so painful that, at times, he had difficulty seeing clearly. Worried about his condition, his secretary, Celia Barrett, cautioned the other staff members about his previous "breakdowns" at their old law firm.[127] Whittaker may have enjoyed his judicial duties more than corporate counseling, but this change in routine neither relieved the pressure he put himself under nor diminished his anxieties.

The work atmosphere in Whittaker's chambers resembled his old law office, quiet preoccupation with nervous energy just below the surface. No one who worked for Whittaker felt relaxed on the job, at least, they did not think they should because he would not allow their interest or his expectations to lag. Treating his subordinates with civility, never comradely, Whittaker maintained a discreet detachment with those who worked closest to him. At times, though, his temper showed, especially if someone in his office interfered with his work. One day, retired Judge Albert Reeves returned to his old chambers and asked Whittaker's clerk if he could borrow a book from Whittaker's library. As a retired federal judge, Reeves still had an office in the courthouse, and the clerk felt obligated to give him the book. The next day as Whittaker conducted a pretrial conference with two lawyers in his library, he went to look up a point of law only to discover the book missing. After learning what had happened from his clerk, he pointedly declared, "*Nothing* leaves this office without *my* permission!" Rattled, the clerk sought to retrieve the book from Reeve's office, but it was locked. In desperation the clerk went to the chambers of Circuit Court Judge John Caskie Collet and borrowed his copy. Ironically, Whittaker soon replaced Collet on the circuit bench.[128]

On another occasion Whittaker's clerk received a lashing because he failed to interfere with what Whittaker was doing. It was a Saturday, and although court was not in session Whittaker was in his chambers working. Since there was no bailiff present on Saturdays to keep visitors from interrupting Whittaker, that task fell to his clerk. When an elderly-looking man wearing a jacket, plaid shirt with no tie, and carrying a disreputable looking hat came to Whittaker's chambers, the clerk told him the judge was too busy for visitors. "If it's important, he can be interrupted," the clerk said. "No," replied the man, "Have the judge call me when he's not busy. Tell him Caskie Collet was here." Stunned by the realization that he had just dismissed a federal judge, Whittaker's clerk tried to explain why he had sent Collet away, but Whittaker was already out the door. As he left to see Collet personally, Whittaker admonished his clerk," You *always* interrupt when Judge Collet is here!"[129]

In spite of the pressures he put on himself, the long hours and unrelenting pace, Whittaker was happiest serving on the district court. Looking forward to a comfortable retirement without the hassles and bureaucracy of private practice, he had returned to the one arena that still interested him— the trial courtroom. As a judge, though, Whittaker had to give up some of his former contacts, like his clients. A former associate of his has remembered how Whittaker's close association with other lawyers also diminished. "Occasionally he stopped by the [Watson] firm," this associate has said, "He always wanted to chat. He used to bemoan the fact that he had lost contact with his clients and with other lawyers. Because of the restraints on him as a judge, his conversations and friendships were impaired."[130] That did not stop Whittaker from eating lunch everyday at Wolferman's restaurant in downtown Kansas City; he still felt he could remain impartial, even surrounded by men who might end up arguing a case in front of him. Twice as a district judge Whittaker listened to arguments from Watson associates, but it could not be argued that he showed partiality toward his former law firm since in both cases the motions he sustained were not an end to the litigation.[131]

Although he felt restraints as a judge, Whittaker also felt immense satisfaction at the district court. So passionate was his love of the district court that, even after he had served on both the appeals court and Supreme Court, his greatest desire was to return to the district court. During his last year on the Supreme Court, in fact, Whittaker revealed just how much he missed serving on the district court. His former research assistant from 1952, future District Court Judge Joseph Stevens, Jr., was visiting Whittaker in Kansas City and mentioned his desire to fill a vacancy on the Jackson County Circuit Court. Whittaker advised him to be patient, though, predicting that one day Stevens would become a district court judge. "And let me tell you something, young man," Whittaker said, "When you get there—stay there!" Years later when Judge Stevens received the "Whittaker Award," presented annually by the Lawyers Association of Kansas City, he remembered Whittaker's regret and said, "There was some pathos in his remark. He longed for the district court but his friends and supporters would not let him stay where he really wanted to be."[132] Whittaker's pleasure at the district court was evident to those who worked closest to him, especially his clerk who followed him to the court of appeals. "Judge Whittaker loved the camaraderie of the district court," his clerk has said, "especially the pretrial conferences, the trials, and second guessing the jury. The Eighth Circuit was more cloistered."[133]

When Judge John Caskie Collet of the Eighth Circuit Court of Appeals died suddenly on December 5, 1955, at the age of fifty-seven, Charles Whittaker did not consider himself a candidate for appointment. He was content at the district court and intended to stay there. His intentions, though, were of little consequence. The people and policies that put him first on the court of appeals and then on the Supreme Court were already in place. There was little Whittaker could do to stop the process since he would not decline. It was not pride or vanity that compelled him to accept each subsequent appointment, but a strong sense of duty. Although he did, he felt as though he did not have a choice.

One of Whittaker's supporters for the circuit court appointment, Missouri Senator Thomas Hennings, wrote to both the president and the attorney general three weeks after Collet's death arguing for a Missourian to fill the vacancy. Although Hennings was a Democrat, there was still a sense of entitlement among senators for representation on the circuit courts, and Collet had been the only Missourian on the Eighth Circuit. Hennings and fellow Democratic Senator John McClellan of Arkansas—the only two states not then represented on the Eighth Circuit—both recognized that the majority of cases emanating from the Eighth Circuit originated in Missouri. As the fourth ranking member of the Senate Judiciary Committee, Hennings threatened to delay consideration of any nominee from another state. Supporting Whittaker's promotion, Hennings wrote the president, "Although Judge Whittaker and I are not of the same political faith, I know him as one of Missouri's ablest lawyers and I am well aware of his outstanding record as a federal district judge."[134] Certainly Hennings's endorsement of Whittaker helped smooth the way for his promotion, but there were additional factors that gave Whittaker a decided edge over other possible candidates. Eisenhower's elaborate set of criteria for the selection of federal judges had still another element implemented in late 1953 that ensured Whittaker's promotion: all appellate court appointments, including the Supreme Court, would have prior judicial experience. Eisenhower especially favored nominees already working within the federal judiciary or on state supreme courts because, to his military mind, such hierarchical promotion made sense.[135]

The introduction of prior judicial experience as a criterion for nomination made Whittaker's promotion to the Eighth Circuit Court of Appeals a near certainty. He had met Eisenhower's other criteria once already, and now that he had the necessary court experience for promotion, few other candidates satisfied both Eisenhower's expectations and Hennings's appeals for a fellow Missourian. Again, Roy Roberts offered considerable influence on Whittaker's behalf (this time unsolicited), using the *Star's* Washington correspondent, Duke Shoop, to appeal repeatedly with Brownell at the Justice Department.[136] Considering the circumstances, Charles Whittaker seemed the "perfect fit," with one slight drawback: no one had asked him if he wanted it. Whittaker later claimed he was unaware of his nomination until he read about it in the newspaper. He told an interviewer,

> I knew Collet had died and there was a vacancy. I didn't even know they were considering me. The appointment was announced before I was consulted. I was in St. Louis that day and saw in the St. Louis paper that I had been nominated by the president for the vacancy. No one had spoken to me about it.... It wasn't until I arrived home in Kansas City the next day that I was reached by telephone to ask if I would accept the nomination. They said they hoped it would be all right. I calculated it would be.[137]

Whittaker may have been reluctant to consider himself a candidate, but he certainly understood the *possibility* of promotion to a higher court. He admitted as much to his clerk at the time, who has remembered Whittaker telling him that Brownell mentioned the possibility of promotion to the circuit bench while they were still discussing Whittaker's district court appointment.[138] Using lower federal district and appeals court appointments as "stepping stones" to higher court appointments, then, became the standard

procedure during Eisenhower's presidency. Both Potter Stewart and John
Marshall Harlan were appeals court judges like Whittaker before Eisenhower
elevated them to the Supreme Court. Herbert Brownell, in fact, convinced
Harlan to join the Second Circuit Court of Appeals only as a means of getting Harlan on the Supreme Court. When Eisenhower considered appointing Brownell to the Supreme Court, he, too, suggested first putting Brownell
on the Second Circuit to prepare for promotion.[139] Eisenhower's fascination
with promotion from within the judiciary made Whittaker's advancement
possible. All someone like Roy Roberts had to do was decide he wanted
Charles Whittaker on the Supreme Court to make it happen.

Although several months passed between Whittaker's nomination and
final Senate confirmation, his prospects were never in jeopardy. Confirmation came swiftly and effortlessly. The Senate Judiciary Committee did receive
one protest during its deliberations, a "crank letter" from a man in St. Louis
who accused Whittaker of taking part in a "criminal conspiracy" in the death
sentence of Arthur Brown, but since the writer never appeared to testify the
Committee did not consider it.[140] On May 31, 1956, the Judiciary Committee
gave Whittaker unanimous approval without discussion, and the following
week, June 4, the full Senate unanimously approved his appointment. Praising the Senate's action, the *Kansas City Star* reported, "From all we have heard
he is recognized for the ideal combination of a keen legal mind and judicial
temperament. You hear lawyers comment on the fact that the 'new' legal problems aren't new to Judge Whittaker, a tribute to his reservoir of knowledge.
While he thinks faster than most lawyers he is known for patience. His help-
fulness with young lawyers has attracted special attention."[141] Less than three
weeks later in Kansas City retired Circuit Court Judge Kimbrough Stone,
who had been succeeded by Judge Collet, submitted the judicial oath.

Even before he began his new judicial service, at the news of his nomination Whittaker remarked how reluctant he felt at the prospect of leaving
the district court. "I am moving up to the court of appeals with mixed emotions," he told reporters, "During my two years on the bench I have had to
keep a rein on myself to keep from joining in with the lawyers trying the case.
I will miss the more active role of a district judge."[142] Around this same time
Whittaker issued another statement considerably less adverse about going to
the court of appeals, but still his words carried a note of doubt: "While I did
not seek the promotion and was in no sense a candidate for it, I recognize it
to be a great honor. I hope that I will be as happy on the United States court
of appeals bench as I have been on the federal district court bench. I must
say that this comes to me as a bolt out of the blue."[143] During his swearing-
in ceremony, following his judicial oath, Whittaker's words suggested a des-
perate tone, even trepidation, as he said, "I am sorry to leave the bench of
the district court…. I have never ceased praying to God. I will never cease
praying. He'll always see me through."[144] While it seemed everyone who had

a stake in his nomination came away satisfied with his appointment, Whittaker himself dreaded making the move. He had not sought a federal judgeship to be in the presence of other judges while they considered whether the law was correctly applied, but rather to be in the company of other lawyers during the actual trial of cases when judgments were first made. Feeling pushed into his new position, Whittaker approached the circuit court apprehensively, regretful at leaving the district court but determined not to disappoint his supporters. Soon he discovered his apprehensions were well founded. Life on the Eighth Circuit, what he considered "a rather drab existence," was not at all like working on the district court.

The Eighth Circuit Court of Appeals operated at a much slower pace than the district court principally because of the collegial nature of the institution. Comprised of seven judges who sat all together (*en banc*) only on rare occasions, the court met in three-judge panels. Making accommodations for other court members constrained someone like Whittaker who preferred his own pace. The judges heard appeals in St. Louis, Missouri, which became the permanent site in 1948. The chief judge, Archibald Gardner, randomly assigned three judges to hear cases together and then appointed one of them to write the opinion. According to his son, Kent, Whittaker looked forward to the intellectual exchange and debate of discussing cases with two other judges, but he became disappointed when he realized that it rarely occurred. The other judges simply stated how they would rule—nothing more.[145] While another judge on the panel could dissent from the majority, Gardner discouraged them, and in the thirty-three cases in which Whittaker participated there were only three dissents—two of those were Whittaker's.[146] Because of the accommodations necessary when an assignment placed him in the company of two of his colleagues, Whittaker grew frustrated working on the Eighth Circuit. As Theodore Fetter, historian for the Eighth Circuit, noted, "His strong beliefs sometimes made it difficult to function smoothly as one of several members of an appellate bench."[147]

Contributing to the slower pace of the Eighth Circuit were the relative ages of some of the judges. Of his six colleagues, three of them, Gardner, Joseph Woodrough, and John Sanborn, were all a generation older than Whittaker. Chief Judge Gardner, who was eighty-nine years old, had been on the court for twenty-seven years, and his eyesight had become seriously impaired. One time after hunting with his new gun, Gardner became indignant with Whittaker for asking if he had hit anything. Woodrough, age eighty-three, had been on the court for twenty-three years and was suffering hearing loss, although in time he would use a hearing aid. Despite his advanced age, Woodrough was best known for his long walks, sometimes outlasting even his own law clerks. Sanborn, considered the intellectual on the court, was seventy-three years old and had been on the court twenty-four years. These men, as well as Harvey Johnsen, who had been on the court for sixteen years, were part of an earlier era known as "the Stone Court" for its chief judge, Kimbrough Stone. This earlier court was considered more of a "family" than seven individuals each working in their home chambers. Staying in the same hotels, the judges in the 1940s deliberated in different cities around the Eighth Circuit. Following lunch they took long walks together and later in the evening discussed cases informally over dinner. There were few dissents then, and seldom the need for an *en banc* sitting. It was a time marked by long service and close relationships. By the time Whittaker joined the Eighth Circuit, the camaraderie of "the Stone Court" had begun to slip away due to changes in personnel, court procedures, and increasing court dockets.[148]

Although he spent only nine months serving on the Eighth Circuit, Whittaker became frustrated by the slow pace, long delays, and sense of isolation. Working from his chambers in Kansas City, Whittaker spent most of his time doing research, no doubt feeling like Judge Sanborn's comparison of an appellate judge to a "gnome in the library." Eager for assignments, Whittaker worked so quickly that in time he sensed a need to slow down. "He was sensitive to the fact that the other judges were much older," his clerk has said, "and he didn't want to appear to be 'showing off.'"[149] When district courts in the circuit became backlogged with cases, Whittaker jumped at the chance to assist them in clearing their dockets, and Gardner assigned him first to go to Iowa and then to Arkansas for additional duties.[150] It was during the trip to Iowa in late summer with just his clerk for company that Whittaker became unusually sociable, revealing a personal side few of his subordinates ever saw. "It was just the two of us riding together in his Cadillac," his clerk has remembered, "I learned then that he liked to ballroom dance when he was young. The judge told me that this was the first time in his life when he didn't feel like he was 'scratching' to get ahead. The work was more relaxed. Now that his sons were all adults, he said he felt like he had missed their growing up."[151]

Whittaker's record as a circuit court judge, while not laudatory, certainly was not impeachable. Although none of his circuit court opinions exerted the kind of influence as some of his district court decisions, none of them was ever overruled or condemned. Four of his circuit court opinions were later appealed to the Supreme Court, but two of those were denied *certiorari*, effectively upholding Whittaker's rulings, and the other two were both affirmed.[152] Since Whittaker's service on the Eighth Circuit was so short, he actually arrived at the Supreme Court before his four decisions on appeal did, preventing him from participating in their consideration. Having to sit through the consideration of four of his own appeals court opinions so recently decided must have been somewhat discomforting for him. So rapid was Whittaker's advancement through the federal judiciary that Justice Frankfurter reportedly quipped, "We can get a judge from the district court quicker than we can get a case from that court."[153]

What made Whittaker's judicial career so remarkable was that he served at all three levels of the federal judiciary and that he served such short terms at each level—so short, in fact, that each of his judicial commissions were signed by the same president. Every one of his colleagues on both the district and appeals courts served longer at just one level of the federal judiciary than Whittaker did at all three. Having served such a short time on the lower courts it would have been surprising for Whittaker's work to have made any impact on the development of law, but it did. Several of his decisions as a district court judge continued to exert their influence long after Whittaker ceased judging, and to his credit not one of his lower court decisions was reversed by a higher court. Considering his success as a lower court judge, many anticipated Whittaker would make an exceptionally well-qualified choice for the Supreme Court, that is, once he was appointed. Anticipating Whittaker would distinguish himself on the Supreme Court, Marlin Volz concluded that Whittaker's lower court decisions made him eminently qualified for the high bench: "His opinions were models of orderliness, of the use of direct, exact and concise language, of logical, careful and persuasive reasoning, of the expert analysis and application of legal authorities. They were readable and to the point. There could be no doubt as to what the court had held. In short, he showed himself to be a top-flight judicial craftsman."[154]

It was not Whittaker's skills as an opinion writer, though, that propelled him so rapidly through the federal court system. He needed the backing of influential Republican leaders, and, most importantly, he satisfied the complex, rigid requirements that Eisenhower promulgated for the selection of federal judges. Initially Whittaker sought a district court judgeship to return to the closeness of the trial courtroom, but, because he satisfied the political designs of interested parties in both Washington, D.C., and Kansas City, Whittaker was compelled to advance up through the federal judiciary however unwillingly. With each "promotion" up the judicial ladder, he found himself farther removed from his home and those pleasures that made him want to become a lawyer in the first place. Following his resignation from the Supreme Court, in subtly poignant phrases, Whittaker used one of his favorite analogies—baseball—to describe for bar association audiences his "run around the bases,"

> I was enabled to touch three bases in three years. I went to first on a walk, to second on a fielder's choice, and on the second pitch thereafter I was sacrificed to third. First base, the district court, being close to the dugout of the home team and its fans, was a perfect delight; second base, the United States Court of Appeals—particularly the Eighth Circuit—while a little more removed from the people, was a very quiet and comfortable position. But third base, I found truly to be, as the fans say, "the hot corner." Then came the most solemn quest for light that can proceed from the broodings of a human soul.[155]

Ready or not, Whittaker was about to embark on that quest.

4

Arriving at the Supreme Court

The Supreme Court in 1957 became the center of national controversy just after Charles Whittaker arrived there portending, coincidentally, the personal difficulties he suffered as a justice. The focus of national attention on the Court in the summer of 1957, which considerably diminished media attention on its newest member, concerned recent Court decisions regarding Communism and its supporters. Controversy surrounding Court decisions had been prevalent for the last three years since the Court announced its historic decision desegregating America's public schools, but this new controversy over Communism was by far the most serious threat to the Court's integrity since the constitutional crisis of 1937. Southern Democrats had led earlier attacks on the Court following its desegregation decisions, but this new threat came from a broader contingency having greater bipartisan support in Congress. Whittaker's arrival at the Court just prior to its showdown with the Eighty-fifth Congress marked the beginning of a new phase in the history of the Warren Court, one which separated the earlier period, highlighted by the desegregation decisions, from the later period, marked by unprecedented expansions in civil liberties—what history has remembered as "the Warren Court." This intermediate period, which included the longest time of uninterrupted membership on the Court during Earl Warren's tenure as chief justice, coincided with Whittaker's five years of service and has been recognized less for producing important landmark decisions (although there were a few) and more for providing a pause between the earlier and later periods.[1] That Whittaker served during this comparatively unremarkable period has seemingly rendered his five years of service all the more insignificant; yet, inside the Court during this intermediate period long fought battles, both personal and professional, were waged—battles that ultimately had a profound impact on Whittaker causing him considerable difficulty as a justice.

Whittaker's appointment to the Supreme Court came in the middle of the Court's 1956 term, unexpectedly to some but not to Justice Stanley Reed of Kentucky who had considered retirement for the last two years. The second of President Franklin Roosevelt's eight appointments to the Supreme Court, Reed served on the Court for nineteen years before announcing his retirement on the anniversary of his judicial oath, January 31, 1957. With his health and mental faculties still in good shape, at age seventy-two it seemed odd that he would announce his retirement during the middle of a court term, waiting until just after the Court's winter holiday break. The usual explanation for Reed's "jumping ship" in the middle of the term has been that he was dissatisfied with the "direction" the Court was taking. According to Reed's biographer and former clerk, John Fassett, "Only [Justice Sherman] Minton could be depended upon consistently to join him in resisting pressures to support krytocratic positions advocated by the activist bloc [consisting of Justices Black, Douglas, and Chief Justice Warren]."[2] After Minton left the Court for health reasons at the start of the 1956 term, it seemed that Reed would be all alone in dissent that term in cases involving subversive Communist activities. Fassett's most reasonable explanation for Reed's announced retirement in the middle of the term, then, was that Reed "foresaw nothing but defeat and frustration to come by his participation in the significant number of major cases scheduled to be argued and decided during the balance of the term."[3]

By leaving the Court halfway through the term, Reed was able to disassociate himself from those decisions where he anticipated he would be in the minority, but many of the cases to which Fassett referred had not yet been argued and their outcomes were in no way certain.[4] Besides, while Chief Justice Warren could be found voting most consistently with Justices Hugo Black and William Douglas, the positions of other recent appointments were then unclear. John Marshall Harlan had served on the Court for only one full term, and William Brennan had replaced Minton just a few months earlier. By retiring when he did, Reed not only avoided participation in some highly publicized, controversial decisions, he also denied himself and his successor the opportunity to place in the record an opinion positively stating their contrary views. Not unless the Court delayed arguments in most of these cases could a replacement be appointed and confirmed in time to participate in them. (Of course, reargument was unnecessary because in none of the controversial decisions handed down at the end of the 1956 term was the outcome a split Court.) Furthermore, the Court's historic decision in *Brown v. Board of Education* ending segregation in the nation's public schools just three years earlier gave ample proof that Reed had little compunction about writing a sole dissent in a highly controversial case if he believed the Court had exceeded its legitimate authority. The fact that he could be persuaded not to issue his proposed dissent in that case also served as an indication that case outcomes were never certain until their announcement. Considering Reed thought about retirement for nearly two years, there must have been other factors leading to that decision than his concern over participation in certain cases scheduled for argument during the latter part of the 1956 term.[5]

When the press asked Reed why he was retiring, he smiled and said, "Because I'm seventy-two years old."[6] It appeared Reed was being facetious with reporters, but his age was, in fact, one of the principal reasons for his departure. At the time of his announced retirement, few people took note of the fact that as solicitor general in 1937 Reed had publicly supported President Roosevelt's plan to "pack" the Supreme Court by adding another justice for each one over age seventy who refused to retire. While Reed's involvement in developing the plan has been open to speculation, his public support of the plan became apparent in the months following its announcement.[7]

This public involvement in the "Court-packing" controversy of 1937 lay heavy on the conscience of Justice Reed following his seventieth birthday almost twenty years later. Confiding to his clerk at the time, Reed explained his reason for retiring: "He told me he had been on the steps of the Court when the press asked him what he thought of Roosevelt's plan. He thought it was inappropriate for him to comment, but, feeling like he should say *something*, he said anyone at age seventy should retire. No one remembered that he had said this."[8] By January 1957 Reed had turned seventy-two years old, and his conscience had caught up with him. Although he did not want to leave, he remembered his public statements about required retirement and felt as though he had no choice. While the news of Reed's retirement came as no surprise to his own clerks, some of those working for other justices were caught off guard. The day Reed's retirement was announced, one of Justice Felix Frankfurter's clerks strode into Reed's office, bypassing completely the usual protocol of waiting first to be announced, and started shouting at Reed, "How can you leave the country to the Communists?"[9]

Reed's announced retirement so soon after Minton's departure and timed to follow the Court's holiday break seemed abrupt to some observers, but the chief justice, the president, and the attorney general certainly knew of Reed's plans before he went public.[10] In fact, not only were Reed's plans a well guarded secret between the Justice Department, the White House, and the Court, but for several months it seemed probable that Whittaker's selection as Reed's replacement was considered long before Whittaker ever got the call. According to John Fassett, Reed wrote to the president and discussed with Eisenhower his plans to retire before the actual announcement, but, more important, Chief Justice Warren probably knew of Reed's plans during the holiday break once Reed had made up his mind.[11] Furthermore, Warren may have suspected that Whittaker was next in line for appointment to the Supreme Court. When Whittaker's first clerk at the Supreme Court, Alan Kohn, a graduate of Washington Law School in St. Louis, first applied to the Court in November 1956 he sent applications to both Justice Tom Clark of Texas and Chief Justice Warren, hoping to improve his chances of being selected. After Clark rejected his application, Kohn made plans to begin his law practice in St. Louis, having heard nothing from Warren all through December and January. As far as Kohn was concerned, his application had been overlooked or discarded, either way he was sure by mid–March that it was too late to receive a clerkship. Then, a few days after Whittaker took his seat on the Court, Kohn received an invitation from him for an interview. Shocked and confused how his application addressed to Warren from four months earlier ended up in the hands of the Court's newest appointee, Kohn later suspected that Warren intentionally held his application aside because Warren knew that Reed was planning to retire and that Whittaker might be on tap to get the appointment. According to Kohn, when Whittaker arrived in Washington for his nomination announcement, Warren asked him if he had a clerk, and Whittaker replied, "I don't even have a place to stay yet." Warren reassured him, saying, "I've got one for you from Missouri," and he gave Kohn's application to Whittaker, noting that Kohn would be available to start his clerkship in April, about the same time Whittaker began his duties at the Court.[12]

No doubt, Whittaker, too, had his own suspicions that he might be headed for the Supreme Court. Not that he wanted to go—he dreaded the possibility, but he could not ignore it. As soon as Reed's retirement was announced, far less attention was paid to his nineteen years on the Court as to the field of likely successors and their philosophical orientations. The day after Reed's announcement, the *New York Times* ran a front page story speculating on possible candidates. Among those listed were Charles Whittaker and future Supreme Court Justice Potter Stewart, both federal appeals court judges at the time. Federal appeals court judges were prominent on the list of potential candidates (since Eisenhower's policy of judicial promotion had become widely known), especially those from middle America because geographical representation on the Court was then considered an issue.[13] Just as important, though, Eisenhower's policy of promotion was communicated personally to Whittaker; he knew his chances were good to move up the judicial ladder. One of Whittaker's former colleagues has remembered Whittaker telling him that when discussing the district court appointment with the attorney general, he was told if it worked out he could go to the Supreme Court: "He knew he might be going to the Supreme Court and had a hard time keeping it to himself."[14]

Evidence that Whittaker suspected he might be promoted to the Supreme Court can also be found by looking at his appeals court decisions. He failed to write one of his last opinions as an appeals court judge, a dissent in *Milwaukee Insurance v. Kogen*, rendered more than two weeks before he received official notification of his nomination. This seemed unusual given that insurance was a field of law in which Whittaker had considerable experience and that he had a predilection for writing thorough, well-researched opinions. Whittaker was too proud of his writing, his command of language, not to compose a dissent clearly stating his views. His disdain of misinterpretation would have compelled him to at least announce his rationale for dissenting, even if he could not find precise supporting details for his arguments. As Theodore Fetter, historian of the Eighth Circuit, noted, as a judge, "[Whittaker] was an advocate, earnestly pressing the points with which he agreed."[15] Whittaker had already dissented once before on the court of appeals, and he was anxious for writing assignments due to the slower pace of appellate judging. What could have caused Whittaker to neglect his written opinion in this dissent, his last opinion as an appeals court judge? The call from Attorney General Brownell recommending his nomination for the Supreme Court did not come until February 28. Were there other indications that he might be elevated to the Supreme Court before the formal announcement was made, other than the persistent encouragement from his friends reassuring him that he would be the one? The day he was nominated, Whittaker's wife, Winifred, told reporters, "We had all heard rumors that the judge might be appointed to the Supreme Court." Whittaker, though, may have had more than rumors to fuel his suspicion. His sister, Dorothy, who met with him at least a week before the formal announcement was made, even before the phone call from the attorney general, said Whittaker had hinted then that he might not "be around long."[16]

Once again, just as his promotion to the court of appeals was all but assured, Whittaker's appointment to the Supreme Court seemed predestined because of two compelling factors: Eisenhower's insistence on a set of restrictive criteria for the selection of federal judges and the incessant urgings of Eisenhower's close friend and confidant, Roy Roberts, president and general manager of the *Kansas City Star*. Ironically, Eisenhower's first three appointments to the Supreme Court had not necessarily followed his preferred set of criteria for choosing the most highly qualified candidates for the position. His first choice, Earl Warren as chief justice, fulfilled a political promise. His second choice, John Marshall Harlan, was an abdication to the personal preference of his attorney general. His third choice, William Brennan, was designed to meet the demands of several disparate constituencies just before Eisenhower's re-election: Catholics, state court judges, and Democrats.[17] Not that these appointments proved unworthy (Eisenhower later became disappointed with the judicial positions of both Warren and Brennan), but none of them yet satisfied completely Eisenhower's objective, impersonal set of criteria, what he believed would yield the best candidates. With his re-election just three months behind and Brennan's confirmation still pending in the Senate, Eisenhower had for the first time an opportunity to let his criteria-driven selection process choose who he believed was the most qualified person to join the Supreme Court. That person would undoubtedly be a moderate to conservative Republican sharing Eisenhower's "middle of the road" philosophy of governance. He would have to be relatively young (under age sixty-two) and possibly from the Midwest, which was under-represented on the Court, although geography was not determinative of the choice. The paramount concern was prior judicial experience, and that had to come from one of the federal courts of appeals.[18]

Eisenhower devised several compelling reasons for insisting on prior judicial experience as a qualification for Supreme Court appointments. First, he thought that lower federal court service provided some guidance when judging a candidate's judicial philosophy, based on their lower court opinions. As he later admitted, "Prior judicial experience did not stem primarily from the belief that the experience *per se* would be valuable. Rather, ... looking at what a man had done as a judge was the best way to get a good reading on what he would do in his new post."[19] Eisenhower's attorney general, Herbert Brownell, suggested other purposes behind Eisenhower's preference for candidates with judicial experience. According to Brownell, judicial experience exhibited a candidate's judicial temperament, their judicial craftsmanship, and their willingness to sacrifice personal income for public service.[20] Taken together, these two perspectives suggested that Eisenhower was just as concerned with finding good judges as he was with finding the right kind of judges. Although he would be criticized for relying so heavily on prior judicial experience as his lodestar for selecting Supreme Court justices, Eisenhower remained committed to finding only qualified candidates, without letting personal attachments or patronage considerations guide his decision.[21]

In order to find the best possible candidate for the new Court vacancy, Eisenhower continued to rely entirely on his attorney general to come up with recommendations, yet Brownell was limited in the use of his own discretion by Eisenhower's restrictive criteria when searching for qualified candidates. This greatly simplified Brownell's task. He had to find the most highly recommended moderate Republican judge under the age of sixty-two then serving on the federal courts of appeals, preferably one from the Midwest. His search yielded few candidates, only fourteen, and, as Brownell later admitted, none of them struck him as being above the rest. Early on in their search the administration was interested in Judge Elbert Parr Tuttle of the Fifth Circuit, but Brownell had his doubts about nominating a southern judge who had loyally enforced the Court's recent desegregation decision.[22] So it appeared initially that there was no obvious front-runner, that is, none of the judges who met Eisenhower's criteria also impressed Brownell as being suited for selection to the Supreme Court. Rather than expanding their search by loosening Eisenhower's criteria, Brownell had to come up with a good reason to recommend someone from his short list of potential candidates. Whittaker's name rose to the top of the list because Roy Roberts put insistent pressure on the Justice Department to get Whittaker named to the Supreme Court, not because of the quality of Whittaker's work on the lower federal courts. According to Brownell, just after Reed's announced retirement, Roberts began to literally "pester" Brownell about a Whittaker appointment. Throughout the next month Roberts had his Washington correspondent, Duke Shoop, petition Brownell on behalf of Whittaker. Giving in either to Roberts's persistency or Roberts's considerable influence with the president, Brownell decided to look over Whittaker's record. What he found did not impress him. Whittaker was a good judge, but not an outstanding one.[23] Brownell made the recommendation, though, because Whittaker fit Eisenhower's criteria as well as any other federal judge on the list, and Whittaker had something the other candidates did not: an enthusiastic booster who happened to be good friends with the president. Without first consulting Whittaker, Roy Roberts decided he wanted to place someone on the Supreme Court, and, thanks to Eisenhower's limiting set of criteria, Whittaker was in the right place for Roberts to achieve his goal.[24]

Four weeks after Reed's announced retirement Whittaker first learned of his nomination. When he arrived home Thursday evening, February 28, his wife greeted him at the garage door and told him the attorney general had called. Whittaker was supposed to make contact with the attorney general that same day. Aware of the possible implications, Whittaker phoned Washington, and Brownell told him either he was prepared to make a recommendation to the president or he had already made one, Whittaker could not remember which. "He didn't specifically mention the Supreme Court," Whittaker later said, "but that was needless."[25] Although his name had been mentioned in the press as a possible candidate for the appointment and his friends in Kansas City had endlessly speculated on his promotion, Whittaker still was shocked at the news because he could not see himself on the inside track. He had been on the Eighth Circuit Court of Appeals for only eight months—hardly the experience one needed to prepare for the Supreme Court. Other possible candidates, like Potter Stewart from the Sixth Circuit, had been appeals court judges for more than two years. It was inconceivable that Whittaker could move so rapidly from the court of appeals to the Supreme Court. Besides, only once before had a justice of the Supreme Court sat previously as both a district and later appeals court judge, and it had taken fifteen years and three presidents to move him through all three levels. How could Eisenhower put Whittaker on three different courts in less than three years? Not only did Whittaker have difficulty taking seriously the suggestion that he could go to the Supreme Court, but he earnestly did not want to go—no more than he had wanted to go to the court of appeals. Had it not been for Roy Roberts's ambition, Whittaker could have remained content as a district court judge the rest of his life.

Even with his staff at the court of appeals, Whittaker did not speculate on his chances for promotion, and they first learned of his nomination from the newspaper. When Whittaker failed to report to his office on Friday morning, no one there guessed he was on his way to Washington for a press conference. (Whittaker later enjoyed telling his law clerks how he had to get the owner of the dry cleaners store to open early Friday morning so he could retrieve his only blue suit for the trip to Washington.)[26] On Saturday, March 2, Whittaker arrived at the White House without ceremony; he had met Eisenhower only once before, a pro forma meeting following his appointment to the court of appeals. Without notice of the nomination, newsmen gathered in the press secretary's office, becoming aware of the announcement only when they saw Whittaker seated at a desk. After hearing the announcement read, Whittaker lit a cigarette and puffed on it slowly. "I am almost rendered numb," he told the newsmen, "I was just stunned. I had no indication. I had heard rumors that I might be appointed, but I had no reason to take them seriously."[27] Whittaker was not the only one shocked to learn of his appointment. The man he replaced, Stanley Reed, thought his good friend, Potter Stewart, would be his replacement; at least, Reed got that impression from Eisenhower. According to Reed's former clerk at the time, it was important to Reed to have Stewart replace him, and Reed was disappointed with Whittaker's selection.[28]

Praise at the news of Whittaker's nomination came from both political and legal circles. In the House of Representatives, Republican Congressman William Avery of Kansas expressed his particular satisfaction that the nominee hailed from the Midwest. Acknowledging Whittaker's humble beginnings, Republican Representative Thomas Curtis of Missouri applauded Whittaker's professional success, first as a lawyer and then as a judge, saying

> There is one feature above all others that makes this appointment so timely and heart-warming. In this age of sophistication and specialization there is a growing tendency to believe that the old virtues of perseverance and hard work are insufficient to bring about success.... Justice Whitaker's [*sic*] career as a student, a lawyer, a jurist, and now his elevation to an Associate Justice of the Highest court in our land demonstrates that the basic human virtues still play a vital part in our society.[29]

In its investigation of Whittaker's professional qualifications the same association that forty years earlier had hoped to prevent someone like Whittaker from even attending law school, the American Bar Association (ABA), found Whittaker eminently qualified for the Supreme Court. Bernard Segal, chairman of the ABA's standing committee on the federal judiciary, highly praised Whittaker's nomination, saying, "Judge Whittaker has served with distinction and to the complete satisfaction of the bar. His judicial service has been marked by outstanding legal ability, industry, and judicial temperament."[30] Aside from the customary applause attending his nomination, Whittaker also received accolades from the man he replaced on the district court, retired Judge Albert Reeves, who said at the news of Whittaker's nomination, "I think Judge Whittaker was the finest selection the president could have made. I daresay there isn't a man on the bench better qualified than Judge Whittaker.... [He] represents what lawyers want on the courts."[31]

Not everyone was as thrilled at the news of Whittaker's nomination. Fyke Farmer, the Nashville lawyer who assisted Horace Davis in his failed attempt to sue the University of Kansas City in Whittaker's courtroom two years earlier, made the trip to Washington to testify against Whittaker before the Senate Judiciary Committee. Claiming Whittaker had a "personal predilection, amounting to a prejudice or bias, against fundamental principles of the Constitution," Farmer contended in his prepared testimony that Whittaker's ruling against Davis was "the most fell judicial blow that has been struck on this continent against human liberty."[32] Committee members, however, were not as interested in discussing Whittaker's ruling in the *Davis* case as they were with examining the writings and activities of the witness and his sympathy with the Communist Party. Questioning Farmer at length about his participation in various Communist "front" groups, Committee members hoped to establish his "character" before they gave any weight to his testimony. Once the exact nature of the questions Davis refused to answer before the Board of Trustees of the University of Kansas City was determined, Democratic Senator John McClellan of Arkansas, for one, expressed his satisfaction with Whittaker's ruling in the case, saying, "Any private institution or any public institution has a responsibility ... to eradicate from their staff, to remove from their staff, and to refuse to hire people on their staff who will not openly and frankly state their position with respect to whether they belong to or support an organization that is in a conspiracy to destroy this Government. And failure to do it, in my opinion would be a lack of fidelity to their country, and I commend them and I commend the judge for this opinion."[33] What became clear from the hearing was that Whittaker's appearance was merely a formality—his actual testimony was short, even cursory—since no one on the Committee had any misgivings whatsoever about his qualifications. Instead, Committee members pilloried Farmer for his support of Communism, chiding him for never appealing Whittaker's decision in the *Davis* case and openly criticizing him for suing former President Truman to prove that Truman had never legally committed the nation to war in Korea. Ironically, a great portion of the hearing was devoted not to discussing Whittaker's qualifications to be a judge but rather to discussing Horace Davis's qualifications to be a teacher and Fyke Farmer's qualifications to be a witness before a Congressional Committee. Following Whittaker's brief statement defending his decision in the *Davis* case (as well as strong recommendations from the Missouri Bar Association and Missouri's two Democratic Senators, Thomas Hennings and Stuart Symington), the Judiciary Committee unanimously approved Whittaker's nomination and sent it the next day to the full Senate.[34]

There were several reasons Whittaker's Supreme Court nomination seemed to sail effortlessly through the Senate, not the least of which because the Senate had twice before approved his lower court nominations. To have acted any differently would have seemed like admitting a mistake.[35] After Missouri Senator Symington announced the nomination to the Senate, Republican Senator Frank Carlson of Kansas commended the president for it, exclaiming Whittaker had "the background, the experience, the character, and the judicial temperament to become one of the outstanding members of the United States Supreme Court."[36] On the same day the Senate considered Whittaker's nomination it also considered the recess appointment of William Brennan, who already had served on the Court for five months without Senate approval. Being a recess appointment, a Catholic, and a Democrat, Brennan faced more scrutiny from the Senate than Whittaker, but both were easily confirmed. Understandably, Whittaker's nomination went unopposed; he met Eisenhower's criteria for the selection of federal judges, he had no blemishes on his professional record—at least none that conservative Republicans found damaging, and he had twice before been confirmed by the Senate. There was no reason to doubt that both Whittaker and Brennan would pass inspection. Prior to 1957, every Supreme Court nominee since 1930 had been confirmed; the Senate approved every one of seventeen appointments, including every justice then serving on the Court.[37] Praising Whittaker's selection, Senator Hennings of Missouri announced, "He is a man of the highest character, a man of unimpeachable integrity, and a man of courage. He is scrupulously fair in his decisions and understanding of the law. In addition to all these qualities, he has proved himself to be one of the hardest working members of the federal bench."[38] Without a dissenting vote, the Senate confirmed Whittaker on March 19 (Brennan was also confirmed that same day, with the only "no" vote shouted audibly by Republican Senator Joseph McCarthy of Wisconsin), and one week later he took the oath of office.[39]

The three weeks between Whittaker's nomination and his swearing-in as an associate justice were especially hectic—and exciting—for his family. When Whittaker's nomination was announced, his wife, Winifred, was at home in Kansas City tending to their youngest son, Gary, a senior at Rockhurst

Keith — a momentus day — your Dad's inauguration day
Fondest Regards
Walt G.

Whittaker's family en route to his swearing-in. For the flight to Washington the Whittakers relied on their long-time friends, Russell and Mabel Gunn, whose nephew, Walt, flew the plane. Making all the arrangements herself to move their family to Washington, Winifred was without Charles for this trip because he remained in Washington following their dinner with the president, the chief justice, and the rest of the Court. *Left to right*: Mabel Gunn, Winifred, Walt Gunn, Keith, Pat (Keith's wife), and Gary. (Photograph courtesy of Dr. C. Keith Whittaker)

High School who had the flu. The week after Whittaker returned to Kansas City he received a call from Chief Justice Warren inviting him and Winifred back to Washington to have dinner at the Supreme Court with the president and the other justices. Winifred was busy making all the arrangements for the family to travel to Washington for the swearing-in ceremony as well as plans to move to Washington. She lost four pounds in all the excitement (insisting she would rest after the swearing-in) and did not have time to go shopping for a new dress. Described as vivacious and charming, Winifred later remarked to reporters, "I was in a twit. I didn't know what to wear, but I didn't want to bring anything showy. After all, we are newcomers and I want to be as inconspicuous as possible."[40] Winifred's best friend, Mabel Gunn, who first met Whittaker during his fraternity days at law school, offered Winifred a navy taffeta evening dress, explaining that it had been worn only once in Mexico City and would be appropriate for the nation's capital as well.[41] When they arrived in Washington, Chief Justice Warren took the Whittakers on a tour of the Court building. That evening the Whittakers ate dinner in the justices' conference room where they met the Eisenhowers, the Brownells, and the justices and their wives, including retired Justices Reed and Minton. Afterwards, riding in the chief justice's limousine back to their hotel, the Whittakers were giddy with excitement. Charles commented, "This last week has been like a dream," and Winnifred said, "I've just got to pinch myself to think that all this is true."[42]

Since the judicial conference of the eleven courts of appeals was being held in Washington later that same week, Whittaker decided to stay and represent Chief Judge Gardner of the Eighth Circuit and then remain for his hearing before the Senate Judiciary Committee. Winnifred returned to Kansas City to make final arrangements to fly the whole family back to Washington for the swearing-in. Because Whittaker was staying in a different hotel as the rest of his family, all their luggage had to be rearranged for the flight. Winifred and Gary returned to Washington with Keith, who was then an intern at Kansas City's General Hospital and about to begin his residency at the University of Kansas Medical Center, and Keith's wife. The other son, Kent, a senior at Dartmouth College, drove his 1955 red Corvette convertible from Hanover, New Hampshire, to Washington so the family could have a vehicle during their stay. Kent flew back to Kansas City with the rest of the family and returned to Washington with his father's maroon Cadillac before driving his own car back to college. As it turned out, Whittaker arrived to work his first few days as an associate justice in his son's red Corvette convertible.[43]

After Whittaker's nomination was announced, he joked with reporters about his brief terms at both the district and appeals courts, saying, "It looks like I can't hold a job."[44] Once the initial shock and excitement over his elevation began to dissipate, though, there was little humor to his predicament. Without warning or solicitation, Whittaker was thrust into the national spotlight, an unnerving experience. He was now a member of the Supreme Court, the highest judicial office in the country. At least within the Missouri legal community Charles Whittaker had been *somebody*. Others respected what he had accomplished considering his background and legal training. He was a self-made man who could be proud of his own success. Being a district court judge was his life's one ambition, yet here he was, the junior member of one of the most powerful decision-making bodies in the country where, ironically, he would sink into obscurity.

Whittaker felt keenly the awesome power of his new responsibility, and he did not want it. Furthermore, he did not want to leave the only place he had ever known as home. Whittaker had deep roots in Kansas City, both personal and professional, and he hated to be so far away from his family and friends living in Washington where everything was different and seemed strange to him. Trying to hold on to the life he once knew, Whittaker returned to the Kansas City area as often as he could during his five years on the Supreme Court as a way of replenishing his spirit. One of his former law associates has remembered how disconcerting life in Washington was for Whittaker: "The situation was not what he expected. He did not realize the difference between his background and the society in the East. He was not cultured in the eastern sense. He was shocked by what he found."[45] Hoping to overcome his disappointment and reluctance over his "promotion," Whittaker made light of his situation, telling bar association audiences that he "felt clean" going though J. Edgar Hoover's laundry three times in the last three years.[46] Privately, though, Whittaker believed he had made a mistake ever accepting the president's offer, and it took some time for him to change his mind about that.

The Whittakers never were completely satisfied living in Washington. During his first three months in Washington while the Court finished its 1956 term, Whittaker lived "the lonesome life of a bachelor in a little apartment." Winifred remained in Kansas City, and when their youngest son, Gary, graduated from high school in early June, Whittaker was there for the occasion. His mind was elsewhere, though, as a newspaper reporter noted: "He leaned far forward with his head down, as if in deep thought. Occasionally he sat upright, then leaned forward again and made several pencil notations."[47] In addition to the work of the Court, Whittaker was preoccupied with finding a new home in Washington for his family. Over the Court's summer "vacation," the Whittakers moved into a new house in Washington's fashionable Spring Valley. Whittaker glumly remarked to reporters that the new home was half as big and comfortable as his home in Kansas City but cost him twice as much.[48] Now Charles and Winifred were part of Washington's socially elite, a role ill-suited to either of them. They seldom attended social affairs and rarely entertained at home. Not caring for the glamour of "official life" in Washington, Winifred cooked their family's meals and cleaned their home herself. One reporter described her as a "refreshing ocean breeze in the stilted and stuffy atmosphere of Washington's frenzied social life. She is free of pretense."[49] Winifred had little to do in Washington but the cooking and shopping, and once their youngest son went away to college she needed to find other outlets for her energy than cleaning an empty home.

Winifred had been active in Catholic affairs in Kansas City, and so to recapture that part of her life before moving to Washington she continued to assist charitable organizations affiliated with the Church. Dissatisfied living in Washington, being so foreign and far removed from her experience, on her first visit to a Washington church she told a friend, "This is not my church."[50] Winifred also volunteered to work at area hospitals. Since no one recognized her as the wife of a Supreme Court justice, her presence at Georgetown University Hospital attracted little attention, that is, until John Kennedy recognized her. In late November 1960, president-elect Kennedy returned to Washington from a trip to Florida to visit his wife and newborn son in the hospital. Well-wishers and hospital workers were kept cordoned off so Kennedy could easily pass through hospital corridors. Recognizing Winifred in the crowd of spectators, Kennedy paused briefly as he strode through the hospital to say, "Hi, Mrs. Whittaker." Hospital administrators were taken by surprise: she knew the next president! Masking their embarrassment at having treated her like any ordinary volunteer, soon hospital administrators wanted to know just whom they had in their volunteer services.[51] Not that it would have made any difference to Winifred to have them know she was married to a Supreme Court justice. She did not volunteer to be publicly recognized. In fact, during the five years they lived in the capital, the Whittakers were seldom recognized, not even Charles, who was the one appointed to the Court.

As an associate justice of the Supreme Court, it was surprising how little Whittaker was recognized outside the courtroom, considering the intense news coverage his appointment carried. Once the media frenzy quieted, however, the most junior justice fell into relative obscurity. Most of the news stories relating Whittaker's anonymity were intended to be light-hearted, illustrating the irony of the situation. People who came into contact with him might have been more impressed had they realized just what he did for a living. For example, after Whittaker had been on the Court for more than a year, he and Chief Justice Warren were in Los Angeles attending a meeting of the ABA when a law student stopped them and said, "I've always wanted to have my picture taken with the Chief Justice of the United States, would you mind?" Warren answered, "Not at all." The student then turned to Whittaker and asked him to take the picture.[52] A few months later, Whittaker was in Kansas City on one of his annual holiday visits riding in a car with a friend. His friend continued to address him as "justice," so when the car stopped in front of Whittaker's hotel the chauffeur opened the door for him, bowing grandly as he stepped onto the curb. The next day as the car passed by Whittaker's hotel again, the chauffeur remarked to the friend's wife, "That's where I took that Justice of the Peace yesterday."[53]

Whittaker's public obscurity was more than mistaken identity, though; he was too modest to flaunt his position. Although he had rank and privilege, he did not expect special treatment. A rugged individualist, Whittaker preferred to perform his own labors. A classic example of this occurred during his first summer in Washington. As a lawyer Whittaker had a habit of offering rides home to his associates, as much to impress them with his automobile as to continue their conversations, and during his first year on the Court he drove his clerk, Alan Kohn, to a Washington bus stop. Kohn has remembered that the tire valves on Whittaker's Cadillac were exceptionally long, and on one unbearably hot day during rush hour one of the valves snapped off when

Whittaker pulled up too close to the curb. The tire was immediately flat. Kohn suggested they call a service station to come repair the tire, but Whittaker took off his jacket saying, "We can fix this ourselves." Struggling in the heat, it took both men to change the tire. None of the traffic that passed that day gave them any notice. Kohn has said, "No one at that bus stop had any idea who we were." It was then that Whittaker first confided to his clerk that his move to the Supreme Court had been a big mistake. He said he had "sold himself down the river for a pot of porridge," and Kohn thought Whittaker was ready to quit the Court right then.[54] Changing his own tire during rush hour traffic was not the most daring stunt Whittaker performed in the service of his automobile. As a lower court judge, about the time he moved to the Court of Appeals, Whittaker saved his car from costly damage when he put out an engine fire. It happened a few blocks from his home in Kansas City; his car had stalled near the fountain at Meyer Circle and Ward Parkway. Passionate about his cars, Whittaker was not about to abandon his vehicle when smoke appeared under the hood, so he used his straw hat to carry hatfuls of water from the fountain to put out the fire.[55]

Being a member of the Supreme Court entitled Whittaker to a lifestyle to which he was unaccustomed. He was now a member of Washington's politically privileged. The Whittakers, however, spent their nights at home, avoiding the countless invitations they received to attend any number of parties reserved for Washington's elite class. Not that they were unsociable; the Whittakers enjoyed the company of close friends, who all still happened to live in Kansas City. Feeling outclassed, Whittaker remained the perennial outsider in Washington. Besides, the tremendous workload of the Court provided a reasonable excuse for not going out more often, and as one of Whittaker's clerks has explained, "They had to be careful of the diplomatic swirl and the military swirl. They could not afford to make the wrong impression."[56] On one of the rare occasions when Whittaker accepted an invitation to be a guest at a formal cocktail party, he happened to be the highest-ranking government official present. Washington protocol required that other guests remain until the highest-ranking official departed. Whittaker spent most of the evening off to one side speaking with his friend the Australian Ambassador, completely unaware of his prerogative or the other guests' discomfort waiting on him to leave. The hostess finally had to ask Winifred to persuade Whittaker to leave so the other guests could depart. After a fair interval driving around in his car, Whittaker returned to the party to continue his conversation.[57]

According to Whittaker's youngest son, Gary, there were other privileges to having rank. During one of his college breaks, Gary was riding in Whittaker's car when Whittaker made a right turn on a red light. Since Whittaker had a two-digit license plate (forty-seven), reserved for high-ranking government officials, he was surprised when a motorcycle policeman pulled him over.

Whittaker tried to explain how right turns on red lights were permitted in some places, but the policeman flatly stated, "Not in Washington." Rattled and somewhat embarrassed at receiving a traffic ticket in Washington, Whittaker confided to the policeman, "Let me tell you who I am." When he showed his identification, the policeman backed away from the car and said, "You go right ahead, sir."[58]

Whittaker's position as an associate justice garnered for him numerous invitations to return to the Kansas City area where he was regarded as a kind of celebrity. His new status also brought renewed interest in him as a public speaker or guest presenter. This celebrity status back home combined with his dislike for Washington's high society compelled Whittaker to return to the Midwest as often as his schedule permitted. During the Court's winter and summer breaks the Whittakers returned to Kansas City and rented rooms or stayed with friends rather than remain in Washington. When they traveled abroad to Europe, their long-time Kansas City friends, Russell and Mabel Gunn, served as companions. Whittaker returned to Kansas City during his five years on the Supreme Court as much to surround himself with familiar environs as to surround himself with awed onlookers. He loved to return home, both to be at home and to be revered at home. His trips back to Kansas City always found Whittaker at his favorite haunts surrounded by friends, leading the lunch time round table discussion at a downtown restaurant or sitting in the library of his former law offices, leaning back with his feet on the table describing life on the Supreme Court to his former associates. On one of his many visits back to his old law firm, Whittaker even remarked to his former associates how their brief in a case before the Supreme Court involving Safeway stores had been helpful in the justices' deliberations. Apparently Whittaker had no compunction about deciding a case where his former associates represented one side, considering his vote was determinative in the five to four decision relieving Safeway of charges of price discrimination.[59] Since Safeway had not been one of his clients at the firm, Whittaker felt he could remain impartial, and in all of his discussions with former associates he never disclosed confidential information about the Court.[60]

These visits with former associates gave Whittaker a chance to relax and be himself, something he found impossible to do at the Supreme Court. In Washington, Whittaker never felt he measured up to the other justices, but in Kansas City he was the measure against which all other lawyers were judged—the proverbial big fish in a small pond. No wonder he enjoyed returning to Kansas City, where he was admired not so much because he was on the Supreme Court but because he, more than others, *deserved* to be on the Supreme Court. For his part, Whittaker remained as unpretentious as ever, especially among those he had known for so long. Following his nomination, when Whittaker first returned to Kansas City, friends at a businessman's breakfast at the University of Kansas City asked him, "What do we call you now?" Whittaker responded, "Its Charley Whittaker to you boys."[61] Once Whittaker began his duties at the Court, his former clerk at the district and appeals courts encountered him in Kansas City and greeted him as "Judge" out of habit. Realizing his error, the clerk corrected himself, saying, "Justice." Whittaker, though, became reassuring, telling his former clerk, "I'm still 'Judge' to you."[62]

Whittaker also received considerable recognition from colleges and universities following his Supreme Court appointment. In June 1961 he traveled to Huntingdon, Pennsylvania, the town of his forebears, to deliver the commencement address at Juniata College where he received the honorary degree Doctor of Laws. Twice Whittaker's Alma Mater honored him with its "Alumnus of the Year" award (in 1955 he received it from the University of Kansas City, and in 1966 he received it from the University of Missouri-Kansas City). His Alma Mater also bestowed on him an honorary Doctor of Laws degree, as did Central College in Fayette, Missouri. Certainly, Whittaker must have felt tremendous pride with all of this recognition. Still, he may have had misgivings about his own legal education; receiving honorary degrees only served to accentuate the fact that he had prepared for a career in law by attending a part-time "night" law school. The Kansas City School of Law Whittaker attended no longer existed (it had since been incorporated into the University of Kansas City and then the state university system), but its progeny continued to claim Whittaker as one of its own. Whittaker, likewise, felt a strong attachment to his former law school. Just after his nomination to the Supreme Court, he donated about five hundred books from his own collection to the school, saying, "Young lawyers here working with these volumes might be reminded that in this land of opportunity, the zenith still can be reached the hard way from humble beginnings."[63] Although much of what he accomplished in his life was due to his own dogged perseverance, Whittaker still felt indebted to his old school for starting him on his life's work. At a banquet in honor of his fifty-seventh birthday hosted by the University of Kansas City Law School, Whittaker said, "The vistas opened to me by the law school have been so great that I have given up trying to repay them."[64]

Another public honor came to Whittaker in November 1958 when the Kansas City Bar and Lawyers Association of Kansas City jointly sponsored to have his portrait placed in the capitol building at Jefferson City, Missouri. Considered an "extraordinary honor" to have his portrait displayed in the Missouri capitol, Whittaker planned to be in Jefferson City for the unveiling. He was reluctant, though, to invite the president or the other eight justices to the event (as suggested by its promoters). Scheduled to hang in the south entrance of the house chambers, the portrait was presented to the state legislature, but then plans got sidetracked because house members had other ideas about the use of that space. So for two years the governor's office temporarily stored the portrait until the Missouri Supreme Court unanimously accepted it. Surprised to find the portrait hanging in the Supreme Court instead of the capitol building, Missouri Supreme Court Judge Laurance Hyde explained to Whittaker that the dispute over the capitol space was due to "personalities and petty jealousies."[65]

Despite the public recognition he received, Whittaker still regretted his decision to accept his Supreme Court appointment, and he fell into an ever deepening melancholy. A *Kansas City Star* reporter revealed, "Only Charley Whittaker himself, his wife, Winifred, and perhaps a few trusted friends have been aware of the frustrations and disappointment, the sense of loneliness and homesickness that beset him at times after he took his seat on the bench."[66] Once on a return trip to his hometown of Troy, Kansas, to commemorate the 100th anniversary of the Pony Express, Whittaker let slip the tremendous difficulty he encountered every day in his work at the Court. Not that anyone in the crowd of 1,500 perceived the poignancy of his remarks; they had come to encounter the festivities or to catch a glimpse of their most celebrated former citizen. Organized by the Doniphan County Bar, the event included a public reception to honor Whittaker, who was the featured speaker at the Pony Express commemoration. Speaking off the cuff, Whittaker responded to criticisms of the Court taking so long to reach decisions, reminding his audience, "To make a mistake in a court whose decision is ultimately the law of the land is to make a mistake that will haunt the court member forever after."[67] Considered an entertaining speaker, Whittaker's address was well attended, although few in the audience realized then how much he was bothered by such a heavy burden. His every decision affected the law of the land, and it haunted him constantly that he might make a mistake.

Evidence of Whittaker's difficulty accepting the burden to make decisions that profoundly affected American law—or American lives—can be found in his first three months on the Court. Because of his mid-term appointment, Whittaker was unable to participate in every case decided at the end of the 1956 term; he missed out on oral arguments and conference discussions in many of the cases already that term. Whittaker could only participate in those cases scheduled for argument beginning his first day on the Court, March 25, 1957, leaving just three months until the end of the term. During that time, Whittaker participated in twenty-nine cases with written opinions, writing three of those opinions himself, and in all but four of those cases he voted with the majority. Whittaker's greatest difficulty involved those cases where his vote determined the final outcome of the case. For example, twice during his first three months on the Court, Whittaker's vote contributed to five to four majorities, making him feel like his was the only vote that mattered.[68] Even the clerks working for other justices noticed Whittaker's discomfort his first year, and when some of them teased one of Whittaker's clerks, saying, "Your boss looks nervous," Whittaker's clerk answered, "You would be, too, if you had to decide every case in the building!"[69] More important, though,

1957 Supreme Court of the United States, shortly after Whittaker's arrival. *Left to right*: Douglas, Brennan, Black, Clark, Warren, Harlan, Frankfurter, Whittaker, and Burton. Whittaker joined a Court steeped in controversy and embroiled in bitter personal disputes. As the newest member, he felt enormous responsibility despite the fact that he missed out on many of the most controversial decisions at the end of the 1956 term. (Collection of the Supreme Court of the United States)

to understanding Whittaker's difficulty were those cases where Whittaker failed to act at all. During his first three months on the Court at the end of the 1956 term the justices split four to four in four separate cases, and, unable to bring himself to settle the issue in favor of one side or the other, Whittaker asked that the cases be held over until the next Court term to give himself more time to carefully weigh the arguments involved—the same arguments that the other justices had no trouble deciding. Since Whittaker was new, with the outcome balanced four to four, the other justices were willing to give him the time he required to reach a decision.[70]

One of the cases held over from Whittaker's first three months on the Court was illustrative of the kinds of cases that caused him the greatest difficulty making decisions; it showed how he struggled between competing claims and how the Court operated to secure victory for one group of justices over another. The case involved Everett Green, an elderly man accused of setting fire to his Washington apartment and killing his female companion in the blaze. At his first trial Green was indicted for arson and first-degree murder, to which he pleaded not guilty, but the jury found him guilty of arson and second-degree murder, which was not a capital offense. On appeal, Green's lawyers argued that the trial judge had erred in allowing a second-degree murder conviction when Green had been indicted on first-degree charges. The case was then remanded back to the trial court, where a new jury found Green guilty of arson and first-degree murder, and the judge ordered him to be executed. Green's lawyers again appealed, this time contending that Green had been placed in double jeopardy, since at his first trial the jury had essentially acquitted him of first-degree murder when they brought back a guilty verdict for second-degree murder. The appeals court this time disagreed, citing a Supreme Court decision, *Trono v. United States*, which held that a person convicted of a *lesser included* charge was not consequently then acquitted from the greater offense.[71]

When the case came before the Supreme Court one month after Whittaker joined the bench, at the Court's first conference on *Green v. United States* the justices split four to four. The chief justice, joined by Justices Black, Douglas, and Brennan wanted to reverse Green's conviction because they considered it double jeopardy. On the other side, Justices Frankfurter, Burton, Clark, and Harlan relied on the government's contention that *Trono* controlled and wanted to uphold the conviction.[72] That left Whittaker, the last justice to speak at conference, to determine the fate of this one man. If he voted to affirm the conviction, Green would die by electrocution. Whittaker was not comfortable sending another man to his death, remembering the one time as a district judge when he had ordered the death of an admitted rapist and murderer. Here, the accused had pleaded not guilty and had been subjected to two trials, and Whittaker's vote could send him to the electric chair. But how could Whittaker ignore the *Trono* precedent? Whittaker was a strong adherent of the principle of *stare decisis*, which compelled him to follow the rulings in prior cases regardless of his personal feelings or predilections. In fact, Whittaker felt an obligation to President Eisenhower who he believed had picked him primarily because of his devotion to following the law as laid down in prior decisions rather than fashioning law to suit the exigencies of each case.[73]

Whittaker could not ignore what he believed to be his duty as a judge (neither could he ignore the persistent entreaties from both sides to join their position), but he did not want to be responsible for sending another man to die. And that was exactly how he felt; if he voted to affirm the conviction, then he alone was responsible for another man's death. Sure, four other justices also had voted to affirm (i.e. execute Green), so Whittaker, in fact, would not have been solely responsible for Green's death, but that was not the way he viewed it. Whenever the other justices split four to four, which they did with some frequency, in his own mind Whittaker himself became the Supreme Court, making final decisions with no possibility of appeal. Sometimes, as in this case, it was almost too much for him to bear. Unable to make up his mind at the first conference, Whittaker asked to discuss the case again at the Court's next weekly meeting. For eight weeks this continued; the other eight justices held to their views and Whittaker remained undecided. Finally, on the last day of the term, the Court scheduled the case for re-argument the following term. No one outside the Court realized then that the delay was to give Whittaker time to make up his mind.

Over the summer recess Whittaker returned to Kansas City, hopefully to gain a better perspective, and corresponded with his one law clerk, Alan Kohn, who remained in Washington. Kohn had written the original memorandum on Green's case for Whittaker recommending reversal of the conviction, and Whittaker wanted Kohn to continue to do more research on the issues involved in the case. Whittaker needed some way to break this deadlock. When he returned to Washington for the start of the new Court term, Whittaker announced he was ready to reverse Green's conviction, but to do so the decision in *Trono* had to remain undisturbed. That way, Whittaker could feel like he had upheld his obligation to *stare decisis*, and he could relieve himself of the executioner's burden. Justice Black's first draft opinion in *Green*, however, stated that *Trono* was overruled. Whittaker responded that he could not join the opinion if the majority overruled *Trono*, so, to keep Whittaker's vote, Black altered the opinion. To save Green's life and the *Trono* ruling, Whittaker asked that *Trono* not be extended beyond its particular factual setting.[74] *Trono* was not applicable to *Green*, not exactly, because it arose in the Philippines, which had a tradition in Spanish law, and therefore *Trono* could be distinguished, though just barely, from *Green*. With his conviction reversed, Everett Green went free. He lived another four years. When he died, Justice Frankfurter reportedly said to Whittaker, "He went to his death without knowing you saved his life."[75]

The pressures of being thrust onto the Supreme Court so unexpectedly in the middle of a Court term amidst such a divergent group of personalities took its toll on Whittaker almost immediately. By the end of his first three months on the Court, Whittaker was so nervous he could hardly concentrate anymore. One of his clerks at the time, Alan Kohn, observed, "He was not just unhappy. He was distraught and in serious emotional distress. At the Court, the other Justices were aware of his condition and were sympathetic."[76] Whittaker became highly agitated, leading to severe bouts of anxiety, even depression. It was apparent to the other justices that something was terribly wrong with him. Near the end of the term, Justice Burton observed in his diary, "Justice Whittaker has been on the edge of a nervous breakdown but hopes to finish the term and then recuperate."[77] So apparent was Whittaker's distressed condition that the clerks at the Court could not help but comment upon it, speculating as to whether he could recover. One of Justice Burton's clerks, Roger Cramton, at the end of the 1956 term communicated to a friend of his working as a clerk on the Second Circuit Court of Appeals that Whittaker was so overawed and insecure after his first three months on the Court that it was unlikely he would last another year.[78]

During his first year on the Court, Whittaker tried to reassure his family and friends back home that he was recovering from his initial disappointment and becoming adjusted to his new position. To his sister, Hazel, he wrote, "I am very much improved. My nerves are fairly steady again and I believe I am making steady progress."[79] To a friend of his in Kansas City, Whittaker wrote, "I am becoming more adjusted to the work here, and I am considerably more philosophic about it than I was last spring, and I am trying to take it more calmly and in stride, with the realization that it is simply impossible to cover the vast ground in the same detail that I have been accustomed to in the past."[80] After witnessing Whittaker's depressed state during one of his trips back to Kansas City, this same friend responded, "I was very happy you were 100 percent better in all respects than when you were in Kansas City last.... I am sure you are now fully adjusted to the limitations you must accept as your duty."[81]

Whittaker's correspondence merely masked the continuing difficulty he suffered, and his recovery took longer than his letters indicated. About this same time early in 1958, before Whittaker completed one full year on the Court, on two separate occasions he called the new attorney general, William Rogers, complaining that he wanted to quit the Court. As deputy attorney general, Rogers was not much impressed with Whittaker, but he advised him to give the job more time.[82] Committed to staying because of a sense of duty, Whittaker communicated an optimistic tone to his friends in Kansas City, writing to one of them, "I have become familiar with my new surroundings and have gotten my feet squarely on the ground and am now enjoying the work and getting along, I think, very well. I certainly feel far better about the move than I did at the end of last term."[83] This may have been more wishful thinking, the words of a man trapped in a situation from which he could not escape but where he desperately wanted to leave. The truth was, Whittaker agreed to stay on the Court for only five years; that was his self-imposed time limit. He considered his service on the Court more of a sentence, and he mockingly described for his clerks how he was "serving out a five year sentence." So disgusted was he about ever leaving the trial bench in Kansas City that, at times, five years seemed too long to wait. One of his friends in Kansas City, worried that he was taking his disappointment too hard, wrote to him, "[B]ut try and don't get that five year idea in your head its bad to dwell upon it, [sic] get some kind of a hobby or diversion from that awful grind, but you can do it."[84]

By the fall of 1957 Whittaker was under the care of a Kansas City physician to help him cope with his condition. Unfortunately, Whittaker's condition, most likely acute anxiety and depression, was misdiagnosed and improperly treated. Physicians did not then have available appropriate treatments for a disease like depression, and they lacked a thorough understanding of the effects of depression, so the drugs Whittaker's physician prescribed ended up causing more harm than good. Whittaker spent the Court's summer recess recovering in Kansas City where his former colleagues at this old law firm sensed he remained under enormous pressure. When he returned to Washington for the start of the Court's 1957 term Whittaker brought with him a wide variety of sedatives designed to treat hypertension and insomnia. The combination of drugs may have created counteractive effects causing his condition to worsen, and Whittaker wrote to his physician just after the start of the Court term complaining of certain side effects.[85] One was considerable weight loss. Not a large man to begin with, any weight loss on Whittaker would have made his appearance ghastly. When Whittaker's former law clerk from the district and appeals courts, Clyde Rayburn, had a chance to see Whittaker for the first time since he left Kansas City at an event honoring Whittaker's appointment, Rayburn was appalled at what he saw. "I saw a crowd around a man in a dark suit, but I did not at once recognize him," Rayburn has said, "Then I heard his voice; he had a strong voice that projected, and even with people around him it carried. It was not until I looked him in the face that I knew it was him. He had lost a lot of weight, and he looked terrible."[86]

Whittaker's condition, while not widely reported outside the Court, caused grave concern for those who worked with him. Whittaker's secretary, Celia Barrett, who had made the move to Washington with him from the district and appeals courts, kept in contact with Rayburn and indicated in her letters how Whittaker was under considerable stress. Remembering previous episodes when Whittaker had suffered nervous breakdowns as a lawyer while she worked for him, Barrett confided to Whittaker's two law clerks at the Court that this kind of reaction to stress had happened before. Although Whittaker needed medication to control his anxiety, Whittaker's clerks that first term have maintained that neither his work nor his judgment were impaired.[87] Whittaker's letter to his physician indicated that he was probably being overmedicated, causing detrimental, even addictive effects. Whittaker was not himself, and his behavior became erratic. One of his former colleagues from his old law firm has remembered visiting the Whittakers in Washington and riding in the car with both of them. From the back seat he could see how Whittaker's wife, Winifred, kept her hand just on the steering wheel as Whittaker drove around Washington, aware that Whittaker was having difficulty concentrating.[88] On another occasion one of Whittaker's family members became offended when audience members at a local bar association meeting in Kansas City commented how Whittaker appeared to be drunk. Knowing Whittaker did not drink alcohol, she frankly admitted that Whittaker had been taking tranquilizers to control his nerves.[89]

From his first day at the Court, Whittaker worried that his legal training had been insufficient, leading to intense feelings of inferiority. Although his appointment marked the first time in the Court's history when all nine members were law school graduates, compared to the other justices, Whittaker's legal training seemed ridiculous.[90] The other eight justices then serving on the Court all had university diplomas in addition to their law degrees from full-time accredited law schools. Three of the justices, Frankfurter, Burton, and Brennan, graduated from Harvard Law School, considered one of the best in the country. Frankfurter also taught classes at Harvard where Brennan was one of his pupils. Justice Douglas, likewise, taught law, first at Columbia where he received his law degree and then at Yale. Justice Harlan had attended Balliol College in Oxford, England, on a Rhodes scholarship and then received his law degree from New York Law School.[91] All in all, the justices possessed impressive legal education credentials, that is, all but Whittaker. Back home in Kansas City his attendance at the Kansas City School of Law was regarded with pride—someone from such an undistinguished law school ended up on the Supreme Court—but at the Court Whittaker's legal education became a source of embarrassment. Once, Justice Douglas, who could be particularly cruel to colleagues, was overheard during a heated conference discussion to say derisively, "What do you expect from a hick lawyer born in Troy, Kansas, and coming from the Kansas City School of Law?"[92] Such a comment would have hurt Whittaker deeply, making his struggle to overcome his feelings of inferiority all the more difficult.

When Whittaker arrived in Washington he was nervous about going to the Court in large part because he had such a reverence for its members that he could not help but feel inferior. Just after the Court's 1956 term ended, Whittaker told reporters, "I have the greatest humility as I approach the job. I have a humbleness I have not known heretofore. I do not profess to be able to come up with all the answers, but can only say that I will do the best I can."[93] It took some time for Whittaker to realize that his place at the Court, seated at the end of the bench reserved for the Court's newest member, was one among equals. According to Whittaker's son, Kent, other Court members experienced the same doubts and frustrations as Whittaker early in their service. Kent has remembered both of his parents describing how Whittaker's closest colleague on the Court, Justice Harlan, tried to assure and comfort Whittaker by relating several stories about his own agonies when he arrived at the Court. Whittaker himself noticed Justice Stewart, who arrived over a year after Whittaker, had an equally difficult time adjusting.[94] These other men, though, possessing differing talents and experience differed from Whittaker in one key respect: not one of them doubted that they belonged on the Supreme Court. Whittaker did, however, and his doubt became manifest even as he took his judicial oath. All justices upon completing the oath have said, "So help me, God." One observer at Whittaker's swearing-in ceremony has remembered how oddly emphatic Whittaker said, "So, *help me*, God."[95]

Although there was little reason to doubt himself, Whittaker's fear of failure became a self-fulfilled prophecy from which he could not at first disentangle himself. When he arrived at the Court and Justice Black asked him how he felt about being a justice, Whittaker replied, "Mr. Justice, I am scared to death." Black reassured him, saying, "Well, there is no reason for that. You will find that these justices are all just boys grown tall."[96] Whittaker, though, could not shake the feeling that these other "boys" were somehow giants, and he marveled at their abilities. Next to Justices Black, Frankfurter, and Douglas, who had all arrived at the Court when Whittaker was still defending insurance and streetcar companies back in Kansas City, Whittaker felt overawed. He was completely out of his element. So insecure did Whittaker feel around some of the other justices that he could not admit his difficulty except to their clerks. On his first day at the Court, as he approached the bench, Whittaker confided to two of Chief Justice Warren's clerks, "Boys, I have never felt so inadequate in my entire life."[97] Later during his first three months as a justice, Whittaker received a note delivered by one of Frankfurter's clerks. Asked to sit down in Whittaker's chambers, the clerk could tell Whittaker was having difficulty. "He labored under serious feelings of inferiority," this clerk has said, "and he said to me, 'Your justice is a genius, and I am totally inadequate.'"[98]

The timidity Whittaker felt going to the Supreme Court was somewhat justified. Besides being on the Supreme Court considerably longer than Whittaker had served as a lower court judge—all but Harlan and Brennan were already on the Court before Whittaker received his first judicial assignment, and Brennan brought seven years judicial experience in the New Jersey state court system with him—several of his colleagues on the Court had experience working closely in the president's administration or in the United States Senate. The range of experience and knowledge that his colleagues brought to the Supreme Court comprised a collective force that made Whittaker feel alienated. Furthermore, several members of the Court commanded respect and recognition through the strength of their personalities; their confidence in their own abilities and the rightness of their decisions was unshakable. Some of Whittaker's colleagues had been intimate associates of the president who appointed them to the Court (Whittaker had met Eisenhower only once when promoted to the Court of Appeals) or had established national reputations as scholars or statesmen.

Whittaker also suffered doubts about his ability to contribute in any meaningful way to the Court's work. He had no philosophy of governance to guide his decision-making, no policy preferences, and little experience grappling with the most important kinds of questions brought to the Supreme Court. His judicial philosophy, if he had one, was best summarized in the words of one of his former associates as, "The law means what it says and says what it means." Many of Whittaker's colleagues on the Court, though, had very definite, well-defined philosophies about how the law should be read, and understood, apart from the printed text. Following his appointment, the *Dallas Morning News* observed that Whittaker would "not have too much company among his eight prospective colleagues," if he "read the law only for understanding of its meaning," but, the paper concluded, "if [he lived] up to that single quoted sentence, a Daniel [had] indeed come to judgment."[99]

The other court members at the time of Whittaker's appointment varied as much in their experience and abilities as they have in the judgment of history. While there has been no objective measurement devised to gauge the importance of any Court member, the opinions of sixty-five law school deans and professors of law, history, and political science were used in a 1970 survey to rank the first one hundred justices appointed to the Court using five categories: great, near great, average, below average, and failure. The majority of justices were rated as "average" by the evaluators, but only two of Whittaker's colleagues were (Clark and Stewart). First published a couple of years before his death, this survey revealed Whittaker's rating as one of only eight Court "failures" (along with Burton); three of his colleagues were considered "great" (Black, Frankfurter, and Warren) and three "near great" (Douglas, Harlan, and Brennan).[100] Not everyone has agreed with Whittaker's classification as a "failure," though, or with the results of the survey generally, observing how Whittaker did make meaningful, though not extraordinary, contributions to the work of the Court and how the survey results actually revealed more about the biases of the evaluators,[101] but the overall consensus was that Whittaker was overshadowed on a Court comprised of some of the most distinguished justices of the twentieth century. Frankfurter's reputation may have diminished and Brennan's improved somewhat since the initial survey, but there could be no doubt that Whittaker served on a Court composed of remarkably able men.[102] Much of the legacy of these men was due in large part to their long service on the Court. After serving for more than three decades, Black, Douglas, and Brennan each undoubtedly had far more influence on the Court as an institution and the public's perception of the Court than Whittaker's five years of service. In fact, all of Whittaker's Court colleagues (with the exception of Burton) in time surpassed his total length of service by more than a decade, making his contributions seem all the less significant.[103] Whittaker's "failure" may have been that he served so short a time on the Supreme Court with what could arguably be considered one of the finest lineups of justices to sit together. To better understand their influence on the Court at the time of Whittaker's appointment, their philosophical differences, and their lasting impact on American law, each of Whittaker's colleagues should be examined in their order of appointment.[104]

Hugo Black of Alabama had been the senior associate justice since 1945 when Harold Burton replaced Owen Roberts, the last of the "Nine Old Men" present during the days of Roosevelt's "Court-packing" plan and the constitutional revolution that followed. Considered the most intellectually formidable member of the Court at the time of Whittaker's appointment, Black had served on the Court already for over nineteen years and would continue to serve another fourteen. By the time Whittaker joined the Court, Black had witnessed the departure of fifteen different justices; altogether in his long service he would serve with thirty individuals. Already past the recommended age of retirement by Roosevelt's proposal (Black was seventy-one), Black had been a strong supporter of Roosevelt's New Deal legislation while serving in the Senate (1927–1937). When the aging Justice Willis Van Devanter, one of the "Four Horsemen" who consistently voted to strike down New Deal legislation, announced his retirement from the Court, Roosevelt nominated Black to fill his first Court vacancy. As one of their own, there was little the Senate could—or would—do to oppose his nomination, although there was considerable grumbling about Black's qualifications. Soon after he took his seat on the bench, the press revealed that Black had once been a member of the Ku Klux Klan. Criticisms of his appointment were heard immediately, and, unable to deny the accusation, Black conceded that it had been politically expedient to join the Klan. His membership, though, lasted only two years. Some twenty years later when most of the country had long forgotten about the uproar over Black's appointment, one of the clerks at the Court asked Black over lunch if it were true that he had once been a member of the Klan. One of Whittaker's clerks who witnessed the conversation was initially shocked at the impertinence of the question. Black, however, was not the least offended. "He smiled, and in his southern drawl, replied that, yes, when he was young and running for office in Alabama, he had joined the Klan," this clerk explained, "He added that he would have joined B'nai B'rith and the Knights of Columbus also if they would have admitted him."[105]

Black's great legacy to the Court during his thirty-four year tenure was his insistence that the due process clause of the Fourteenth Amendment incorporated all of the protections of the Bill of Rights against infringements by state lawmakers. He also advocated a "preferred position" for the First Amendment among the guarantees protected by the Bill of Rights. For the first half of his Court career, though, Black struggled to gain acceptance of these views, writing more often in dissent, but in time much of the Bill of Rights was incorporated by the Fourteenth Amendment. Although total incorporation remained out of his reach, Black settled for selective incorporation, as, one by one, different guarantees of the Bill of Rights were made applicable to the states. This victory did not come until the 1960s, though, after Whittaker left the Court, when Black's views finally commanded a majority.

Justice Black led what came to be known as the "liberal" or "activist" bloc of the Court while Whittaker served there. This group, usually in the minority, was more apt to ignore legal precedents if they thought that an earlier decision had been wrongly decided. Their principal concern was the protection of civil liberties in the face of government intrusion, and they were more willing to allow their personal policy preferences to determine what constituted a "just" decision in the area of civil liberty. Of course, such a broad generalization of the principal aim of the "liberal" bloc serves simply to illustrate, in broad strokes, what differentiated it from the "conservative" bloc, led by its chief proponent, Felix Frankfurter. Certainly none of the justices voted strictly along either "liberal" or "conservative" lines, and at times two justices with almost completely opposing views on most issues could be found voting together, such as in *Kent v. Dulles*, where Frankfurter joined the so-called "liberals" to form a Court majority.[106] More often, though, if the Court split five to four, undoubtedly the "conservatives" constituted one side and the "liberals" the other, giving more centrist justices like Tom Clark the balance of power. Therefore, during Whittaker's service, there were two recognized, opposing groups on the Court, and throughout Whittaker's five-year tenure they maintained a precarious balance between them.

Leading the conservative forces on the Court for eighteen years before Whittaker's appointment was Felix Frankfurter, considered at the time of his own appointment to be one of the country's leading law professors and Court expert. Espousing the virtues of judicial restraint, Frankfurter and his adherents believed that the judiciary, as a co-equal branch in the federal system, should defer to the legislative judgment unless there was a clear constitutional violation. In other words, even bad laws were permissible as long as they did not run afoul of the Constitution. Supporters of judicial restraint sought to reach decisions without considering constitutional questions whenever possible. Therefore, if one disagreed with the effects of legislation, the proper course was to have the law changed through the legislative-deliberative process rather than resort to the courts. By contrast, activist justices like Black considered the courts the last recourse for those deprived of their rights once the legislative process failed to act or acted arbitrarily or capriciously. While Frankfurter considered deference to the popularly elected branch the proper role of a judge, Black considered it an abdication of the judicial duty not to correct the abuses of legislative discretion. These two positions formed the principal rivalry between liberals and conservatives during Whittaker's Court service, and their differences were as much personal as they were ideological.[107]

Felix Frankfurter, the champion of judicial restraint, was one of the most fascinating and infuriating members of the Court during his twenty-three years of service. Three years older than Black, at age seventy-four Frankfurter was the oldest member of the Court when Whittaker joined it. A study in contrasts, Frankfurter's early career was a far cry from his conservative position on the Court. As a faculty member at Harvard Law School, Frankfurter became a leading reformer during the 1920s, aiding the National Association for the Advancement of Colored People and helping to found the

American Civil Liberties Union and the *New Republic*. He defended victims of the first "red scare," including the notorious Sacco and Vanzetti, and became active in the Zionist movement. An intimate advisor to President Franklin Roosevelt as well as having close contacts with Justices Oliver Wendell Holmes and Louis Brandeis on the Court, Frankfurter seemed an obvious choice for Roosevelt's third appointment. Considered a brilliant conversationalist, Frankfurter's friendships were legion. Besides politics and law, Frankfurter cultivated friendships in all areas of the social sciences and humanities. With this breadth of learning, Frankfurter understandably had an inflated opinion of himself. He had no trouble demonstrating to others that they were not his intellectual equals. One of Whittaker's clerks recalled how, when invited to have lunch with the clerks, Frankfurter "played a little trick to show off his intellect and his professorial skills. Usually the Justices would simply answer questions from the clerks as they were asked. Justice Frankfurter waited until all eighteen questions had been asked, and then proceeded to answer them, pretty much in the order asked."[108]

The dispute between Black and Frankfurter over the proper role of the Court, raging as it did almost twenty years, became one of the most contentious battles of the modern Court. Ultimately, Black's position prevailed, making its greatest strides once Frankfurter left the Court. The battle between the activist justices and the adherents of judicial restraint raged on mercilessly throughout Whittaker's short tenure, but what made this battle so difficult to endure was the combatants themselves, particularly Frankfurter. An enormously insecure man, Frankfurter took personally every perceived "loss" in his quest to restrain the activist justices on the Court, and he held in contempt all those who joined the other side. According to one Frankfurter biographer, "Frankfurter would mentally divide his colleagues into three categories—adversaries, allies, and potential allies. He would react to adversaries as he had throughout his life—with heated anger and frustration, with attacks on their integrity and motives, with a search for vindication."[109] In correspondence with his friend and confidant, Judge Learned Hand of the Second Circuit Court of Appeals, Frankfurter degraded those justices who belonged to the liberal bloc as well as those who might be tempted to join them; he even spoke disparagingly about other Court members to his own clerks, especially about Black. Frankfurter respected Black's intellect, but when Frankfurter received a copy of a Black opinion he might say, "Let's see what kind of drivel is here."[110] Although opinions differ, some clerks who worked at the Court considered Frankfurter a "bully" who preyed on the insecurities of others, yet Frankfurter's own clerks found nothing intimidating about the diminutive Frankfurter. "His way of getting you off his back was to accuse you of not reading this or that book, article, case, etc.," one of them has said, "Then, after you read it and discovered it had nothing to do with his argument, he would be on to another argument."[111]

The one characteristic that Black and Frankfurter shared in common was their determination to forge majorities, whatever the cost. Both Black and Frankfurter were notorious proselytizers, constantly pressing their points on the other justices to gain acceptance. Black, however, was far less irritating personally, making him all the more persuasive. While Black used calm, deliberative argument to get his point across, Frankfurter lectured his colleagues, often speaking condescendingly to those, which included most, justices he considered inferior. Typically Frankfurter appealed to his colleague's lack of learning, which caused their misunderstanding of the issues presented, telling them if they only read more they would agree with him. Of course, Frankfurter himself, the consummate teacher, would supply them with the requisite material. As one Frankfurter biographer observed, "Frankfurter was in constant search of new recruits; he treated every newly appointed justice as a potential convert or ally…. All received the familiar Frankfurter treatment— flattery and instruction…. Frankfurter constantly instructed new brethren, telling them to read this case or that article, calling attention to the inadequacies of their opinions, wooing their votes."[112] Depending on the personalities involved, Frankfurter's approach yielded just as many enemies as it did allies. Part of the reason Frankfurter worked his colleagues so hard (apart from being supremely certain of the correctness of his position) was the sense that after twenty years of battling activist justices like Black, Frankfurter was starting to lose ground. He began to see about the time of Whittaker's appointment that the edifice of judicial restraint he had sought to preserve was beginning to crumble. One of Frankfurter's clerks from the 1959 term has remembered, "When I was there Frankfurter understood he was losing long fought battles, and he became stronger, even more aggressive in his arguments to hold his ground. This created a major crisis for him. He needed justices Clark, Stewart, and Whittaker (Harlan was always on his side), to hold on to a majority. That may be why he worked them so hard."[113]

One case from the 1958 term illustrated most clearly the difference in philosophical positions between Black and Frankfurter as well as their handling of other justices to garner majorities. Alfonse Bartkus was acquitted in federal court on charges of robbing a federally insured savings and loan association, but then federal officials assisted the state of Illinois in indicting Bartkus on identical charges in state court where he was convicted and sentenced to life in prison. Clearly the Fifth Amendment's ban on double jeopardy prevented Bartkus from standing trial again in federal court, but could he be charged in a state court with the same offense for which a federal jury had just acquitted him? The answer to that question depended on whose side one followed, Black's or Frankfurter's. To Black, the Fifth Amendment's prohibition of double jeopardy applied in this case because the Fourteenth Amendment incorporated it through the due process clause, which applied to the states. Frankfurter, on the other hand, in the final court decision, argued that Bartkus was not subjected to double jeopardy because he committed not one but two crimes—one against the federal government and one against the state of Illinois—each punishable by different sovereignties. To lend further credence to his position, Frankfurter noted how every state supreme court but one to consider this very issue had ruled in favor of "dual sovereignty." Twice Bartkus was charged with robbery, and afterwards he appealed twice to the Supreme Court. Both times he lost.

The first time the Court considered Bartkus's claim, during Whittaker's first full term, the justices split evenly four to four (Brennan did not participate) on whether to reverse his conviction. Because of the tied vote, the Court upheld the conviction in a short *per curiam* order. What made this first vote so unusual was that Whittaker joined the three remaining liberal justices (Black, Warren, and Douglas) to reverse the conviction just as he had in the case of Everett Green decided that same term. Frankfurter later tried to convince Whittaker to sustain the conviction by explaining to him the difference between invalidating and sustaining a state conviction based on the Fourteenth Amendment, writing, "A particular instance of hardship may be so offensive to fundamental notions of fairness that the due process clause may be invoked by the victim of such individual outrage. That is the essence of due process: a shock to the conscience in a particular case."[114] Certain though that Bartkus was treated unfairly, Whittaker responded, "After a trial in a federal court resulting in acquittal, to permit a second trial and a conviction in a state court upon precisely the same issues seems quite unfair.... All of this 'shocks (my) conscience' and, in my view, constitutes a denial of due process."[115]

By the second time Bartkus's case came before the Supreme Court, significant changes had taken place in the personnel and voting of the justices. This time Brennan participated in the decision, which was a sure vote to reverse the conviction, and Burton had been replaced by Potter Stewart, who was not at all sure which way he should vote. Without Stewart's vote the Court remained evenly split four to four because Whittaker changed his mind from the previous term and now voted to affirm the conviction. Frankfurter was primarily responsible for Whittaker's switch, as Roger Newman noted, "'Felix really went after Whittaker in *Bartkus*,' recalled Black's clerk, Guido Calebresi, telling him he *had* to agree. Hugo similarly tried, his purpose just as transparent, but his manner much more gentle."[116] Black tried using his reasoning from the previous term to appeal directly to Whittaker, saying, "It doesn't say twice put in jeopardy by the same government, but for the same offense.... When the 'feds' do what was done here, we have a direct violation of the Fifth Amendment or it is so shocking to the conscience that we can't take it under the Fourteenth."[117] Frankfurter persisted, though, and after browbeating both Whittaker and Stewart was able to hold on to a bare majority to sustain the conviction. Black, on the other hand, decided enough was enough. He stopped trying to win back Whittaker's vote; not because Whittaker's mind was set the other way or because Black grew weary of Frankfurter's verbal sparing, but because Whittaker had reached a breaking point. "Whittaker found himself trapped between the pressures put on him by Justices Frankfurter and Black," Black's clerk that term has explained, "He found each of them convincing, moving from one to the other. This frustrated Black and Frankfurter…. At a certain point, though, Black said to me that he could not do that anymore to Whittaker; he was coming apart. So Black stopped trying to get Whittaker's vote and lost those cases. He may have concluded the fight was no longer worth it. Although Black stopped trying to win Whittaker's vote, he continued to argue with the other justices even after he lost their vote or never had it to begin with."[118]

The final outcome in *Bartkus* was a five to four vote to sustain the conviction, and, as happened more often, Stewart, not Whittaker, held the decisive fifth vote.[119] Frankfurter kept together his bare majority by lecturing first Whittaker and then Stewart into submission, and Black led the liberal justices in dissent.[120] *Bartkus* typified the doctrinal dispute between Frankfurter and Black and highlighted their efforts to hold on to votes. Frankfurter was much more demanding, desperately trying to preserve a tradition of judicial restraint that he had maintained for twenty years. Black was just as passionate in his views, but his manner was more relaxed. He did not grate like Frankfurter. Within ten years, though, Black's view prevailed; although it was not expressly overruled, *Bartkus* did lose all force and practical effect after *Benton v. Maryland*, which made the double jeopardy prohibition of the Fifth Amendment enforceable against the states through the Fourteenth Amendment.[121] The tide had already started to turn while Frankfurter was still on the Court, and he lashed out violently at those who sought to destroy his legacy. Once Frankfurter left the Court, the country was awash with liberal Court decisions.

Possibly the most activist justice during Whittaker's tenure because of his flagrant disregard for legal precedents was William Douglas. As the youngest person ever appointed to the Court, Douglas set the record for the longest term of service, over thirty-six years. By the time Whittaker arrived at the Court, Douglas had served already almost eighteen years, having been appointed just three months after Frankfurter. Douglas, however, being so young at the time of his appointment, was a generation younger than Frankfurter, really more Whittaker's contemporary, and the personal antagonism between Douglas and Frankfurter was one of the most vicious in the Court's history. Frankfurter and Black disagreed intensely on substantive issues, but they maintained a respectful relationship, even reconciling their differences somewhat toward the end of Frankfurter's life. In contrast, Frankfurter hated Douglas, and Douglas had no hesitation revealing his feelings were mutual.[122] During the 1958 term, Whittaker's second, clerks at the Court have remembered Douglas and Frankfurter refusing to speak to each other. Two years later Douglas drafted a memorandum explaining how Frankfurter's violent outbursts at conference compelled him not to participate in any more conferences together lest their rivalry became too much for Frankfurter to bear.[123] Chief Justice Warren convinced Douglas not to circulate his memorandum to the others and Douglas returned to conferences, but his behavior at conferences only infuriated Frankfurter. Just as passionate in his views as Frankfurter, Douglas behaved irreverently, steadfastly refusing to defer to Frankfurter on any score. During conferences, just to aggravate Frankfurter, Douglas might get up and leave while Frankfurter spoke, or, if he stayed to endure Frankfurter's pontification—lasting precisely the length of a Harvard Law School lecture—Douglas, who spoke right afterward, would say he had been prepared to vote one way, but Frankfurter had talked him out of it.[124] This type of "needling" between Douglas and Frankfurter remained prevalent throughout Whittaker's tenure and contributed to heightened tensions among the justices.

William Douglas was a product of the vast Pacific Northwest, where he hiked in the mountains near his home at Yakima, Washington. His love of the outdoors made Douglas an ardent environmentalist and conservationist and became the central feature of his personality. Moving east to attend law school at Columbia University, Douglas became a disciple of the new "Legal Realism," which encouraged a more results-oriented kind of judging— a philosophy that would have been foreign to Whittaker. Like Frankfurter, Douglas had been an intimate associate of President Roosevelt's New Deal advisors. After two years serving as chairman of the Securities and Exchange Commission, Douglas became Roosevelt's fourth pick for the Supreme Court. There he developed a reputation as a maverick justice, one who behaved differently presumably for the purpose of being different. More active than any of his colleagues on the Court, Douglas engaged in extensive nonjudicial activities. Traveling worldwide, he wrote numerous books on fields as wide-ranging as civil liberties, wilderness preservation, and U. S. foreign policy. Criticized for his outspoken beliefs both on and off the Court, more than once there were calls for his impeachment. Politically ambitious, twice while he served on the Court Douglas was considered as a vice presidential running mate. In 1944 Douglas's name was among a field of likely candidates to run with Roosevelt, and in 1948 President Truman offered Douglas a place on the ticket, but Douglas turned it down. When Douglas later boasted to clerks at the Court over lunch that Roosevelt had wanted him as his running mate, one clerk asked him how he would have selected justices if he had become president. According to one of Whittaker's clerks, Douglas replied the answer was easy: "He would have appointed persons who would vote the way he wanted them to vote."[125]

As the most results-oriented justice on the Court, Douglas's reputation has been tarnished considerably because of his scant regard for scholarship.

Many of his written opinions lacked adequate supporting legal reasoning, and, according to one biographer, "often appeared superficial or just plain sloppy." The reason for this was Douglas's irreverent disregard for Court conventions. He wrote his opinions hastily, as he did all his work on the Court, and rarely altered them—even if it meant winning more votes. Douglas disapproved of the lobbying that went on between other justices, especially Black and Frankfurter, and he wrote exclusively for himself. He was just as satisfied to file a one-person dissent as he was to persuade four to join him in a majority.[126] In fact, during Whittaker's five years on the Court, Douglas dissented without written opinion eighteen times, and four of those were against Whittaker decisions. Douglas did not seek consensus; at conference he presented his views succinctly without concern for compromise. By all accounts, though, Douglas was brilliant, and, in time, many of his views did win Court majorities, but that was the result of changes in Court personnel and not because of Douglas's own efforts.[127] In many ways, Douglas could be just as infuriating as Frankfurter. Both men had overblown egos, and neither had any qualms suggesting that their colleagues were intellectually inferior. All the other associate justices had two law clerks (the chief justice had three), but Douglas insisted he needed only one. Always the first to finish writing opinions—and the first one out the door when, sometimes before, the Court term ended—Douglas scoffed at his colleague's complaints that they were being overworked, claiming the Court's work required only four days out of the week to complete. During the Court's sessions while other justices listened to oral arguments, Douglas could be seen addressing letters or scribbling notes for his next book, and then, without warning, he would ask a pointed question that went to the heart of the issue.[128]

Far more than any other justice with whom Whittaker served, even Frankfurter, William Douglas was not a likable person. The most reclusive member of the Court, Douglas preferred it that way. He treated his colleagues, his clerks, and his staff brusquely, even harshly. One of Douglas's own clerks has admitted that interpersonal relationships were difficult with Douglas: "He had a forbidding personality; he was moody, demanding. Not always straight, you did not know sometimes what he wanted."[129] Clerks who worked in other chambers have not recalled Douglas forming close relationships with any of the justices, even Black, who was easily Douglas's closest ally in terms of ideology. Both men were strong proponents of a "preferred position" for First Amendment freedoms in relation to other guarantees of the Bill of Rights, and both of them accepted a literal reading of that document. Douglas, however, was willing to go even further than Black in extending the Bill of Rights beyond a literalist interpretation and making its provisions applicable to changing times and circumstances—what was considered a "living" Constitution. Despite their liberal, activist tendencies (and their high percentage of voting together), Black and Douglas were not close personally. Black disapproved of Douglas's personal lifestyle, which included four marriages, the last two to women one-third his age, and Black thought little of Douglas's scholarship. Once when Black had one of his clerks draft a minor dissent for him, Black would not let the first draft circulate. After reading over his clerk's work, Black said, "This is good enough for Bill [Douglas], but not the others."[130]

Next in seniority on the Court was eleven-year veteran Harold Burton. Generally considered conservative in his views, the Republican Burton became President Truman's first appointment to the Court, presumably to improve relations between the White House and Republican leaders in Congress. Many believed, though, that Burton's appointment was another example of the kind of political cronyism that marked Truman's presidency. Burton had been a leading member of the renowned "Truman Committee," or Senate Special Committee to Investigate the National Defense Program during World War II. Before Burton's one term in the Senate, he was engaged in local and state politics, serving one term in the Ohio legislature and then filling three terms as Cleveland's mayor. On the Court, Burton's reputation suffered because the press portrayed him as more involved with Washington's social scene than with his Court duties, yet he was well respected by the other justices and their clerks because of his pragmatism. He approached each case on its merits with no predilections. When the clerks in the 1956 term polled themselves to pick the one justice to represent them if they were on trial—or, as one clerk put it, who they would pick if they had to have nine of the same person on the Court—their choice was Burton.[131] Not highly regarded as a legal technician or prolific opinion writer, Burton gained a reputation outside the Court as being at best a mediocre justice. Before his service on the Court ended, Burton's inferior image was further tarnished when Yale law professor Fred Rodell publicly criticized Burton for being "ploddingly conscientious," suggesting a weakness of mind unfitting for a justice. It was just this conscientiousness, though, that earned Burton the esteem of his colleagues. As his biographer, Mary Frances Berry, noted, Burton recognized his own weaknesses and worked all the more carefully so as not to prove to be a disappointment. "Knowing that he was not brilliant and that writing came hard and was not likely to be filled with flowing phrases," Berry wrote, "Burton thought the best he could do for the practicing lawyers was to outline every precedent that he had considered and rejected and the process by which his result had been reached."[132]

Whittaker might have had a sympathetic companion and steadying force on the Court had Burton stayed, but after thirteen years Burton retired before Whittaker began his second full term. Suffering the effects of Parkinson's disease, by the spring of 1958 Burton decided to leave the Court at the end of the term, and he informed Eisenhower in March. Eisenhower, though, did not want the pressures of selecting a successor at that time, so, according to one of Burton's clerks, Burton's plans were kept a secret while he considered staying another year.[133] In the meantime, arrangements were made for Burton's clerks to go to work in the Justice Department if he left before the start of the next Court term and his successor did not use them. By June Burton's condition had worsened, and his doctor advised him to retire. Deciding to wait until after his seventieth birthday, June 22, to inform Eisenhower, Burton finally met with the president on July 17 to formally offer his resignation. Still, Eisenhower delayed announcement of Burton's retirement until a successor was found, and not until the opening of the new Court term in October did the public learn Burton was leaving. In large part the delay was designed to avoid complications during the Court's special summer session to consider arguments in the Little Rock school desegregation controversy. After the Court issued its ruling in the Little Rock case, *Cooper v. Aaron*, Burton informed his clerks and the rest of the Court of his retirement.[134] To replace Burton, Eisenhower selected another Ohioan, Judge Potter Stewart of the Sixth Circuit Court of Appeals. At age forty-three, Stewart was the youngest member of the Court at the time of his appointment. By waiting until the start of the Court's 1958 term to nominate Stewart, Eisenhower was able to make his third recess appointment, an unprecedented number for any president.

The other Truman appointee on the Court, Tom Clark of Texas, was best remembered for his incessant good-humor and penchant for bow ties. Described by one of his own clerks as "an old Texan-frontier type," Clark was modest, warm, and gracious. So gracious, in fact, that another clerk has remembered what a struggle it was to go through a door in Clark's home: "You were his guest so he would stand aside inviting you to go first. Yet, he was the justice so you naturally stepped aside so he could proceed first. Often it would be a standstill."[135] Clark began his public service in Texas as the assistant district attorney for Dallas County. Later Clark joined the Justice Department in Washington, and during World War II he was on the west coast supervising the evacuation of Japanese-Americans to relocation camps. As a justice Clark more often supported the government in the field of subversive activity, but he later came to regret his role in the Japanese relocation. After serving four years as Truman's attorney general, Clark became Truman's third pick for the Court. Truman later became disappointed with Clark on the Court, especially after Clark joined the majority to find Truman's actions unconstitutional when Truman ordered his secretary of commerce to seize and operate the nation's steel mills to avoid the potential harm caused by an impending steel strike during the nation's participation in the Korean conflict.[136] Already on the Court for seven and a half years when Whittaker arrived, Clark occupied a centrist position on a Court split between the two competing philosophies of Black and Frankfurter. During Whittaker's tenure, in fact, Justices Clark and Stewart were called upon more often than Whittaker to write for both sides in five to four cases, ostensibly to hold on to their votes. The impression has persisted, however, that Whittaker was somehow the "swing vote." In reality, Whittaker's vote was far more reliable for the conservative bloc than either Clark's or Stewart's. During Whittaker's first term Clark cast the deciding vote in important cases, and later either Clark or Stewart became the pivotal votes in determining the outcomes of five to four decisions.[137]

The remaining Court members were all relative newcomers when Whittaker joined their ranks and, with the exception of Earl Warren, were relatively unknown at the time. Each of President Eisenhower's first three appointments to the Court, however, has been ranked among the leading justices of the twentieth century, and each of their careers on the Court extended well beyond Whittaker's term of service. Moreover, much of their acclaim as justices occurred because of their role on the Court following Whittaker's departure. The first of Eisenhower's appointments to the Court, naming California Governor Earl Warren as chief justice, will forever be remembered as inaugurating a distinctive period in Court history known as "the Warren Court." In his first term as chief justice, Warren focused national attention on the Court when he declared segregated public schools unconstitutional in one of the most celebrated (and, in some parts of the country, most reviled) decisions of modern times, *Brown v. Board of Education*. Considered a landmark case, *Brown* gave added impetus to the burgeoning Civil Rights movement in America and marked the beginning of the end of a way of life many southerners were loath to change. What made Warren's role in the *Brown* decision so remarkable was not so much his written opinion, which was accused of lacking sufficient legal support, but his resolve to forge a unanimous decision, one that would have been impossible under his predecessor.

The *Brown* decision, however, did not mark the beginning of what was later considered "the Warren Court." That phase of Warren's legacy did not begin until first Whittaker and then Frankfurter left the Court. Not until the 1962 decision in *Baker v. Carr* (made without Whittaker's participation) holding that legislative apportionment was justiciable did history's "Warren Court" come into being, sparking a rights revolution that redrew American political boundaries, incorporating more of the Bill of Rights into the due process of the Fourteenth Amendment, and dramatically altering our criminal justice system. With the exception of *Mapp v. Ohio* (decided during Whittaker's tenure), the hallmarks of "the Warren Court"—cases like *Engel v. Vitale* that prohibited prayer in public schools, *Gideon v. Wainwright* that incorporated the Sixth Amendment's guarantee of the right to counsel for all indigent defendants charged with a serious crime in state courts, *New York Times v. Sullivan* that extended First Amendment protection to prevent libel suits without proof of actual malice, the reapportionment decisions *Wesberry v. Sanders* and *Reynolds v. Sims* that declared Congressional and state representation must be based on population, *Griswold v. Connecticut* that established a "right to privacy" not explicitly found in the Constitution, and *Miranda v. Arizona* that provided significant safeguards for criminal defendants—were all decided after Whittaker's departure from the Court. Whittaker missed out on the substantial changes in American constitutional law wrought by "the Warren Court," situating his five years of service between the uproar following *Brown* and the attendant applause of *Baker*.[138]

When Earl Warren took over as chief justice the Court was riven by the Black–Frankfurter debate over the proper role of the Court. Not until after Whittaker's departure, when Arthur Goldberg replaced Frankfurter, did the pendulum finally swing one way giving the liberal bloc the necessary five votes to constitute a majority. Accepting the guidance of the Court's two senior members, Warren at first allowed Black to preside over conferences until he felt prepared to do so, and he accepted Frankfurter's tutelage, asking for and receiving abundant reading material. Warren's relationship with Black, both personally and jurisprudentially, grew closer over time, but his relations with Frankfurter quickly chilled and the two became distant and resentful of each other. Soon Warren found his niche with the liberal bloc, and he, too, became a results-oriented justice, using his own sense of fairness to lead him to his decisions. For Warren, principle became more important than precedent, and in conference discussions he cut through the most tangled legal arguments by asking simply, "Yes, but is it fair?" Not considered a profound legal thinker or scholar, once Warren made up his mind he relied on his liberal colleagues to craft a proper legal explanation for his decisions. In fact, Warren came to rely on the two colleagues he respected most, Black and Brennan, to help him both before and after conferences. It was well known at the Court that before conferences Warren stopped at Brennan's chambers to discuss his strategy for presenting cases, and after conferences Warren went to Black to decide opinion assignments when the two of them were in the majority together.

Warren's greatest asset at the Court and what made him such an effective chief justice was his political skill. The Court did not need another legal technician, what it needed was leadership, a quality in which Warren excelled. Warren's political career began in 1925 when he became the district attorney for Alameda County, gaining a reputation as a tough, incorruptible prosecutor and becoming in 1931 "the best district attorney" in the country. Before the outbreak of World War II Warren became the California attorney general, securing the nominations of all three state political parties, and during the war he executed the evacuation of Japanese–Americans from the state. Like his Court colleague, Tom Clark, Warren later regretted his participation in the Japanese relocation. Popular with both political parties, Warren got elected to three terms as governor of California. Recognized nationally as a leading Republican, in 1948 Warren became Thomas Dewey's running mate in the presidential election, and in 1952 Warren was a serious contender for the presidential nomination. Following Eisenhower's presidential victory in 1952, Warren was promised the next Court vacancy, and in preparation for that position he accepted Eisenhower's invitation to become solicitor general. As luck would have it, the first vacancy was as chief justice when Fred Vinson died unexpectedly, and, although reluctant at first, Eisenhower kept his promise to Warren. Like Clark before him, Warren disappointed the president who appointed him. Eisenhower never fully supported the Court's desegregation decisions (a point that aggravated Warren), and in the field of subversive activity many of the Court's decisions left Eisenhower disgusted. The members of the Court, though, came to appreciate Warren's decisive leadership, his warm, friendly personality, and his commanding presence. During his fifteen years as chief justice, there was never any doubt as to who was in charge.[139]

Eisenhower's second appointment to the Court, John Marshall Harlan, was the only other Court member in 1957 besides Whittaker with any federal court experience. Harlan had served as a judge on the Second Circuit Court of Appeals for only eight months (which was seen as a necessary stepping-stone before advancement to the Supreme Court) before Eisenhower chose him in 1955 to fill the vacancy created when Justice Robert Jackson died suddenly. Prior to that, Harlan had been one of New York's leading Wall Street lawyers representing major corporations like Du Pont in antitrust and commercial litigation. Much like Whittaker, who was only one year younger, Harlan had little political experience prior to his Court appointment, devoting most of his professional career to private practice. Unlike Whittaker, Harlan was more refined, better educated, and had gained a national reputation among corporate lawyers after successfully arguing important cases before the Supreme Court. Patrician in his manners, Harlan was courteous, correct, and sincere in his concern for others, making him one of the most personally respected members of the Court. Aligned most closely with Frankfurter's views, together they formed the core of the conservative bloc on the Court. Personally, Harlan got along well with Frankfurter, accepting Frankfurter's tutelage, and his clerks have attributed this as much to his easy-going manner as to his gratitude at having such a gifted teacher. A persistent advocate of federalism, Harlan was willing to allow for greater latitude of state experimentation in fashioning laws, and, like Frankfurter, he did not think that courts should substitute their will for that of the popularly elected legislatures. Unlike Frankfurter, though, Harlan was more even-tempered, and rather than trying to badger or cajole his colleagues into accepting his views, Harlan used lengthy, well-written, persuasive memoranda to present his arguments. Because of his gentle personality, Harlan was well liked by his colleagues, especially Justice Black, who, as a member of the liberal bloc, was diametrically opposed to Harlan's views. Even though they disagreed, Black and

Harlan were close, admiring the strength of each other's arguments and their skillful presentation. One of Black's clerks has remembered, for example, that in one trivial commerce case, initially the justices had voted six to three, and Harlan got the opinion assignment. After Black's dissent circulated, though, two justices switched their votes, giving Black a majority, but instead of redrafting his majority decision into a dissent, Harlan rewrote it using Black's line of analysis. Although he did not agree with Black's outcome, Harlan wrote from Black's point of view. Another vote switched, and Harlan kept the majority. According to this clerk, "The two of them were delighted with each other."[140]

Rounding out the liberal bloc and becoming a dependable fourth vote for Black, Douglas, and Warren was Eisenhower's third appointment, Judge William Brennan of the New Jersey Supreme Court. Joining the Court at the start of the 1956 term, just five months before Whittaker's arrival, Brennan became Eisenhower's second recess appointment. Brennan's selection seemed custom-made for the unique set of criteria Eisenhower devised during an election year for choosing the next justice. He was Catholic, a Democrat, and had experience as a state court judge. Prior to his judicial service, Brennan had been a member of a prominent Newark law firm representing corporate clients. The youngest member of the Court at the time of his appointment at age fifty, Brennan became the third longest serving member appointed to the Court in the twentieth century (almost thirty-four years), just behind Black and Douglas. Because of his three decades of service, his charming unassuming manner, and his ability to forge coalitions through compromise and conciliation, Brennan has been regarded as one of the most influential members of the modern Court. His role as a consensus builder and leader of the activist wing of the Court, however, was not that apparent during Whittaker's five years of service. Like Whittaker, he was a newcomer, serving in the shadows of the acknowledged leaders of the Court—Black, Frankfurter, and, of course, Warren. In fact, during Whittaker's tenure, clerks at the Court have admitted that it seemed unlikely at the time that Brennan would achieve the kind of stature he subsequently did, being regarded as what one clerk called "a smart alec lightweight." When Brennan arrived at the Court he aligned himself almost immediately with the other liberal justices, developing a special rapport with Chief Justice Warren that the other two, Black and Douglas, did not have. With Brennan's appointment, the judicial philosophy of Black and Douglas—that the Fourteenth Amendment incorporated all of the protections of the Bill of Rights against the states—finally had four solid votes, just one vote shy of a majority. Like Douglas, who accepted the idea of a "living" Constitution, Brennan, too, was willing to look beyond the literal words of the Constitution's text to find implied rights; unlike Douglas, Brennan was an accomodationist, willing to modify his written opinions if it meant gaining a majority, and Brennan's great legacy was his remarkable ability to fashion majorities. Nicknamed the "Four Framers" [of the Constitution] by Whittaker's law clerks, this activist group—Black, Douglas, Warren, and Brennan—throughout Whittaker's tenure were continually in search of the decisive fifth vote to give sanction to their view of the Court as the final guardian of individual rights.

This was the Court Whittaker joined in the spring of 1957, torn by ideological rivalries, personal antagonisms, and composed of men with widely diverse backgrounds who, with few exceptions, had far more experience in state and national politics than Whittaker. Further complicating his situation, Whittaker joined the Court in the middle of its term, a term that concluded as the most controversial since the Court's outlawing of segregated schools three years earlier. Not that Whittaker became embroiled with the controversy over the final decisions of the 1956 term (he joined the Court too late to participate in most of those decisions), but like the other justices he could not ignore the public outcries against the Court or the chilling effect those accusations had on the direction of the Court. These responses, coming so close after Whittaker's appointment, were directed at recent national security decisions.

In the months following Whittaker's appointment, the Court handed down a series of decisions that not only disabled much of the country's loyalty-security program but also outraged members of Congress, who responded with a spate of anti–Court measures designed to strip the Court of its jurisdiction or restrict its rulings in similar cases. In May 1957 the Court announced two state bar admission cases, ruling that bar associations could not deny membership to applicants based solely on their having joined the Communist Party prior to World War II.[141] Membership in the Communist Party was not *per se* evidence of poor moral character, and, besides, joining the Communist Party before 1950 was legal. Then in June the Court reversed the federal conviction of a labor union president, Clinton Jencks, after government witnesses testified he had falsely filed a required non–Communist affidavit. When the government refused to reveal to Jencks confidential FBI files corroborating their witness's testimony, the Court rebuked the government's efforts, asserting that without revealing the files the government had to give up its prosecutions.[142] The final blow came on June 17, what critics dubbed "Red Monday," when the Court handed down a quartet of cases, including *Service v. Dulles* (which appeared mild compared to the other three announced that day) that all ruled in favor of suspected Communist Party members or its sympathizers.[143]

In two of the anti–Communist cases handed down on "Red Monday" the Court questioned the scope of federal and state legislative-investigative inquiries, reversing the contempt convictions of those who refused to testify. In *Watkins v. United States* a labor union officer refused to answer questions before the House Un-American Activities Committee about persons no longer members of the Communist Party, and in *Sweezy v. New Hampshire* an economist refused to answer questions put to him by the state's attorney general about, among other issues, a lecture he had delivered. In both cases the Court set limits on the investigative powers of legislative bodies, declaring in *Watkins* that "there is no congressional power to expose for the sake of exposure." In the final case, *Yates v. United States*, the Court reversed the Smith Act convictions of fourteen Communist Party leaders charged with conspiracy. What distinguished this case from the Court's earlier decision in *Dennis v. United States*, where eleven Communists had all been convicted on the same charge, was the distinction the Court now made between advocating a political belief and advocating a course of action. Without overruling *Dennis* or holding the Smith Act unconstitutional (a course preferred by Black and Douglas), the Court made further conspiracy prosecutions virtually impossible, and none were ever made. The net result of the Court's 1956 term was, in the words of Lucas Powe, "nothing short of astounding."[144]

Ironically, despite the uproar over its decisions, in none of the Communist related cases mentioned did the Court declare an act of Congress unconstitutional or even rule on a constitutional question. In addition, in the three federal cases, *Jencks, Watkins,* and *Yates,* only one justice dissented (Clark supported the government's loyalty programs more as a matter of principle), and in the state cases there were never more than two or three justices in dissent. Of course, Whittaker did not participate in any of these decisions, his appointment coming too late for him to listen to oral arguments, but with the votes so far apart even if he had joined the dissenters it would have made no difference in the final outcomes.[145] The question remained, though, would the Court continue to defend those accused of Communist sympathies, or could Congress effectively turn back the Court's direction?

A few outspoken supporters of the Court applauded its recent decisions, but the Court's detractors exceeded them in numbers and passion. These decisions did not capture the current of the country or of the Congress, and in Congress anti–Court sentiment ran high. The need to respond to recent decisions was keenly felt. Calling the Court a "great menace to this country," Democratic Senator Strom Thurmond of South Carolina called for the impeachment of those justices who supported anti–Communistic decisions, and Democratic Senators Olin Johnson of South Carolina and James Eastland of Mississippi, who was then chairman of the Senate Judiciary Committee, proposed a constitutional amendment to require justices be reconfirmed every four years.[146] Although it would not have changed any of the contested decisions, numerous bills were also introduced in both houses to change the qualifications for *future* Court appointments, clearly indicating that the *present* members were somehow unfit for the office. The reason the Court made such poor decisions, its critics believed, was a lack of adequate judicial experience; in other words, the Court was comprised of too many politicians and law professors. For example, H.R. 304, which prohibited members of Congress, heads of federal agencies, and governors from appointment for five years after leaving office, would have disqualified Black, Burton, Douglas, Clark, and Warren; and H.R. 320, which required justices be natural born citizens, would have disqualified Frankfurter.

Most of the measures designed to curb the Court never made it out of committee; only one anti–Court measure successfully passed though Congress, the so-called "Jencks Act," but it was less a rebuke of the Court's decision and more a confirmation of its ruling in *Jencks*. There were, however, two close calls for the Court, too close, in fact, for the justices to ignore. During the first session of the Eighty-fifth Congress, just one month after "Red Monday," Republican Senator William Jenner of Indiana introduced the most sweeping measure to curb the Court, effectively stripping the Court of its appellate jurisdiction in the field of internal security and reversing those decisions. Because of some astute political maneuvering, Missouri Senator Thomas Hennings was able to stop the Jenner bill from coming out of the Judiciary Committee. The following year, Republican Senator John Butler of Maryland amended the Jenner bill (S. 2646) by dropping most of the jurisdiction-stripping measures while creating what Robert Steamer considered "one of the most vitriolic and ungracious attacks ever made on the Supreme Court."[147]

The Jenner-Butler bill made it out of the Senate Judiciary Committee by a vote of ten to five, and, despite his best efforts to stall any floor action on anti–Court measures, Democratic majority leader Lyndon Johnson of Texas had to allow a vote on it. On a motion from Senator Hennings the bill was tabled indefinitely by a close 49 to 41 vote, but the message was clear. Had it passed, anti–Court feelings ran so high in the House that it would have become law. With all the commotion over the Court's recent decisions and the uproar in Congress, it was no wonder Charles Whittaker felt apprehensive about his new position. Hardly had he been there a few months when *Time* magazine summarized the public hostility against the Court: "Not since the Nine Old Men shot down Franklin Roosevelt's Blue Eagle in 1935 has the Supreme Court been the center of such general commotion in newspapers and in the bar. If anyone doubted before, following recent cases, the Court made it clear that it was building a new wing to the temple of American law — even at the cost of razing an old wing, hard-built."[148]

Ultimately the Court came through the conflict with the Eighty-fifth Congress relatively unscathed but not unreformed. Beginning with Whittaker's first full term, the justices in the conservative majority beat a hasty retreat in the field of national security, and throughout Whittaker's tenure, with the major exception of the Little Rock controversy, race related cases were nearly avoided completely. Instead of losing every time, the government began to win more often when prosecuting suspected subversives, and, according to

Lucas Powe, the change in direction was intentional. Frankfurter decided to save the Court from itself.[149] Although the majority in future national security cases insisted that the Court had not changed directions, the change was so apparent that by 1960 the *New York Times* commented, "What Senator Jenner was unable to achieve the Supreme Court has virtually accomplished on its own."[150]

While the change in the Court's direction was not, as Herman Pritchett characterized it, "another 'switch in time to save nine,'" Powe contended that the crisis facing the Court at the time of Whittaker's appointment was potentially more dangerous than Roosevelt's efforts to transform the Court in 1937 because measures that would have stripped the Court of its appellate jurisdiction in 1957-58 stood a better chance of passing congressional approval than did Roosevelt's "Court-packing" plan.[151] Led by Frankfurter, the Court's conservative majority entered what Powe described as a transitional period, somewhere between stalemate and retreat. While there were notable exceptions, like *Cooper v. Aaron* and *Mapp v. Ohio*, for the most part the time encompassing Whittaker's service on the Court did not see many landmark decisions. This transitional period, beginning with the Court's retreat from controversial rulings in national security cases and ending with the Court's entry into the "political thicket" of legislative reapportionment, coincided with Whittaker's arrival to and departure from the Court, making his five years of service seem uneventful. The uproar over *Brown* had subsided as the South embarked on endless delaying tactics to stall desegregation efforts, and history's "Warren Court" still awaited the appointment of a reliable fifth vote giving the liberal minority a solid majority.[152]

When Charles Whittaker arrived at the Supreme Court, rather than taking Justice Reed's old chambers, he settled into Frankfurter's because Frankfurter wanted Reed's for himself. As the junior member of the Court, Whittaker was expected to show deference to his senior colleagues, and Whittaker was just as pleased to occupy the former chambers of the venerable Frankfurter. Just the same, there was a certain pathos to the situation. It had been, after all, this kind of deference that landed Whittaker at the Supreme Court in the first place. Without consultation, Roy Roberts decided that Whittaker would become his man on the Court, and with a little prompting both the attorney general and the president concurred. Although deep down he had misgivings about his own qualifications, Whittaker did not refuse the invitation. Once he was on the Court it did not take long before his anxiety nearly broke him. He would have to prove, as he did to get into law school, that he could measure up. No one doubted he could more than Whittaker himself.

This, then, was his predicament as he anticipated serving out his self-imposed five-year sentence: the Court was embroiled in a conflict with Congress over national security, two competing philosophies fractured the Court as justices chose up sides, personal antagonisms between some justices continually threatened to disrupt the Court, and, not least of all, Washington's high-profile, elite society left the Whittakers feeling out of place and far from home. Ironically, about the time he entered law school Whittaker had changed his name to sound more "judicious," more like his ideal of a great trial lawyer. Almost forty years later he came to occupy the same "seat" on the Court that had once belonged to his adopted namesake, Charles Evans Hughes, who occupied the "seventh seat" from 1910 to 1916.[153] Now it was Whittaker's turn. Had he known where his new name would take him, he might have opted to take his father's advice and remained Charles Ernest Whittaker, gentleman farmer and country banker.

5

Finding a Higher Law

"Lots of things have happened since I received that fateful call," Charles Whittaker told a reporter in March 1960. After three years on the Supreme Court, Whittaker was a different person than when he arrived. He was more relaxed, he had overcome his disappointment over leaving Kansas City and the district court, and, best of all, he was beginning to enjoy his work. Something had changed for Charles Whittaker—something so pronounced that he freely admitted, "I did not like it at first, but now I am getting a big kick out of my work. Although the life of a justice is hard and exacting, it provides the opportunity for service of the highest order, and I am getting results."[1]

The typical view of Whittaker's five years of service on the Court has been that he struggled incessantly the entire time, that he arrived on the brink of a nervous breakdown and five years later finally had one. This view, however, overlooked the fact that halfway through his tenure Whittaker made a complete turn around, becoming a more active and influential justice. When he first arrived at the Court Whittaker was timid, insecure, and overawed. After two full terms, though, he became accustomed to his new role and determined to overcome his earlier difficulties. Contributing to Whittaker's new attitude about the Court was the appointment of Potter Stewart in October 1958, relieving Whittaker of the burden of being the most junior justice. Stewart was a pragmatist with no clearly defined judicial philosophy, and, like Whittaker, both the liberal and conservative sides courted his vote. More significant, however, to Whittaker's improved outlook was a new confidence in his own abilities. No longer content to join the opinions of others, Whittaker began writing separately more often. He discovered, moreover, that his opinions could sway the other justices. On occasion his views changed the outcome of a case. No longer reluctant about making his views known, Whittaker began to enjoy his work.

The greatest difficulty evaluating Whittaker's Court service has been that his contributions were so easy to overlook. In the few memorable landmark decisions rendered during his tenure Whittaker took a backseat, joining other justices' opinions rather than writing his own. His majority assignments for the Court usually did not involve cases considered of great national import or lasting significance (few of them were even close decisions). In fact, what has been remembered about Whittaker's service was his indecision—his inability to make up his mind or changing back and forth from one side to the other. Several of his concurring opinions revealed how hopelessly he felt stuck in the middle, wanting to accommodate both sides without completely giving in to either. This view of Whittaker as incapable of making decisions, as continually struggling to overcome his own deficiencies, has obscured any meaningful contributions he made to the Court. Though not as historically momentous as ending segregation in public schools or redrawing the country's political landscape, there were a few Whittaker opinions that were important—at least, the law as then interpreted was substantially changed. Several of Whittaker's opinions set new precedents, and a few continued to have a lasting impact on American law. Whittaker's difficulties early in his Court service, however, have persisted affecting public opinion about his effectiveness and ability as a justice.

For the first two years he was there, Whittaker was miserable on the Supreme Court. Speaking frankly about his difficulties those first two terms, Whittaker told an interviewer, "The demands are tremendous and unless one can learn to pace himself to do the work of this importance under great pressure he is likely to be miserable."[2] Whittaker was in his office at the Supreme Court by nine every morning and did not go home until six thirty or seven at night. He took an armload of work home with him every night, staying up past midnight reading. Instead of slowing down or planning for his retirement, Whittaker kept the same relentless pace he had set for himself as a lawyer twenty-five years earlier, and the effects showed on him. One of the clerks at the Court Whittaker's first term has recalled, "I never saw Whittaker smile. He was a dour individual." Other clerks have agreed that Whittaker seemed overwhelmed his first two terms. Justice Douglas's clerk in Whittaker's second term has commented, "Whittaker was a sympathetic figure; he was obviously overwhelmed. He acted like it. During oral arguments he rarely spoke. His written output was a mere fraction of the other justices. There was nothing to distinguish him."[3] Another clerk that same term who wished to remain anonymous has written, "[Whittaker] always seemed to me physically quite different from the other justices—less intellectual in appearance.... To call a spade a spade, I think he found—indeed he at least once indicated in my hearing—that he found certain aspects of his job intolerably hard."[4]

Much of Whittaker's difficulty lay in his devotion to completing his work thoroughly. There simply was never enough time to read everything he thought he should read, which was why he took so much work home with him. Whether it was inadequate preparation for the task or his intense conscientiousness to fulfill what he thought was his duty, Whittaker exhausted himself at first by trying to read and do everything that other justices left to subordinates. Blaming his difficulties, in part, on the volume of work, a decade after he left the Court Whittaker wrote, "I think the volume of the Court's work is overwhelming; there would be fewer dissents and a better product if the Court were to have substantially more time in which to do its work."[5]

Unlike other justices who relied more on their clerks to do some of the reading and writing for them, Whittaker relinquished little responsibility to his two clerks. In Whittaker's chambers, clerks were most often found doing research or writing memoranda, rarely if ever did they draft an opinion. Whittaker wanted that responsibility for himself even though it put him under enormous pressure. "He seemed receptive to our views," one of Whittaker's former clerks has remarked, "but he was very much his own man. He accepted some of our comments in the opinion. Other justices would not work on an opinion without their clerks."[6] Another one of Whittaker's former clerks has remembered how if they were allowed to draft an opinion, it never retained its original form. "Bill Canby and I thought we drafted some good opinions," this clerk bluntly stated, "Whittaker accepted parts of them. Words like 'an' and 'the.' In fairness, though, he had difficulty delegating responsibility; he did not want to accept our 'prose' on how a case ought to be decided."[7]

Accepting the responsibility for writing every decision inevitably took its toll on Whittaker. He labored over every word, which caused delays and frustration for the rest of the Court. Even Stewart, who was young and vigorous, had to abandon after his first term his intentions of writing every opinion assigned to him. By the end of the term Stewart had his clerks drafting dissents for him.[8] No justice, with the possible exception of William Douglas, who boasted he needed only four days to complete the Court's work each week, could easily keep pace if they worked on every opinion themselves, but Whittaker tried. There were several underlying reasons for Whittaker's commitment to writing his own opinions without assistance from his clerks, not the least of which was an article he read in *U. S. News & World Report* that insinuated law clerks exercised too much influence over the justices' opinions. This article appeared just after Whittaker arrived at the Court, following the Court's end of the term decisions supporting civil liberty claims of suspected Communists, at a time when Congress and the rest of the country thought the Court had overstepped its bounds in dismantling much of the domestic security program. Criticism of the Court was rampant. "What you find in a close look at the Supreme Court," this article observed, "is that, instead of the popular picture of nine men upholding or changing the laws of the country, there are 18 others who participate more or less actively in paving the way for important decisions.... The question that is raised at this time, when the Supreme Court is deploying its power in the fields formerly controlled by other branches of the Government, is whether the influence of these young law clerks—some not yet admitted to the bar—is reflected in Court opinions."[9]

The message was clear and unmistakable, and it was not lost on the justices. Both Whittaker and his first term clerk, Alan Kohn, remembered the content of the article long after they left the Court. This one article, however, written in response to recent Court decisions, was not alone responsible for Whittaker's commitment to writing his own Court opinions without assistance from his clerks. For thirty years Whittaker practiced law largely without assistance from subordinates, and it was unlikely he would rely on them once he got to the Supreme Court. He derived greater satisfaction from what he alone accomplished, which was why he relished so much his role as a district court judge—it gave him the opportunity to be in complete control. Whittaker would not abdicate to his clerks what he saw as his duty to fulfill, not after a lifetime of relying on himself.[10] Too proud of his own abilities, Whittaker never realized he could have benefited from his clerks' assistance; because they were recent law school graduates Whittaker held his clerks' abilities in low regard. "You must realize," he once told an interviewer, "that these are just youngsters, bright boys but [they have] no experience practicing law [and are] necessarily quite immature and not very adequate as a sounding board. Besides, I don't think justices of the Supreme Court need a sounding board. He knows what sounds right to him."[11]

Because of his disdain for his clerks' assistance, Whittaker remained aloof with them, maintaining a professional detachment that precluded social intercourse. Described as a private man, conversations with his clerks concerned the business of the Court and little else. After conferences, he told his clerks how the justices voted, but that was all. One of Whittaker's second term clerks has remembered, "He was circumspect. He would have found it unseemly to tell us how he felt about the other justices." This same clerk recalled how at the end of their year together he told Whittaker how grateful he was to serve as Whittaker's clerk, how that experience was the highlight of his legal career. Still disappointed and disillusioned by his own appointment, Whittaker offhandedly asked his clerk, "Why would you say that?"[12]

Whittaker's clerks all agreed that working for him meant doing an inordinate amount of research and little else. To function effectively as a justice, Whittaker should have relied on his clerks more. Instead, he tried to do all of the work himself. One of his former clerks remembered how Whittaker used to comment that it would be impossible for his two clerks to read all of the material they were required to read each week, yet Whittaker somehow managed to read every word himself after his clerks finished.[13] "His problem was not his legal ability," one of Black's former clerks has commented, "I don't think Whittaker used his clerks much. I think he was afraid to. Black and Frankfurter used their clerks enormously, but you still knew the work would be theirs. That job was tough enough using clerks who worked; it had to be worse if you did not trust your clerks."[14] Whittaker was often abrupt with his clerks, especially early in his Court service. One of his first term clerks, Ken Dam, has remembered, "He was sometimes curt, that was his style. I learned then to know ahead of time what I was going to say before I said anything."[15] Once during his first term at the Court Whittaker became so enraged at his clerks that he lost control of himself. It was the only time when anyone at the Court remembered seeing Whittaker out of control, and he quickly recovered, but the episode indicated that below the surface Whittaker was in turmoil.

The incident occurred near the end of the term in a relatively insignificant case, *Byrd v. Blue Ridge Rural Electric Cooperative*, a workmen's compensation case raising procedural questions. Whittaker drafted his separate opinion himself concurring in and dissenting from William Brennan's majority decision, and the time it took the Court to reach a final decision (just three weeks) indicated this was not a difficult case for any justice. Whittaker left his draft opinion for his clerks to read, and they, of course, were expected to approve it. Instead, one of his two clerks, Ken Dam, turned to the other and said, "What are you going to do about this? It cannot be circulated as it is. We'll get crucified at the lunch table."[16] All the clerks ate lunch together at the Court, and Dam worried that the other justices' clerks, who generally held a low opinion of Whittaker, would heap scorn on Whittaker's clerks if they allowed the rest of the Court to see his opinion. According to Whittaker's other clerk that term, Alan Kohn, Whittaker's sentences were exceedingly long, and, although he summarized the facts of the case well, he failed to synthesize the facts with the applicable law in a well-reasoned, pithy conclusion. Whittaker's clerks had no doubt that he reached the right decision in the case, but they did not want his already weakened reputation to suffer any more because of insufficient writing skills. Another justice's clerk has confidentially admitted, "[His] abilities were not held in high esteem by the other clerks. I think his own clerks perceived him to be the least intellectually capable."[17]

Since Kohn had drafted the bench memo for *Byrd*, it was agreed that he should tell Whittaker it needed more work. When Kohn explained his concerns about sentence length and the rationale for the decision, Whittaker became so angry that he picked up the opinion and threw it at his clerk, screaming, "If you can do better, you take a crack at it!"[18] In the next room Whittaker's secretary, Celia Barrett, who overheard the exchange, became so upset she immediately collected her belongings and went home. It had been a horrible day in Whittaker's chambers, and Kohn had until the next day to work on redrafting the opinion. After cutting down in size some of the longer sentences and adding a final paragraph to clarify the opinion's rationale, Kohn left his revised copy on Whittaker's desk the next morning. Celia Barrett awoke that day to find Whittaker's limousine waiting to take her to work. At the office, no one spoke to Whittaker when he arrived, and after he finished reading the revised opinion he came out of his chambers announcing, "Send it to the printer!" He thought Kohn's revised opinion was excellent—no further changes were necessary. Obviously Whittaker regretted his earlier behavior, and without discussing it further his office staff understood his intentions. In his own way he was trying to apologize.[19]

This one example of Whittaker losing control of himself and lashing out at his staff was a rare exception. At no other time did he berate his clerks like this, and no one who ever worked with him has remembered him ever losing his temper with a subordinate. In fact, the general impression among clerks at the Court (his own as well as others) was that Whittaker was a gentleman, always courteous towards others. For example, one of Frankfurter's former clerks has remembered, "Whittaker was extremely polite, sweet, open. He was less dynamic than the other justices…. He seemed shy, withdrawn, overawed. The other justices all had strong personalities. Whittaker was not a strong personality."[20] To speak unkindly about his staff or the other justices was not in his nature, and none of his family ever heard him speak critically about how he was treated at the Court. Whittaker had too much reverence for the men with whom he served to harbor ill feelings towards them, and he described the Court as "a closely-knit family, a congenial and happy family notwithstanding the great differences and heated debates we have over controversial issues."[21]

Although at first he felt uncomfortable in his role as a justice and regretted ever leaving Kansas City, Whittaker did not let his personal feelings interfere with his professional decorum. Justice Douglas in his autobiography considered Whittaker an "affable companion" as well as a "quiet recluse."[22] Others have similarly remarked how Whittaker was gracious but kept mostly to himself. Douglas's former clerk during Whittaker's last term has written, "I knew Justice Whittaker when I was at the Court and liked him very much. I though he was a very kind, considerate, and thoughtful man. He was one of the finest human beings with whom I have come in contact."[23] Generally, Whittaker got along well with everyone at the Court, and he was best remembered for his cordial manners. In the fall of 1959 he took up playing golf after a fifteen-year absence to help him relax. His usual companions were Justices John Marshall Harlan, Tom Clark, and retired Justice Stanley Reed, who he considered his closest friends in Washington. Even after he left the Court, Whittaker maintained a high regard for the institution and protected its integrity, telling bar association audiences, "It is too much to expect, in the myriad of circumstances involved in these cases, that even nine men, though equally dedicated, devoted, and competent, will view all things alike. Hence the Court frequently divides, and firm dissenting views are often stated in strong language. But I am happy to say to you that mutual respect is such that this is always, or nearly always, done without personal rancor or ill will, and that, at least outside the conference room on Fridays, the Justices are a reasonably happy family."[24]

Whittaker may have held his brethren in high regard, but reciprocal sentiments were not shared. In fact, some justices like Felix Frankfurter went out of their way to show their disdain for Whittaker's work. During their first term together Whittaker and Frankfurter had a difficult relationship, in part because of Frankfurter's overbearing tutelage, the effect being to embarrass more than to instruct. A clerk that term has remembered one incident when Whittaker circulated a draft opinion to the other justices and Frankfurter used it to humiliate Whittaker's already fragile ego. As sometimes happened in Whittaker's writing, the first sentence was so long that it covered the entire first page and ran into the second page of his opinion. Frankfurter asked the print shop to make a copy of the draft in triple space so he could make corrections directly above Whittaker's printed text. He then had nine copies printed and circulated.[25] Whittaker's own clerks agreed that his written opinions lacked the style of other justices who wrote in broader philosophical terms. "He had a terrible style—too much procedure," one of Whittaker's clerks has remarked, "He tended to put too much into the opinion. He treated them as though they were district court litigation, and he kept reminding the other justices of that responsibility."[26]

Not everyone at the Court appreciated Whittaker's unique perspective, his thirty years of trial court experience. Some found fault with his courtroom performance. One of Douglas's clerks noted how during oral arguments Whittaker barely spoke while the other justices peppered lawyers with questions. Other clerks have remembered with derision Whittaker's habit of reading his opinions in their entirety, word for word, including footnotes and citation numbers.[27] All of this gave the impression of a justice who was unprepared for the nation's highest court and ill equipped to carry out his duties. Whittaker thought if he read enough law, if he exhausted every possible argument (and himself in the process), then he could find the one indisputably correct answer.[28] The problem for Whittaker was realizing that few questions brought to the Supreme Court had one indisputably correct answer. The law did not remain fixed and unchanging, following predictable certainty, and Whittaker had to overcome his feelings of self-doubt and self-pity before he could find his place on the Court.

Observations that Whittaker participated little in the Court's work or had little influence on the Court's decisions were at best exaggerated. The *Kansas City Star* described Whittaker's courtroom performance as interactive and useful: "Thin faced and of severe aspect, he listened intently to arguments and frequently interrupted attorneys to ask questions, putting complex legal situations on a more down-to-earth level."[29] Several of Whittaker's colleagues on the Court paid him tribute following his retirement, emphasizing his dedication to his work and his skill as a lawyer. "His entire preoccupation was with the law," Chief Justice Warren wrote, "He refused to leave time for any diversion. I am sure no Justice who has sat on this Court was more conscious of his great responsibility, more diligent in performing it, or more concerned about the result of his efforts." Douglas, likewise, seemed impressed with Whittaker's devotion to detail: "Each and every case he processed was done with a thoroughness never exceeded. He exposed every facet of a question, whether minute or major, and gave it intensive scrutiny.... His care in scrutinizing even the humblest petition was one indication of his dedication to evenhanded justice." Calling Whittaker "an expert legal technician," Clark praised Whittaker's contributions to their conferences, writing, "Abhorring subterfuge he sought for the truth as he saw it and in our conferences fought for it with all his might. He sensed facts—events—and mastered them.... He could drive a quarter horse through a fallacious argument and never use a spur."[30] One of Douglas's clerks has remembered how Whittaker's interactions with lawyers appearing before the Court made an impact on him. "He paid attention to the lawyers," this clerk has said, "He got their points and asked good questions. That is where I learned how to present oral arguments."[31]

Whittaker's writing, while technical, even bland by comparison, was neither inappropriate nor embarrassing. He understood his audience—the lawyers and judges who would read his opinions—and his style reflected his concern for their understanding and acceptance of his reasoning. "He wrote his decisions for the people who would need them—the district court judges," one of his former clerks has commented, "He did not think it was his responsibility to convince others on the Court to accept his views. He had his own special role for himself."[32] That special role meant deciding each case based on his own understanding of the law, regardless of how well he understood it. It also meant standing by his convictions rather than aligning himself with one side or one particular philosophy. When asked if Whittaker had been a failure at the Court, all of his clerks agreed that such a subjective term did not apply to Whittaker. His influence over the direction of the Court or over the other justices was immaterial to such an assessment because, as one of his former clerks put it, "He could not fail to influence his brethren when he had not joined the Court intending to influence any of them."[33]

Court sessions opened the first Monday in October and lasted until late June. The justices heard arguments in cases for two weeks at a time and then had two weeks to conduct their research and writing. Under the leadership of Earl Warren the Court's schedule changed; instead of starting sessions at noon and holding conferences on Saturdays, Warren began sessions at ten in the morning and held conferences on Fridays. Mondays were decision days when the Court announced its rulings.[34] At the weekly Friday conferences only the justices themselves attended. Here the justices decided which cases from the docket to set down for argument and considered the final outcome of cases already argued. By all accounts Warren, who led these discussions, was a supremely effective presiding officer, making sure all the justices had time to state their views without interruption. After the chief justice spoke the most senior justice, Hugo Black, who sat at the opposite end of the justices' long conference room table, spoke next. Each justice in order of seniority then took his turn, ending finally with the most recent appointment.

Whittaker's first full term was the only time he sat in the conference room chair reserved for the most recent appointment (who was also expected to answer the door if the justices received a message from outside the conference); by his second term he moved over one seat to make room for Potter Stewart. While in conference, each justice made notes on the arguments raised and the votes cast, and, according to one of Whittaker's first term clerks, Whittaker kept incredibly complete notes of these discussions.[35] When discussion on a case ended, the justices cast their votes on the final outcome in reverse order of seniority, beginning with the most junior justice.[36] This way the Court's recent appointees were relieved of the burden of casting the deciding vote on a split Court. After he left the Court, Whittaker once remarked that the position of speaking last but voting first "put the monkey on the junior's back," an uncomfortable position.[37] During his first full term Whittaker felt enormous pressure being the junior justice. As one of Warren's clerks that term has explained, "Whittaker was always the potential fifth vote, which meant he was courted more than the others, adding to his woes. He had adequate intellectual skills, but the job was tough for him, whether he was the fifth vote or the ninth."[38]

Casting the "fifth vote," or being on the majority side in five to four decisions, led some to conclude that Whittaker was the "swing vote" on the Court, that justice who could vote either way in a close decision. Leon Friedman, for example, considered Whittaker the swing vote on the Court, claiming, "Whittaker cast the crucial vote in a number of significant cases. In no less than forty-one instances he voted with the conservatives in a five to four decision denying a claimed civil right or liberty."[39] Friedman may have exaggerated, though, since one of the cases he claimed carried Whittaker's "crucial" fifth vote, *Draper v. United States*, was, in fact, a six to one decision.[40] Being on both sides of what appeared to be identical cases or encountering indecision wrestling with weighty constitutional issues did not make Whittaker the swing vote. That role belonged to someone who could be found more often on both the conservative and liberal sides of the Court, someone whose vote more often made a difference in the final outcome of a case. Friedman himself admitted, "Whittaker contributed merely one of five votes to the conservative group and in one sense it was no more decisive than any others," so why consider it "crucial"? Justices Clark and Stewart, in fact, held the decisive swing vote throughout Whittaker's tenure because of their pivotal position between the conservative and liberal blocs.[41]

Potter Stewart joined the Court at the beginning of Whittaker's second full term, October 14, 1958, and became one of the most enigmatic of justices during his twenty-two years of service. A graduate of Yale Law School, Stewart was a skilled trial lawyer in his hometown of Cincinnati, Ohio, before Eisenhower appointed him as a judge to the Sixth Circuit Court of Appeals in 1954, making Stewart at age thirty-nine the youngest judge in the federal judiciary. When he joined the Supreme Court four years later Stewart refused to be identified with either the conservative or liberal sides and instead based his decisions on his own independent analysis of the issues involved. This "middle position" on a Court that was often torn between the two competing philosophies of Black and Frankfurter often made Stewart the swing vote.[42]

Whittaker generally tended to be more conservative; at least, his votes most often lined up with that philosophy espoused by Frankfurter and Harlan. He was not, however, what one of Brennan's clerks called a "knee-jerk conservative." Instead of adhering to one particular philosophy, this clerk continued, "Whittaker gave careful thought to every case and was well-respected for that."[43] As a result, on rare occasions Whittaker could be found voting alongside the liberal justices. Another one of Brennan's clerks has confided, "I think Whittaker wanted to join the left, more liberal wing of the Court, but he had trouble emotionally and intellectually doing that." Like Stewart, Whittaker used an independent analysis of each case to determine what he thought was the correct result absent an overriding philosophy of judging. Before he took his seat on the Court the *Washington Post* correctly predicted that Whittaker would be "a dedicated jurist rather than an advocate of any particular doctrine or line of reasoning."[44] This frustrated justices like Black and Frankfurter who relied on their personal philosophies to guide them in their decisions; it also made it more difficult for Whittaker to reach a decision. One of Whittaker's first term clerks has remarked, "He tried to avoid labels; he did what he thought was right according to the law. As a trial lawyer he was very good at assembling the facts of a case and the applicable law. I think he should have taken a position; he needed a philosophy."[45]

Without a judicial philosophy to guide him, decisions were often difficult for Whittaker. According to his son, Kent, there were three compelling factors that caused Whittaker serious difficulty at the Court: First, Whittaker went to the Court with an inferiority complex; his modest beginnings and legal education were continually a source of embarrassment for him. Second, the volume of work was exhausting, and Whittaker made the mistake of trying to do all the work himself without relying on subordinates.

Finally, Whittaker lacked a "philosophy of governance," which other justices used to decide the outcome of a case even before it arrived at the Court.[46] Whittaker's "philosophy of law," if one could call it that, made the task of judging even more difficult. He told reporters just after his nomination to the Court was announced, "Justice cannot be produced through any system of procedures alone. In the main it is, and must always be, the product of long hours of hard, diligent, painstaking labor by highly competent, experienced, careful and practical lawyers.... *The practice of law is a deliberate science and must be recognized as such.* Its product will not be any better, regardless of the system used, than the lawyers who do its work."[47]

At its core, this "science" of law involved the discovery of facts, and these facts, in turn, led to the controlling legal precedent by which a case should be decided. The difficulty with this type of judging was that slight differences in fact could lead to widely different results, and, as Whittaker himself later admitted, "Precedents for almost any proposition can be found, and questions presented are often so razor sharp that they might be decided either way with almost equal support of precedent and reason."[48] Because Whittaker lacked a philosophy of judging to help him make decisions in those cases where precedents could be found for both sides, he struggled most with constitutional questions. One of Harlan's former clerks has remembered how Whittaker agonized incessantly over constitutional cases, telling Harlan he was simply unable to decide them.[49] "His basic problem was he was extraordinarily conscientious," one of Whittaker's clerks has explained, "He had a background in railroad negligence cases; he felt he had to get his mind completely around a question. This could be taxing for him with constitutional questions because of his thirty years of experience as a trial lawyer. He had to understand everything about these novel questions. A Yale law graduate had a better perception of constitutional questions than his thirty years as a trial lawyer."[50] Instead of developing a comprehensive judicial philosophy, Whittaker relied on the facts of each case to lead him to what he considered was the correct decision. Describing his obsession with uncovering the facts, one of Whittaker's former associates said, "He insisted that the facts be copper riveted to the foundation upon which he relied to sustain his position. He was reluctant to decide an issue until he all but exhausted himself in trying to be absolutely sure he was right. Everyone ... that knew him well and long has heard him say, 'If you are going to tell it—tell it right.'"[51]

While his philosophy of judging made it difficult for him to reach decisions, it also meant that Whittaker could at times be found on the liberal side when the Court split along philosophical lines. His first clerk at the Court, Alan Kohn, fairly described Whittaker's political leanings, summarizing how he could be found on both sides of the philosophical rift within the Court: "At his core, he was probably a Libertarian. A raw-boned farmer from northeastern Kansas, he had a strong distrust of government. This made him a conservative on economic issues. If a man owned a business he should be allowed to run it any way he pleased. In the area of individual rights he sympathized with persons caught in the governmental web. In his first years on the Court, that outlook found him siding with the Four Framers [Black, Douglas, Warren, and Brennan] in several cases even though he felt more comfortable with the conservatives."[52] Another Whittaker clerk, James Edwards, has described Whittaker's inconsistency and the problems it presented: "He turned out on some issues to be more liberal than the Republican right-wing would have liked. I attributed this to his 'populist' background—I always understood him to have come from comparatively humble beginnings—which caused him to be more philosophically aligned with Black (and some of the other more liberal justices from more comparable backgrounds) than with Frankfurter and even Harlan.... This used to frustrate Frankfurter who was constantly lobbying Whittaker to try to keep him to the strict constructionist position."[53]

Those cases where Whittaker was in the company of the "Four Framers" typically involved civil liberties, but since his overall record on civil liberties was generally conservative (three-quarter of his votes in civil liberty cases denied the claimed right) Vestal concluded that in the area of civil liberties Whittaker was difficult to classify as a justice. What was clear, however, was that Whittaker based his decisions (and his votes) on the particular factual circumstances that arose in these cases. In the areas of denaturalization and alien deportation, for example, Vestal noted that Whittaker voted both for and against aliens' claims and that he "carefully balanced competing claims in the frequently odd and unique circumstances involved in these cases." Similarly, in criminal defense cases, especially the right to counsel, Vestal found that the particular facts involved "indicated that Whittaker determined violations of due process on a case-by-case method."[54] As a result, Whittaker joined the "Four Framers" in cases like *Bonetti v. Rogers*, where he ruled for a six-person majority that an alien who had entered the country for permanent residence in 1923 could not be deported according to the Internal Security Act of 1950, despite the fact that he had been a member of the Communist Party from 1932 to 1936. Written during his first full term on the Court, *Bonetti* was exceptional; later in his Court service Whittaker bowed to Frankfurter's intense lobbying and remained more on the conservative side.[55]

There were examples, however, in Whittaker's third and fourth terms that pitted him against Harlan and Frankfurter, suggesting that Whittaker did not slavishly follow Frankfurter's doctrine of judicial restraint, but none of these involved civil liberties and so were often overlooked. In each case, Frankfurter, Harlan, and at least one other justice, notably Stewart or Clark, dissented from Whittaker's majority opinion, leaving Whittaker on the side of the "Four Framers." In three decisions his third term Whittaker met opposition from Frankfurter and Harlan in cases from such diverse fields as failure to file income tax,[56] change in venue,[57] and a criminal conviction for mail fraud.[58] In his fourth term twice the core of the conservative bloc did not join Whittaker, once in a patent infringement case[59] and again in an income tax case involving an interpretation of the Federal Rules of Civil Procedure.[60]

The most significant decisions where Whittaker joined the liberal bloc were both decided in his first term as a justice. Known as the expatriation cases, in *Trop v. Dulles* Whittaker became the fifth vote to reverse the loss of citizenship of a defendant convicted by military court-martial of desertion during time of war, and in *Perez v. Brownell* Whittaker dissented alongside three of the "Four Framers" in another five to four decision, this time to reverse the loss of citizenship of a defendant who voted in a foreign election. These two cases were significant on their own merit because they challenged an act of Congress, something that happened far less frequently than challenges to state legislative action, but they were also significant for what they revealed about Whittaker.

First, Whittaker's reputation as a justice has suffered because he changed his mind about the outcome of these cases. Other justices also changed their minds about the outcome, so Whittaker's behavior was not that aberrant. It was the nature of the Court's operation for justices to change their votes; after a draft opinion was circulated it was not unusual for a justice to request changes to the text to stay with the opinion or to change his view of the case and vote a different way, possibly writing separately or joining another opinion. Second, Whittaker's dissent in *Perez* (written as a Memorandum rather than a dissent, which demonstrated how difficult it was for him to write) revealed Whittaker's middle-of-the-road position, analyzing each case on its particular facts without succumbing to the doctrinal positions of either Warren or Frankfurter, that either expatriation was forbidden in all cases by the Fourteenth Amendment or that deference should be paid to Congress unless there was a clear constitutional abridgment of rights. Whittaker often found himself caught in the middle between the activist posture of the liberal side and the restraint urged by Frankfurter and Harlan, finding appealing yet conflicting arguments in both. Unable to embrace wholly one side or the other, Whittaker then wrote for himself, most often in concurrence or, as in this case, in a memorandum disguised as a dissent.

Perez and *Trop* were first argued before the Court on May 1 and 2, 1957, just six weeks after Whittaker arrived there, and although Warren initially had five vote majorities in both cases they were held over until the next term to give more time to the dissenters to draft opinions. According to Bernard Schwartz, the first vote in these cases showed Whittaker along with Clark, Burton, and Frankfurter on the side to strip United States citizenship from both Clemente Perez and Albert Trop. On the other side, Brennan, Harlan, Douglas, and Black joined Warren to retain citizenship for both Perez, who had voted in a foreign election, and Trop, who was court-martialed for wartime desertion. The central issue in both cases was whether or not Congress possessed the power to proscribe citizenship. At the first conference, Warren argued that the Fourteenth Amendment guaranteed citizenship for life, which Congress could not touch unless a person voluntarily gave it up. On the other side, Frankfurter urged judicial deference to a co-equal branch of the government. Since not everyone in the majority was satisfied with Warren's draft opinion because he failed to clearly explain why denaturalization was outside the bounds of Congressional authority the cases were held over.[61]

When the justices returned the next fall to hear reargument in the cases, Harlan, Brennan, and Whittaker each changed their minds. Harlan decided to join the side stripping both Perez and Trop of their citizenship; Brennan decided to switch in only one case stripping Perez of his citizenship; and Whittaker decided to switch in one case to retain Trop's citizenship. That left different outcomes in each case: Warren still had a five to four majority in *Trop*, but Frankfurter now had a six to three majority to strip Perez of his citizenship for voting in a foreign election. With the justices now in the unusual position of justifying congressional authority in one case to deprive a person of their citizenship but not in the other, both sides set about drafting opinions. Following Frankfurter's draft of the new *Perez* majority, Whittaker decided to change his vote in *Trop* back to his original stance, giving Frankfurter a majority in both cases. That left Warren to redraft dissents in both cases. After Warren's drafts circulated, Whittaker again switched sides, this time joining Warren's side to retain citizenship in both cases. The final outcome was Perez lost his citizenship by a five to four vote but Trop kept his by an equally divided Court. What had caused this conflicting result? Brennan joined both majorities, one justifying loss of citizenship but not the other.[62]

Because Whittaker switched his votes in these and other cases he has been characterized as weak or indecisive, yet changing votes subsequent to a draft circulation was not uncommon at the Court. In *Perez* and *Trop* both Harlan and Brennan changed their views following reargument, a fact often overlooked.[63] That Whittaker switched his vote in *Trop* three different times was not at all unreasonable considering that both Harlan and Brennan had a change of mind following reargument and that Warren and Frankfurter in their draft opinions continued to alter or modify their arguments in the hopes of swaying votes and gaining majorities. Numerous examples abound of justices changing their votes following the circulation of a draft opinion, but Whittaker's reputation has been especially tarnished because of other justices' comments regarding his indecision. Justice Douglas in his autobiography observed, "Whittaker would make up his mind on argument, only to be changed by Frankfurter the next day. In conference, Whittaker would take one position when the chief or Black spoke, change his mind when Frankfurter spoke, and change back again when some other Justice spoke.... No one can change his mind so often and not have a breakdown."[64] Douglas, however, was not the most charitable man or the most reliable source when it came time to write his autobiography. Chief Justice Warren, likewise, reportedly quipped after Whittaker's retirement, "Charlie never could make up his mind about decisions until he left the Court."[65] These comments, however, belied Whittaker's intense convictions once he made up his mind. As should be evident, Whittaker was not satisfied with a decision until he had mastered every fact and exhausted every conceivable argument, which took time and allowed for the potential to vacillate from one position to another. Once his mind was decided, though, nothing could shake his convictions. For example, Justice Clark related a humorous incident when the Court was divided and Stewart went to see Whittaker to persuade him to change his mind. As Clark described the scene, "He came back announcing defeat and adding, 'He not only disagrees, but violently; in fact, I think he must have eaten raw meat for breakfast!' To which, one of the other brethren said, 'No, we may as well give up. If he feels this keenly about it, it's from conviction and *not* raw meat. He's ruined every steak I ever served him.' You see, we sometimes host special luncheons in the Justices' Dining Room and this particular Justice had flown in some very special steaks which, he thought, were best served quite rare and Charlie, as we all knew, likes his burned to a crisp!"[66]

Warren's majority opinion in *Trop*, joined only by Black, Douglas, and Whittaker, ruled unconstitutional that section of the Nationality Act of 1940 that provided for loss of citizenship if the accused was dishonorably discharged from military service after a court martial convicted him of desertion during time of war. Congress had no power over denaturalization, Warren asserted, but even if it did, that section of the Act violated the Eighth Amendment's ban on cruel and unusual punishment. This second statement was necessary because Frankfurter in his *Perez* majority ruled that Congress did possess authority in certain areas. Black and Douglas concurred in Warren's opinion, but, they stated, if citizenship could be divested then this power should not belong to military authorities, a point Warren refused to handle in order to keep Whittaker's vote.[67] The tension between Frankfurter and Warren over these two cases was felt in the courtroom the day of their announcement. According to Anthony Lewis, correspondent for the *New York Times*, Warren read in his *Trop* opinion, "In some eighty-one instances since this Court was established it has determined that congressional action exceeded the bounds of the Constitution. It is so in this case."[68] Frankfurter responded from the bench that those eighty-one cases were "nothing to boast about since many of them have been overruled."[69]

Frankfurter's majority opinion in *Perez*, joined by Harlan, Burton, Clark, and Brennan, found that Congress acting under its foreign relations powers had the authority to divest a person of their citizenship after they voted in a foreign election. Brennan's vote was the weakest of the five. Initially he planned to write a separate concurring opinion rather than join Frankfurter's opinion, but Frankfurter revised enough of his opinion to keep Brennan's vote. As the decisive fifth vote in both cases, Brennan's position was the least consistent. He agreed with Frankfurter's *Perez* opinion that Congress possessed authority to divest a person of citizenship in the exercise of its foreign relations powers, but in *Trop* he concurred with Warren, claiming that military desertion did not necessarily effect the war powers of Congress and so denaturalization was beyond its powers. Whittaker, on the other hand, voted consistently in the end to retain the citizenship of both Perez and Trop, although he did not do so on the absolutist position first posited by Warren and supported by Black and Douglas that the Fourteenth Amendment prohibited expatriation unless voluntarily requested.

Whittaker's dissent in *Perez*, a two-page memorandum, sought to find a middle position between the two extremes of Warren on the one side and Frankfurter on the other. Warren's dissent in *Perez*, joined by Black and Douglas, stated that the Fourteenth Amendment guaranteed permanent citizenship to all native born and naturalized citizens. Voluntary surrender of citizenship was possible, but voting in a foreign election was not sufficient to show a voluntary abandonment. Besides, Warren observed in his dissent, the United States had allowed aliens to vote in presidential elections up until 1928. Douglas joined by Black also dissented in *Perez*, following much the same line of arguments as Warren but stressing that Congress was wholly without power to expatriate unless to prescribe how voluntary expatriation could occur. Whittaker could not join these liberal dissents because, like Frankfurter, he believed that Congress did have the power to expatriate a citizen if there were danger of embroiling the United States in an international dispute or of embarrassing it in the conduct of foreign affairs, but he could not strip Perez of his citizenship simply for voting in a foreign election because that ran none of those risks. As long as it was legal at the time for Perez to vote in Mexico, and since the United States had allowed aliens to do so until 1928, Whittaker saw no risk of an international dispute. Whittaker also agreed with Warren's proposition that voting in a foreign election did not, as such, indicate a voluntary abandonment of citizenship, but he could not accept the view shared by Black and Douglas that Congress was wholly without power to expatriate. As a result of his misgivings about both the majority and dissenting views, Whittaker wrote his separate memorandum explicating his partial agreement with both. In the end, Whittaker voted to preserve the citizenship of both Trop and Perez (his back and forth voting in *Trop* indicated that may have been where he wanted to be all along), and within a decade Frankfurter's opinion in *Perez* was expressly overruled by the later "Warren Court" activists.[70]

To a large extent Whittaker's difficulty on the Supreme Court centered on this willingness to accept divergent points of view as equally valid and compelling. As he did in *Perez*, at times Whittaker could not come down firmly on one side or another, preferring instead to write separately. His separate concurring opinions generally sought to explain how he found reasonable arguments on both the liberal and conservative sides. In several cases the Court waited on Whittaker to either pick a side or write separately, during which he was continually implored by both sides to finally decide. His commitment to finding the one indisputable, correct result at times left him hopelessly stuck between these two rival factions, when the only way to free himself from their entreaties was to write on his own.

Whittaker's struggle to accommodate both sides of the philosophical divide also led him to write separately in *Frank v. Maryland*, a question of search and seizure by civil authorities. Ultimately his position came closer to the Court's final position eight years later on the question of civil searches than either the initial liberal or conservative reactions. When *Frank* was first presented to the Court on appeal, the justices split on whether to accept the case: Warren, Black, Douglas, Brennan, and Stewart voted to note probable jurisdiction while Frankfurter, Harlan, Clark, and Whittaker voted to dismiss it. Once the case was argued, though, the initial conference vote was eight to one to affirm Frank's conviction for refusing to allow entry to a Baltimore, Maryland, health inspector. Neighbors had complained that there were rats around Frank's home, and when the health inspector received no response on his first visit he examined the area outside the house where he found a pile in the rear of the house identified as "rodent feces mixed with straw and trash and debris to approximately half a ton." Later Frank refused to allow the inspector in the basement without a search warrant, and he was arrested the next day and fined twenty dollars.

The question for the Court was whether Frank had been denied due process of law as required by the Fourteenth Amendment. Ten years earlier in *Wolf v. Colorado* the Court had held that the core of the Fourth Amendment—"the security of one's privacy against arbitrary intrusion by the police"—was incorporated against the states by the Fourteenth.[71] *Wolf*, however, like other leading Fourth Amendment cases, dealt with police searches looking for evidence of a crime, not with health inspections. The question of due process in *Frank* then became inextricably tied to the question of whether administrative searches conducted by civil authorities required the same procedural safeguards as criminal searches conducted by police. At the Court's first conference, Warren led the discussion by stating that Baltimore's ordinance was not unreasonable provided the fine was not excessive and no jail time was involved. Black could not draw a distinction between the amount of the fine and the reasonableness of the statute, but he concurred with Warren—Baltimore officials had acted reasonably. Frankfurter, on the other hand, believed the amount of the fine represented the reasonableness of the ordinance. Other justices stressed the long history of health inspections in the United States without a search warrant. Only Douglas disagreed with the prevailing view, and, with the vote eight to one, Warren assigned Frankfurter the majority opinion.[72]

During the drafting of opinions in *Frank* three justices—Warren, Black, and Brennan—abandoned the majority and joined Douglas's dissent instead. According to Melvin Urofsky, Douglas had asked his clerk to research the dissent, but when the clerk could not find materials to support a dissent Douglas told him to "bring in all the books you got, and let me see what I can do."[73] Douglas then drafted a ten-page dissent that eloquently extolled the virtues of the Fourth Amendment and the dangers of warrantless searches, and immediately his three liberal-minded colleagues joined him. The vote now stood five to four, and Whittaker announced that he wanted to reconsider his vote. The Court remained split four to four for weeks with Whittaker undecided. According to Douglas's clerk, the lobbying Whittaker suffered was severe. Eventually Warren persuaded Whittaker to make up his mind. At the Friday conference Whittaker said he would reach a decision by Monday.[74] He spent the weekend in the country with his clerk and came back announcing he would stay with his original vote—Frank had not been deprived of due process, but Whittaker could not swallow whole the majority contention that no search warrants for civil inspections were required. Eight years later neither could the rest of the Court, and Frankfurter's majority opinion was overruled. Ironically, no one at the Court had a change of mind about the issue, but, like so many changes that took place during the "Warren Court" era, changes in Court personnel brought about the new decision.[75]

By concurring in the majority decision rather than joining Frankfurter's opinion, Whittaker clearly had misgivings about the principal argument used to sustain Frank's conviction, namely that search warrants were not a requirement in civil inspections. The needs of modern society, a long history of health inspections, and dominant public opinion as to the necessity of conducting regular inspections led the majority to conclude that civil authorities should not be held to the same procedural requirements as police officers. Frankfurter wrote for the majority,

> Time and experience have forcefully taught that the power to inspect dwelling places, either as a matter of systematic area-by-area search, or, as here, to treat a specific problem, is of indispensable importance to the maintenance of community health; a power that would be greatly hobbled by the blanket requirement of the safeguards necessary for a search of evidence of criminal acts. The need for preventive action is great, and city after city has seen this need and granted the power of inspection to its health officials; and these inspections are apparently welcomed by all but an insignificant few.[76]

Whittaker's concurrence in *Frank* was too brief (one paragraph) to easily discern precisely his misgivings related to Frankfurter's opinion, but the crux of his opinion seemed to be, "that the health inspector's request for permission to enter petitioner's premises ... was not a request for permission to make ... an *unreasonable* search within the meaning of the Fourth and Fourteenth Amendments."[77] In other words, as long as the search was reasonable, not arbitrary or unwarranted in some way, then a search warrant was not necessary. Otherwise, it did not appear that Whittaker was ready to preclude all search warrants in civil inspections.

What constituted a reasonable search without a warrant in civil inspections? Whittaker's replacement on the Court, Byron White, gave the answer eight years later in *Camara v. Municipal Court* when the Court overruled Frankfurter's opinion in *Frank*, holding instead that search warrants in civil inspections were a reasonable requirement of the Fourth and Fourteenth Amendments. White wrote for a six-person majority, "Since our holding emphasizes the controlling standard of reasonableness, nothing we say today is intended to foreclose prompt inspections, even without a warrant, that the law has traditionally upheld in emergency situations.... [I]t seems likely that warrants should normally be sought only after entry is refused unless there has been a citizen complaint or there is other satisfactory reason for securing immediate entry."[78] As a result, Whittaker's concurrence in *Frank*, though less explicit than White's opinion, came close to the reasonable standard the Court advocated when it overturned *Frank*. According to *Camara*, when Frank refused the health inspector entry there were still reasonable grounds for the inspector to enter the premises without a search warrant: first, there had been complaints about rats around the house, and, second, there was satisfactory reason for securing immediate entry, namely, the health risk of a half ton of rat feces mixed with debris just outside the house. By supporting the reasonableness of the health inspector's request, Whittaker's concurring opinion should be regarded as an appropriate middle ground between the two rival blocs on the Court.

Whittaker's reliance on the reasonableness of the health inspector's request in *Frank* demonstrated a key characteristic of his jurisprudence: the plain meanings of words, as he understood them, could be instrumental in his decisions. At times the dispute over a word's meaning was not necessarily a matter of its legal or strictly literal definition, but rather what Whittaker understood as its commonly accepted or "plain meaning." While some have considered this type of lexicological wrangling beyond the pale of the Supreme Court, preferring instead to think that minor legal minutia like defining words was better suited to the lower courts, this was precisely the kind of work Whittaker enjoyed and in which he excelled.[79]

In the construction of statutes and the application of procedural rules Whittaker found his niche. Since other justices on the Court were more comfortable than Whittaker wrestling with larger constitutional questions, and there was no doubt but that Whittaker's greatest difficulties making decisions involved cases where a person's rights or liberty were at stake, he contented himself with writing more often on those technical questions of procedural rules that occupied most of the Court's docket. In many of those cases the final decision turned on the Court's interpretation of one particular word. For examples, in his first full term Whittaker dissented alone from the majority in a worker compensation case because he did not believe that an injured worker could be, or be legally compensated as, both "totally and permanently disabled" and "temporarily totally disabled" at one and the same time.[80] At the opening of the 1958 term Whittaker joined Black and Douglas in dissent because the definition of what constituted a "home" was left unresolved in the Court's *per curiam* order, thereby denying construction workers a tax deduction for travel expenses.[81] Whittaker dissented again from the Court's decision, this time joined by Brennan and Stewart, because of the difference of opinion over whether a group of Maine homemakers knitting articles for sale were "members" of a cooperative as defined by state law, or were they "employees" for the purposes of the Fair Labor Standards Act.[82]

The disagreement between Whittaker and Frankfurter over the meaning of "plain words" in *Commissioner of Internal Revenue v. Acker* gave rise to an amusing editorial in the *Washington Post* entitled, "Antics in Semantics." Whittaker's majority opinion in *Acker* relied on congressional history and the construction of revisions to the Internal Revenue Code to determine that the failure of a taxpayer to file a declaration of his estimated tax, which would subject him to a penalty, did not also subject him to further penalties for filing a "substantial underestimate" of his tax. Frankfurter, joined by Clark and Harlan, dissented because of Whittaker's interpretation of congressional intent, writing, "The Court's task is to construe not English but congressional English. Our problem is not what do ordinary English words mean, but what did Congress mean them to mean.... Here we have the most persuasive kind of evidence that Congress did not mean the language in controversy, however plain it may be to the ordinary user of English, to have the ordinary meaning."[83] In a letter to a friend Whittaker responded to Frankfurter's ridiculous syllogism by writing, "It is gratifying to me that this [*Washington Post*] editorial said that my Brother's view toward plain words was reminiscent of the chapter in *Alice in Wonderland* entitled 'In the Looking Glass,' to the effect that 'words mean what I say they mean, because I say what words mean.'"[84]

The plain meanings of words, at least how Whittaker understood them, underscored many of his separate concurring opinions. He examined each case individually from a practicing lawyer's point of view, building his analysis of the case first upon the facts presented and then upon the legal precedents supporting those facts. There were examples of Whittaker writing separately not because he found equally controlling arguments on both sides of an issue but because he found what he believed was an acceptable alternative argument from what the majority presented. This did not make him inferior to the other justices; on the contrary, many on the Court appreciated Whittaker's views. As one of Black's clerks has stated, "Whittaker's work did not reveal any weakness. He might stop by and read an opinion to us. He took his work seriously.... He was one of nine; not bigger than life, or idiosyncratic, or as personable as some of the others, but he held his own."[85] One of Douglas's clerks put it this way: "Whittaker had good abilities. No one was embarrassed by his opinions. The Court was better for having him on it. He was from mid–America; he had trial court experience. He brought a unique perspective with him."[86]

This unique perspective caused Whittaker to write separately in *McElroy v. United States,* where the Court ruled that neither civilian employees of overseas military forces nor the dependents of military servicemen were subject to court-martial jurisdiction for either capital or noncapital offenses. This case together with its companion, *Kinsella v. Singleton,* presented to the Court three different categories of cases: civilian military employees charged with noncapital offenses; a civilian military employee charged with a capital offense; and a civilian military dependent charged with a noncapital offense. Justice Clark ruled for the five-person majority that each of these categories of cases was outside the jurisdiction of a general court-martial and required the protections of the Fifth and Sixth Amendments. Not raised in these cases but instrumental to their outcomes was the question of civilian military dependents charged with a capital offense; that issue had already been settled by the Court three years earlier in one of its more controversial decisions, *Reid v. Covert,* decided during Whittaker's first three months as a justice. The controversy surrounding *Reid* and leading to the Court's difficulty deciding *McElroy* involved the Court overruling one of its own precedents in little less than a year.

The Court first heard *Reid* at the end of the 1955 term when Justices Stanley Reed and Sherman Minton were still on the bench. Clark's majority opinion the first time the case was heard upheld the convictions of two women accused of murdering their husbands. The dissenters, Warren, Black, and Douglas, did not have time at the end of the Court term to draft their opinions and so announced their decisions would follow the opening of the next Court term. (Frankfurter, likewise, issued a separate opinion denouncing the haste used to prepare the majority opinion before the end of the term, although it was unclear if he intended to dissent.) Before the opening of the next term, however, events unfolded that changed the eventual outcome of *Reid,* and the Court overruled itself. Frankfurter and Warren convinced Harlan, who had voted with the majority, to vote to rehear the case, and Brennan replaced Minton, giving the dissenters one more vote to reverse the convictions. When the case was reargued one month before Whittaker took his seat on the bench, Reed had already left and Whittaker could not participate. In the second *Reid* decision the majority agreed only to the proposition that courts martial for civilian military dependents charged with capital offenses were unconstitutional.[87] The groundwork was thus laid for the difference of opinion that resulted in the *McElroy* and *Kinsella* decisions.

Assigning Clark the majority opinions in *McElroy* and *Kinsella* was clearly a strategic move by Warren to keep Clark's vote with the majority. Although Clark had voted in both *Reid* decisions to uphold the convictions of civilian military dependents charged with a capital offense, he was now prepared to apply the Court's recent precedent from the second *Reid* decision to other categories of civilians and offenses. For Clark, once the Court made courts martial out-of-bounds for any civilian, then the protection of federal courts applied to all civilians living overseas with the U. S. military. Relying on their earlier concurrence in *Reid*, Frankfurter and Harlan concurred with the majority in *Kinsella* only to extend the protections of federal courts to civilian military employees charged with *capital* offenses; the other categories of cases, they believed, were all within the purview of Congress to prescribe and the military to punish. Whittaker, however, joined by Stewart, concurred with the majority in *Kinsella* only to the extent that civilian military *dependents* charged with noncapital crimes should receive the protection of federal courts. Ironically, Whittaker also relied on the second *Reid* decision as precedent but reached a different result. Instead of relying on the nature of the crime to extend federal court protection to civilians who worked for the military, Whittaker reasoned that *Reid* offered protection to civilian dependents because of their special relationship to the military. Civilian military employees, even those who committed capital offenses, should still be subjected to court-martial jurisdiction because, according to Whittaker, one did not need to be a "member" of the armed forces to fall within the constitutional meaning giving Congress the authority to "make rules" for the "land and naval Forces" (Constitution, Article 1, Section 8). Civilian employees were an integral part of the functioning and operation of the military, so for Whittaker they belonged to it and should be subject to its jurisdiction. In the end, four justices (Frankfurter, Harlan, Whittaker, and Stewart) all dissented in *McElroy* where the Court prohibited civilian military employees charged with noncapital offenses from being subjected to courts martial.[88]

The unique perspective Whittaker brought to the Court also led him to concur in the result in *Gomillion v. Lightfoot*, one of the few race-related cases the Court accepted during his tenure. The decision in *Gomillion* was easy enough and all the justices agreed to the outcome; the difficulty lay in choosing a rationale for the decision while avoiding any connection to the Court's decision in *Colegrove v. Green* where the Court had held that apportionment of a state's congressional districts was a nonjusticiable question. *Colegrove* presented several problems for the Court, not the least of which was that reconsideration of it would have deeply fragmented the Court into its two rival blocs, something the Court could not afford when confronted with a race-related case. The only justices remaining on the Court since *Colegrove* was decided were Frankfurter, considered the majority author although only two other justices had joined his opinion, and Black and Douglas, who both had dissented from Frankfurter's opinion. *Colegrove* had served for more than a decade as the leading precedent for keeping the Court out of the "political thicket" of state reapportionment, and with its four to three decision resting on a shaky majority and three justices still harboring intense personal feelings about its outcome, the Court decided to make clear how it could be distinguished from *Gomillion*, which was a clear case of the worst kind of racial gerrymandering. The Alabama state legislature had redrawn the municipal borders of Tuskegee, Alabama, in such a way as to turn it "from a square to an uncouth twenty-eight sided figure," with the effect that all but four or five of the city's four hundred African American voters were living outside the new city boundaries, but not a single white voter was so displaced. Clearly what the state legislature had done was motivated by a discriminatory purpose, but because the issue involved redistricting of municipal boundaries, considered exclusively an exercise of state power, the state argued that *Colegrove* prevented federal courts from accepting jurisdiction.

When *Gomillion* first arrived at the Court three justices—Clark, Whittaker, and Stewart—voted to deny *certiorari*, possibly believing that the case was nonjusticiable. Once the Court accepted the case for argument, though, the question became not one of justiciability but upon what grounds should the Court base its decision. The justices were unanimous in their conclusion that Alabama had acted in a discriminatory way, but should their decision rely upon the Equal Protection clause of the Fourteenth Amendment, which had been consistently used as the rationale in state discrimination decisions, or upon the Fifteenth Amendment's protection of the right to vote? These two constitutional bases for reversing the state's municipal redistricting were equally defensible considering that they were both raised in the briefs representing African American voters of Tuskegee, in oral arguments, and in the Court's conference discussion. The African American petitioners presented *Gomillion* as a racial discrimination case, relying on other discrimination cases as precedents and distinguishing *Gomillion* from the kind of reapportionment issues raised in *Colegrove*. In every mention of constitutional violations the petitioners paired together the Fourteenth and Fifteenth Amendments. In addition, during oral arguments Robert Carter, the lawyer on behalf of petitioners, several times admitted that changing the city's boundaries in no way impaired the right to vote of those excluded African Americans from voting in all other state and county elections. In fact, when Carter stated that dividing citizens based solely on race was a violation of the Constitution and a member of the Court asked based on what, Carter responded with the Equal Protection clause. One of the justices then summarized

Carter's position: "They are left with such rights to vote as those in the county outside of the municipality have—I presume what you have to meet here is—although the state has a right to change the areas of its cities, you have to look at its purpose. That's your argument: to see, and if you find that the purpose was to put colored people out of that area so that they could not vote in that area, although they could vote outside of that area, that that violates the equal protection or due—whichever clause you say it does."[89]

At the Court's first conference on *Gomillion*, October 21, 1960, the justices all agreed that Alabama's redistricting of Tuskegee was racially motivated and therefore unconstitutional, but the rationale for the decision remained an open question. While Warren and Frankfurter saw no connection between *Gomillion* and *Colegrove*, Black did not believe that the two could be so easily distinguished. He proposed that the Court treat *Gomillion* as a new field, one unrelated to the apportionment question, thereby avoiding *Colegrove*. Black also saw no problem with deciding the case on either the Fourteenth or Fifteenth Amendments, although he worried about the potential political backlash from the Court's decision whatever the rationale. Other justices, including Brennan, Whittaker, and Stewart, felt the best basis for the decision was to rely on the Fifteenth Amendment protecting citizen's right to vote.[90] With all the justices agreed that Alabama had acted unconstitutionally, Warren assigned the opinion to Frankfurter, a strategic move designed to give the author of *Colegrove* a chance to distinguish the two cases.

In his majority opinion Frankfurter summarized the petitioner's claim, announcing that by changing the municipal boundaries of Tuskegee the state had discriminated against its African American citizens in violation of the Due Process and Equal Protection clauses of the Fourteenth Amendment and had denied them the right to vote in defiance of the Fifteenth Amendment, but then Frankfurter completely sidestepped the Fourteenth Amendment claims and instead based his decision solely on the deprivation of the right to vote *in municipal elections*. This singular focus on the municipal franchise clearly suggested, as Carter admitted in oral arguments, that the right to vote per se in other state and county elections was not at issue and the only harm done to petitioners was to take away their municipal vote in Tuskegee. Frankfurter never answered the Fourteenth Amendment claims, explaining how they were not at issue, and so left them hanging.

Sometime between the first conference and the Court's final decision, Douglas and Whittaker began to doubt Frankfurter's opinion, and both prepared separate concurring opinions. In order to keep Douglas from issuing a full opinion (and to prevent Black from defecting as well) Frankfurter changed language in his discussion of *Colegrove*, which had become a point of contention between the two sides on the Court.[91] Frankfurter went to great lengths to show how *Gomillion* could be distinguished from *Colegrove*, obviously because Black and Douglas continued to pressure for a reconsideration of the *Colegrove* precedent, not because the petitioners from Tuskegee had asked for it. When asked directly at oral arguments if the petitioners wanted to overrule *Colegrove*, Carter stated no, that was not an issue. The state of Alabama, however, relied on *Colegrove* as its defense of a nonjusticiable issue, to which Frankfurter replied, "When a legislature thus singles out a readily isolated segment of a racial minority for special discriminatory treatment," the case was then lifted out of the "so-called 'political' arena and into the conventional sphere of constitutional litigation."[92] This made it possible for the Court to decide *Gomillion* without reconsidering *Colegrove* by claiming that *Gomillion* was somehow beyond the bounds of those cases governed by *Colegrove* (as far as Douglas and Black were concerned it was the opening they needed to begin dismantling the edifice built around the "political question" doctrine and the issue of reapportionment). Frankfurter made clear that the racially motivated issues presented by *Gomillion* were easily distinguishable from the dilution of voting strength found in *Colegrove* because, he summarized, "[T]he inescapable human effect of this essay in geometry and geography is to despoil colored citizens, and only colored citizens, of their theretofore enjoyed voting rights."[93] In other words, the motive behind the legislature's action was discriminatory, leading to a violation of a constitutionally protected right.

Whittaker found a different rationale for opposing Alabama's actions against African Americans, and he wrote his own concurring opinion despite entreaties from both Warren and Frankfurter to reconsider. Whittaker considered the Fourteenth Amendment claims, specifically the Equal Protection clause, the proper vehicle for reversing Alabama's racially motivated actions. He had three sound reasons for basing his decision on the Fourteenth rather than the Fifteenth Amendment: First, by avoiding the question of voting rights the Court could escape conflict with *Colegrove*; second, the Court had already established unanimous precedents with *Brown v. Board of Education* and *Cooper v. Aaron* upon which to rest an Equal Protection claim since Alabama's actions were clearly an unlawful segregation of the races; and third, Whittaker could not believe that the African American voters displaced by the redistricting of Tuskegee had been deprived of their right to vote if they continued to enjoy voting rights following the redistricting. They could no longer vote in municipal elections, but they could still vote in all other state and county elections, the very point brought up in oral arguments that Frankfurter passed over in his opinion. By relying on the Equal Protection clause of the Fourteenth Amendment, Whittaker's *Gomillion* concurrence focused attention on the racially motivated segregation that took place in Tuskegee rather than the loss of certain voting privileges. Whether or not the rest of the Court agreed with him was immaterial; they all agreed that Alabama's actions were unconstitutional.[94]

Since the Court's historic *Brown* decision desegregating America's public schools, maintaining unanimity on the Court became a priority in racial discrimination cases, and in numerous *per curiam* decisions issued following *Brown* desegregating other public facilities the general impression was of a Court united against the evils of racial prejudice. Maintaining unanimity, however, in every case motivated by racial considerations, as *Gomillion* proved, became increasingly difficult on a Court torn by personal feuds and doctrinal differences. The one resounding success in this area during Whittaker's tenure became a landmark decision reaffirming the Court's role as final arbiter in questions of constitutional interpretation, yet the final outcome in *Cooper v. Aaron* still proved to be less satisfactory than complete unanimity. *Cooper* originated when the school board of Little Rock, Arkansas, sought to delay any further desegregation efforts for another two and a half years after the first attempt ended in a showdown between Governor Orval Faubus and President Eisenhower. At the start of the 1957 school year Faubus sought to prevent nine African American students from entering Central High School by calling in the National Guard. Once the Guardsmen were removed and angry white mobs threatened to disrupt the students' entrance, Eisenhower responded by ordering troops from the 101st Airborne Division into Little Rock to protect the students. The school board decided in February 1958 to seek a delay of desegregation, convinced that violence would ensue if it moved forward with its plans, and in June a federal district judge agreed. On appeal, the Eighth Circuit Court of Appeals in August reversed the district court decision but stayed its order for thirty days to give the school board time to petition the Supreme Court.

Because the Court was not yet in session, counsel for the African American students, represented by Thurgood Marshall of the National Association for the Advancement of Colored People (NAACP) and its Legal Defense Fund, then filed a motion with Whittaker in Kansas City (he was assigned the Eighth Circuit) to stay the Eighth Circuit's postponement and to stay the order of the district court. Rather than decide such a grave matter on his own Whittaker contacted Warren, who was in California attending a convention of the American Bar Association with Clark and Brennan, and the decision was made to convene a special session of the Court on August 28 to come up with a decision in time for the start of the new school year. Justices returned to Washington from all over the country (Harold Burton was vacationing in Switzerland), and within two weeks they prepared a *per curiam* decision supporting the NAACP just days before the scheduled opening of school. By the end of September, one week before the start of the new Court term, the justices crafted an extraordinary opinion supporting the principles announced in *Brown* and declaring that further delay would not be tolerated. Furthermore, the strength of the decision lay in its pronouncement that the Court's interpretation of the Constitution was binding on all office holders who swear an oath to uphold the Constitution. No governor or state legislature could defy an order of the Supreme Court.[95]

Initially Brennan drafted a memorandum at Warren's request that later became the basis for the final opinion in *Cooper*. All of the justices were then invited to make modifications to the opinion, turning authorship into a joint effort. Apparently Whittaker demonstrated his concern for the wording of the opinion by suggesting form and word changes on every page of Brennan's draft.[96] Whittaker's concern for the precision with which the Court operated was not lost on others, and one of Douglas's clerks has written, "He was a true gentleman and an asset for the Court.... I would not agree with any comment that Justice Whittaker's work was ineffective. I had the good fortune to review Justice Douglas's notes of the conference each week and found on many occasions that Justice Whittaker made very thoughtful, incisive comments that helped to put issues in perspective."[97] During the drafting of the *Cooper* opinion, Harlan suggested that it contain mention of the three newest justices who were not present for *Brown* but who still fully concurred in its holding. Though one of those justices, Brennan, objected to it, this suggestion made its way into the final opinion. Harlan also came up with the idea to have the opinion issued in every justice's name rather than just one—an unprecedented move—and, despite Douglas's opposition when Frankfurter proposed it at conference, every justice signed the opinion thereby strengthening its tone of resolve.[98]

Throughout the special session, which lasted more than four weeks, security tightened at the Court. Fears of retaliation against the justices themselves became real, and Whittaker's secretary at the time has remembered how both she and the justice had their lives threatened.[99] Threats from outside the Court, however, did not cause the justices as much unease as the trouble within. Just days before the final *Cooper* opinion was announced, Frankfurter revealed his intention to write a separate concurrence, and, speaking for the liberal Court members, Brennan remembered, "We almost cut his throat!"[100] So furious were Black and Brennan at Frankfurter's diminution of a unanimous Court opinion in the face of what was sure to be hostile southern reaction that they threatened to issue their own separate opinion condemning his separate opinion. In the end, though, Harlan persuaded Black and Brennan to withdraw their threats, and Frankfurter's appeal to moderate southern lawyers, many of whom were his former students, waited until the start of the new Court term for its announcement.[101]

In other race-related cases considered during Whittaker's tenure, the Court not only lost the semblance of unanimity it sought to preserve in *Cooper* and *Gomillion*, but several justices including Whittaker balked at the insistence of the liberal justices that the NAACP and African American petitioners necessarily had to prevail simply because the case presented a question based on race. In the first such case, *Harrison v. NAACP*, decided at the end of Whittaker's second full term, the justices split on whether to accept jurisdiction over a question that threatened the survival of the NAACP in many southern states or whether to send the case back to the state court for its interpretation of new state law. Here the state of Virginia had enacted five new statutes that on their face were meant to improve the ethical conduct of lawyers but in fact were designed to foreclose further legal activities of the NAACP operating within the state. Before state courts had a chance to rule on the constitutionality of the new statutes the NAACP sought and received a declaratory judgment from a federal district court that three of the statutes were unconstitutional. The question put before the Supreme Court was one of judicial comity: would the Court allow Virginia's courts to authoritatively interpret all five laws before exerting federal jurisdiction? If it did then Virginia's state courts could delay indefinitely NAACP activity in the state until a decision was reached. Many on the Court could not accept such a blatant attempt to put the NAACP out of business.

At the conference, March 27, 1959, several justices seemed torn; they believed that Virginia's laws were unconstitutional but felt obligated to allow the state to interpret its own laws first. Harlan, Clark, and Stewart insisted that the case go back to the state courts for interpretation, although Harlan admitted it would be easier to affirm the district court. Black preferred to affirm, but for the sake of unanimity he was prepared to go along if a majority wanted to send the case back to Virginia. Whittaker also sought unanimity, and although he preferred to send the case back to the state he would vote for affirmance.[102] In the end, Black and Frankfurter both switched their original votes to give Harlan a six-person majority to send the case back to Virginia. Harlan made clear in his opinion that no retaliatory action should be taken against the NAACP during litigation, and Douglas, Warren, and Brennan dissented, claiming that all five statutes were unconstitutional. In time, once Virginia courts had a chance to interpret the new laws, this case was back before the Court in a new guise, and the justices split even more severely over the fate of the NAACP.

Two years after *Harrison* the Court heard a pair of race-related cases and in each case upheld the claims of African Americans who charged racial discrimination, but, unlike previous discrimination cases that could point to the Equal Protection clause of the Fourteenth Amendment for support, these cases presented more complicated legal issues. They were also notable because Whittaker was the only justice who voted with the minority and dissented in both. Such a position has raised questions about Whittaker's personal views related to desegregation, but close examination of the two dissents reveals that Whittaker objected to the majority's handling of the issues presented more so than the desegregation of privately run businesses. In the first case, *Boynton v. Virginia*, an African American law student traveling by interstate bus from Washington, D. C., to Montgomery, Alabama, refused to leave the "whites only" section of a restaurant in a Richmond, Virginia, bus terminal and move to the section reserved for "colored." After his arrest and conviction for violating state law he appealed in the Virginia state courts that his right not to be discriminated had been violated according to the Due Process and Equal Protection clauses of the Fourteenth Amendment, the Commerce clause of the Constitution (Article 1, Section 8, paragraph 3), and a provision of the Interstate Commerce Act (ICA), which made it unlawful for a motor carrier while engaged in interstate commerce "to subject any particular person to any unjust discrimination." At the Supreme Court this case presented two separate problems: the grounds upon which to base a ruling and the correct statutory interpretation of the ICA.

Whittaker, joined by Clark, disagreed with the Court's handling of both issues. On the first issue, the proper grounds for basing its ruling, the petitioner had relied on the two constitutional claims in his petition for *certiorari* but had not raised any violations based on the ICA. Black, writing for the majority, decided to base the Court's decision on a statutory interpretation of the ICA rather than reach the constitutional questions. Whittaker objected, claiming that Court rules prohibited it from considering issues not presented or argued. If, however, the Court wished to decide the case based on a construction of the ICA, then Whittaker still objected. According to the ICA, if the restaurant was "operated or controlled by any [bus] carrier," then it could not discriminate in its service. Whittaker believed, and the majority agreed, that the record in the case showed that the bus company did not, in fact, own or actively operate or directly control either the bus terminal or the restaurant in it. For Whittaker that was enough, and he refused to extend the meaning of the ICA beyond what he understood as its "plain language." The majority, however, construed the ICA to apply to those facilities the bus carrier chose to use as an integral part of its transportation services, whether or not directly "operated or controlled" by the carrier. Black reasoned that because the petitioner had purchased a Trailways bus ticket and the bus had stopped at a "Trailways Bus Terminal" for an announced stopover, then this was proof of an integral relationship between the bus carrier and the restaurant. (There was some question in the record over which bus carrier the petitioner had actually used and its relationship to the ownership of the bus terminal and the restaurant.) In response to Whittaker's dissent, Black made clear what the Court was not deciding, writing, "We are not holding that every time a bus stops at a wholly independent roadside restaurant the Interstate Commerce Act requires that restaurant service be supplied in harmony with the provisions of that Act," just what Whittaker intimated was the logical outcome of the Court's holding.[103]

The outcome of *Boynton* led to the "Freedom Rides" of the summer of 1961 as protesters for civil rights decided to test the decision. Whittaker's position in *Boynton* did not indicate that he held personal feelings against desegregation or the purposes behind the Civil Rights movement; he based his dissent on what he believed the law required. What had prompted the Court majority to overlook the only two issues raised by the petitioner, the constitutional claims? Perhaps the outcome would have been less solicitous to the cause of desegregation, considering the owners of a private facility had acted in accord with Virginia law, which permitted them to forbid any person to remain on their premises. The Court may have also hoped to avoid any entanglement with state law, and so by construing a federal statute the majority achieved their real purpose, which was to continue to lend support to desegregation efforts.[104]

Decided the same term as *Boynton* was another race-related case, *Burton v. Wilmington Parking Authority*, where, like *Boynton*, the issues involved were more complicated than previous desegregation decisions involving state action, and Whittaker again disagreed with the majority. This time, however, Harlan wrote the dissenting opinion, joined by Whittaker and Frankfurter. Here the fundamental issue was the same as that in *Boynton*: an African American had been denied service in a restaurant because of race, only this time the Court majority relied upon the Equal Protection clause of the Fourteenth Amendment for its decision. Since the Fourteenth Amendment applied only to discriminatory action by the state, the question became how much state action had occurred at the Eagle Coffee Shop of Wilmington, Delaware? The Delaware Supreme Court denied petitioner relief on two grounds: first, the restaurant's actions were incidents of private discrimination and did not involve state action triggering the Fourteenth Amendment, and second, Delaware state law permitted the restaurant owner to refuse service to anyone who "would be offensive to the major part of his customers, and would injure his business."[105] The petitioner appealed to the Supreme Court of the United States on the ground that Delaware's Supreme Court had construed state law unconstitutionally. At first the Court dismissed the appeal over Stewart's dissent, but then it accepted the case as a discretionary petition for *certiorari* so it could rule on the Fourteenth Amendment claim.

Clark's opinion for the majority found that because the restaurant leased space from a publicly owned and operated car park it was physically and financially an integral part of that public project, built and maintained by public funds and devoted to public use. Therefore, its refusal to serve an African American amounted to discriminatory state action. Stewart concurred in the judgment but would have accepted the case on appeal; he thought the Delaware Supreme Court had authoritatively interpreted state law to mean that African Americans were offensive to a majority of patrons. The state court's action violated the Fourteenth Amendment, Stewart argued, in a more direct and obvious manner than the majority's contention that leasing from a tax-supported public enterprise constituted state action. Harlan, on the other hand, with Whittaker and Frankfurter, dissented from the majority (as well as Stewart's more direct approach), preferring instead to refer the case back to the Delaware Supreme Court to ascertain its interpretation of state law. Was it taking judicial notice, as Stewart claimed, that African Americans were an offensive group—if so, then state action was involved—or was it incorporating the common law notion that businesses can serve whom they please, in which case the Fourteenth Amendment could apply. For the dissenters, the real issue was not so much a question of private versus public accommodations, but rather proper regard for the decisions of state courts: exactly what had the Delaware Supreme Court meant when it construed state law? Without that understanding, the dissenters believed, the majority ruled prematurely when reaching for the Fourteenth Amendment claim.[106]

The following term, Whittaker's last, the Court considered a pair of race-related cases involving the survival of the NAACP as it worked to compel compliance of court-ordered desegregation in the South, but Whittaker retired before the cases were decided. In each case the justices split along ideological lines, voting at conference five to four with Warren, Black, Douglas, and Brennan in dissent. Since a split vote would have been disastrous for the NAACP the cases were held over for reargument the next term. By then, both Whittaker and Frankfurter were off the Court, and a more activist Court supported the claims of the NAACP. In the first case, *NAACP v. Button*, the Court considered only one of the five Virginia statutes originally presented in *Harrison v. NAACP* (the other four had been struck down by state courts) concerning antibarratry, a prohibition on stirring up lawsuits. The conference discussion revealed a split in the justices over how much consideration to give the perceived discriminatory purpose of the law, which was designed as part of a package to prevent the NAACP from operating within the state. Warren, Black, Douglas, and Brennan found the law discriminatory and irrational, designed to circumvent the Court's *Brown* decision. Black conceded that if the law stood in force then the NAACP was through in the state. Those justices in the majority, especially Frankfurter, Clark, and Whittaker, felt that to strike down the law as a violation of the Constitution was to give African Americans a favored position with the Court. According to Brennan's conference notes, Frankfurter said, "I can't imagine a worse disservice than to continue being the guardians of the Negroes.... There is nothing in the record to show that this statute is aimed at Negroes as such!" Clark took a similar position, stating, "To strike this law down, we would have to discriminate in favor of Negroes." Harlan recognized the purpose of the law was to thwart the NAACP in its school desegregation efforts, but, he said, "A state has that right." Whittaker saw no difference in how the law could be applied, whether to a white supremacy group or the NAACP, and he urged the Court to be "color blind" in its interpretation.[107] That left Stewart, who initially found the law constitutional but then switched his vote after reargument, only to switch back again joining Clark and Harlan in dissent.

Whittaker's retirement similarly caused the Court to reschedule arguments in *Gibson v. Florida Legislative Investigating Committee*, where the final outcome again differed markedly from the initial vote. In *Gibson* the Florida legislature requested NAACP membership lists to see if Communists had infiltrated that organization. At the first conference, the justices split five to four along the same lines that divided them in *Button*, and a majority including Whittaker agreed that the state had a legitimate interest in investigating Communist infiltration. Whittaker retired before the Court's final decision, though, and a four to four deadlock compelled the Court to schedule reargument. With the loss of both Whittaker and Frankfurter the following term, a new Court majority found no compelling state interest in acquiring the membership lists, which had been designed as an ingenious way to hamper the NAACP. As a result of Whittaker's retirement, both *Button* and *Gibson* were restored to the Court's calendar, and once Arthur Goldberg replaced Frankfurter the liberal justices had a reliable fifth vote to assure the survival of the NAACP.[108]

During Whittaker's service to the Court there were few truly memorable or landmark decisions. Besides *Cooper v. Aaron*, the unanimous decision reaffirming the Court's authority during the Little Rock school desegregation crisis, undoubtedly the most important decision during Whittaker's tenure was *Mapp v. Ohio*, a five to four decision that sparked a revolution in criminal procedure.[109] In *Mapp* the Court completed the incorporation of the Fourth Amendment into the due process of the Fourteenth and applied the exclusionary rule against illegally seized evidence to state criminal procedure. In landmark cases such as *Mapp*, Whittaker's role remained on the periphery; he was not part of the majority that revolutionized state criminal procedure, and he chose to join Harlan's dissent rather than write his own. He played a similar role in another important case involving illegal searches, *Elkins v. United States*, decided one year before *Mapp*, where he again joined Harlan's dissent. In *Elkins* the Court put an end to the "silver platter" doctrine, where evidence illegally obtained by state officers and barred from state prosecutions could be turned over to federal officers for trial. Whittaker's views on questions of search and seizure, though, were not as apparent as his dissenting votes in *Mapp* and *Elkins* indicated. In one case, *Chapman v. United States*, decided the same term as *Mapp*, Whittaker ruled for an eight-person majority that the warrantless search made of rented property with the landlord's permission was illegal and the evidence seized should have been excluded. In *Chapman* a landlord smelled a strong odor of whiskey coming from his rented property, and he directed local police to enter the house where they found an illegal still in operation. When the tenant returned home police arrested him and later turned him over to federal authorities so he could be prosecuted under federal liquor laws. Although local police conducted the initial search and arrest without a warrant and then turned the evidence over to federal officials, the decision in *Elkins* did not apply, Whittaker wrote, because lower courts had relied on federal standards for evaluating the search. As such, Whittaker found this search violated the requirements of the Fourth Amendment. Relying on previous Court decisions where officers detected "scents" indicative of a crime being committed, Whittaker ruled that in this case there was likewise ample time for the police to procure a search warrant without the risk of losing any of the evidence.

On average Whittaker wrote fewer majority opinions than any other Court member (the Court average was 11.4 opinions per term; Clark had the highest at 13.5 opinions and Whittaker the lowest at 9.25 opinions), yet some have ascribed to him far fewer majority opinions than he actually wrote. Arnold Rice, for example, wrote, "Of the dozen or so opinions he wrote during a short tenure, none is of abiding prominence."[110] Henry Abraham, likewise, claimed, "In his brief tenure ... the eight majority opinions he did author were of no genuine consequence. In fact, he managed to average little more than one a year—thus breaking Justice Van Devanter's modern record of barely three annually."[111] These overblown assertions, meant to discredit Whittaker as a justice and his impact on the Court, further damaged his reputation, making him seem a pathetic figure and his contributions negligible. Whittaker did, in fact, write forty-two majority opinions for the Court and just as many dissents for more than one hundred total opinions in his five years of service. Moreover, his total opinion output increased over time, eventually reaching levels comparable to other justices. For example, in his first two full terms while other justices usually exceeded Whittaker's numbers of majority and dissenting opinions, by his last two full terms Whittaker's total opinion output was on average or above average for the Court.

Part of the reason that Whittaker's opinion output was so low his first two terms and then saw a sizable increase his last two terms was that he experienced greater dissatisfaction and difficulties early in his service. By his third full term Whittaker felt better about his abilities, and consequently his opinion output went up. His first two terms, however, Whittaker suffered because of low self-esteem, he was depressed, and he overmedicated to compensate. The effects of Whittaker's difficulties were not lost on the other justices or their clerks. One clerk who wished to remain anonymous has observed how his justice was reluctant to spend any time with Whittaker because of his distressed mental condition. This same clerk has acknowledged that the justices may have treated Whittaker gingerly because they were sensitive to his problems and did not want to further aggravate him. Statistics have confirmed that Warren, at least, considered Whittaker less capable than other justices when assigning opinions. As chief justice, Warren's responsibility included assigning opinions when he was in the majority and giving each justice his fair share to write (dissents or separate opinions were a personal choice and so did not count). Warren, however, did not consistently strive for numeric equality in opinion assignments.[112] Therefore, in the 1957 and 1959 terms, for examples, Clark wrote twice as many majority opinions as Whittaker, presumably because Warren was reluctant to give Whittaker further responsibility. Whittaker had less opportunity to make an impact on the Court and leave a lasting impression unless he was willing to write separately. As one of Douglas's clerks has said, so much of a justice's work and legacy depended on the assignment of opinions.

Not only was Whittaker assigned fewer opinions than other more experienced justices, but his assignments were usually not close decisions or had few dissenters. According to one of the clerks at the time, this fit the pattern of most new justices early in their careers; they were "tossed nine to zero dry stuff." To say, however, that none of Whittaker's decisions were "of abiding prominence" or "were of no genuine consequence" was to assume, first, that he wrote few opinions and, second, that those opinions he did author had little significance. To the contrary, several of Whittaker's Court opinions established new legal precedents or altered the Court's interpretation of long-standing precedents. These cases generally involved economic issues or technical questions of court procedure and so were easily overlooked. For example, in a patent infringement case, Whittaker set a new rule for distinguishing repair from reconstruction in combination patents. If a component part of a combination patent did not hold its own distinct patent, then its replacement, Whittaker ruled, did not lead to direct or contributory patent infringement unless the entire combination were reconstructed at one time.[113] Praising Whittaker's decision for offering desirable economic effects, the *New York University Law Review* noted how, "In terms of practical judicial administration, as well, the new standard of reconstruction appears superior to the former approach which required consideration of several rather indefinite factors. Since total reconstruction is now necessary to constitute infringement, it should be relatively simple in the future to determine whether there has been an infringement."[114]

In another case setting new precedents, Whittaker restricted the constitutional prohibition against state imposts or duties on foreign imports (Article 1, Section 10, paragraph 2) and considered when an import commodity ceased to be an import and became subject to state taxation. Whittaker moved the point in time of a state's power to tax closer to the point when the product entered the country. By so doing, Whittaker modified the "original package" doctrine promulgated by Chief Justice John Marshall in 1827, which held that as long as imported goods retained their original form they were immune from state taxation.[115] Whittaker found such a doctrine constituted only one factor in determining whether goods imported for manufacturing lost their immunity as imports. Even goods in their "original package," Whittaker ruled, were no longer exempt from state taxation if they were put to the use for which they were imported. Considered a "profoundly significant" decision at the time,[116] Whittaker distinguished between those imports stored in a warehouse *intended* for use in manufacturing and those that were "so *essential* to current manufacturing requirements that they must be said to have entered the *process* of manufacture."[117] Whittaker's decision here paved the way for future Court decisions to expand further states' taxing powers over imported goods.[118]

Each of these decisions at the time was significant because they changed the prevailing law, but Whittaker did not earn many accolades because they were limited to economic concerns and not the civil liberty claims that attracted widespread attention. Questions of individual rights, particularly those protected by the First Amendment, generally gained greater public attention, yet Whittaker wrote far less frequently in civil liberty cases than on economic issues. The one First Amendment case that Whittaker authored for a Court majority, *Staub v. City of Baxley*, presented two problems for him: First, Frankfurter wanted Whittaker to avoid any references to the First Amendment in a state case since it supported the incorporation doctrine advocated by Black.[119] Whittaker, however, was undeterred, writing, "This freedom [of speech] is among the fundamental personal rights and liberties which are protected by the Fourteenth Amendment from invasion by state action."[120] Whittaker's second problem involved jurisdictional questions, which proved more difficult to answer. Summarizing the key jurisdictional issue of the case, Frankfurter wrote in dissent, "This is one of those small cases that carry large issues, for it concerns the essence of our federalism—due regard for the constitutional distribution of power as between the Nation and the States, and more particularly the distribution of judicial power as between this Court and the judiciaries of the States."[121] The case began when Rose Staub solicited labor union membership in the city of Baxley, Georgia, in violation of a city ordinance that prohibited such solicitation without a permit. On appeal, lawyers for the City of Baxley urged the Court to dismiss the appeal because, they claimed, Staub lacked standing to challenge the validity of the ordinance. She had never applied for the permit. Furthermore, state procedure required her to attack specific provisions of the ordinance rather than the whole. Whittaker turned these arguments aside, though, ruling instead that the ordinance was a prior restraint on free speech since the issuance of the permit was discretionary with the mayor and city council. Considered Whittaker's "most notable decision for the Court," *Staub* presented specific solicitation for the first time under the protection of the First Amendment.[122]

As Frankfurter mentioned in his dissent, *Staub* was a "small case," the kind that Whittaker could expect to receive his first two years on the Court. Ironically, in a case remembered for its defense of free speech, the jurisdictional issues were, in fact, paramount to the First Amendment claims. Questions of jurisdiction, tax regulation, labor relations, and patent infringement—these were the issues on which Whittaker wrote most often. During his first

two terms Whittaker received more than his share of "nine to zero dry stuff."
Then during Whittaker's third full term (1959–60) he found new satisfaction
for his work, something that had eluded him his first two terms. This new
satisfaction was derived, in part, because Whittaker became more accustomed to the workload—the never diminishing stacks of papers as well as
the heightened sense of responsibility. He relied more on his clerks (their
advice more than their drafts), which meant that decisions came easier for
him. Of course, many of the decisions that term were also made easier because
they involved highly technical aspects of the law, what one clerk has described
as "lawyer-type cases, bread and butter litigation." The questions raised in
these cases did not depend upon having a broad philosophical framework
for interpreting the Constitution (since fewer constitutional issues were
raised) as much as sifting through the legislative history of a statute to find
its meaning or discovering the legal precedents to support that particular
understanding. These were tasks for which Whittaker felt wholly capable.
Before if the issues raised involved substantive questions of individual rights,
Whittaker lacked the experience to feel confident in his decisions. Now, however, with so many of the cases involving "lawyer-type" questions—questions
concerning the legal machinery by which the law was maintained—Whittaker
felt more in his own element. He found the confidence to state his views
definitely and to stick to them. As he told an interviewer later that term, "I
decided not to be unhappy about my views not prevailing at first and to stand
on my own two feet and let the chips fall where they may."[123]

A good example of the kinds of cases that Whittaker felt most comfortable deciding and most confident about his decisions were those involving
the Internal Revenue Service (IRS) and questions of federal tax law. This was
an area where Whittaker had gained considerable experience as a corporate
lawyer, which did not go unnoticed on the Court. While other justices,
notably Warren and Frankfurter, preferred in tax-related cases to defer to
the majority, Whittaker admitted that he enjoyed these cases more than others. As a result, Warren assigned to Whittaker more tax-related cases to write
for the Court than any other; nearly thirty percent of all of Warren's assignments to Whittaker were tax-related cases. So confident was Whittaker in
questions concerning federal tax laws that at least a fifth of his total opinion
output related to this one area, and over half of his nine dissents written his
first term were on tax-related issues. The other justices recognized Whittaker's
ability and experience in this field, and near the end of his first term Douglas wrote to Whittaker, "You know this much better than any of us."[124]

Although Whittaker still had difficulty writing opinions during his first
term, one case, *Flora v. United States*, a tax-related question, demonstrated
how he successfully overcame his earlier difficulties and became more productive and influential during his third term. When *Flora* was first argued
before the Court near the end of Whittaker's first term, it became clear at

conference that the other justices were in unanimous agreement to support the government—all, that is, except Whittaker. Warren accepted the opinion assignment himself and, writing for the majority, upheld the government's contention that federal courts lacked jurisdiction to hear suits against the Commissioner of Internal Revenue (CIR) unless the taxpayer paid the full amount due for a tax deficiency. "[T]he legislative history ... and related statutes," Warren's opinion declared, "leaves no room for contention that their broad terms were intended to alter in any way the ... principle of 'pay first and litigate later.'"[125] Unfortunately for Warren, his clerk copied directly from the government's brief, "There does not appear to be a single case before 1940 in which a taxpayer attempted a suit for refund of income taxes without paying the full amount the Government alleged to be due."[126] There were, of course, numerous instances where this had occurred, but Whittaker failed to mention that in his dissent. Outnumbered eight to one, Whittaker issued a one-sentence dissent stating his belief that the case should have been decided the other way, relying on three appeals court decisions as precedents. He did not try to buttress his dissent with more compelling arguments, neither did he attempt at conference to persuade other justices that his position was valid. Instead, the majority relied entirely on the government's claims, and Whittaker, certain of himself but unable to persuade, dissented almost without notice.

Near the end of Whittaker's second term he felt vindicated when the losing party in *Flora* cited dozens of cases in its request for rehearing where, contrary to Warren's original opinion, a taxpayer had attempted a suit for refund without paying the full amount due. The Court granted a rehearing the following term, and this time, instead of being all alone with a barely recognized dissent, Whittaker put Warren on the defensive and found three more votes to join him in dissent.[127] The change was dramatic and had a profound impact on Whittaker's self-image. Other justices recognized his expertise. When the new term began, Frankfurter sent one of his clerks to Whittaker to learn all he could about *Flora*. This clerk, Paul Bender, after studying the petition for rehearing convinced Frankfurter that the Court had made a mistake relying on the government's claims. Ordinarily Frankfurter paid so little attention to tax-related cases that he voted mechanically with the majority, but this time Frankfurter had good reason to take interest. He had become so disgusted with Warren's embrace of the liberal-activist posture that he relished an opportunity to embarrass Warren in *Flora*. Prompted by Frankfurter's support (and considerable supporting memoranda) Whittaker filed a twenty page dissent, which began, "A deep and abiding conviction that the Court today departs from the plain direction of Congress, defeats its beneficent purpose, and repudiates many soundly reasoned opinions of the federal courts on the question presented, compels me to express and explain my disagreement in detail."[128] So impressed was Frankfurter with Whittaker's second dissent that he appended a short memorandum to it, which read, in part,

> For one not a specialist in this field to examine every tax question that comes before the Court independently would involve in most cases an inquiry into the course of tax legislation and litigation far beyond the facts of the immediate case. Such an inquiry entails weeks of study and reflection. Therefore, in construing a tax law it has been my rule to follow almost blindly accepted understanding of the meaning of tax legislation.... Once the basis which for me governed the disposition of the case was no longer available, I was thrown back to an independent inquiry of the course of tax legislation and litigation for more than a hundred years, for all of that was relevant to a true understanding of the problem presented by this case. This involved many weeks of study during what is called the summer vacation. Such a study led to the conclusion set forth in detail in the opinion of my Brother WHITTAKER.[129]

In his revised *Flora* opinion for the majority, Chief Justice Warren felt compelled to answer Whittaker's dissent, noting, "Normally a brief epilogue to the prior opinion would be sufficient to account for our decision. However, ... because our dissenting colleagues have elaborated upon the reasons for their disagreement, we deem it advisable to set forth our reasoning in some detail."[130] Then in a substantially longer opinion than his first effort, Warren held on to a bare majority by shifting his emphasis, deciding instead that the statutory language was "inconclusive" and the legislative history "irrelevant" in order to reaffirm his prior decision. Whittaker was undeterred, though, and he stressed the plain language of the statute involved. "Nor can it be denied," he wrote, "that congress has provided ... that: 'The district courts shall have original jurisdiction of any civil action against the United States *for the recovery of any sum alleged to have been excessive or in any manner wrongfully collected under the internal-revenue laws.*' (Emphasis added.) English words more clearly expressive of the grant of jurisdiction to Federal District Courts over such cases than those used by Congress do not readily occur to me."[131]

This time Whittaker made his case so convincingly that two of the justices (Frankfurter and Harlan) who were prepared to follow unquestioningly Warren's first decision now changed their minds. Stewart had not been present for the first decision but joined Whittaker following reargument. With just one more vote, Whittaker might have had a majority, but that was beside the point. Whittaker found that he could influence other justices, and that was enough. As one of Whittaker's clerks has remarked, "He was more pleased when other justices accepted his view than he was about getting their votes."[132] For Whittaker, unlike some other justices, it was never about winning majorities but about having the courage to stand by your convictions. Frankfurter's clerk, Paul Bender, who worked with Whittaker on the second

Flora opinion, has remarked, "Whittaker was the best tax lawyer on the Court, but no one listened to him. Frankfurter was delighted that Warren had made a mistake. He was far more interested and enthusiastic than Whittaker to point out the error of the majority. Whittaker was more retiring and shy. He may have erred by not being more assertive the first time the case was argued."[133]

By his third term Whittaker was no longer reluctant to "stand on his own two feet." He was prepared to make his case, emphatically when necessary, once he realized that being in the minority was not a mark of failure. At times what began as the minority position ultimately prevailed as justices changed their votes following the initial conference. Whittaker experienced this first-hand during his third term, quite unexpectedly, in a relatively minor case involving jurisdictional questions, *Florida Lime & Avocado Growers v. Jacobsen.* What happened during the consideration of this case had a profound impact on Whittaker, one that entirely changed his perspective on the Court and his self-image. Following argument of the case, Whittaker went to the Friday conference with his mind made up how he would vote. After all the justices stated their positions, a majority of seven voted the other way. When Warren assigned Frankfurter the majority opinion, Whittaker was reluctant to even attempt a dissent. There seemed little point to it: the case was an entirely procedural matter with little significance beyond the parties involved, the majority casually concluded that federal district courts lacked jurisdiction in the matter, and Frankfurter was sure to offer compelling reasons to support such a conclusion. Whittaker's clerks, however, believed that his rationale for dissenting was sound, and they encouraged him to draft a dissent. Prompted by his clerk's enthusiasm, Whittaker circulated his dissent without expecting any replies. When notes came back to Whittaker's chambers from justices ready to join his dissent, he was caught completely off guard. He had not hoped to change votes, and with each note of acceptance his self-confidence rose precipitously. In the end, Whittaker gained five additional votes, his dissent became the majority opinion, and Frankfurter was left to re-draft his opinion into a dissent, which only Douglas joined.[134]

Whittaker's success at influencing other justices through his written opinions during his third term, especially in relatively technical questions about the law's operation, led to a new enthusiasm for his work. The *Kansas City Star* reported midway through the term, "Whittaker began to feel that the tide had turned for him and his professional life once more was one with direction and with its share of triumphs and satisfactions. He now finds himself inspired by the challenge before him and happy in his work and environment."[135] Spurred by his successes in *Flora* and *Florida Lime*, Whittaker began writing more dissents his third term, so many, in fact, that his total dissents were more than twice as many in the previous term. Although Whittaker still received fewer majority assignments than other justices, his dissents that term

Whittaker relaxing with his grandchildren. Taken in the summer of 1960 at his oldest son's home in Texas, this photograph shows the justice enjoying a rare moment of family togetherness. By this time, Whittaker had "found his feet" and was enjoying his work on the Court. The summer recess away from Washington always refreshed him. (Photograph courtesy of Dr. C. Keith Whittaker)

brought his total opinion output up to average levels with the rest of the Court. The next term, Whittaker's fourth, his opinion production reflected his change in outlook: for the first time he received just as many majority opinions as other justices, and his total opinion output was slightly above average for the Court. Whittaker had turned a corner. He had finally found his feet.

No longer reluctant to circulate his dissents, Whittaker nearly repeated his performance in *Florida Lime* by attracting votes away from the majority position in another relatively insignificant case, *Federal Trade Commission v. Henry Broch*. After the initial conference Whittaker again found himself voting with a minority of justices, but once he circulated his dissent he attracted enough votes from Douglas's majority opinion to change the outcome of the case. This time, however, with the vote so close, five to four, Douglas uncharacteristically changed just enough of the language of his original opinion to retrieve one of the lost votes and retain his majority. Unlike Douglas, who on occasion could horse trade as well as the other justices, Whittaker refused to change one word of his opinion in the hope of winning back a majority. To do so would have cost him his convictions. "Analysis is built block by block," Whittaker often reminded his clerks, and he would not negotiate a correct outcome. As a result, his original dissent garnered only three other votes (Frankfurter, Harlan, and Stewart), but Whittaker was enjoying his work now. Having startled his clerks earlier that term by describing his Court service as a "five year sentence," Whittaker now softened that decree, and by midterm he was joking with his clerks that maybe he could make it ten years.[136]

This new outlook during his third term caused Whittaker to dissent more often whether or not other justices accepted his position. Once he found that he could exert influence over other justice's decisions, he gained the confidence to stand by his convictions even if it meant he was standing alone. Three times during the 1959 term Whittaker was the sole dissenter, something he had done only once in each of the two preceding terms. In three labor-related cases Whittaker stood by his understanding of what the law required and supported business interests in each case. While it was easy to assume that his pro-business position in these cases was colored by his thirty years as a corporate defender, his dissenting opinions relied more on the particular language of the statutes involved and the course of legal history to support his conclusions than on a predisposition to favor employers. He could not base his decisions on a favored outcome and then find the precedents to support it. That approach (favored by Douglas and the Legal Realists) flew in the face of how Whittaker believed the law operated. His formalistic approach examined the legislative history, legal precedents, and plain language of a statute, which he believed led to one inescapably correct result. Of course, relying on different precedents could lead to different results, which only gave encouragement to those like Douglas to find the support needed for a favored outcome. It would be a mistake, however, to assume Whittaker intentionally dissented in favor of employers as a personal preference.[137]

Whittaker's three solo dissents during his third term were not so significant for their holdings since none of them later became precedents for restricting federal labor law, but they were significant in terms of Whittaker's own well being. By his third term Whittaker felt confident enough in his abilities to write dissents that no one else joined, when before he would have been reluctant to write at all unless assigned an opinion, preferring instead to join other justices' dissents. Now that his opinions proved he could sway votes, now that he felt his opinions mattered, he wrote separately more often. As a result, Whittaker had the opportunity through his separate opinions to influence the direction taken in future court rulings.

In one tax-related case involving union benefits, *United States v. Kaiser*, Whittaker's dissent had greater influence in future Tax Court decisions than the majority opinion. The case began when a non-member who joined in a worker's strike went to the union seeking financial assistance. Since the union's assistance was not based on membership, the union paid his rent and provided him food vouchers. The non-member then claimed on his federal tax return that the union's assistance was a "gift" and, therefore, was not taxable income. Justice Brennan for the majority agreed that within the meaning of the Internal Revenue Code there was sufficient reason for a jury to find in favor of the taxpayer. In his dissent, joined by Harlan and Stewart, Whittaker questioned the union's motives in offering assistance to a non-member, finding no rational basis for believing that the union's assistance was based on "detached and disinterested generosity." To be considered a "gift" in order to avoid paying income taxes on it, the Court had established in a related case that financial assistance had to be offered "out of affection, respect, admiration, charity or like impulses."[138] Whittaker found no such impulse for the union's assistance: "It seems plain enough that those payments were made by the union to enable and encourage respondent and other striking workers to continue the strike which had been called or approved by the union, and were not motivated by benevolence.... Because of the economic advantages to be obtained by the union from winning the strike, the union had a manifest self-interest in financially sustaining the strikers while they carried on its strike."[139]

Fifteen years after the decision in *Kaiser*, Whittaker's former associate at the Watson law firm, Judge Bruce Forrester of the U. S. Tax Court, restricted the majority opinion in *Kaiser* to the sole proposition that the determination of what type of assistance constituted a "gift" was within the province of a jury to decide. Like Whittaker, though, Forrester believed that the intent, or motive, behind the assistance should weigh heavily in that determination. Of all the factors that could compel a union to offer assistance to a worker, financial need, not the success of a strike, should be the paramount consideration. Inquiry into the worker's financial status, then, became the minimum requirement to indicate the union's motive was based on "detached and disinterested generosity." Relying on Whittaker's characterization of a union's purpose in offering assistance to striking workers, Forrester noted, "Strike benefits inherently are designed to meet economic need only because of the strike. They are paid precisely to help those unemployed by a strike, not from charitable impulse, but from the self-interested desire to ensure the economic feasibility of the strike. [see dissenting opinion of J. Whittaker]."[140] A decade later Whittaker's dissent in *Kaiser* still continued to exert its influence in Tax Court decisions as judges narrowly interpreted Brennan's majority decision concerning the jury's prerogative in determining whether a money transfer was a "gift" for income tax purposes. Once again, the motive behind the transfer, as Whittaker first questioned, became the overriding concern.[141]

In another tax-related question Whittaker's dissent garnered votes from both Black and Douglas, and even though it offered a more common sense solution this time his position failed to prevail. In *James v. United States* the

Court split three ways, with two different majorities reaching two separate results. The first result, and the least significant in terms of federal tax law, had six justices voting to reverse the defendant's conviction: Warren, Brennan, Stewart, Black, Douglas, and Whittaker. The second result, and the one with lasting significance, had a different majority of six overrule the Court's previous decision in *Commissioner of Internal Revenue v. Wilcox*. That case, decided fifteen years earlier when Black, Frankfurter, and Douglas were Whittaker's only colleagues serving on the Court, was a nearly unanimous decision with only Burton in dissent. There the majority had held that embezzled money did not constitute taxable income to the embezzler even though he used it for his own purposes and the embezzlement may have given rise to a deductible loss for the original owner. Burton's lone dissent in *Wilcox* later came to prevail in *James*, where the Court ruled that embezzled money did constitute taxable income to the embezzler. Black and Douglas, though, held to their original views in *Wilcox* and joined Whittaker's dissent to uphold it. Apparently Frankfurter had a change of heart about *Wilcox*, since he was the only justice who heard both cases and voted to overturn it.

In his dissent, Whittaker argued persuasively that although the Internal Revenue Code defined "gross income" as "gains or profits and income derived from *any source* whatever," an embezzler obtained no "legal or equitable claim" to the money at the time of the unlawful taking. The illegal acquisition of funds created a debtor-creditor relationship, and the money should not be taxable until it *becomes* his money. "An embezzler," Whittaker wrote in dissent, "like a common thief, acquires not a semblance of right, title, or interest in his plunder, and whether he spends it or not, he is indebted to his victim in the full amount taken as surely as if he had left a signed promissory note at the scene of the crime."[142] Besides, Whittaker urged, taxes had already been paid on the money when the company originally acquired it. What the government sought to do was collect twice on the same amount. Unfortunately for Whittaker, neither the Court nor Congress later changed the majority's interpretation in *James*. Embezzlers can still expect to report as taxable income the money they fraudulently acquire, even though that action itself is punishable by statute. Once their misdeed was discovered, by requiring them to pay taxes on it their legal claim to the money was secured, and the company to which it was owed would fail to recover the loss. Although his dissent did not prevail, Whittaker's reasoning in *James* made more practical sense.

The impact of Whittaker's Supreme Court opinions, whether his dissent ultimately prevailed as in *Florida Lime* or his dissent influenced the direction of future judicial rulings as in *Kaiser*, has been difficult to discern for two reasons. First, most of Whittaker's significant decisions were complex legal questions involving court procedures or highly technical aspects of federal tax law, for example. Whittaker did not make his mark in any landmark decisions, he was not assigned many majority opinions involving constitutional questions, and his record on civil liberty issues was comparatively poor. Historians typically have focused on these three classes of cases: landmark decisions, constitutional questions, and civil liberty claims. By looking almost exclusively at these types of cases, it has been easy to overlook Whittaker's contributions. Major constitutional questions and landmark decisions, however, were not the staples of the Court's work. In the five years that Whittaker served, less than twenty percent of all the cases decided by written opinions involved constitutional questions; comprehensive studies of the Warren years have named even smaller percentages. Civil liberty issues, often the lodestone of Court historians, have accounted for just as small a percentage of the Court's work.[143]

Criticizing Whittaker because his "narrow and exclusively conceptual view" was better suited to a district court judge than a Supreme Court justice, Leon Friedman emphasized how Whittaker confused the distinctive roles of the two.[144] Friedman's characterization of a justice as "expounding a Constitution" was relevant only if constitutional questions were raised. Most of Whittaker's opinions did not involve constitutional questions, making his more significant opinions easier to overlook. Besides, Whittaker did understand the difference between judging at the district court and the Supreme Court, as he told an interviewer during his third term: "Service on the Supreme Court is very different from service on any other court. One of the important differences is that a justice is immediately impressed with the idea that this court speaks the last word and hence what is said is of vital effect upon the whole country and upon the lives and liberties of the people. On this court you do the blazing yourself, which the lower courts have to follow."[145] Friedman also criticized Whittaker's civil liberty record, ascribing to him the same kind of activist posture that someone like Douglas adopted when deciding cases, as though Whittaker's purpose was to vote against a claimed right per se rather than base his decision on an understanding of what the law required.[146] By focusing so much attention on Whittaker's civil liberty record and the relatively few constitutional questions raised during his five years of service, Friedman, among others, overlooked other more meaningful, though less fascinating, contributions Whittaker made to the Court's work.

The second reason historians have been unable to discern the impact of Whittaker's opinions was the close attention given to his personal problems at the expense of examining more of his written opinions. Typically, historians have considered Whittaker's difficulties making decisions in cases like *Perez v. Brownell* and *Frank v. Maryland* indicative of the kinds of difficulties he suffered throughout his Court service. Compounding this perception was the revelation that Whittaker suffered emotional strain and retired from the Court following a nervous breakdown. Since he had difficulty deciding significant cases like *Perez* and *Frank*, both decided in his first two terms, and then left the Court in the middle of his fifth term suffering from emotional exhaustion, the conventional view of Whittaker's service has been that he struggled with every decision, constantly hated his work, and therefore never made any real, lasting impact on the Court's decisions. Such a generalization no longer seems appropriate.

Whittaker did, at first, have difficulty in his new role on the Court, and he suffered at times tremendous emotional and mental strain, but that should not completely obscure the fact that during his third and fourth terms he adjusted to his new role and began to enjoy success at his work. By his third term Whittaker was more comfortable on the Court, and he frankly admitted to a reporter, "It takes some time to adjust to this type of work and to get over becoming awed by the tremendous importance of every word written or spoken.... After awhile you learn the pivotal and decisive things to look for."[147] During his last two full terms Whittaker wrote more separate opinions, his self-confidence climbed, and he derived greater satisfaction from his work. Certainly the decline in major constitutional cases at that time contributed to Whittaker's increasing satisfaction and comfort, but throughout Whittaker's five years of service he made significant contributions. That Whittaker made any lasting contributions at all would have surprised his critics, who claimed that few of Whittaker's decisions lasted after he left the Court and that the opinions he did author "were of no genuine consequence."[148] Contrary to these claims, Whittaker did, in fact, author several Court opinions that continued to exert their influence long after he left the Court; at least, other judges relied upon them and recognized their value.

Most of Whittaker's significant opinions for the Court, those with lasting impact, involved purely procedural matters or obscure questions of federal tax law. Their relative anonymity concealed their significance as leading precedents in those fields. Two such cases occurred during Whittaker's first term. In Whittaker's first assignment to open the new Court term, *Lawn v. United States*, several defendants were charged with evading and conspiring to evade payment of large amounts of their federal income tax. The significant issue for the Court, however, was a question of procedural due process, causing Harlan, Frankfurter, and Brennan to concur in the convictions of some of the defendants but not all of them. Whittaker, on the other hand, found sufficient evidence to sustain the convictions of all the defendants. More to the point, Whittaker ruled that prejudicial statements made by the government prosecutor during his closing summation when viewed within the entire context of the trial did not deprive the defendants of a fair trial. These statements were provoked by the defense council when the trial judge failed to step in and stop it, and Whittaker developed what came to be called the "invited response" rule. Twenty-seven years later the Court continued to rely on Whittaker's ruling in *Lawn* and the "invited response" rule.[149]

Whittaker's second significant decision during his first term, *United States v. F. & M. Schaefer Brewing*, also involved federal tax collection, but like *Lawn* the key issue was a procedural matter. This time Frankfurter and Harlan dissented. The question for the Court was when to begin calculating the time limit for the losing party in a civil action to file a notice of appeal. Whittaker interpreted the Federal Rules of Civil Procedure to make this date begin when the judge ordered a final "Judgment" specifying the exact amount to be paid, rather than an earlier date when the judge granted a motion for summary judgment without specifying the exact amount. Thirty years later the Second Circuit Court of Appeals still found Whittaker's reasoning in *Schaefer* persuasive. Speaking for the court, Judge Frank Altimari remarked, "[I]t is obvious that a final judgment for money must, at least, determine, or specify the means for determining, the amount."[150] In 1993 the Second Circuit again relied on *Schaeffer*, noting that although the mention of a specific dollar amount in a judgment was not a *sine qua non* of finality, it was a significant indicator; the intent of the judge more than the presence of a dollar figure indicated finality of judgment.[151]

Several of Whittaker's opinions over the next three terms also became leading precedents, but because they involved questions of taxation or tort their value has been overlooked. Ironically, in each of the following cases only one justice dissented from Whittaker's opinions, and that was Douglas. Whether it was his haste to complete his Court work, his disdain for Whittaker, or his general irreverence for the process, Douglas dissented in each case without a word of explanation—he just dissented, period. In *Commissioner of Internal Revenue v. Hansen* Whittaker settled a conflict between the circuit courts in a tax-related question involving finance companies that used the accrual method of accounting. Long after he left the Court, the U. S. Tax Court still cited Whittaker's ruling in *Hansen* with approval.[152] In another tax-related question, *Bulova Watch v. United States*, Whittaker relied on the specific provisions of the Internal Revenue Code rather than a more general tax statute to determine the date on which to begin calculating interest for an overpayment of taxes. Two and a half decades later, the U. S. Tax Court still relied on Whittaker's decision in *Bulova Watch*, noting at the time how it was well settled that a specific statute controlled over a more general one.[153]

In the field of federal tort claims Whittaker's decision in *United States v. Neustadt* became a leading precedent. In that case, homeowners sued the federal government after relying on an inaccurate inspection and appraisal by the Federal Housing Administration, causing the homeowners to purchase their home in excess of its fair market value. Whittaker instead found that the United States was not liable to the homeowners because the Federal Tort Claims Act precluded suits against the United States arising out of "misrepresentation." Over the next thirty years first the Court of Claims and then the U. S. Claims Court continued to hold the United States exempt from liability in claims resulting from misrepresentation.[154] In each of these cases Whittaker's careful analysis of federal tort or tax laws produced opinions that remained the standard by which future cases in those fields were decided.

The above-mentioned cases all became precedents for later court decisions; they have not yet been repudiated or replaced. They remain relatively unknown, though, due to their limited application. These cases did not involve constitutional rights or individual liberty, making their significance somewhat understated. There was one Whittaker opinion, however, decided during his second term, that did gain lasting significance and raised serious Fourth Amendment questions; it became the first instance of the Court upholding a criminal conviction based on the word of a police informer. That case, *Draper v. United States*, began two years earlier in Denver when a federal narcotics agent there received detailed information related to the arrival of narcotics from Chicago. The informer, a paid "employee" of the narcotics bureau, was known for reliable and accurate information. When James Draper stepped off a train from Chicago on the date given and matching exactly the physical description and mannerisms described by the informer, the narcotics agent arrested him without a warrant and then searched him. The narcotics found in his possession were later used as evidence at his trial. The question for the Court was whether, considering the circumstances, the narcotics agent had probable cause within the meaning of the Fourth Amendment to believe that Draper was committing a crime at the time of his arrest. If so, then the arrest without a warrant was legal and the subsequent search that turned up the evidence was incident to a lawful arrest.

Draper contended in his petition for the Court that the informer's knowledge of narcotics arriving from Chicago was "hearsay," and that there were insufficient grounds to establish probable cause for his arrest because the only evidence of a crime being committed was the word of an informer. Whittaker easily dealt with Draper's first contention, reminding him that "hearsay," while inadmissible at trial to establish guilt, could be used to establish probable cause for an arrest because the requirements of the two, guilt or probable cause, were so different. The Court had never before considered the key issue in the case, though, whether the word of a paid informer, taken alone, was sufficient to establish probable cause for an arrest without a warrant.[155] Whittaker's treatment of that issue was both simple and direct: because the informer was known for providing reliable and accurate information, the narcotics agent had a duty to act based upon that information. Once the agent personally verified all of the observable facets of the informer's story, he had reasonable grounds to believe that the one nonobservable facet of unverified information, namely the crime itself, was being committed.

As with Whittaker's other significant decisions, Douglas again was the only justice to dissent in *Draper* (Warren and Frankfurter did not participate), only this time he explicated his views in a written opinion. Douglas decried "the mere word of an informer" as the basis for a warrantless arrest, claiming that without more there was insufficient ground for believing a crime was being committed. Not until after Draper was arrested and searched did the narcotics agent have reason to believe Draper possessed narcotics, and, Douglas argued, once narcotics were found it would be "difficult to adopt and enforce a rule that would turn him loose."[156] Law reviews were generally critical of Whittaker's decision in *Draper* and sided with Douglas. One claimed, "The danger of this decision seems obvious.... The unverified word of an informer should not be sufficient basis for probable cause when that information is a *prediction* that a crime will be committed and a description of the person that is supposed to commit it.... No magistrate would issue a warrant for arrest on the facts here."[157] Another predicted that the Court's decision was limited by the particular circumstances involved and that the Court would restrict its ruling to narcotics violations.[158] If they were not critical of Whittaker's decision, law reviews were suspicious of its application. Few considered Whittaker's opinion capable of withstanding closer scrutiny, and given the dramatic expansion of civil liberties for criminal defendants wrought by the later "Warren Court" it was surprising that *Draper* continued to exert its influence as a leading precedent for the next thirty years.

The agitation over *Draper* was due in large part because the word of an informer was used to arrest and search a defendant without a warrant. Many believed, like Douglas, that had the police sought a warrant on "the mere word of an informer," no magistrate would issue one without more evidence of a crime. At the time *Draper* was decided the Court had yet to state that the word of an informer was sufficient to establish probable cause when requesting a search warrant, but by the next term the Court was able to rectify that. In another nearly unanimous decision, *Jones v. United States*, Frankfurter lent support to Whittaker's *Draper* opinion, stating that an informant's story was reasonable grounds for issuing a search warrant so long as the police corroborated it with other independent observations within the officer's own knowledge. Instead of limiting or abandoning the *Draper* precedent, the Court over the next three decades used it to develop new standards for determining the extent to which police informers could be used to justify searches and arrests.[159]

Of all of Whittaker's decisions for the Court, *Draper* had the greatest lasting impact, leading the way for the Court to establish and then modify its standards for evaluating the use of police informers in criminal cases. Still considered "the classic case" as late as 1993 for first stressing the importance of corroborative efforts by law enforcement officials to substantiate the claims of informers, *Draper* became Whittaker's most celebrated opinion in terms of its long-standing application as a precedent.[160] In the decade following *Draper*, the Court fashioned the "two-pronged test" to determine whether an informer's words could provide reasonable grounds for issuing a search warrant. First, in *Aquilar v. Texas* a majority of six justices agreed that without direct personal information, law enforcement officials could expect a search warrant based on hearsay information provided they could substantiate the informer was both credible and reliable.[161] Five years later in *Spinelli v. United States* the Court established the second prong of the test, ruling that in addition to the reliability of the informer, officials had to corroborate the informer's story through the use of independent sources.[162] Although the two-pronged test was used to determine if probable cause existed for the issuance of a search warrant, which had not occurred in *Draper*, Harlan noted in his majority opinion in *Spinelli*, "The detail provided by informant in *Draper* ... provides a suitable benchmark.... A magistrate, when confronted with such detail, could reasonably infer that the informant had gained his information in a reliable way."[163]

Draper provided not only the basis for determining the reliability of the informer, Harlan continued, it also set the standard for how authorities were to corroborate the informer's story through their own observations: "Independent police work in [*Draper*] corroborated much more than one small detail that had been provided by the informant.... [I]t was perfectly clear that probable cause had been established."[164] More than a decade later the Court abandoned its two-pronged test in favor of what it called "totality of the circumstances analysis," but Whittaker's opinion in *Draper* continued to serve as an illustration of the value of corroborative efforts by law enforcement officials to substantiate the details of an informer's story.[165] Considered a "classic" among Fourth Amendment decisions questioning whether an informer's story constituted probable cause, *Draper* became the most prominent of Whittaker's opinions to contradict those who claimed his decisions did not survive after his departure from the Court or were "of no genuine consequence."

Whittaker's opinion in *Draper*, although still valued by federal judges as a leading precedent thirty years after he left the Court, did not establish him as an accomplished justice, at least, not in the arena of public opinion. Nor did his other notable decisions involving federal tort or tax law improve his reputation. These were not areas of the Court's work often recalled with admiration—if considered at all. Therefore, Whittaker's contributions to these areas, as well as his acknowledged expertise in them, have been overlooked entirely. Not that questions of federal tort or taxation, for example, have historically distinguished the work of the Supreme Court. Certainly questions of individual liberty, constitutional rights, and congressional authority deserved greater attention, yet it was in these areas that Whittaker made little impact. Whatever lasting influence *Draper* continued to exert has been overshadowed by the historically significant ruling in *Mapp v. Ohio*, where Whittaker ended up on the "losing side" without a word of his own in dissent. In those historically important cases where Whittaker did author an opinion, other justices received all the recognition.

Whittaker's concurrence in *Frank v. Maryland* and his dissent in *Perez v. Brownell*, for examples, were generally ignored because Frankfurter's majority opinions in both cases were later overruled giving the dissenting views of Douglas and Warren greater distinction. In both *Frank* and *Perez* Whittaker had sought a middle ground, a position that proved inconsequential when the Court's two philosophical sides battled for divergent outcomes. In both cases his difficulty reaching a decision came to characterize his contributions more than his separate opinions. Likewise, Whittaker's concurrence in *Gomillion v. Lightfoot*, while arguably more defensible than Frankfurter's majority opinion, escaped notice. As a race-related case *Gomillion* was easy to decide. On the question of legislative reapportionment, it was obliterated by the landmark decision in *Baker v. Carr*, announced just five days before Whittaker's retirement and beginning what came to be remembered as history's "Warren Court." That Whittaker did not participate in this momentous decision or the subsequent rights revolution that followed further obscured his contributions to the Court.

While he served, the Court considered relatively few historically significant cases, and of those that it did consider Whittaker's participation was marginal. Where Whittaker made his most meaningful contributions, in those "lawyer-type cases" that constituted the bulk of the Court's work, he has received little recognition. Certainly Whittaker was, at best, a mediocre justice when it came to the Court's most historically significant cases; yet, in the majority of cases that came to the Court Whittaker continued to excel in those areas that had distinguished him as a district court judge. He was arguably the undisputed tax expert on the Court, and his thirty years of experience at the bar made him one of the best lawyers there as well. There was no doubt but that had he survived his fifth term, he might have continued to serve in comfortable mediocrity for many more years. Court history is replete with mediocre justices who served on unnoticed, their contributions long since forgotten. Whittaker escaped such a fate, though. His contributions *have been* overlooked, but he was not considered even mediocre by most standards. Typically Whittaker was judged a "failure" as a justice. No doubt his "failure" rating was due, in part, to his undignified departure from the Court. Whatever contributions he made, however his opinions had a lasting impact, Whittaker's personal problems attracted far more attention than his written opinions. In the middle of his fifth term Whittaker unexpectedly suffered a complete nervous breakdown, forcing him to retire and ending any chance he had of gaining a favorable reputation.

6

Failing Justice

Considered one of the worst justices appointed to the Supreme Court in the twentieth century, Charles Whittaker has been routinely degraded in assessments of his Court service. Beginning with Leon Friedman's contribution to a collected work on the lives of Supreme Court justices published four years before Whittaker's death, reactions to Whittaker's five years of service have generally been harshly critical. Recognized at the time as the most comprehensive evaluation of Whittaker's life and work, Friedman's analysis consequently led sixty-five Court "experts" to conclude in a 1970 survey by professors Albert Blaustein and Roy Mersky that Whittaker was a "failure" as a justice. Undoubtedly, this "failure" rating colored any subsequent appraisal of Whittaker's service, and, understandably, Whittaker's difficulties at the Court became far more conspicuous than his achievements there or elsewhere.[1]

Much of the criticism used to perpetuate Whittaker's image as a judicial "failure" has been misguided, irrelevant, or simply overexaggerated; thus, it served little purpose but to further damage his reputation. Granted, Whittaker suffered numerous problems as a justice, the least of which was his strong dislike of Washington and being so far from his family and friends in Kansas City, but a fair assessment of Whittaker's problems and their underlying causes has been neglected. Instead of being ridiculed and maligned because of a few highly improbable or circumstantial incidents, Whittaker's difficulties need to be understood in the full context of the circumstances that eventually led to his hospitalization. He did not in the middle of his fifth term decide that his "five year sentence" was at an end. Neither did his fifth term necessarily contribute an inordinate amount of strain that was not present in previous terms—the pressures were the same although the stakes seemed higher. Whittaker suffered a near complete physical and emotional breakdown for two principal reasons: First, the intra- and interpersonal conflicts that pervaded his Court service, particularly Frankfurter's influence and antagonism, gave rise to intense feelings of inadequacy and resentment. The irony of Whittaker's situation making his plight all the more pathetic, as summarized by one of Brennan's clerks, was that Frankfurter left the Court shortly after Whittaker, dramatically altering both the personality and jurisprudence of that institution. Had the situation been reversed, had Frankfurter departed before Whittaker, then quite possibly Whittaker might have remained on the Court another five years.[2] Second, Whittaker brought to the Court a pre-existing medical condition: he suffered from recurrent depression. Misdiagnosed and poorly treated, this condition ultimately impaired him completely.

To gain a sensitive understanding of Whittaker's difficulties as a justice, first, criticisms of his work need to be addressed. Some of the evidence used to portray Whittaker as a judicial "failure" has been repeated with such regularity as to appear valid when, in fact, critical examination of all the relevant circumstances raises questions regarding the soundness of the conclusions. One of the most oft-repeated criticisms of Whittaker as a justice was that his votes lacked consistency, particularly in cases involving police interrogations. The cases cited to support this contention were all decided during Whittaker's first full term when his feelings of insecurity were highest and he was more likely to vote on both sides of the philosophical divide. Not that his personal misgivings about joining the Court played any part in his decisions, but his so-called inconsistency occurred in the one term when Whittaker was more apt to join the liberal justices, Warren, Black, Douglas, and Brennan. In two of the cases cited, *Moore v. Michigan* and *Payne v. Arkansas*, Whittaker voted alongside the liberal justices to form a majority upholding the claimed civil liberty (in *Payne* Frankfurter and Harlan also joined them), whereas in two other cases, *Thomas v. Arizona* and *Crooker v. California*, Whittaker joined the conservative side in denying the claimed civil liberty. Ironically, some of the same critics who found fault with Whittaker's consistency in these cases also chided him for being too conservative, that is, having a poor civil liberties record. Questions concerning Whittaker's consistency in these cases were initially raised while Whittaker was still on the Court. Professor Daniel Berman compared Whittaker's opinion in *Payne* with his vote in *Thomas*, both related to coerced confessions, and his vote in *Moore* with his vote in *Crooker*, cases raising right to counsel questions. These comparisons at first seemed reasonable considering *Payne* and *Thomas* addressed coerced confessions while *Moore* and *Crooker* considered the right to counsel, yet some critics confounded the issue by comparing *Thomas* to *Moore*, ostensibly because in both cases the petitioners claimed they feared retribution at the hands of their captors; the issues to be decided, though, namely coerced confession or right to counsel, were significantly different enough to make these cases as well as Whittaker's votes easily distinguishable.[3]

The difficulty ascertaining Whittaker's consistency in these cases was that he authored no opinion except for the majority in *Payne*, so his views on what distinguished his seemingly contradictory votes can be found only by comparing the majority opinions of other justices. If Whittaker were to be faulted, then failure to author a separate opinion explicating his views might suffice, but a close reading of the majority opinions demonstrates that these cases can be distinguished. To understand how Whittaker could vote differently in what appeared to be similar cases, one needs to find his *ratio decidendi*, or the reason for his decision. This vague and elusive term will not necessarily be stated in a Court opinion, but by reading the opinion in its entirety one can grasp the basic reason for the Court's decision. To find the essence of Whittaker's *ratio decidendi* in these cases, one must account for all the relevant facts that proved determinative to the final decision. Only then will Whittaker's vote in *Moore* to set free a confessed murderer make sense when compared to his vote in *Crooker* to condemn a confessed murderer to die. In both cases the petitioners claimed they had been denied counsel. Taken alone, that fact certainly made Whittaker's votes appear inconsistent, yet that was not the determinative fact in the Court's final decisions. There were other more intricate details that made all the difference to someone like Whittaker who carefully weighed and considered such details. Not that Whittaker's *ratio decidendi* as described here should be considered more proper than the dissents in *Moore* and *Crooker* (he was, after all, the only justice to join the majorities in both cases), but there were reasonable grounds for him to vote differently based on the differing facts of each case. Since Whittaker did not write separately in *Thomas*, *Moore*, or *Crooker*, but did join the majority in each, those majority opinions will have to provide his *ratio decidendi*. When compared to his own written opinion in *Payne*, Whittaker's reasons for casting seemingly contradictory votes should be clear.[4]

In *Moore v. Michigan* Whittaker provided the decisive fifth vote to overturn the state conviction of a confessed murderer who had spent the last nineteen years in solitary confinement at hard labor, the maximum penalty allowed under state law. Writing for the majority, Brennan summarized the essential details of the case providing Whittaker with a *ratio decidendi* for voting with the majority. A seventeen-year-old African American with a seventh grade education was accused of murder, and at his trial he did not have the assistance of counsel because he waived that right. Brennan wrote, however, that the petitioner had not *intelligently* waived his right to counsel, thus invalidating his guilty plea. His refusal of counsel was "motivated to a significant extent" by an "expectation of mob violence." That there was no actual threat of mob violence against the petitioner while held in custody was of no moment because the expectation of it planted in his mind by the sheriff's remarks led to his waiver of counsel. Without the assistance of counsel the petitioner was deprived of an essential element of a fair trial. As a result, his defense raised questions of considerable technical difficulty that someone with a seventh grade education could not handle on their own.

Whittaker also provided the decisive fifth vote in *Crooker v. California*; only this time he upheld the death sentence of a confessed murderer. Because the petitioner in *Crooker* was also denied counsel, along fundamental philosophical lines Whittaker's votes did, indeed, appear inconsistent. Justice Clark's majority opinion in *Crooker*, however, provided significant differences in details, which offered Whittaker a *ratio decidendi* for reaching the opposite conclusion from *Moore*. The petitioner in *Crooker* was a thirty-one-year-old college graduate who had completed one year of law school. He did not waive his right to counsel at trial as in *Moore* but instead requested a lawyer be present during his police interrogation. His first two requests were denied, but on the third request he made contact with a lawyer who represented him throughout his arraignment and trial. During police questioning the petitioner confessed to the murder. At the Supreme Court his lawyer argued that the confession had been coerced, and, even if it was voluntary, it was a violation of due process because the petitioner was without counsel. Considering the totality of the circumstances involved, Clark wrote for the majority, the confession made without the benefit of counsel was voluntary. The petitioner was informed of his right not to answer any questions and, indeed, had shown full awareness of his rights during questioning. Because of his age, intelligence, education, and conduct during questioning his confession was ruled voluntary and the deprivation of counsel during questioning was not considered so prejudicial as to deny him due process.

Although Whittaker appeared inconsistent by virtue of being the only one to vote with the majority in both cases, considering the relevant facts of each case it was not difficult for him to reach contrary conclusions. The petitioners were not of the same age or intelligence, leaving one more vulnerable to the law's machinations than the other. Whereas *Moore* involved the waiver of counsel at trial, *Crooker* involved the denial of counsel during questioning. Fundamentally, if a judge believed that lack of counsel at any stage in the criminal justice process was a deprivation of due process (and the liberal justices did), then these cases appeared similar. For someone like Whittaker, though, who relied entirely on settled law for precedent, judges were bound by prior decisions; personal views were immaterial to their decisions. Finally, the undisputed facts in these cases showed that the petitioner in *Moore* acted out of fear of retaliation, but in *Crooker* the petitioner demonstrated full regard for his rights. Taken together, these distinctions provided enough difference to reasonably expect someone like Whittaker, whose philosophy of judging relied entirely on the relevant facts of each case, to reach opposite results.[5]

Another pair of cases used to substantiate Whittaker's inconsistency as a justice both involved charges of coerced confession. Again, because the claimed civil liberty in these cases was the same, Whittaker has been accused of inconsistency for voting in one case to uphold the petitioner's death sentence but not in the other. In this example, though, Whittaker was not the only justice to reach opposite results; Frankfurter and Harlan voted alongside him. In *Thomas v. Arizona* a five-person majority ruled that the petitioner's murder confession was voluntary and not coerced by fear of being lynched. The relevant facts of the case gave sufficient reasons for believing that the petitioner's oral confession was not induced by fear, considering the confession came twenty hours after the so-called "threat of lynching" and was made in the presence of a Justice of the Peace who advised the petitioner of his rights. The "threat" to the petitioner happened at the time of his apprehension when one of the bystanders with no official connection to the sheriff's posse "lassoed petitioner around the neck and jerked him a few steps in the general direction of both the Sheriff's car and the nearest trees, some 200 yards away." No one in the sheriff's posse mentioned lynching or made any threats, and the sheriff reprimanded the bystander. The petitioner maintained his innocence, accusing another man of the crime, and when the other man was apprehended a short time later a bystander again roped both men and pulled them to their knees. This time others joined the sheriff in protesting such tactics.

Summarizing the facts of the case, Clark concluded for the majority, "Deplorable as these ropings are to the spirit of a civilized administration of justice, the undisputed facts before us do not show that petitioner's oral statement was a product of fear engendered by them."[6] At the time of the ropings the petitioner accused another man of the crime; twice the sheriff intervened and protected the petitioner; no actual force or threat of force was made against the petitioner; and the confession came twenty hours after the ropings in a courtroom where the petitioner was advised of his rights. Furthermore, at his trial, the jury was informed to ignore the petitioner's oral confession unless it was found entirely voluntary. The totality of these circumstances was sufficient for the majority to rule the confession voluntary. Surprisingly, the four dissenters in this case, Warren, Black, Douglas, and Brennan, issued no opinion expressing their collective outrage that the majority chose not to consider that the trial judge ruled the petitioner's two written confessions made subsequent to his oral confession were involuntary and "procured by threat of lynch."

Because Whittaker's vote in *Thomas* sustained the conviction of a confessed murderer but in *Moore* his vote reversed the conviction, these two cases have been compared to further demonstrate his inconsistency although the principal claims, coerced confession in *Thomas* and benefit of counsel in *Moore*, were significantly different. Granted, there were similarities in the petitioner's claims that their actions had been prompted by fears of retaliation:

in *Thomas* the petitioner claimed his confession was coerced because of fear of lynching, and in *Moore* the petitioner claimed he waived his right to counsel because of fear of mob violence. In *Thomas* the petitioner was twice roped during his apprehension, yet in *Moore* there was no actual threat of violence. What compelled Whittaker to vote with a conservative majority in *Thomas* but with a liberal majority in *Moore*? If one accepted the supposition that he simply voted inconsistently, unable to make up his mind or incapable of making a considered judgment, then the answer was easy. A critical reading of the two majority opinions, however, which Whittaker would have made, reveals one substantial difference in the cause that prompted the petitioners' fears, a cause that made all the difference in cases based upon the Fourteenth Amendment's application to state action. In *Moore* the sheriff holding the petitioner custody planted the idea that an angry mob was waiting to get him. In *Thomas*, on the other hand, the petitioner acknowledged that the sheriff intervened to stop the ropings and acted to protect the petitioner. In one case an agent of the state prompted the fear leading to a deprivation of rights, in the other the state's agent acted to dispel the fear. If Whittaker's vote in these cases was inconsistent because both raised questions of fear and retaliation, then the cause of that fear and the agent responsible for it should be considered when comparing them.

The only case where Whittaker wrote an opinion in the quartet used to show he acted inconsistently was his majority opinion in *Payne v. Arkansas*. Here Whittaker ruled for a seven-person majority that the petitioner's confession was not an expression of free choice and was therefore invalid. The vote in *Payne* might have been much closer was it not for some adroit legal maneuvering by the Court to keep Frankfurter and Harlan from dissenting. As Whittaker's first term clerk, Alan Kohn, recalled the situation, Frankfurter believed the Court should dismiss the case because Payne's lawyer failed to cite a violation of the federal Constitution, specifically the Due Process clause of the Fourteenth Amendment, in his appeal. Without a federal question for decision, Frankfurter argued, the Court should not accept the case. This upset members of the liberal side, particularly Warren, who argued that if the justices all agreed the confession was coerced, how could they send a man to his death? This was justice decided by "technicalities and procedural niceties." Frankfurter, however, could not be persuaded, and Harlan, a staunch supporter of federalism, would have followed him in dissent. According to Kohn, everyone on the Court agreed that the federal question was not properly raised before the Court, but not all were willing to see a man executed because of it. As a compromise, Whittaker directed the clerk of the Court to obtain all the records of Payne's appeal in the Arkansas state courts, and if the federal question were raised by any means whatever then Whittaker would write the decision reversing the conviction. As it turned out, there was one reference to a federal case that relied on federal law and involved coerced confession, and that satisfied the justices that the federal question had been raised.[7] There was, however, no mention of the federal issue in Whittaker's final opinion or in the dissents by Burton and Clark, who deferred to the judgment of the trial court and found the confession voluntary. Clark further argued that there was other evidence besides the confession for a jury to find Payne guilty. Whittaker, on the other hand, dismissed that contention because there was no way to gauge how much weight the jury gave to the confession compared with the other evidence. Writing for the majority, Whittaker set forth in detail his reasons for finding Payne's confession coerced, providing his *ratio decidendi* in this case as well as revealing his reasons for voting to sustain the convictions in cases like *Thomas* and *Crooker*.

Summarizing the circumstances leading to Payne's confession, Whittaker described Payne as "a mentally dull 19-year-old youth" who was arrested without a warrant, was denied a hearing before a magistrate, was not advised of his rights, was held incommunicado for three days, was denied food for long periods of time, and was told by the chief of police that there was an angry mob waiting to get him. Of course each of these actions was objectionable, some even violated Payne's rights; yet, to discover Whittaker's *ratio decidendi* one must bear in mind the question before the Court. Was Payne's confession coerced, and, if so, how? Considered individually, as objectionable as they were to just treatment, none of these actions on their own necessarily led to Payne's confession. "It seems obvious from the *totality* of this course of conduct," Whittaker wrote, "and particularly the culminating threat of mob violence, that the confession was coerced."[8] The totality of the circumstances was the key to Whittaker's decision, with emphasis on the threat planted in the petitioner's mind by the chief of police, an agent of the state. That Payne suffered no physical torture was no answer because, Whittaker recognized, "There is torture of mind as well as body; the will is as much affected by fear as by force."[9]

Whittaker reached his decisions in these cases by considering the relevant facts and applicable precedents. His supposed inconsistency in cases of coerced confessions can now be distinguished. Comparing *Payne* to *Thomas*, both cases claiming coerced confession, the relevant details were so different that when considering the totality of the circumstances it was reasonable for Whittaker (and Frankfurter and Harlan, as well) to reach opposite results. Payne was considered "mentally dull," but Thomas had normal intelligence; Payne was threatened with mob violence by the chief of police, but Thomas was threatened with lynching by bystanders while the sheriff protected him; Payne confessed to murder immediately after the threat of violence was disclosed, but Thomas confessed twenty hours after the roping incident; Payne was not given an initial hearing or advised of his rights, but Thomas was accorded both; in *Payne* the jury could give any weight to the confession in its consideration of guilt, but in *Thomas* the jury was instructed to ignore the confession if it believed the confession was involuntary. Arguably Whittaker's principal reason for voting opposite ways in these cases, the totality of the circumstances, was not the best or only legitimate rationale for judgment, but it did offer reasonable grounds for his decisions and blunts the claim that he was inconsistent.

Rather than accepting the view that he was inconsistent, if one considers *how* Whittaker could reasonably cast opposite votes in cases raising similar civil liberty claims, then his seemingly contradictory votes made sense. The above-mentioned cases made similar claims, but they were not based on the same relevant facts so opposite results were possible. The possibility that Whittaker voted consistently within a framework for weighing the relevant facts of each case has yet to occur to his critics. That he was inconsistent better suits his classification as a judicial "failure." If one is to gain a realistic perspective on Whittaker's difficulties, though, then his perceived inconsistency needs to be viewed in relation to this framework for weighing the relevant facts of each case. Not that this process necessarily suited the rest of the Court; each justice, after all, had their own basis for making decisions. Whittaker's may have been less appropriate than others, but that was beside the point. In terms of consistency, he cast his votes in a manner that seemed wholly consistent with his framework for weighing the facts of each case.

Other evidence used to sustain Whittaker's "failure" classification was limited to a few regularly repeated anecdotes that, if true, made him appear somewhat naive, even pathetic, but these isolated incidents certainly did not justify the wholesale condemnation of his judicial service that critics promulgated. These anecdotes by themselves were insufficient to warrant censure of Whittaker's Court service; considered together with his contributions to the Court's work they become almost trivial. The story about his failure to write his own majority opinion was, at best, suspect, and the others related to his relationship with Frankfurter revealed more about how difficult it was to work with Frankfurter than about Whittaker's shortcomings. The circumstances surrounding these stories call into question both their veracity and, more importantly, their relevance to an appraisal of Whittaker's work. Moreover, reliance on these anecdotes to characterize Whittaker as a "failure" has diverted attention away from the actual, underlying causes of his distress and final breakdown and has focused too much attention on inconsequential, highly improbable events. That his critics failed to account for more serious, potentially disruptive problems Whittaker suffered on the Court was not surprising. These anecdotes reinforced the view that Whittaker was unqualified to sit on the Court, so they satisfied his "failure" rating. A critical examination of the relevant circumstances was unnecessary, and Whittaker's image as a "failure" perpetuated itself.

The one story cited most often to demonstrate Whittaker's disability as a justice described his failure to write the majority opinion in *Meyer v. United*

States. Instead (if one believed the story), Whittaker allowed Douglas, who had already written his own dissent, to write the majority opinion for him. The source for this story was Douglas himself, and the account presented in his autobiography offered the only confirmation that the incident actually occurred. Because of its extensive use to castigate Whittaker, Douglas's account is presented in its entirety:

> In one case when the vote was five to four, Whittaker was assigned the opinion of the majority. I had already written the dissent and went to his office to discuss a wholly different matter. When I entered he was pacing his office, walking around his desk with pursed lips as if possessed. I asked him what was wrong. He said, referring to the five to four decision, that he had been trying to write the majority opinion but simply could not do it.
>
> "That's because you are on the wrong side," I said.
> "Not at all. Not at all. I am right but I can't get started."
> "Would you like me to send you a draft of the majority opinion?"
> "Would you, please?"
>
> Within an hour the draft was in his office, and when the opinion came down (*Meyer v. United States*, 364 U.S. 410) it was one of the few in which the majority and minority were written by the same man.[10]

With no written records other than the majority and dissenting opinions in *Meyer* to confirm Douglas's story, this account has received widespread recognition as evidence of Whittaker's inadequacy as a justice. There was, however, considerable circumstantial evidence to suggest that Douglas's account was a gross overexaggeration of his assistance in *Meyer*, thereby making Whittaker appear far less pathetic than conventional portrayals. First, consider Douglas's repeated claim that the decision in *Meyer* was by a five to four vote. The actual vote in *Meyer* was six to three; only Clark and Brennan joined Douglas in dissent. Perhaps Douglas's memory was faulty on this point, but the final outcome was easily verifiable. Even Douglas's literary assistant who aided him in preparing his two-volume autobiography, Dagmar Hamilton, related that *Meyer* was decided by a split Court. More important, though, in a personal interview the year before Douglas's account was published Hamilton offered a slightly different story, suggesting Douglas's recitation altered with each retelling. In her version, Hamilton had Douglas offering to write a few notes to help get Whittaker started on the opinion, and within a few hours Douglas sent the material to Whittaker.[11] Compared to Douglas's claim that in less than an hour's time he drafted the entire opinion for Whittaker, taking a little longer to prepare a few notes on the case seemed far more reasonable. Not that Hamilton's version more closely approximated the truth; she had no firsthand knowledge of the incident. She got the story from Douglas, whom she trusted implicitly, although there were good reasons not to trust Douglas.

By the time the second volume of his autobiography containing this account came out Douglas had suffered a stroke and his mind was failing. During the five years he spent revising the manuscript his mental condition deteriorated to the point that former Justice Abe Fortas remarked, "They never should have published that second volume of his memoirs. People don't realize that Douglas was a very sick man by then."[12] Even though his editor noted that the greater part of the book had been written by 1973, that is, before his stroke, there was little reason to believe that Douglas's memoirs were above suspicion. When he first contacted Hamilton to work on the manuscript for his autobiography in the spring of 1972 Douglas was already paranoid, suspicious that his office had been plundered and was being bugged (he had Hamilton hide the manuscript in a secret location). More significant, however, the story of Douglas's life contained in his memoirs was a fantastic re-creation of the person he wanted the world to remember, not the truth. One Douglas biographer could not find a single person to confirm a single account dealing with them in one of Douglas's books. Even the first volume of his autobiography published before his stroke and describing his pre–Court years contained tales that one of his law school classmates called "stretching hyperbole beyond its limits."[13] Clearly, Douglas's recollection of *Meyer*, whether his mind was failing or not, should not be accepted at face value.

There were other factual circumstances surrounding Whittaker's majority opinion in *Meyer* besides the six to three vote that made Douglas's story seem much less plausible. The timing of the circumstances offered several compelling reasons for believing Whittaker was not as hopelessly stuck in the writing process as Douglas made out. First, *Meyer* was argued during Whittaker's fourth full term on the Court, not his first, and Whittaker was then fully adjusted to the work of the Court and far more productive. He was no longer reluctant to issue separate opinions, nor was he disillusioned anymore by his appointment. More significant, however, there was no evidence that he was dependent upon prescription medications to cope with his anxiety or depression, causing him to pace round his office "with pursed lips as if possessed." Second, *Meyer* was argued during the opening week of oral arguments, making it one of the first assignments Whittaker received. The summer recess always refreshed Whittaker, especially after trips back to Kansas City, making the opening of a new Court term seem less demanding than the closing eight months later. Finally, the time it took Whittaker to complete *Meyer* amounted to no more than five weeks, which was a reasonably short period of time considering that many Court decisions were held up for months waiting on the drafting of opinions. Even unanimous decisions could wait two to three weeks from the time they were argued until their announcement as the justices drafted and re-drafted opinions. Since no opinions were announced until all the justices were satisfied with their separate majority, dissenting, and concurring opinions, there was no time limit on when opinions had to be announced. It seemed inconceivable in retrospect that at the beginning of his fourth full term Whittaker desperately sought the assistance of another justice on an opinion after just a few weeks of work.

To further support the contention that Whittaker was capable of completing *Meyer* on his own, consider the content of the case and the context in which it was completed. *Meyer* was not legally complicated (in all of their five separate pages, neither Whittaker nor Douglas cited a single legal precedent); the difference between the majority and dissenting opinions involved differing interpretations of the Internal Revenue code and an overpayment of federal estate taxes. This was one area of law in which Whittaker excelled; he was a recognized expert on the Court in the field of federal tax law. Statutory interpretation of Internal Revenue codes and examination of the legisative history behind such codes were not daunting tasks for Whittaker—he enjoyed that part of his work more than any other. Furthermore, the language of the majority opinion is quintessentially Whittaker's style, that is, exceedingly dull, formal, convoluted, and wordy. Comparing separate sections from Whittaker's majority opinion and Douglas's dissent, each concerning the correct interpretation of the Internal Revenue code, the differences in style and sentence length become abundantly clear. In ten sentences, Whittaker wrote,

> Petitioners correctly concede that if the policy constitutes but one "property," within the meaning of the statute, it would not qualify for the marital deduction because the wife's interest in it would be a "terminable" one, within the meaning of the statute, inasmuch as the wife may die before receipt of the 240 guaranteed installments, in which event the unpaid ones must go to the daughter if then living. They concede, too, that the $17,956.41, shown on the insurer's books as necessary to fund the monthly payments for the 240 months certain, does not qualify for the marital deduction for the same reasons. But they contend that, although the policy made no provision therefor [*sic*], the insurer's bookkeeping entries constituted a real division of the insurance proceeds into, and created, two "properties"—one of $17,956.41 and the other of $7,231.09—and that the latter qualifies for the marital deduction under the statute because it is payable, if at all, only to the wife—during her lifetime beyond the 240 months—and no other person has any interest in it.
> Whether a policy of life insurance may create several "properties" or funds, either terminable or nonterminable or both, we need not decide, for we think the policy here involved constituted only one property, and made only so much of its proceeds payable to the wife as she might live to receive in equal monthly installments, and made any guaranteed balance payable to the daughter. Hence, under the terms of the policy, the "interest passing to the surviving spouse [may] terminate or fail" and a "person other than [the] surviving spouse may possess or enjoy [a] part of such property after such termination or failure of the interest so passing to the surviving spouse." Therefore the policy and its proceeds—considered apart from petitioners' claim that the insurer's bookkeeping division of the proceeds of the policy

into two parts created two "properties"—are disqualified for the marital deduction by the express provisions of § 312 (e) (1) (B) of the Internal Revenue Code of 1939. The legislative history of the section further supports and compels this conclusion. Illustrating applications of the terminable interest rule, the Senate Committee Report gave an example that is in no relevant way distinguishable from this case, and makes it very clear that the marital deduction is not allowable in the case of an annuity for the surviving spouse for life if "upon the death of the surviving spouse, the payments are to continue to another person (not through her estate) or the undistributed fund is to be paid to such other person."

We think petitioners' argument—that the insurer's bookkeeping division of the proceeds of the policy into two parts created two properties—cannot withstand the provisions of the policy and the actual facts respecting the insurer's bookkeeping division of its proceeds, under the clear terms of the statute and its legislative history. The policy made no provision for the creation of two separate properties—one a property sufficient to provide payments for 240 months, to the wife while she lived and any remainder to the daughter, and another property sufficient to provide an annuity to the wife for the period of her actuarial expectancy beyond the 240 months—and no such separate properties were in fact created.[14]

In the same number of sentences, Douglas more succinctly summarized his position:

> The Court, with all deference, errs in making its decision turn on whether the wife's *interest* after the 20-year term is a separate "property" within the meaning of the statute. The ruling of the Court is on a statutory provision that does not exist. Under the statute the question is not whether "property" is terminable; it is whether an "interest" is terminable. The statute indeed draws a marked distinction between "property" and "interest." Section 812 (e) (1) (A) speaks not of "property," but of any "interest" in property. Section 812 (e) (1) (B) speaks only of an "interest passing to the surviving spouse" that will "terminate or fail." The statute at these points is concerned with "interest" in property—not with "property." Yet the Court, disregarding the statutory scheme, looks only to "property" and finding but one insurance policy denies the deduction.
>
> Plainly there may be more than one "interest" in a single "property." A deduction is not denied merely because the surviving spouse and someone else each have an "interest" in the same "property."[15]

After a more thorough, critical reading of the two opinions, it is beyond belief that they were, as Douglas claimed, "written by the same man."

The Court's calendar also offers clues to refute Douglas's version of events. When the justices sat for oral arguments to open the 1960 term, they heard seven other cases the same week as *Meyer*. Following the Friday conference that week, Whittaker received three majority assignments including *Meyer*; Warren also assigned him to write the majority opinion in *Aro Manufacturing v. Convertible Top Replacement*, and Frankfurter assigned him the majority in *McPhaul v. United States*. Clearly the chief justice and the senior member of the conservative bloc had no misgivings about Whittaker's capabilities at the start of his fourth full term. After the first two weeks of oral arguments, Whittaker's three majority assignments were still more than any other justice (while each of the other justices received two assignments, Douglas received one from Warren and Clark received one from Frankfurter). Typically the chief justice has the responsibility to see to it that the assigning of opinions for the Court remains equitable among the justices, so it was not surprising that Whittaker did not receive any more majority assignments until after *Meyer* and *McPhail* were announced in November. By the Court's Christmas holiday break Whittaker received two more assignments, and his five majority assignments were still more than Douglas, Warren, Frankfurter, and Clark received. Whittaker was pulling his load along with the other justices, and the fact that he announced his majority opinion in *McPhail* and a dissent in *United States v. Hougham* before *Meyer* was ready indicated that he was not having difficulty writing. Moreover, if he was overburdened with three majority assignments at the start of the new term, why then would he work on separate dissenting opinions in *Hougham* and in *Boynton v. Virginia*? How can Douglas's account be accepted at face value when it appeared on the record that in his fourth term Whittaker was assigned more or chose to write more than in the three preceding terms?

That Douglas had his dissent in *Meyer* completed before Whittaker's majority opinion was not surprising. Douglas was well known for finishing his separate opinions weeks, if not months, before majority opinions were circulated. Even before conference discussions when the justices voted on the outcome of a case Douglas dictated to his clerks how he thought a case would come out, and in his haste to finish his work he drafted opinions immediately following conference discussions, usually in one setting, and then refused to alter them.[16] That Douglas went to Whittaker's chambers to discuss a case with him also came as no surprise. The justices at this time were far more willing to frequent each other's chambers than at a later time, and Whittaker was among the few Court employees who had any kind of rapport with Douglas. Whittaker admired Douglas's brilliance, and, according to one of Whittaker's last clerks, the two men were close personally. "I think they liked each other," this clerk has said, "Although they differed on civil liberties, they were close on business cases. If Whittaker had a concern about a case, turning to Douglas would be no surprise."[17] Allowing Douglas to draft an entire opinion for him, however, was out of the question. Whittaker was too proud of his own ability and too determined to prove his worth than to permit another justice to complete his assignment.

One of Whittaker's clerks at the time, James Edwards, had no recollection of the events described in Douglas's autobiography, and he found it hard to believe that Whittaker would so easily acquiesce to relinquishing responsibility for an opinion. "It's hard to imagine that he would let another justice write an opinion for him," Edwards has remarked, "He was too proud of his opinions. If he did let anyone else write his opinion, he would not let anyone in his office know about it."[18] Giving Douglas free reign to draft his majority opinion in *Meyer* not only seemed out of character for Whittaker, but it ran counter to the kind of tightly reasoned, thoroughly explicated opinions Whittaker favored. Not known for brevity, Whittaker wrote his opinions the way he read them—with exacting detail. Turning to Douglas, who had little regard for exactitude or precision, and saying, "Would you, please [send over a draft of the majority opinion]?" was, indeed, "stretching hyperbole beyond its limits" and resembled another one of the tall tales Douglas used throughout his autobiography.[19]

So what did happen in *Meyer*? Would Whittaker turn to another justice for assistance on an opinion? Certainly Whittaker had immense respect for other members of the Court, particularly those at the time considered giants—Black, Frankfurter, and Douglas. Whittaker did, in fact, rely on other justices for jurisprudential guidance as well as emotional support. Although he was writing more and admitted to enjoying his work more during his fourth term, some clerks thought he looked tired and strained much of the time. One of Harlan's clerks has remembered how Whittaker visited Harlan's office when he was working on a case. "He seemed out of his depth," this clerk has recalled, "He was the least confident of the justices (Douglas the most). He found some cases very difficult—he agonized over them."[20] In the previous term Whittaker had gone to Black's chambers during a death sentence appeal, one he had to decide on his own, worried about his decision. One of Black's clerks at the time remembered the contrast between the two men: while Whittaker fidgeted waiting on death sentence appeals, Black seemed calm. Black took these decisions seriously, but over time he had come to terms with them. Instead of pacing, Black might be home having dinner while he waited.[21] If Whittaker were having trouble getting started on *Meyer* and Douglas had offered to assist, undoubtedly Whittaker would have been grateful. Most likely Douglas sent over a copy of his dissenting opinion already prepared in advance of the majority opinion or, at most, scribbled down a few notes to give Whittaker direction. That was exactly what happened in Whittaker's first term when he was having difficulty completing another case, *United States v. Hvass.*

A more difficult case for Whittaker considering his background and experience, *Hvass* involved a question of perjury and whether or not the local rules promulgated by a district court constituted a "law of the United States." Considered midway through his first full term as a justice, Whittaker worked on *Hvass* at a time when he was still disappointed by his appointment, was overawed and insecure, and relied on medication to control his anxiety. According to one of Whittaker's first term clerks, Alan Kohn, *Hvass* was a relatively insignificant case that proved technically difficult to answer. Several times Kohn drafted sentences to assist Whittaker with the decision but to no avail. While Whittaker labored over the opinion, Douglas stopped by his office and agreed to help with it. A short time later Douglas sent Whittaker two key sentences that Whittaker adopted into the opinion.[22] Decided by an eight to one vote, Douglas was the only justice to dissent in *Hvass*. Unlike his five-page dissent in *Meyer*, this time Douglas summarized his views in one brief sentence. Chances were Douglas had no hesitation about going to visit Whittaker and willingly offered assistance if Whittaker expressed difficulty with an opinion. The two were in agreement in a surprising number of cases, and both felt somewhat isolated on the Court (although Douglas probably preferred it that way). Douglas's recollection of *Meyer* was probably accurate up to the point of writing the majority opinion himself. Therefore, criticisms of Whittaker because Douglas claimed he drafted the majority opinion in *Meyer* ignore other relevant circumstances and give Douglas's account too much credit.[23]

Another story used to discredit Whittaker's abilities as a justice involved a single incident at the beginning of his first full term. Unlike Douglas's account in *Meyer*, though, this story did not rely on a single unreliable source for verification. Here the evidence was contained on three scraps of paper, or Court memoranda, found in Frankfurter's Court papers. The veracity of the incident was undeniable. One question remained, though: what did it tell us about Whittaker? Was it good reason, as Bernard Schwartz claimed, for putting Whittaker on the list of the ten worst justices ever appointed? Schwartz related this incident as evidence of just how "dumb" Whittaker was, using it to confirm his own suspicions about Whittaker—that he became no more than Frankfurter's lackey, intellectually incapable of thinking on his own and hopelessly retarded when it came to comprehending Frankfurter's subtle, sophisticated humor. Here is what happened: at the opening of the 1957 term, Whittaker's first, Frankfurter circulated a mock opinion in a movie censorship case, which read,

No. 372.—October Term, 1957.

Times Film corporation,   )
    Petitioner,   )
)
        v.   )
)
City of Chicago, Richard J.   )
    Daley and Timothy J. O'Connor.   )

The Court of Appeals in this case sustained the censorship, under an Illinois statute, of a motion picture entitled, "The Game of Love." The theme of the film, so far as it has one, is the same as that in Benjamin Franklin's famous letter to his son, to the effect that the most easing way for an adolescent to learn the facts of life is under the tutelage of an older woman. A judgment that the manner in which this theme was conveyed by this film exceeded the bounds of free expression protected by the Fourteenth Amendment can only serve as confirmation of the saying, "*Honi soit qui mal y pense*" [Evil be to him who evil thinks].

Shortly afterwards Whittaker sent Frankfurter a note, reading, "I join in your *per curiam* in this case." Frankfurter then replied, "This was intended as a joke."[24]

Used to demonstrate Whittaker's "lack of intellectual capacity," Schwartz considered the evidence found on these memoranda "the incident that best illustrates why Whittaker is on this list [of the ten worst justices]." That Frankfurter had to explain this "joke" to Whittaker was not remarkable; albeit amusing, it merely showed how naively gullible Whittaker was in this one incident. What was remarkable was not that Whittaker failed to grasp the subtly mocking tone of Frankfurter's witticism, but that Schwartz used this one incident to classify Whittaker as "a travesty of what a judge ... should be."[25] Without more, it was ludicrous to consign Whittaker to the bottom of the judicial heap, as it were, because he did not get a "joke." Certainly there was more, and if one wanted to criticize Whittaker, then a more thoughtful and thorough examination of the relevant circumstances was necessary. Whittaker had served on the Court for only three months when this occurred, the final three months of one of the Court's most controversial terms. Upon returning to Washington after the Court's summer recess Whittaker was agitated and distraught; he was nervous about his new position; he regretted ever accepting the appointment; and he was medicating himself to cope with the strain. Just as important, Whittaker had an almost childlike reverence for men like Frankfurter, whom he considered the paragon of judicial virtues. Such conditions inevitably led Whittaker to misperceive Frankfurter's supposed levity (whether or not this mock opinion provoked amusement was, after all, a matter of taste).

That Frankfurter's true intentions could be easily misunderstood was not that unrealistic. Frankfurter courted sophisticated, intelligent people. He enjoyed lively debate and witty repartee. Circulating ridiculous doggerel styled after lesser-known literature to the rest of the Court for his own amusement was not uncommon. These memoranda for the Court served no purpose other than to give Frankfurter further opportunity to demonstrate his worldly wisdom and oddly amusing views on matters before the Court. As early as 1943 Frankfurter revealed his penchant for writing mockingly satiric opinions never intended for publication, although his concurrence in *Interstate Commerce Commission v. Inland Waterways* never circulated among the other justices. If it had, would they have taken him seriously?[26] To a novice like Whittaker, who no more knew of Franklin's letter to his son than he could translate *honi soit qui mal y pense*, Frankfurter's opinion must have seemed reasonable for a *per curiam* order, which were meant to briefly dispose of a case.

So, Whittaker was not as sophisticated (some might say snobbish) as Frankfurter. Did that make him a "failure"? Would a satirical bent have meant Whittaker was more capable as a justice? Certainly experience dispelled any misgivings Whittaker had about circulating his own wry dissenting opinion two years later in a worker injury case. As he informed his good friend in Kansas City, Roy Roberts, he wrote *Inman v. Baltimore & Ohio Railroad* "in a satirical and semi-humorous vein." Asking Roberts to keep the opinion in confidence, Whittaker explained, "A number of Justices, on both sides of the controversy, have had a measure of fun out of this dissent and I thought you might get a 'chuckle' out of it."[27] Once the alignment on the Court shifted to Whittaker's favor in the case he revised his dissent into a concurrence and announced it from the bench, causing a murmur of laughter through the courtroom. It seemed, then, that Whittaker did have a recognizable sense of humor when it came to insignificant cases. That he misunderstood Frankfurter's arcane references for an actual Court opinion was neither unreasonable nor contemptible. What was surprising was that Frankfurter in an uncharacteristic sympathetic gesture corrected Whittaker instead of ridiculing his naiveté.

Whittaker's relationship with Frankfurter was fraught with contradictory sentiments on both sides and therefore is difficult to characterize. Depending on the source, Whittaker either greatly admired Frankfurter or resented Frankfurter's incessant lobbying for votes.[28] Certainly Whittaker admired Frankfurter as a justice, as was evident in a heartfelt letter he composed after learning of Frankfurter's retirement from the Court. Writing just five months after his own retirement, Whittaker was unabashed in his expression of devotion towards Frankfurter:

> The news last evening of your retirement filled me with emotion. I am sure your decision was right. Seldom have I disagreed—as you well know— with your decisions and in this one, as in most others, I am satisfied you have taken the wise course.
>
> Adequate words for the proper expression of my affection for you, and for the true expression of my appreciation of your contribution to the Court and to our Country, do not readily come to mind. I am sure I need not dwell on the depth of my affection for you as a friend, a man, and a Justice, for upon these matters I have so often, and perhaps to an embarrassing extent, expressed my views to you and to others. As respects your contribution to the Court and to our Country, let me say that, in my view, no other man, not even your beloved Holmes or Brandies [*sic*], has had such great and good influence upon, or has made a more lasting and beneficial contribution to, the work of the Court and the law of the land. What a great satisfaction it must be to you to look upon a record so enviable and unsurpassed.[29]

Whittaker's own clerks have acknowledged that Frankfurter lobbied Whittaker for votes, but none ever heard Whittaker speak critically of Frankfurter. Whittaker prized their relationship. In fact, when the Whittakers hosted what was for them a rare social gathering at their Washington home in the spring of 1961 for all the justices and their wives, Whittaker was overjoyed when Frankfurter arrived. Because his wife was bedridden during most of his Court tenure and could not accompany him, Frankfurter rarely, if ever, attended mixed social gatherings. Whittaker considered Frankfurter's attendance a testament to their friendship.[30]

Had he been more cynical, however, there were sufficient reasons for Whittaker to resent Frankfurter's efforts to secure his vote. Described as a "proselytizer," Frankfurter was relentless in his quest to line up votes for his position. Not all of the justices pushed as hard to sway votes, but several former clerks have agreed that securing votes and pressing their points was a primary concern for some justices. According to one of Black's former clerks, some justices had no hesitancy about going to see another justice to argue for votes. Black and Frankfurter were recognized leaders in this effort. "Frankfurter was a powerful advocate," this clerk has said, "Black was as well, although he was more soft-spoken. Both of them knew how to control their emotions. They were both logical, but there was a strong moral force in their arguments." Concerning other justices' participation in lobbying efforts, this clerk has said, "Harlan would not participate in this kind of persuasion. Douglas did not care for it. The chief did not see that as his role to be partisan. He was more concerned with appearances. Black would, though. He saw it as part of his job to argue."[31] Although Clark was not interested in lobbying for votes, according to one of his former clerks, "He was far more open than the other justices to negotiating on wording to reach a consensus. Sometimes he would negotiate directly with another justice. Other times he would send us to the clerks for another justice to determine what wording had to be changed to obtain agreement."[32] Brennan became the supreme accommodationist, capable of crafting an opinion that could attract enough votes to comprise a majority. Twice during the 1960 term one of Brennan's former clerks has remembered how cases were argued on constitutional grounds but Brennan came up with a statutory interpretation that managed to get a fifth vote.[33]

All of this negotiating on case outcomes must have been a heady experience for Whittaker, who still lived by the credo: "The law means what it says and says what it means." Unfortunately for Whittaker, too often what Black said made sense and what Frankfurter said made sense, leaving Whittaker gripped by indecision. In such a condition, Frankfurter used whatever means were at his disposal to obtain Whittaker's vote. According to Schwartz, "Frankfurter was a born lobbyist and would go out of his way to influence colleagues, law clerks, and even clerks' wives. No one, indeed, could match Frankfurter in his incessant attempts to curry favor in the Court."[34] Douglas, especially, resented Frankfurter's efforts, writing, "Frankfurter used his law clerks as flying squadrons against the law clerks of other Justices and even against the Justices themselves. Frankfurter, a proselytizer, never missed a chance to line up a vote. His prize target was Whittaker, ... Whittaker was duck soup for Frankfurter and his flying squadrons of law clerks."[35] Certainly Frankfurter was relentless in his efforts to obtain votes, but were his efforts sufficient to warrant Whittaker's resentment?

The impression of many at the Court was that Frankfurter dominated Whittaker, even, some might have said, abused him. According to Michael Parrish, Frankfurter was an enormously insecure man who was "frequently consumed and crippled by rage, vanity, and self pity."[36] Despite his refinement and recognized intellect, Frankfurter was arrogant and had a volatile temper. Once he screamed at Warren during a Court conference, "Be a judge, god damn it, be a judge."[37] Another time Black told his son following a conference, "I thought Felix was going to hit me today, he got so mad."[38] Known to dominate those in a subordinate position, one Frankfurter biographer, H. N. Hirsh, suggested that Frankfurter's personality contributed to his wife's mental breakdown. According to Hirsh, Marion Frankfurter was an astonishingly bright woman and every bit her husband's intellectual equal. "Although we cannot know the extent to which Marion's psychological condition arose independently," Hirsh wrote, "the evidence ... suggests that Frankfurter's personality unquestionably intensified her condition. It is absolutely clear that Frankfurter dominated his wife and that this affected her profoundly. Frankfurter's other personal relationships show evidence of disturbance as well."[39]

Undoubtedly Frankfurter's treatment of Whittaker contributed to Whittaker's mental breakdown and disability. Perceiving Whittaker's insecurity and dependency, Frankfurter used both flattery and intimidation to ensure Whittaker's compliance. Early in his Court service Whittaker received complimentary notes from Frankfurter, who expressed "how gladdened I was by the clear-sightedness" that Whittaker displayed "so early in your days on the Court."[40] Two years later Frankfurter was still complimenting Whittaker, writing, "No one on the Court more than you searches more consistently to reach results in cases solely on relevant judicial grounds."[41] Schwartz considered such comments "ludicrous" since Whittaker was, Schwartz estimated, "one of the weakest Justices in Supreme Court history."[42] Transparent as this flattery was, Whittaker accepted it gratefully, pleased to be in Frankfurter's good graces. Law clerks at the time recognized it as a ploy to gain votes, even if Whittaker did not. "Frankfurter really went to work on Whittaker from day one," one of them said, "and Whittaker was just overwhelmed by ... the notion that this great intellect was actually complimenting him.... It was clear to everybody on the Court with the exception of Whittaker that he was being used by Frankfurter and that Frankfurter was ingratiating himself in order to secure Whittaker's vote."[43] Whether or not Whittaker recognized Frankfurter's affectation was a matter for conjecture, but Whittaker did feel the effects of the lobbying that regularly occurred, and he admitted in a 1971 interview, "There [was] a good deal of politicking. For example in a four to four case, the one hold-out will be impleaded and beseeched ... by both sides. That's a very uncomfortable position to be in but it [did] happen with some frequency."[44] That it probably happened to Justice Stewart as often was little comfort for Whittaker. At those times he felt like he was *the* judge making *the* decision and the collective views of his four like-minded colleagues made little difference.

Frankfurter's intense lobbying, some believed, was the principal reason behind Whittaker's breakdown and departure from the Court. "I heard from the other clerks that Frankfurter was badgering Whittaker over *Baker v. Carr*," one of Harlan's clerks has written, "It was the view of the other clerks that Frankfurter had driven Whittaker off the Court."[45] One of Brennan's clerks from the previous term stated the reason more forcefully: "Whittaker was driven crazy by Frankfurter, who wanted to uphold congressional action in the Communist cases. Frankfurter went to see Whittaker. He frightened him. He was unrelenting, unforgiving. I attribute Whittaker's difficulty to Frankfurter. There was pressure from Frankfurter, pounding Whittaker all the time."[46] This constant lobbying was not limited to the Court in conference or the justices' chambers; Whittaker received solicitations at his home, as well. One of his former law associates who visited Whittaker in Washington and witnessed Whittaker's physical disintegration has remembered how Whittaker received phone calls from other justices wanting to discuss pending cases. "No, I'm not surprised he had a nervous breakdown," this associate has said, "That evening in Washington when he got calls from other justices you could tell it disturbed him. They seemed to be offering to vote one way for him if he would vote another way for them.... To other members of the Court it was meaningless what prior cases said, but that was not how Whittaker thought."[47]

Another anecdote routinely used to impeach Whittaker's character highlighted his difficult relationship with Frankfurter and the depth of his emotions. The source for this anecdote was Justice Stewart, and Schwartz was fond of relating it as evidence of Whittaker's "defects" as a justice. According to Stewart, Whittaker "used to come out of our conference literally crying." "You know," Stewart continued, "Charlie had gone to night law school, and he began as an office boy and he'd been a farm boy and he had inside him an inferiority complex, which ... showed and he'd say, 'Felix [Frankfurter] used words in there that I'd never heard of.'"[48] Was this one observation evidence, as Schwartz claimed, that Whittaker was "bewildered by the law's complexities"?[49] Such an *ad hominem* characterization tells us less about Whittaker's abilities as a justice than about his personal insecurities and his infuriating relationship with Frankfurter. Certainly Whittaker felt encumbered by his modest origins; other legal professionals had called into question his legal training the day he enrolled at the Kansas City School of Law. There was more to consider, though, with Whittaker's insecurities than his rural upbringing and part-time legal education. Despite all that, he still achieved distinction as one of the finest corporate lawyers in the Midwest. He earned a reputation among trial lawyers as an accomplished advocate possessing a command of language. Arguing over the meaning of words became one of his favorite pastimes. At the Supreme Court, however, none of that mattered. Possessing a command of language among midwestern corporate lawyers from moderate-sized law firms did not measure up to the Harvard-bred, self-assured bibliophile Frankfurter. Whatever distinction Whittaker achieved before going to the Court only made his service with Frankfurter all the more humiliating. Therefore, it was as much his anguish over losing his former renown as his modest, rural beginnings that fed his feelings of discomfort.[50]

Because Whittaker felt such intense admiration for Frankfurter, any disapprobation from Frankfurter would have cut to the quick. Eighteen years Whittaker's senior, Frankfurter both intimidated and inspired. His own mastery of language gave Frankfurter a superiority complex, causing him to take umbrage with lesser wordsmiths. According to Parrish, "Next to the *U. S. Reports*, [Frankfurter] treasured most the *Oxford Unabridged Dictionary* and routinely criticized those who used words such as impact, seminal, and semantic. But he larded his own prose with eschew, bifurcate, and eventuate, and he could describe a draft opinion by Justice Tom Clark as 'this farrago of irresponsible, uncritical admixture of far-reaching needlessly dangerous incongruities."[51] That Whittaker felt overwhelmed to the point of tears following one of Frankfurter's Harvard-styled lectures was due, in part, to his conviction that he *should* understand Frankfurter's locution. The pity for Whittaker was not realizing that Frankfurter's linguistic fecundity was mere showmanship. Had Whittaker felt less reverence and more indifference toward Frankfurter, then maybe he could have avoided such pronounced expressions of self-loathing as tears.

The abuse he suffered from Frankfurter's fury and the continual entreaties to sway his vote were both significant factors leading to Whittaker's final breakdown and departure from the Court. In addition, there were other, more subtle, less direct influences that potentially added to his personal stress, and these, too, contributed to the overall patterns of stress pervading his Court service. These other influences concerned the justices' conduct, their personal feuds and dramatic outbursts. In time, one interpersonal conflict entangled Whittaker in his own minor quarrel and inevitably led to heightened tensions over the smallest matters. The leading antagonists in these doctrinal and personal battles were Douglas and Frankfurter, who carried on one of the longest-running bitter personal feuds in Court history. Caught in the middle of this rivalry and often compelled to take sides were the other justices, who, at times, became just as impatient and annoyed with Frankfurter and Douglas as they did with each other. Under such circumstances, Whittaker's personal difficulties were further exacerbated by the petty bickering taking place all around him.

Following his retirement from the Court, Whittaker frequently entertained bar association meetings with recollections of his Court service. Never one to cast aspersions on the Court or its members, Whittaker's recollections of conference discussions gave only hints of the tensions that underlay the justices' deliberations. "These discussions are always orderly, and are most seriously conducted," Whittaker told his listeners, "While they often generate much emphasis and heat, they are always, or nearly always, so far as I can tell, conducted objectively and without rancor or personal ill-will."[52] Whittaker's recollections were colored by his reverence for the institution and his deeply felt loyalty to preserving in the public's mind the justices' integrity. As already mentioned, Douglas and Frankfurter could make conference discussions acutely uncomfortable for the other justices, if not unbearable. Phillip Cooper described how Douglas used to send Frankfurter "into apoplectic rage" during conference discussions—so much so that by Whittaker's fourth term Douglas threatened to stop attending conferences altogether.[53] Douglas was not the only one who found Frankfurter's insolence insufferable. According to Roger Newman, early in the 1958 and 1961 terms, Black walked out of conference because of Frankfurter, picking up his hat and telling his startled secretary, "Felix kept on talking and talking."[54]

In addition to Frankfurter's endless orations, he also aggravated his colleagues each term with memoranda urging procedural changes in the conduct of Court business. These memos, Cooper reported, "grew like Topsy over the years," and while "[s]uch lectures would not have been welcome from virtually any member of the Court ... Frankfurter's pedantic attitude and condescension were particularly unbearable."[55] Reactions to Frankfurter's memoranda went from indifference to intolerance as other justices grew increasingly impatient or offended by his written harangues. At the beginning of the 1957 term, Whittaker's first, Warren challenged Frankfurter's suggestion that the controversy engulfing the Court at the end of the previous term could have been prevented were it not for the "massing" of important cases by the chief justice at the end of the term.[56] Three years later, Douglas launched a "memo war" in response to Frankfurter's annual missive, sending copies of his remarks to all the other justices. "We are not first-year students who need to be put under strict restraints," Douglas informed his colleagues, "The blowing of whistles, the counting to three or ten, the suspension of all activity for a stated time may be desirable and necessary on playgrounds or in sports. But we are not children; we deal not with trivia; we are not engaged in contests. Our tasks involve deliberation, reflection, meditation. When opinions have jelled, the case is handed down.... I resist the effort to foist one system on all of us."[57] The use of Court memoranda to vent their ideological differences, which by Whittaker's final term had degenerated into petty personal squabbling between Frankfurter and Douglas over ridiculously trivial matters, continued unabated up until the time Whittaker left the Court.[58]

The most dramatic exchanges between two justices were those that occurred in open court, particularly between Warren and Frankfurter. Beginning about the time Whittaker arrived at the Court, relations between Warren and Frankfurter had cooled considerably, and during Whittaker's tenure the two men's suspicions of each other turned to loathing. Their public outbursts during Court sessions, at times under the cover of delivering Court opinions, revealed the deep divisions and personal antagonisms that permeated the more secluded conferences. One of their first public outbursts occurred on the last day of the 1957 term. Warren announced the outcome in *Caritativo v. California*, a six to three *per curiam* decision to affirm the execution of Luis Caritativo, who was sentenced to die in the California gas chamber. Relying on a single legal precedent to support California's policy of granting to prison wardens sole discretion to determine an inmate's sanity at the time of their execution, the majority including Whittaker offered no other rationale for its decision. Frankfurter then announced his dissent (joined by Douglas and Brennan); only he enhanced his written opinion with extemporaneous remarks, as was his habit, which took the chief justice completely by surprise. Summarizing Frankfurter's views, Whittaker's clerk that term, Alan Kohn, wrote, "California, he said, had a procedure that shocked the conscience and was intolerable in a civilized society. It was profoundly abhorrent to execute an insane man and Luis was entitled to a hearing on the question of his sanity. The state of California would have on its conscience a barbaric execution. The Justice was a great orator and made a compelling argument worthy of the finest lawyers."[59] Unprepared for Frankfurter's polemic and offended that his home state was being publicly pilloried in open court, Warren responded, "Neither the judgment of this Court nor that of California is quite as savage as this dissent would indicate."[60] Warren then issued his own extemporaneous rebuttal against Frankfurter's charges, which Kohn described as "entirely unheard of and stunningly unprecedented." According to Kohn, who witnessed the entire exchange, "Frankfurter was furious. He literally spun around in his chair. The Chief had no right to issue a rebuttal. It breached fundamental traditions of the Court."[61]

Open conflict between Warren and Frankfurter quelled somewhat for a few years, although privately the two became resentful of each other. Then in the year before Whittaker's breakdown the two were at it again in front of the public. Near the end of Whittaker's last full term, in April 1961, the Court decided *Stewart v. United States* by a five to four majority with Stewart joining the four liberal justices. Black announced for the majority that Willie Lee Stewart was deprived the protection of the Fifth Amendment against self-incrimination when the prosecutor at his third trial asked him, "This is the first time you have gone on the stand, isn't it?" The majority found the question prejudicial and reversed his murder conviction. The four dissenters were willing to overlook the question as inconsequential within the context of the entire trial, and Clark in his dissent made clear from the opening line his disdain for the majority's conclusion: "It may be that Willie Lee Stewart 'had an intelligence in the moronic class,' but he can laugh up his sleeve today for he has again made a laughingstock of the law."[62] It was Frankfurter's dissent, however, that angered Warren enough that he responded from the bench, and, according to one of Brennan's clerks that term, "That just doesn't happen—Warren gave him a dressing down in front of reporters."[63] Once again Warren responded to the manner in which Frankfurter embellished his dissent with comments not found in the written opinion. Frankfurter had called Black's majority opinion an "indefensible example of judicial nit-picking" and "excessively finicky appellate review." Without an opinion to read in the case, Warren followed Frankfurter's peroration with his own extemporaneous remarks: "I must say that although I did not file an opinion in this case, that was not the dissenting opinion that was filed. This is a lecture. This is a closing argument by the prosecutor to the jury. It is properly made perhaps in the conference room, but not in the courtroom. As I understand it, the purpose of reporting an opinion in the courtroom is to inform the public and is not for the purpose of degrading this Court. I assure you that, if any written opinion had said these things, I would have had much to say myself. But unfortunately the record will not show it."[64]

These open exchanges were the only visible signs the public had that tensions were seething inside the Court. Underneath the Court's placid veneer, tensions mounted to the breaking point over personalities and petty squabbling. In conference discussions, no justice was immune from the strain attending the sharp divisions in ideology or loyalty. By the fall of 1961, with one of the most important cases ever decided looming on the horizon, Warren and Frankfurter were bickering again over Frankfurter's behavior. At conference, less than three months before Whittaker entered Walter Reed Hospital, Warren was answering a procedural question by Stewart while Frankfurter snickered and passed a note to Harlan. Warren stopped in his explanation and turned on Frankfurter, saying, "I am goddamn tired of having you snicker while I am talking. You do it even in the courtroom and people notice it." According to Douglas's notes, Frankfurter denied he was snickering, and there followed a long harangue by Warren stating he had reached the limits of his tolerance for Frankfurter.[65]

The tensions created in conference or in court over Frankfurter's eccentricities permeated Whittaker's Court service and became more prevalent with each new term. Not all the justices, however, were embattled with personal hostilities; to the contrary, most maintained detached, dignified relations with colleagues (the consensus among clerks at the time was that Harlan was liked and respected by all the justices), but the close seclusion of the conference and the strong personalities of some justices made cordiality difficult at times. The inescapable consequence was that personal mistrust and dislikes strained the justices' relations, creating an atmosphere of heightened anxiety. In addition to personal antagonism, there were also strongly held views on the nature of the Court's work—those cases considered worthy enough to merit the Court's attention. In this one area, particularly worker injury cases, there was a sharp three-way division among the justices over the Court's proper role. During Whittaker's service different justices in the controversy became increasingly frustrated with the triviality of these cases, as evidenced by their written opinions, and this seemingly minor, insignificant point of contention added yet another level of strain to an already tense situation. Furthermore, it was in this area, arguing the utility of the Court's consideration of the sufficiency of evidence, that Whittaker experienced his only personal encounter with open courtroom hostility from another member of the bench.

The conflict involved cases coming under the Federal Employers' Liability Act (FELA), passed in 1916, which gave to railroad workers the right to recover damages for injuries sustained on the job. According to Newman, Black was the moving force behind the Court's willingness to hear these cases.[66] Joining Black to rule in favor of injured workers were his three liberal-minded colleagues, who usually found a sympathetic vote from Clark to award damages to railroad workers based on the sufficiency of evidence proving negligence on the part of the railroad. Splitting the remaining justices two ways and sparking the debate over whether these cases were worthy of the justices' attention were the views of Frankfurter and Harlan. Frankfurter thought the Court wasted too much of its valuable time on FELA cases, based as they were on a reconsideration of the sufficiency of evidence presented to the jury at trial. Having grown weary of second-guessing juries and believing that the Court's time was better spent wrestling with major constitutional issues or cases of national importance, Frankfurter objected to a minority of justices requiring the Court to consider these claims. He made clear his view just before Whittaker's arrival that the Court should not hear these cases, making a decision on the merits unnecessary. Stating that he believed *certiorari* had been "improvidently granted," that is, the Court made a mistake initially when it agreed to hear the case, Frankfurter preferred to dismiss FELA cases and let the decisions of lower courts prevail.[67] Throughout Whittaker's tenure Frankfurter adhered to the view that FELA cases were a waste of the Court's time and that once accepted for argument they should consequently be dismissed without opinion.[68]

Developing a third line of reasoning in these cases was Harlan, who agreed wholeheartedly with Frankfurter that the Court never should have heard these

cases to begin with, but once accepted for argument the Court was bound
to consider the merits of each one. Relying on the Court's "Rule of Four,"
whereby only four justices rather than a majority were needed to grant *certiorari*, Harlan believed that once a case was argued on its merits, he was duty
bound to decide it on its merits—whether or not the Court had more important matters to consider. Based on this view, Harlan was forced, at times
reluctantly, to concur with the majority to award damages to injured workers because the evidence presented to the jury at trial was sufficient to prove
negligence.[69] The other Court members, Whittaker, Burton, and later Stewart, generally followed Harlan's line of reasoning, agreeing with Frankfurter's
contention that these cases represented a waste of the Court's time but feeling required to pass judgment out of respect for Court traditions. As a result,
in cases like *Moore v. Terminal Railroad Association of St. Louis*, for example,
four justices could disagree with the majority for three different reasons:
Frankfurter wanted to dismiss the case as though it had never been argued;
Harlan grudgingly agreed with the majority although he preferred it had
never been argued; and Whittaker and Burton dissented from the majority
based on the sufficiency of the evidence. Being one to base his decisions on
the particular facts of each case, Whittaker was especially forthright in his
dissent in *Moore*, finding not a "scintilla" or an "iota" of evidence to justify
negligence.[70]

The controversy over whether to accept these cases accounted for only
one portion of the justices' disagreement; there were also strong feelings concerning some of the justices' motives in awarding compensation to the
injured workers. One side voted consistently in favor of the injured railroad
workers even though, as Schwartz noted, at times there was overwhelming
evidence to prove the railroad was not responsible for the worker's injuries.[71]
This single-mindedness of purpose by the liberal justices to consider cases
some felt were insignificant and then to award damages to injured workers
without sufficient evidence to prove negligence further aggravated the justices'
already strained relations. To compensate somewhat for the prevalence of
FELA cases and to relieve the tension attending them, Whittaker in his third
term issued a concurring opinion written "in a satirical and semi-humorous
vein" that "[a] number of Justices, on both sides of the controversy, have had
a measure of fun out of."[72] Considered "one of the most intemperate opinions written by an Eisenhower Court justice,"[73] Whittaker's opinion unexpectedly landed him in an open court clash with Douglas that left Whittaker
completely baffled and revealed Douglas's deep-seated antagonism.

The initial conference vote in *Inman v. Baltimore & Ohio Railroad* was
five to three against the railroad and in favor of the injured worker, a crossing flagman who was struck one night by a drunken driver's car. The injured
worker sued his employer for not providing him with "enough protection"
and won a $25,000 award from the jury. On appeal, the Court of Appeals of

Ohio reversed the verdict, finding that "there was a complete failure of proof to establish the negligence" and that such an accident was not "reasonably foreseeable." With a majority of the view that the Ohio court was in error (Frankfurter refused to participate, believing that *certiorari* was improvidently granted), the justices set about writing opinions. Both Whittaker and Clark prepared dissents, and after circulating them one of the justices in the majority switched his vote to join Clark's opinion, leaving the Court evenly divided. A split Court meant affirmance of the Ohio Court of Appeals without opinion, and Whittaker's dissent became unnecessary. Pleased with his contribution, though, Whittaker informed his close friend in Kansas City, Roy Roberts, "I am not sure that this dissent is solely responsible—but I am sure that it played its part—in inducing the majority to withdraw from their original purpose to reverse the Ohio Court of Appeals."[74] Frankfurter then decided to abandon his improvidently granted position for the sake of a Court majority, and he, too, joined Clark's opinion, but not without stressing his conviction that these cases did not belong at the Supreme Court. Clark accepted the majority assignment; Whittaker revised his original dissent into a concurrence; and Douglas wrote for the four dissenters. The opinions circulated, and on Monday, December 14, 1959, they were announced.

After Clark's announcement of the majority opinion holding that the railroad was not negligent (and Frankfurter's brief statement joining it), Whittaker read his concurrence. In it, he took aim at Douglas's reliance on the "reasonableness" of whether the railroad had done enough to protect its flagmen and whether "reasonable men" could have foreseen the accident that occurred. He wrote,

> I heartily join the Court's opinion. But I derive no pleasure from implying, contrary to the views of my Brothers in the minority, that there was such complete want of evidence of negligence by respondent that "reasonable men" could not differ about it, for, at the very least, I regard my Brothers who dissent as reasonable men.
>
> Notwithstanding this, it seems to me that the facts of this case make it crystal clear that the Court's opinion lacks not a whit in fully comporting with the standards of care of the mythical "reasonable man," for, like the Ohio Court of Appeals, I simply cannot see any substantial evidence—or even a scintilla or an iota of evidence—of negligence on the part of respondent that caused, or directly contributed in any degree to cause, petitioner's unfortunate injury.[75]

Describing the circumstances of the accident, Whittaker asked how the railroad could protect its flagmen from the kind of injury sustained. He answered,

> About the only way, as I perceive, that respondent could protect its crossing flagman against injury from such lawless conduct by third persons would be to provide them with military tanks and make sure they stay in

them while within or moving about cross-intersections in the performance of their duties.

Whittaker then smiled as he read,

> I am not even sure that this method, though iron clad, would be certain protection to a flagman against lawless injury by third persons, for someone might shoot him [A murmur of amusement ran through the courtroom],[76] an act not very different, it seems to me, from the drunken driver's conduct which injured petitioner in this case, and for which injuries he insists, and four members of this Court agree, a jury should be permitted to require respondent to pay damages. How this can be thought to square with any known concept of "negligence" by respondent is beyond me.[77]

When it came time for Douglas to announce his dissent he was visibly upset and spoke angrily. "The case is rather an important one," he began, "it cannot be dismissed by this attempted humor." Without referring to Whittaker by name, Douglas continued, "Those of us who have read the record, as I am sure only a few of us have, recognize that the watchman did not only have to direct traffic. It was like putting a man in an inherently unsafe place and making him juggle." Unlike Whittaker, who read from his printed text, Douglas's reprimand came before announcement of his written opinion. His comments were pointed, cutting, and directed entirely at Whittaker, who had no forewarning. Defending the right of injured railroad men to trial by juries rather than judges, Douglas said the gravity of the issue belied the "rather smart-alecky things that have been said."[78] As noted in the press, none of these comments appeared in Douglas's printed opinion. His display of anger and his self-righteous tone shocked Whittaker. The opinions had circulated in the weeks before; all the justices were aware of Whittaker's opinion—first as a dissent and then as a concurrence. When Douglas finished reading his dissent, he promptly left the bench and returned to his chambers. Whittaker was left reeling; the last thing he wanted was to offend a member of the Court. One of Whittaker's clerks that term has remembered, "What surprised him afterwards was that if it had caused such a strong reaction, why had not Douglas or the others come to him to say he should change it?"[79] Obviously, Douglas's display was a spontaneous reaction to the unexpected murmurs of amusement running through the courtroom, and he was as offended by Whittaker's momentary popularity as by the unusual light-heartedness of Whittaker's words. Such an unexpected (and in Whittaker's mind, unprovoked) public show of hostility must have made Whittaker wary, even nervous about circulating opinions, and it undoubtedly put a strain on his personal relationship with Douglas.[80]

The private feuds, strong ideological differences, and forceful personalities on the Court all contributed to Whittaker's difficulties. In his final term, though, two cases in particular caused Whittaker especial problems. These two, *Brown Shoe v. United States*, a complex antitrust decision assigned to Whittaker just three months before his collapse, and *Baker v. Carr*, the landmark decision inaugurating a revolution in congressional and legislative reapportionment, were both decided without Whittaker. He was not present for the announcement of *Baker* (his retirement became effective one week later) although he was involved throughout most of its deliberation, and he was already home in Kansas City recovering by the time *Brown Shoe* came down. Because of the difficulties he encountered during the consideration of both of these cases and the timing of his retirement so near the announcement of *Baker*, many assumed that these cases, *Baker* in particular, were principally responsible for his nervous breakdown in the middle of his fifth term.[81] This explanation readily supported the view of Whittaker as a "failure": since he struggled perpetually in the most serious of constitutional cases, when *Baker* presented what was arguably the most important and far-reaching question of his entire Court service he buckled under the pressure of indecision. A facile explanation, but one that overlooked other equally significant factors leading to Whittaker's disability. Of course, cases like *Baker* put Whittaker in the middle of a doctrinal dispute that caused both sides to exert tremendous pressure on him in attempts to sway his vote. In fact, Frankfurter reportedly was especially severe with Whittaker during the consideration of *Baker*. This one case, however, as momentous as it was in the history of the Court, cannot be blamed solely as the cause of Whittaker's breakdown. Neither can the circumstances of his fifth term account for the aggregate reasons why he suffered a complete physical and emotional collapse. Underlying the various influences causing strain for Whittaker was a largely misunderstood medical condition that at the time had few successful means of treatment. This disease, complicated by external pressures, was primarily responsible for Whittaker's hospitalization. Unknown to members of the Court, the public, or the administration that appointed him, Whittaker suffered from bouts of severe depression, and by the middle of his fifth term it became so unbearable that he considered suicide.[82]

At the time he served on the Court, there was only one successful treatment for depression, and that, electric shock therapy, was especially cruel to the patient. Early in Whittaker's Court service, his physicians, all residing in Kansas City, instead tried to treat his symptoms with prescription drugs. These medications were unsuitable for a disease like depression, and Whittaker's condition only worsened. Complaining of the side effects of the drugs, Whittaker eventually abandoned his medications. Without proper treatment, though, his depression would eventually return. As his son, Keith, a neurosurgeon, has described it, "Recurrent depression comes and goes by itself. It does not need stress to induce it. My father's depression was familial, genetic. There was no reason to believe his depression had anything to do with his work. Sure, stress exacerbates it, but it's not just a matter of going through tough times. The biochemical reactions are much more complicated. A case like *Baker* could have triggered it, but that was not its backbone."[83] Any number of circumstances his fifth term could have contributed to causing Whittaker's depression to recur. That it happened during the middle of his fifth term may be partly attributed to consideration of *Baker*, but it was just as possible that Whittaker's emotional breakdown merely coincided with the Court's announcement of *Baker*. Although his Court work did not necessarily cause his depression, the stress he experienced grappling with cases like *Baker* and *Brown Shoe* certainly made his depression more difficult to control.

When *Baker v. Carr* first presented itself on appeal to the Court in November 1960, the four liberal justices, Warren, Black, Douglas, and Brennan, voted in favor of hearing it, indicating early on their willingness to consider the claims of Tennessee urban voters who suffered a dilution of voting strength in state politics. According to the Tennessee state constitution, the state legislature was to apportion its membership among the state's ninety-five counties, but for the last six decades it had failed to do so. As a result, forty percent of the population, mostly rural, elected seventy-five percent of the state legislature. Because the Tennessee state courts failed to rectify the inequities in voting, the plaintiffs in *Baker* brought their suit in federal district court as the only remaining remedy. There they argued that the Tennessee apportionment act was unconstitutional because it violated the voters' equal protection rights under the Fourteenth Amendment, and they asked for an injunction to prevent state officers from conducting any more elections under it. The three-judge district court, however, dismissed the case, relying on the Supreme Court's decision in *Colegrove v. Green* as precedent. In *Colegrove* the Court had held that federal courts lacked jurisdiction in state reapportionment and that, even if they could assert jurisdiction, this was a "political question" that federal judges were not competent to address.[84] Reconsidering *Colegrove*, as everyone on the Court was aware, would pit Frankfurter in a clash of wills with Black and Douglas. Considering the magnitude of the case, when the Court first heard arguments on April 19 and 20, 1961, three hours were permitted, threefold as much time as was permitted for most cases.

During the first oral arguments on *Baker*, Whittaker betrayed his own willingness to accept jurisdiction in the case, causing Frankfurter to become instructive on that score. On the second day of oral arguments Whittaker pressed the lawyer representing Tennessee, James Glasgow, to explain how the constitutional provision requiring legislative reapportionment could persist without its ever being enforced. Glasgow relied on state court rulings as determinative, claiming how in *Kidd v. McCanless*, a decision of the Tennessee Supreme Court, the constitutional provision related to reapportionment was neither mandatory nor self-executing. Although it had never been enforced, Glasgow admitted, *Kidd* required that abolishment of the reapportionment provision would render Tennessee effectively without a state legislature. Whittaker then wanted to know how, under the *Kidd* doctrine, the validity of the present state legislature was in any way affected by the *future* compliance of the reapportionment provision. Glasgow again tried to rest his argument on *Kidd*, stating that if "the legislature or the apportionment provisions expired in 1911, then it must be that everything that's been done since 1911 is invalid. As a matter of theory, I don't see how it can be any other way." Whittaker disagreed, however, noting how in Glasgow's own argument the legislature was competent to determine the election and qualification of its own members, and it had done that every term since 1911. Since every one of Tennessee's legislatures had been properly elected in the past, Whittaker wanted to know, how was it possible that courts lacked jurisdiction to effect compliance in the

As only the second person in history to serve on all three levels of the federal judiciary, Whittaker's eight-year tenure in federal service was shorter than that of any of his colleagues. For this reason Whittaker failed to make a lasting impression in the public's mind, but his "failure" rating subsequent to his resignation was colored by inaccuracies and exaggerations without accounting for the real, underlying cause of his difficulties—namely, that he suffered from depression. (Photograph courtesy of Kent Whittaker)

future? Glasgow seemed unable to answer effectively, calling it a political question not meet for adjudication. Frankfurter then tried to extricate Glasgow from Whittaker's rational strait-jacket, prompting Glasgow to rely on *Luther v. Borden*, a nineteenth century decision by Chief Justice Roger Taney, which established the "political question" doctrine.[85] Considering Whittaker's adherence to the principle of *stare decisis*, Frankfurter obviously answered Whittaker's questions with the support of precedent to convince Whittaker that the courts had a long policy of restraint when it came to interfering with the internal politics of the states.[86]

At the Court's first conference on *Baker*, April 20, seven justices were definitive in their positions—only Whittaker and Stewart seemed capable of vacillation. According to conference notes, Warren, Black, Douglas, and Brennan were prepared to reverse the decision of the district court, accepting jurisdiction and even fashioning a judicial remedy for the voting inequities occurring in Tennessee. Frankfurter, Clark, and Harlan were just as determined to support the district court decision. Echoing his views from *Colegrove*, Frankfurter said, "Unless we affirm, we will get into great difficulty and this Court will rue the results.... The costs will be very serious." Undoubtedly for Whittaker's benefit, Frankfurter added, "The Tennessee constitution has nothing to do with the case—this must be a violation of the federal Constitution for the petitioner to get to federal court." "All of these factors," Frankfurter continued, "are not capable of being determined by the courts. Not one state is free of gerrymandering—how can courts determine what is fair in this area? The subject matter is not proper for judicial inquiry."[87] Harlan agreed with Frankfurter, stating that there was no federally protected right based on voting equality and that courts could not solve the problem. Clark refused to go against precedent. Raising the very point Whittaker had argued in court, Clark said, "If we upset the Tennessee system, it would have no legislature."[88] With the vote stalled four to three it came Whittaker's turn to speak. Initially he gave the liberal justices reason for encouragement, stating, "If we wrote on a clean slate, I would say that petitioners have standing to sue and that they are being denied equal protection of the laws—then no relief in the state courts. If there is a constitutional right involved, the chancellor should not withhold relief." Then Whittaker shifted ground, relying on precedent for his decision—just as Frankfurter hoped he would. "Precedents, however, say that this is a 'political issue,'" he continued, "I am reluctant to overrule those cases."[89] Now the Court stood deadlocked four to four, but Stewart would not break the tie. He did not see how voting disproportion was a violation of equal protection, yet he recognized that the Tennessee constitution required equality. Unwilling to choose between the two, Stewart passed.[90]

Following the initial conference on *Baker*, the Court stood precariously poised to go either way. Stewart's vote was unclear, and Whittaker, although he had voted alongside Frankfurter, indicated a willingness to join the liberal side. Recognizing the importance of the case (Stewart compared it to the Court's school desegregation decisions),[91] there was tremendous pressure put on both Whittaker and Stewart. One of Brennan's clerks that term got the impression that Whittaker was the target of intense lobbying by both Black and Frankfurter. "I even heard that they went to his home to see him about it, which was out of bounds," this clerk has recalled, "This must have been disconcerting to him."[92] At one point during conferences on *Baker*, Whittaker admitted that he was willing to be the sixth vote to grant jurisdiction, but not the fifth, clearly indicating that if Stewart were willing, they could both join the liberal side. According to Black's biographer, Roger Newman, "That set Frankfurter off like an alarm clock. 'Felix really berated him,'

Black said later. He talked for four and a half hours, going to the shelves to get cases, reading from them, powerfully arguing that *Colegrove v. Green* had been correct, and looking directly at Whittaker the whole time. After a while Black had enough and walked out."[93]

As a result of Stewart's indecision, the case was set over for reargument the following term. Everyone on the Court recognized the importance of Stewart's vote, Stewart most of all, so there was no hesitancy about taking the summer recess to reconsider the issues involved. That did not mean, however, that Whittaker was off the hook. His willingness to give the liberal justices jurisdiction in the case meant a major set back for Frankfurter's judicial legacy, and it opened the door for the Court to fashion remedies to correct inequities in voting. The only way for Whittaker to join the liberal side, though, was if Stewart did, too, but Stewart was not ready to commit. According to one of Brennan's clerks that term, "Neither one of them wanted to be the fifth vote [to grant jurisdiction]. Stewart, it was believed, would go where Whittaker went; there was a sense that Whittaker was more malleable, which made him the swing vote. Whittaker wanted to do the right thing and take the time to do it right. To his credit, he asked for reargument."[94]

When the justices returned to open the new Court term with three more hours of oral arguments on *Baker*, both Whittaker and Stewart were prepared to finalize their positions. Neither one of them, however, gave the liberals or conservatives the resounding victory that might have been hoped, nor, more importantly, did either of them seem completely beyond persuasion. Arguments were heard on Monday, October 9, but before the Friday conference Frankfurter and Harlan were already trying to influence the Court's two most recent appointments. The day after arguments Frankfurter circulated a sixty-five-page memorandum urging the other justices to consider the "dire consequences" of rejecting *Colegrove*. The following day Harlan, probably at Frankfurter's urging, wrote a direct appeal to both Whittaker and Stewart, asserting that *Baker* was among the most important cases ever to come before the Court. *Colegrove*, he observed, was "among the wisest and [most] farsighted decisions of the Court," and any rejection of it he viewed as a threat to the independence of the judiciary. Concerned with what he saw as the inevitable consequences of overturning *Colegrove*, Harlan asked, "[I]s not the political aloofness of the Court almost as much a matter of appearance as of actual fact? And, were we now to enter this 'political thicket,' would we not inevitably be courting such appearances, however unfounded, as all manner and gradations of apportionment cases come to our door? The only sure way of avoiding this is to keep the gate to the thicket tightly closed." Concluding his letter, Harlan lamented, "[I]t would be a sad thing were we by our own act to plunge this institution into what would bid fair, as time goes on, to erode its stature."[95] These attempts at persuasion were obviously designed to keep Whittaker's vote from wavering and to bring Stewart over to the conservative side. As long as Whittaker voted alongside Frankfurter, it was hoped Stewart would follow. Unknown to Frankfurter or Harlan, their efforts at persuasion proved ineffectual; both Whittaker and Stewart had made up their minds by the time arguments were heard. The end result was worse than Frankfurter might have expected. Whittaker denied that the Court lacked jurisdiction, but he still preferred to vote with Frankfurter. Stewart, too, found the Court had jurisdiction; only he voted with the liberal side.

At the Court's first conference following reargument in *Baker* the justices—all but Stewart—predictably held to their votes from the previous spring; there were, however, new arguments raised by both sides and some shifting of positions. On the liberal side, Warren began the conference by limiting his position solely to the question of jurisdiction, which he believed the Court possessed. Black took issue with Frankfurter's sixty-five-page memorandum, noting how only two other justices agreed with Frankfurter in *Colegrove* on the issue of jurisdiction and how *Luther v. Borden* did not apply under these circumstances. "I agree with *Luther v. Borden*, with each party having claimed to represent the state," Black said, "It wasn't a dispute over a law passed by state, but an argument about which group *was* the state. Congress has the power to resolve that issue.... Here, Congress has no power to give relief to these people, whatever their power may be to pass legislation under the Fourteenth Amendment."[96] Douglas, likewise, wanted to fashion relief for the people of Tennessee; only he stressed the importance of using the Court's decision in *Gomillion v. Lightfoot* as a precedent for reversal. Decided the previous term, in *Gomillion* Frankfurter ruled for a unanimous Court that the gerrymandering scheme of Tuskegee, Alabama, was racially motivated in violation of the Fifteenth Amendment's right to vote. Both Douglas and Whittaker concurred in that decision, but Whittaker preferred to rely on the Equal Protection clause of the Fourteenth Amendment rather than the right to vote of the Fifteenth. To his mind, the African Americans who were denied the municipal vote in Tuskegee were not denied other voting privileges in county and state elections, and therefore equal protection was a sounder bases for decision than the right to vote. In a move designed to attract Whittaker's vote, Douglas used *Gomillion* as a precedent for reversing *Baker* on equal protection grounds. "The equal protection clause is not designed just for Negroes—even he has to show an arbitrary discrimination," Douglas said at conference, "Negroes have no greater right under equal protection than whites."[97] Brennan echoed the chief justice's position, wanting to assert jurisdiction in the case but no more. That way, the Tennessee legislature could act on its own, and the Court could move slowly, incrementally, saving any decision on the merits for a later time. This strategy proved essential to gaining Stewart's vote.

On the conservative side, Frankfurter relied principally on his sixty-five-page memorandum, which later became the basis of his written dissent, deferring instead to Harlan to present their arguments. Harlan struck at

Douglas's interpretation of *Gomillion*, reminding him that it was decided on the right to vote, not equal protection. As for *Baker*, Harlan could find no federally protected right or federal cause of action and therefore no jurisdiction. "If Tennessee had enacted this scheme in its constitution or by statute [rather than by inaction in the enforcement of a constitutional provision], an attack would assert no claim of violation of the Constitution," Harlan said, "If a state can distribute its organs of government as it wishes without subjecting itself to federal judicial supervision or interference, then I can't see why a state may not ... choose the means whereby these organs are to be created and the rules enforced."[98] Clark continued to rely on precedents, particularly *Colegrove*, to deny the Court jurisdiction, but he also raised a point brought up on the first day of oral arguments the previous term—whether the voters of Tennessee had any other recourse besides the federal courts, a point that eventually caused him to switch his vote. "The petitioners failed to show that they had exhausted other avenues of relief," Clark said, "Congress could act to end discrimination in the twenty-odd states where this discrimination exists."[99]

When it came his turn to speak, Whittaker admitted that his vote the previous term had been "very shaky." After writing two diametrically opposed memoranda on the issue, he finally decided to stick with his earlier vote to support the conservative side, but not for the reasons advanced by the other conservative justices. In an unusual show of independence, Whittaker rejected Harlan and Frankfurter's position that federal courts lacked jurisdiction in reapportionment cases or that, even if they exercised jurisdiction, federal courts could not remedy the situation with workable standards. "I now affirm," he said, "but not for lack of judicial power or jurisdiction. The district court dismissed this case on that ground, but it was wrong." Instead, Whittaker reasoned, the district court correctly dismissed the case for failure "to state a cause of action on which relief might be granted." Because the Tennessee Supreme Court had read and interpreted the Tennessee constitutional reapportionment provision as unenforceable by the courts in Tennessee, it effectively amended the Tennessee constitution to make reapportionment nonjusticiable. "If that is so," Whittaker argued, "then the claim here that the petitioners have been deprived of a right granted by state law fails, for no right granted them by state law has been denied. The federal court has jurisdiction to entertain this type of claim, but there is no right to enforce."[100]

Why did Whittaker advance such a novel approach to deciding *Baker*? After all, no other justice subscribed to his reasoning—in fact, Stewart rejected the idea that the decision of a state supreme court could be binding on how federal courts handled a case. By rejecting Frankfurter's side and accepting the idea that federal courts had jurisdiction in these cases, Whittaker left himself vulnerable to attacks from the conservative side. For the same reason, by supporting the Court's jurisdiction but voting to affirm the district court in dismissing the case, he left himself vulnerable to appeals from the liberal side. Once again, Whittaker placed himself in the middle of the two opposing forces on the Court, and they beleaguered him until *Baker* was handed down. Perhaps Whittaker was looking for an alternative because, as had happened before, he could not completely satisfy himself with either side. By voting on Frankfurter's side without embracing Frankfurter's reasoning, Whittaker staked out an independent course, one that he probably came to rue. "Frankfurter thought that Whittaker's vote might be determinative of the outcome," one of Harlan's clerks at the time has remembered, "I was told that Frankfurter would visit Whittaker in his chambers (Frankfurter seldom left his own chambers except to visit his friend, Harlan) and lecture to him, Harvard-professor style, about the harm that would befall the Court if it said that legislative apportionment was justiciable. Some said that Frankfurter drove Whittaker off the Court. The irony, of course, was that Stewart and Clark defected in *Baker*, so even winning Whittaker's vote would have done Frankfurter no good."[101]

With Whittaker's vote on the conservative side to dismiss the case, it was up to Stewart to finally decide the outcome of *Baker*. Like Whittaker, though, Stewart failed to completely embrace one side over the other. His vote lined up with the liberals on the questions of jurisdiction and standing—federal courts could consider the issues, and the voters of Tennessee had cause to complain—but he was not prepared to rule on the merits of the case to determine a remedy. For that, he had to consider the issue further. "Every presumption here is in favor of every state action," Stewart said at conference, "So the state does not have to justify every departure from a one man one vote basis, and the greatest burden of proof is on the plaintiff to show an arbitrary and capricious system."[102] With Stewart's vote joining the liberal side on the question of jurisdiction, Warren assigned the majority decision to Brennan, who had expressed views most closely aligned with Stewart's, and Brennan set about crafting an opinion that could command a majority of five justices. It was another three months before opinions were circulated, and during that time Whittaker's difficulties only worsened.

Before the Court recessed for its annual Christmas holiday break, opinion assignments seemed to be proceeding normally for Whittaker, although signs of his impending disability were already apparent. One of Harlan's clerks that last term has remembered, "Almost from the beginning of the 1961 term, Whittaker was absent, and the clerks in other chambers were just told he was ill."[103] Despite his absence from the Court, Whittaker still completed two majority assignments and one dissent before the break. During the holiday break, Whittaker worked on two other decisions; one became his last opinion, and the other Whittaker never finished. He was in the hospital three months later and Warren had to finish the opinion for him.

The case that Whittaker never finished was *Brown Shoe v. United States*, a complicated antitrust lawsuit brought by the federal government to enjoin Brown Shoe, the third largest shoe retailer by dollar, from merging with Kinney Shoes, the eighth largest retailer by dollar. The district court for the Eastern District of Missouri had ruled that the proposed merger violated the Clayton Act, as amended in 1950, by eliminating one corporation as a substantial competitor in the retail field. The district court also found that the proposed merger increased concentration in both manufacturing and retail, that it established a manufacturer-retailer relationship that deprived all but the top firms in the industry of a fair opportunity to compete, and that it increased a tendency toward monopoly. Ordered to divest itself of its stock acquired in Kinney Shoes and to file in the district court within 90 days a plan for carrying out the decree, Brown Shoe appealed directly to the Supreme Court. Without an appeals court decision intervening, the Supreme Court acquired the entire trial court record, an enormous collection of statistical tables showing the sales of different kinds of shoes and the percent of the industry involved. So complex were the issues in the case that without a thorough understanding of the diverse fields within the shoe industry one could easily become lost in the statistical data. Following oral arguments, December 6, 1961, Frankfurter remarked to the clerks over lunch that the Court was a wonderful place to work, but it lacked something the Metropolitan Opera had—a trap door. "That way," Frankfurter said, "the justices could pull it and Mr. [Arthur] Dean [representing Brown Shoe] could fall to Hell and one of his associates could finish the argument and we could understand it."[104]

At the conference on *Brown Shoe*, December 9, all of the justices agreed with the district court ruling, that Brown Shoe had in some way violated the Clayton Act, although there were differences of opinion on the nature of that violation, leading Clark and Harlan each to concur with the Court's final decision. Harlan also dissented (and presumably Frankfurter would have joined him had he remained on the Court) on the question of jurisdiction, arguing that there was not, in fact, a final decision of the district court upon which the Supreme Court could act. With the justices in agreement on the merits of the case, Warren assigned Whittaker to write for the majority. One of Warren's clerks at the time has remembered how Whittaker struggled writing the opinion, and after just a few weeks Whittaker came to Warren complaining of his difficulty. He told Warren that if he were in his office all day, every day, until the end of the term, there was no way he could get through the entire trial record in time to write an opinion. Warren told him there was no need to read the entire record, just the relevant parts. Whittaker, on the other hand, thought that if the trial record was submitted to the Court, then at least one of the justices should read it, all of it.[105] Whether or not Whittaker's depression aggravated his commitment to examine the entire trial record or his determination to read the entire record contributed to his heightened anxiety was difficult to distinguish. It was clear, however, that Whittaker's condition began to degenerate by the beginning of 1962, and he was not, as Schwartz assumed, simply "overwhelmed by the complexity of the case."[106] It was just as likely that Whittaker was acting irrationally because of his distressed mental and emotional state as because of the enormity of the trial record. Warren's clerk who assisted in finishing the opinion for Warren following Whittaker's retirement has questioned Whittaker's motives in trying to get out of the assignment, asking, "Did he *really* think he had to read the entire record? Or were there other reasons to get out of the assignment to avoid his problem?"[107]

Whittaker's retirement became effective on Sunday, April 1, 1962, and *Brown Shoe* was decided without him. Frankfurter, likewise, was not present for the decision; he suffered a stroke while working at his desk in his chambers on Thursday, April 5. Although he intended to, Frankfurter never again returned to his Court duties, retiring on August 28. Whittaker's replacement, Byron White, did not take his seat on the Court until April 16, too late in the term to participate in many decisions yet to be argued. With Frankfurter in the hospital and no date set for his return to duty, the Court became stalled, unable to hand down any close decisions without his participation. Chief Justice Warren summarized the difficulties the Court was encountering on April 25 in a memorandum to the other justices: "We have handed down no decisions the past three weeks. There are now 15 opinions in circulation and 18 opinions, most of them by a divided Court, which have not been circulated.... There are 24 cases recently argued which have not been assigned.... [U]nless we resolve some factors soon, we will end the Term in a state of confusion or be under the necessity of setting more cases over for reargument. The calendar for the next Term will hardly support such action."[108] The problem, as Warren saw it, was not knowing precisely Frankfurter's plans to return to duty. With no accurate information coming from the hospital on Frankfurter's condition, Warren became increasingly frustrated operating in the dark. (The bulletins coming from Frankfurter's doctors, Warren admitted, were "adequate for the public, but they are not adequate for us. We know that the first bulletin was grossly understated, and ... we must assume that Felix is a very sick man.")[109] The only possible solutions that allowed the Court to resume activity and finish the term on time without setting cases over for reargument were to have Frankfurter return to duty soon or to declare himself out of the cases for the remainder of the term. At the time of Warren's memorandum, neither solution seemed practicable. Compounding the Court's difficulties was not only Frankfurter's absence and White's late arrival, but, as Warren observed, Whittaker had not actively participated in the Court's work since about February 1, four weeks before he entered the hospital.[110] Clearly his condition had deteriorated significantly, and, with the pressure mounting over the Court's decision in *Baker v. Carr*, Whittaker ceased to function effectively.

By the end of January 1962 Brennan had completed his draft of the majority opinion in *Baker* and received Stewart's acceptance. That made a majority of five to accept jurisdiction, repudiating *Colegrove* and the Court's reluctance to enter the "political thicket" of legislative reapportionment. Brennan's draft was careful to avoid any remedy for the Tennessee voters in order to keep Stewart's vote. On February 1 Frankfurter circulated his draft dissent, which was essentially the same in form and substance as his sixty-five-page memorandum following reargument. Over the next four weeks tensions mounted at the Court as opinions circulated and justices changed their positions. Early in February Clark, intending to dissent, began investigating the failure of Tennessee voters to exhaust other remedies before resorting to the federal courts. He sought delay of a decision until he had time to write an opinion, and since he, Warren, and Brennan were going to Puerto Rico for a judicial conference lasting ten days, a decision had to wait until at least early March.[111] During this time Whittaker was also absent from the Court. He had retreated back to the Midwest, but instead of returning to Kansas City he sought refuge at a lodge owned by the *Kansas City Star* in Park Falls, Wisconsin. Located about 50 miles south of Lake Superior in north central Wisconsin, the *Star's* lodge was for the exclusive use of *Star* officials and people visiting the Flambeau Paper Mill owned by the *Star*. According to one of Whittaker's former law associates, Whittaker was the first person to use the lodge without being in the company of a *Star* employee.[112]

Whittaker must have used his influence with his old law firm and their relationship with the *Kansas City Star* (not to mention his personal contact with Roy Roberts who was still president and managing editor of the *Star*) to gain access to the lodge. He chose the *Star's* lodge in Wisconsin because of its easy access and relative isolation, and the purpose of his trip was readily apparent. He had to escape Washington and the pressures of the Court. His depression was becoming unmanageable and interfering with his work. With no other recourse but to leave, he headed west. Once in Park Falls, Whittaker called on one of his former law associates at the *Watson* law firm, a protege of his named Sam Molby who joined the firm in 1938, and asked him to come to the lodge. Unsure why he was being summoned to the lodge or even how long his trip would last, Molby asked a younger associate to look after his desk until his return. Molby stayed at Park Falls for three weeks in early February with Whittaker. For hours on end the two of them sat together in the lodge or along the bank of a nearby lake, barely speaking to one another. Molby later confided to an associate at the firm that it was "frustrating for him to be readily available and attentive to [Whittaker] and at the same time keep from getting bored at doing nothing."[113] When Whittaker remarked that there were cases he had to work on for the Court, Molby reassured him to relax and take it easy. Whittaker was obviously distressed, and it was during this time of reflection, free from external distractions, that he came to a decision.

Those that remembered him from his old law office believed that Whittaker made up his mind to finally quit the Court.[114] He could have contemplated something far more drastic, however, and as his depression deepened Whittaker made arrangements to carry out his plan.

News of his retirement after just five years on the Court raised speculation among his friends in Kansas City that Whittaker took seriously his self-appointed "five year sentence" and that his resignation had as much to do with his personal desire to return to Kansas City as with the difficulties he encountered at the Court. One friend wrote to him, "When I read in the paper that you had resigned from the Supreme Court because of your health, I said to myself, 'Health, hell, I'll bet a horse it was nostalgia.'"[115] Reactions to the news of Whittaker's retirement varied; those who only knew of him were disappointed while those who knew him well were relieved. Because of his dissatisfaction living in Washington and his disappointment at having to leave the district and then appeals courts, Whittaker's friends were grateful—even encouraging—when he left the Supreme Court. One of his Kansas City physicians wrote to him, "When your resignation from the Supreme Court because of health was announced in the news, I remarked to a friend that I was not worried about your health. I would bet a dollar to a donut that you were motivated by a wish to be separated from an unhealthy situation rather than your personal health."[116]

For years the impression persisted that Whittaker's disappointment at ever going to the Supreme Court caused him to resign after just five years. When Whittaker quit his judicial commission three years after his retirement, thus ending his service to the federal courts, *U. S. News & World Report* cited "political observers" who were convinced that Whittaker's public statements following his retirement were "evidence that disenchantment with the Court also may have influenced his 1962 retirement."[117] These were good *excuses* for leaving the Court, but they were not the primary cause of Whittaker's emotional breakdown. Whittaker did not return from Park Falls and tender his letter of resignation because he had had enough. He spent the last two weeks of February suffering from severe depression. Few people inside or outside the Court realized the extent of Whittaker's physical and emotional disability. He was coming apart, and by the end of February he was making plans for his wife's security after his death. On February 26 Whittaker prepared a detailed listing of all of his and Winifred's stock investments and placed it in a safe deposit box where it remained for another ten years. Considering he did this just two weeks before his son, Keith, talked him out of committing suicide made the timing of the incident "damn suspicious," and, Keith believed, indicated that Whittaker was planning to kill himself.[118]

Back at the Court the tensions created by *Baker v. Carr* continued to increase as new opinions were issued and justices shifted their positions. Through the beginning of February Harlan continued to pressure Stewart to reconsider his position, but it was not Harlan that shook Stewart's commitment to Brennan's majority decision; it was Douglas. Assuming the decision would be announced soon, Douglas prepared a concurrence discussing the judicial standards for reapportionment. Stewart was not prepared to go that far, so to limit the majority only to the questions of jurisdiction, justiciability, and standing he prepared his own concurrence. Douglas tried to modify his opinion to keep Stewart from writing separately but to no avail; on the merits of the case Stewart agreed with Harlan's dissent, which rejected the view "that state legislatures must be so structured as to reflect with approximate equality the voice of every voter."[119] Sometime in mid–February Frankfurter re-circulated his draft dissent, this time noting that Clark and Harlan had joined it.[120] That left Whittaker, who had not signed on to any draft opinions and, presumably, was not writing his own. The Court continued to wait on Clark's draft dissent, but with the questions so monumental and the votes still so close, it became increasingly important to determine where Whittaker stood. At one point Frankfurter circulated his draft dissent showing that Whittaker had joined it, but it was unlikely that Whittaker had, in fact, willingly signed on to it. One of Harlan's clerks that last term has remembered, "I think Whittaker was tentatively, though barely, on the Frankfurter-Harlan side. He had not, however, signed on to any opinions in the case by the time he resigned."[121]

As much as Frankfurter wanted Whittaker's vote, there were several reasons why he probably did not get it. First, Whittaker had been prepared since the previous term to grant the Court jurisdiction in the case, and that was precisely the one issue on which the majority agreed. Second, if he were going to join any dissent in the case, Harlan's more closely expressed Whittaker's views from the October 1961 conference: "Once one cuts through the thicket of discussion devoted to 'jurisdiction,' 'standing,' 'justiciability,' and 'political question,' there emerges a straightforward issue which, in my view, is determinative of this case.... [I]n my opinion, appellants' allegations, accepting all of them as true, do not, parsed down or as a whole, show an infringement by Tennessee of any rights assured by the Fourteenth Amendment. Accordingly, I believe the complaint should have been dismissed for 'failure to state a claim upon which relief can be granted.'"[122] There were also arguments in Harlan's dissent concerning the protection of states' agricultural interests and the preservation of local control, both arguments that would have appealed to Whittaker personally. Another reason Frankfurter probably did not get Whittaker's vote was that Whittaker's emotional well being had become noticeably far more distressed by late February 1962, making his commitment to any decision in *Baker* doubtful. So concerned were some of the other justices about Whittaker's capacity to make rational decisions that Harlan and Black reportedly decided to hold over for reargument any case where Whittaker cast the deciding vote. Before they could put their plan into effect, Whittaker retired.[123]

During the first week of March 1962 significant changes took place at the Court. On Friday, March 2, Douglas circulated a memorandum suggesting that *Baker* be decided within the next two weeks in order to give lower federal courts time to prepare for challenges to upcoming elections. Such a suggestion infuriated some Court members, but the most dramatic events were still to come. About this same time Whittaker announced that he wanted to rethink his position from the October conference. According to one of Warren's former clerks, "Frankfurter went berserk about that, and became quite abusive to Whittaker."[124] The potential of losing Whittaker's vote in one of the Court's most historically significant decisions must have been more than Frankfurter could bear. Certainly Whittaker was counted among Frankfurter's allies (in all but six close decisions [5 to 4] Whittaker had joined Frankfurter's side), but in the five years Whittaker served he proved less reliable—and malleable—than Frankfurter would have liked. In over fifty cases decided together Whittaker and Frankfurter voted on opposite sides; in at least a third of Whittaker's written opinions Frankfurter voted the other way. In *Baker* Frankfurter was determined to keep Whittaker on his side. The cost of that determination put Whittaker in the hospital suffering from a complete physical and emotional breakdown. Frankfurter's efforts to control Whittaker finally took their toll. Whether Frankfurter knew or understood about Whittaker's condition did not seem to matter. Frankfurter could not accept defeat after waging war with Black and Douglas for twenty years. "Certainly Frankfurter was a major factor in causing it [Whittaker's breakdown]," remarked Whittaker's son, Kent.[125] There was no doubt but that given Whittaker's predisposition to suffer depression and Frankfurter's intense lobbying during *Baker* that Whittaker's breakdown was unavoidable.

What did come as a surprise and what changed the outcome of *Baker* so irrecoverably was Clark's switch on March 7. Without warning, Clark concluded from his investigation of other remedies for the voters of Tennessee that there were no other remedies. Instead of dissenting, Clark joined the majority with his own concurrence; only Clark went much further than Brennan's majority opinion and offered relief to Tennessee voters (Brennan would not accept remedies yet in order to hold on to Stewart's vote).[126] Informing Frankfurter and Harlan of his changed vote, Clark wrote, "I am sorry I cannot go along, but it does not change the result anyway."[127] The irony, of course, and the tragedy was that Clark's decision came one day after Whittaker entered Walter Reed Hospital. Once Clark made his decision giving Brennan six votes, there was no more fight left in Frankfurter. He may have been seething on the inside, but effecting a change in the outcome of *Baker* was now beyond his reach. Had Clark reached his decision earlier, foreclosing any possibility that Whittaker's vote would make a difference, then perhaps Whittaker could have withstood the pressures he was made to endure. As one of Whittaker's last term clerks said, "Whittaker sort of found himself

1962 Supreme Court of the United States. *Left to right*: Douglas, Whittaker, Black, Harlan, Warren, Brennan, Frankfurter, Stewart, and Clark. Taken near the time of his retirement, this photograph shows no evidence of Whittaker's disability. With Potter Stewart's appointment three years earlier Whittaker was relieved of the burden of being the last to speak at conference, yet his and Stewart's votes were both considered critical to the final outcome of *Baker v. Carr*. (Collection of the Supreme Court of the United States)

the guy who had to decide all these important questions.... His vote was going to decide what the Constitution said."[128]

Whittaker's last day at the Court was Monday, March 5, 1962. At the urging of Justice Douglas he entered Walter Reed Hospital the next day and remained there under observation for more than two weeks. According to press reports one week after he left the hospital, Whittaker lost his appetite, began to worry, and had difficulty sleeping and concentrating. "I was burning the candle at both ends," he said, "to a point where I became completely enervated."[129] His doctors told him that there was nothing organically wrong with him, only a severe case of physical exhaustion. They also warned him that if he returned to the Court he could seriously jeopardize his health. So on the advice of his doctors, "a team of eminent physicians," Whittaker accepted retirement. "I hate to leave the Court," he told reporters following the announcement of his retirement, "This is a distressing experience for me. I wanted to stay and do my duty as long as I could and to maintain my standards of perfection. But after the analysis of the doctors I realized that I was not in a position to return without jeopardizing my health. I had no other choice."[130] According to the *Kansas City Star*, Whittaker at first thought about resigning his commission and leaving the federal judiciary entirely, but on the advice of Chief Justice Warren he instead retired as the result of a disability, which gave him a lifetime pension of half his annual salary, or $17,500. It also meant he could continue to serve as a federal judge in the future if called upon to sit on any district or appeals courts. He could not, however, return to private practice, and the decision whether or not to call him back to service as a federal judge remained the discretion of the chief justice.[131]

Not mentioned in the press releases was the root cause of Whittaker's breakdown or the extent of his disability. Following his announced retirement, Whittaker told reporters that the "great volume and continuous stresses of the Court's work had brought him to the point of physical exhaustion."[132] Several years later while he was still eligible to serve as a federal judge Whittaker again told reporters, "There was no let up in the pressure from the numerous questions which I regarded as extremely important. I suppose they weighed upon me too heavily."[133] As a result, the public continued to believe that the work of the Court proved too difficult or too demanding and that Whittaker simply broke under the strain. That impression explained only part of Whittaker's difficulties. The root of his disability was the depression that overcame him; doctors in Kansas City and Washington compounded his difficulties because they did not completely understand how to treat a disease like depression. "In retrospect, he was severely handicapped by the medical profession," his son, Keith, has commented, "They had the best of intentions, they just didn't know what they were doing."[134] Neither did Whittaker. Relying on a family friend from Kansas City, an orthopedist, Whittaker started taking barbiturates to treat his depression. Such a course led to his physical disabilities landing him in Walter Reed Hospital, but it did not address his emotional state. Once admitted, Whittaker's condition only worsened.

His wife, Winifred, stayed with Whittaker in a suite reserved for high government officials, and she called their son, Keith, an Air Force captain and recent medical school graduate living in Kansas City, to come to Washington immediately. Reluctant to leave his own patients but realizing the seriousness of his mother's request, Keith arrived in Washington and was shocked by what he found. His father was highly agitated, unable to sit still for any length of time. "It was clear to me that the doctors had no decent treatment for his agitation," Keith has said, "It was difficult to decide if he was so agitated because of the disease [depression] or the drugs they were giving him. I realized the drugs were causing his agitation."[135] Whittaker's doctors prescribed Thorazine, which resulted in a condition known as akathisia (extreme restlessness) and compounded his difficulty coping with his depression. By Sunday, March 11, Keith realized his father was suicidal. "When I saw him in Washington he was severely depressed," Keith has recalled, "He was making plans for suicide. I think he was ready to do it.... I'm sure he would have killed himself if I hadn't been there to stop him." It was a tense moment, there in the hospital, as Keith looked his father in the eye and made him promise not to go through with his plan: "He gave me his word that he would not go through with it. I think we were both relieved. He was a man who kept his word."[136]

Understandably, Whittaker's true condition was kept from the public. Even in Whittaker's office, news of his hospitalization came somewhat as a surprise. "We did not know he was ill," one of Whittaker's last term clerks has remarked, "There was not much information about where he was or why he was out of the office."[137] The impression of those who visited him, though, could not have been much different from Keith's; there was something terribly wrong with Whittaker, and the possibility of his recovering soon was remote. The question then became how should the Court proceed—with or without him? According to one of Warren's former clerks, Warren visited with Whittaker in the hospital and discussed the Court's work and Whittaker's difficulties. Upset by Whittaker's illness, Warren asked him, "What's wrong?"

"I just have so much difficulty making up my mind," Whittaker responded, "I agonize over it. Then when I make a decision I worry about it. How do you do it?"

"Early in my career," Warren answered, "I learned to make decisions and not let it worry me."

"That's not in my nature," Whittaker said.

"Your health is the most important thing you have," Warren told him, "Try to be philosophical about it."

"I don't know if I can," Whittaker admitted.[138]

With Whittaker's condition confounding his doctors and his behavior seemingly so erratic, Warren took steps to relieve Whittaker of his Court duties. Convening a panel of military physicians, Warren saw to it that Whittaker had to resign. On Friday, March 16, this panel certified that Whittaker suffered from a "permanent" medical disability and recommended he "be retired from the position of Associate Justice."[139] One of Whittaker's colleagues on the Court, Tom Clark, who was infuriated by Warren's actions, later confided to one of Whittaker's former clerks that the chief justice had acted to protect the Court's reputation, and, although he did not want Whittaker to leave the Court, Warren panicked when he realized the extent of Whittaker's disability.[140] By convincing Whittaker to retire as disabled rather than resigning his commission, Warren also acted to protect Whittaker's well being. As long as Whittaker remained in retired status, he could not aggravate his depression with overwork or financial worries. The terms of his retirement prevented him from engaging in private practice and offered limited financial security. Other than public appearances as a retired justice, Whittaker's professional activities were limited to serving on lower federal courts, and as long as Warren controlled those assignments he could monitor Whittaker's disability.

The same day his doctors certified Whittaker as permanently disabled Warren informed President John Kennedy of Whittaker's status and of his intention to retire as disabled. Whittaker then drafted a letter to the president certifying his disability, as required by federal law, but because his retirement did not become effective until April 1 no formal announcement was made. That gave the Kennedy administration two weeks to search for a successor outside the public spotlight.[141] The man they finally chose to replace Whittaker, Byron White, was then serving as deputy attorney general under the president's brother, Robert, in the Justice Department. Byron "Whizzer" White was widely known as an All-American collegiate football star who earned the highest professional salary in 1938 as a running back for the Pittsburgh Pirates. One of the top graduates in his class from Yale Law School, in 1946 White clerked for Chief Justice Fred Vinson. White first met the future president who appointed him to the Court at Oxford in 1939 while White studied law on a Rhodes scholarship and Kennedy's father served as United States ambassador to Great Britain. Their paths crossed again during World War II when White, a naval intelligence officer, wrote the report on the sinking of Kennedy's PT-109. Because of White's active campaigning and support for Kennedy in the 1960 presidential election, he was rewarded with the number two position at the Justice Department. With no prior judicial experience or elective office as qualifications, at age forty-four White became the youngest member of the Court.[142]

While the Kennedy administration considered its options, Whittaker waited to hear the news of his retirement. On Friday, March 23, one week after he informed the president of his disability, Whittaker left Walter Reed. He had spent the last eighteen days under observation but was nowhere near recovered when he left. As his son, Keith, put it, "There was no progress made when he left Walter Reed. He was far from well." Still depressed and suffering the effects of akathisia, Whittaker was dismissed because he had stayed long enough.[143] With no other medical alternatives available and his retirement from the Court imminent, it was agreed to let Whittaker go. Three days later, Monday, March 26, the Court handed down its historic decision in *Baker v. Carr* in six separate opinions lasting more than 160 pages. Although his retirement from the Court was not yet effective, Whittaker missed the proceedings.[144] He did not return to the Court again until after his retirement became official, making his first public appearance the following week on Tuesday, April 3, seated in the box seats reserved for guests of the justices.

On Thursday, March 29, President Kennedy held a thirty-minute press conference and announced Whittaker's retirement, effective April 1. The next day Kennedy announced his nomination of Byron White to take Whittaker's seat. White, who ordinarily would have headed the selection process for a new justice, was in Colorado at the time, and Kennedy called him two days prior to gain his acceptance.[145] After watching the televised address announcing Whittaker's retirement he and Winifred got into their car and left Washington. They drove for hours through the Maryland countryside, stopping now and then to sit in the sunshine and relax. When they returned to their Washington home Whittaker told a news reporter, "My reaction is one of relief.... Naturally all of this gave me a good deal of distress."[146] One of the many telephone calls that day came from Chief Justice Warren, who wanted to gauge Whittaker's reaction to the president's address. With a note of assurance Whittaker told Warren, "You've been awfully, awfully nice, and I appreciate it. I'm coming right along and the doctors are pleased. I'm a different man from the time you last saw me."[147]

In many respects Whittaker was different when he left Walter Reed. His decision to leave the Court had a restorative effect upon him, and Whittaker could better cope with the depression that had recently overwhelmed him. To people at the Court, the change in Whittaker's demeanor was immediately apparent. One of Whittaker's former clerks who saw him soon after his release from the hospital has remarked, "It may have been his first day back to the Court. I asked him how he felt. He said he felt as though the biggest weight of the world had been lifted from his shoulders."[148] So pronounced was his reinvigoration that Whittaker went to see his friend on the Court, Justice Harlan, explaining that retirement was an enormous relief and recommending it as a way of restoring one's life.[149] Even Whittaker's physical appearance improved. One of Frankfurter's former clerks has remembered seeing Whittaker outside the Court just a few weeks after his retirement and noting, "He appeared relaxed, refreshed, and more robust than I ever recalled."[150] Certainly, leaving the Court marked a dramatic change for Whittaker giving him the opportunity to concentrate on his recovery from depression, but leaving Walter Reed signaled the beginning of his recovery, not the end. Whittaker still had a long way to go before his body and mind were fully restored.

Whittaker's improved outlook so soon after his release from the hospital raised speculation that maybe his illness was not so severe. Some believed his buoyancy indicated a full recovery; others thought that Whittaker's plans to retire after five years were abetted by his hospital stay. If he had intended to retire after five years because of disappointment or discomfort, then he could not have picked a worse time. The truth was, Whittaker had to leave the Court when he did because he suffered from a serious, debilitating illness that threatened to jeopardize his physical and emotional health. According to his three children, it took Whittaker more than a year to fully recover both physically and emotionally. During that time he was still restive and depressed, putting great strain on his family who cared for him. The doctors who treated him at the Kansas University Medical Center in Kansas City had no better idea how to relieve his depression than had the doctors at Walter Reed. Only time and rest were able to restore Whittaker to relative salubrity.[151]

Unlike other living ex-justices in retirement, Whittaker chose not to remain in Washington and occupy an upstairs auxiliary office in the Supreme Court building. Instead, he and Winifred made arrangements to move back to Kansas City, and Whittaker worked out of offices in the downtown federal courthouse where he had served as a district judge. One of the last functions in which Whittaker participated while still in Washington was to be present for the swearing in of his replacement, Byron White. Standing in the conference room on Monday, April 16, as White took the constitutional oath were the members of the Court (except for Frankfurter, who was hospitalized following his stroke) and three recently retired justices, Stanley Reed, Harold Burton, and Whittaker. Four days later Charles and Winifred were back home in Kansas City where they continued to live the rest of their lives. With all of their family and closest friends still living in the Kansas City area there was no reason for them to remain in Washington. In fact, according to one of Whittaker's sons, were it not for attending funerals of former justices Whittaker might never have set foot in the Supreme Court again.[152]

Undoubtedly Whittaker's recovery was speeded by his returning home to familiar places and comfortable company. In time Whittaker anticipated hopefully to be judging again at either the district court in Kansas City or one of the federal courts of appeals. Recognizing the need to slow down and relax for a while, that first summer away from the Supreme Court the Whittakers stayed several weeks at a friend's home in the mountains of Colorado. One of Whittaker's former law associates was renting a cottage nearby, and the two became reacquainted. "He was like a pea on a hot griddle," this associate recalled of Whittaker's condition, "He had an interest span of about twenty minutes. He would play catch, then tire. He would read some, then sit on the porch and talk to my twelve-year-old daughter."[153] Gradually Whittaker's condition improved, and he and Winifred took up residence in an apartment near the stylish Country Club Plaza area of Kansas City as they waited to purchase a home. From his office in the downtown federal courthouse Whittaker conducted correspondence and awaited his next judicial assignment. On occasion former Supreme Court clerks stopped by to see him. Whittaker's first clerk, Alan Kohn, who had been with him through the first three devastating months when it looked like Whittaker might suffer a nervous breakdown, has remembered how Whittaker looked "as though a millstone had been lifted off his neck."[154] Another clerk, Patrick McCartan, from Whittaker's third term when Whittaker began "standing on his own two feet," has recalled how visits to Whittaker's office always ended up in the library talking about cases they had worked on together and how "Whittaker just couldn't keep out of the books!"[155]

As a justice, Charles Whittaker was unremarkable. Had he stayed on the

Supreme Court longer than five years then chances were he would have failed to achieve a standing much higher than that accorded him when branded a "failure" by Court experts. No doubt, his short tenure did not improve his overall rating. There were good reasons for judging Whittaker as less accomplished than others who faced similar challenges. Not destined to become a leading member of the Court, Whittaker was satisfied simply with "finding his feet." To degrade his service, though, with ridicule and contempt because of a few isolated and suspect incidents is to take too narrow a view of his work or the circumstances surrounding his departure. Whittaker was not a "failure" because he was too naive at times, nor did he "fail" because he accepted assistance when offered. Neither was his nervous breakdown the result of continual harassment weakened by indecision. Any judgment of Whittaker's difficulties must be tempered by recognizing the numerous subtle and not so subtle influences causing strain throughout his five years of service. Most important, a sympathetic understanding of the illness that afflicted him and how he struggled to cope with it before it finally forced him to resign surely must mitigate the severity of such an ignoble classification as "failure."

After five tumultuous years, Whittaker's Supreme Court service ended as obscurely as it began. Few people outside of Kansas City ever realized that a Kansas farmboy had once served on the nation's highest court. Whittaker's reputation rested not on the public's recognition, but rather on the limited yet real impact he had made on practicing lawyers. At the news of Whittaker's retirement a Baltimore lawyer wrote to him, "Not only I but a vast number of lawyers throughout the country are deeply conscious of the notable contribution you have made to the work of the Court and the maintenance of its high standards during your tenure on the Court. You have been a stabilizing element and you have never departed from a truly lawyerlike approach to legal issues there."[156] Now Whittaker was back in Kansas City, his home for over thirty-five years, working from an office in the federal courthouse, the one place he still felt at ease. His service to the Court had not remarkably effected its direction, nor were any of his written opinions publicly regarded as profoundly significant. In retirement Whittaker might have been content to watch national events unfold from the comfortable environs of his Kansas City office. He could have spent his remaining years waiting for the chance to judge again, and, for a time, he was willing to bide his time in this way. As a retired justice, however, unburdened from the monastic isolation of his Court duties, Whittaker was free to engage in public appearances, which inevitably drew him into discourse on the most pressing social and legal issues of the day. Free to speak his mind, yet restrained by his sense of propriety, Whittaker gained more recognition and received greater press coverage in retirement than he ever did as an associate justice.

7

Speaking Out

When Charles Whittaker returned to Kansas City, Missouri, following his departure from the Supreme Court his expectation was that, in time, he would resume judicial service as a temporary district or appeals court judge. He looked forward expectantly to such an assignment. At age sixty-one Whittaker had no desire to return to the world of private practice, and with the slower schedule and lighter burdens of temporary appeals court assignments he could look forward to a comfortable and gratifying retirement. His expectations, however, like his plans to continue as a district court judge longer than two years, went unrealized. As much as Whittaker yearned to return to the trial courtroom he had loved since his youth, Chief Justice Earl Warren deprived him of that. Whittaker never again judged a case in federal court. As a result, he began accepting other offers for his services, most notably making public appearances.

At first his status as a retired Supreme Court justice drew attention primarily from the legal community. He enjoyed his newfound celebrity and welcomed opportunities to engage socially with other lawyers and bar leaders. Then two years after his retirement from the Court Whittaker broke onto the public stage with speeches and articles addressing some of the most potent and emotionally charged issues of the day: race relations, civil disobedience, and the pending Civil Rights Act. He followed that up with a speech that many considered an indictment of the Supreme Court, and Whittaker's reputation as the "voice of discontent" spread. The following year he produced his most popular and widely reproduced speech calling for an end to violence and a return to the rule of law. As the demands for justice and equal treatment in the mid 1960s led to widespread violent confrontations between whites and African Americans, Whittaker's call for calm, deliberative discourse to settle differences and the prompt, even-handed enforcement of law appealed to many Americans. With solicitations to write on, speak about, and to endorse a range of causes, Whittaker found himself in retirement more publicly recognized than ever before.

History has not been kind to Whittaker, no more so in retirement than when he served on the Supreme Court. During the social unrest of the 1960s Whittaker became personally involved in public discourse on the ramifications of the Civil Rights movement and expanding federal intervention in that field, yet just after Whittaker's death in 1973 the *New York Times* reported, "Following his retirement, Mr. Whittaker played little part in public life. As the practice of civil disobedience spread in the mid-nineteen-sixties, he wrote an article on it for the F.B.I. Law Enforcement Bulletin."[1] Initially, Whittaker presented his ideas on the Civil Rights movement in June 1965 in a speech before the Tennessee Bar Association. That presentation, at the urging of the association's Nashville president, was then reproduced (over 5,000 copies) and distributed to all the members of the association, the House of Representatives, the Senate, and the president of the United States. Senator Strom Thurmond, a South Carolina Republican, read the speech into the *Congressional Record*, and it reappeared in full text in numerous publications, including *U. S. News & World Report*, the *New York State Bar Journal*, the *Illinois State Bar Journal*, the *Chicago Tribune*, the *Philadelphia Inquirer*, the *New Haven Register*, the *Nashville Banner*, and the *Shreveport Times*. In all, Whittaker estimated that over six million copies of the full speech were printed and circulated.[2] The next year Whittaker rearranged his ideas from the Tennessee Bar address and presented them to the *F.B.I. Law Enforcement Bulletin*, which again received full-text coverage in *U.S. News & World Report* with over two million subscribers.[3] To characterize Whittaker's involvement in the public policy debates of the 1960s as little more than contributing one article to the *F.B.I. Law Enforcement Bulletin* grossly underestimated the extent of his involvement, the wide range of topics he addressed, and the impact of his pronouncements.

To a large extent Whittaker's exposure as a public speaker during the 1960s has been overlooked because he did not espouse the popularly held views of many Americans who supported the aims and strategies of civil rights protests. For example, he objected to the Civil Rights Act of 1964 because he could find no constitutional basis for such an expansion of federal power even though he supported the aims of civil rights leaders who wanted to end state sponsored segregation. Why would Whittaker assume such a controversial stance as a retired justice? According to his son, Kent, "He had no other motive to speak than a genuine concern for society. He sincerely wanted to speak."[4] As a result of his popularity, Whittaker made certain that one of the conditions met when he agreed to go to work for General Motors in 1965 was that he maintained absolute freedom to continue speaking publicly. During negotiations with representatives from General Motors on the terms of Whittaker's employment, he insisted that he retain "complete freedom to speak publicly on any issue not involving General Motors corporation," and in the final contract between Whittaker and General Motors it was agreed that he retained complete independence from General Motors and remained free to speak out on public issues.[5]

Whittaker's position with General Motors as national arbitrator for dealer disputes further weakened his reputation as a retired justice, since it seemed to many that his acceptance of the position followed closely after his retirement from the Supreme Court and constituted the whole of his retirement activities. Del Dickson, for example, in describing Whittaker's departure from the Court, noted how Whittaker "refused to participate in the decision after conference [*Baker v. Carr*], then suddenly quit the Court the following week and went to work for General Motors."[6] Kim Eisler, likewise, summarized Whittaker's retirement by stating, "One week later [after the announcement of *Baker v. Carr*] Whittaker quit the Court and took a job with General Motors."[7] The general impression was that Whittaker's retirement resulted almost immediately in a position with General Motors, or, at least, that his position with General Motors was his most significant activity during retirement.[8] Notwithstanding his many public appearances urging an end to violent demonstrations and a return to peaceful resolution of disputes, Whittaker was also involved in several other extrajudicial activities, serving in an advisory capacity for the American Bar Association (ABA), the American Medical Association (AMA), and the United States Senate. It was in these extrajudicial activities, most notably his public speeches, that Whittaker made his most significant contributions to society during retirement. More importantly, Whittaker did not join General Motors until October 1965, three and a half years after he left the Supreme Court. His decision to resign his judicial commission and go to work for General Motors had more to do with his family's financial well-being than any desire to return to private practice.

Even before Whittaker resigned his judicial commission to go to work for General Motors he made an address that to many observers seemed to publicly disparage the Supreme Court and its recent decisions. At least, that was the impression that later historians presented. Henry Abraham, for example, brazenly asserted, "Whittaker has the rare distinction of being the only modern Supreme Court justice publicly to criticize not only the Court's sitting members, but the institution itself."[9] This impression of Whittaker leaving the Court disappointed and then publicly railing the Court in retirement persisted, leading Theodore Vestal to observe how Whittaker "attacked the Court's decisions and even some of the justices in widely reported remarks, notably in a 1964 speech before the American Bar Association."[10] Such an impression portrayed Whittaker as the disgruntled justice who hated his Court service so much that in retirement he never tired of criticizing it. This impression also established Whittaker as the lone voice of discontent, crying out against the abuses of the Court while other retired justices and sitting justices in particular remained above the fray. Such an impression was largely inaccurate with respect to both Whittaker and other justices. While he served on the Court and long afterwards, several of Whittaker's colleagues spoke openly about their views of the Court and its proper functioning. Some were more considerate in their remarks than others, but the inescapable conclusion was that these justices freely expressed what they thought was wrong with the Court and with some of its decisions.

Whittaker's liberal colleagues on the Court, for example, had no misgivings about criticizing recent Court decisions they believed were wrongly decided, even as they continued to serve on the Court.[11] It was not at all unusual for justices to speak out on the proper functioning of the Court, even to criticize its recent decisions. What was surprising at the time was how Whittaker's reputation evolved to become "a *frequent critic* of the Court's role and of the tendency toward concentrating more power in the Federal Government" by the time he resigned his judicial commission.[12] In the one speech mentioned to support such a claim, his address before the ABA in October 1964, Whittaker made certain to add to the final copy of his draft a statement declining to refer to any recent federal legislative or judicial actions, definitions, or interpretations because, he said, "[T]hey might be thought to be involved in current Judicial controversies or political debates."[13] Confining his remarks to an analysis of the Court's decision in *National Labor Relations Board v. Jones & Laughlin Steel Company,* decided twenty-seven years earlier, Whittaker was careful to avoid even the semblance of impropriety with regards to the Court on which he served and its decisions while he served or afterwards. The impression persisted, however, that Whittaker had lambasted the Court in his 1964 speech, causing many to wonder if he had left the Court disgruntled in order to lash back at it. Responding to a *Washington Post* story covering his speech, Whittaker wrote to Judge Samuel E. Whitaker on the U. S. Court of Claims, "Not only did I not attack the present Court but also how careful I was to avoid any reference to it by referring only to events that preceded the tenure of the present Justices." If Whittaker had wanted to express his disapproval for recent Court decisions, he wrote, "I could have written a stronger, more modern, and better speech."[14] So chafed was Whittaker by press reports that he had "attacked" the Supreme Court that soon after his speech he began to open his correspondence to friends with, "Perhaps I should precede my speeches with a statement of what I am not saying."

Whittaker's public statements addressing social protests, particularly violence accompanying the Civil Rights movement, were far more numerous and widely circulated than his speeches about the Supreme Court, yet accusations of him "attacking" the Court have received greater historical recognition. Instead of "attacking" the Court, Whittaker strove to preserve its integrity and protect it from assault. Around the same time that Whittaker delivered his speech before the ABA he also declined to submit an article to the St. Louis University Law School for a symposium analyzing decisions of the Supreme Court since 1950 because, he explained, of his past and present relationships with members of the Court.[15] A couple of months later, probably in response to the publicity surrounding his ABA speech, Whittaker received a book solicitation from a New York literary agent suggesting the title, "Is the Supreme Court Going Too Far?" Hoping to attract Whittaker to the deal, the agent offered the book "might be a kind of minority opinion such as you might have liked to render had you been on the Court at the time." Whittaker responded immediately with a terse refusal, noting, "I believe it would be an impropriety for me."[16] Even before his October 1964 speech to the ABA Whittaker had a strict policy of not commenting when asked about current Court cases. In an interview just one month before his controversial ABA speech, the *Kansas City Star* reported on Whittaker's refusal to discuss any of the legal aspects of cases then pending before the Court. "I just do not feel it would be appropriate in my circumstances," Whittaker explained, "to express any views concerning the constitutionality of public questions which are now before the Court such as the new Civil Rights Act or the controversial apportionment litigation. Any expression of my views on these matters would be unseemly, might be regarded as intermeddling and would be wholly inappropriate."[17]

Whittaker's defense of the Court began while he was still an active justice, when he began making public appearances speaking before bar association audiences about his experiences as a lawyer. Full of humility and adopting a "just one of the boys" attitude, Whittaker amused his audiences with recollections of his days at trial as he struggled with "pains of inadequacy" and was "almost constantly plagued with doubts about how best to cope with the arts and wiles of opposing counsel."[18] He always opened his remarks with modest self-deprecation, describing himself as a "curio" or "something that they hoped might pack 'em in, a person that people would turn out not so much to hear as to see."[19] Following a long train of reminiscences and clever anecdotes that usually found Whittaker bested by his opponents or confounded by the law's perplexities, Whittaker closed his address with an appeal for understanding and respect for the Court. "Being composed of human beings, the Court has doubtless made mistakes and will make them in the future, regardless of who may be its justices," Whittaker told his audiences, "I cannot ask you to value our work, but I do hope you will understand what it entails, and, when you do, I am sure you will at least respect our endurance."[20]

Once Whittaker was off the Court he continued to make similar speeches before bar association audiences, but his defense of Court decisions became more aggressive. In the fall of 1963 he told the annual meeting of the Nebraska State Bar, "You are entitled to your view. I am not a salesman, nor here for sales purposes. Everyone has the right—indeed, a constitutional right protected by the guarantees of the First Amendment—to speak his mind on all public questions and institutions.... But this thought I wish to leave with you: If criticism is to serve any worthy purpose, must it not be advised, temperate, and responsible? Much of it is not."[21] Whittaker then made reference to three Court decisions, two recently decided since his departure from the Court and the other then a decade old, which presented some of the most emotionally charged issues related to public schools: race and religion. Continuing, Whittaker said, "A fair example is the statement, recently oft repeated, respecting the segregation and the prayer and Bible reading cases, that 'the Supreme Court put the Negroes in and kicked God out of the schools.' Now, my friends, of that type and kind of criticism the most charitable thing I can say is that it is made without understanding of the problems presented, of the commands of governing constitutional provisions, or of what the Court actually decided."[22] Concluding his speech, Whittaker offered his audience the creed by which he had lived as a lawyer, as a judge, and which he still defended as a retired justice: "[I]t is of the essence of orderly government that the Court's decisions, so long as it is charged with the responsibility of decision, must be accepted and obeyed."[23]

Once he was off the Supreme Court, Whittaker's last remaining goal was to return to the lower courts and resume judicial service. Since the conditions of his retirement precluded him from returning to private practice, he planned instead to make himself available to one of the several courts of appeal in the country. Unlike retired Justices Stanley Reed and Harold Burton, Whittaker chose not to remain in Washington and accept assignments to the U. S. Court of Appeals for the District of Columbia or to the U. S. Court of Claims. Instead, he and Winifred returned to Kansas City and took up temporary residence at 1001 West Sixty-first Terrace so he could work out of an office in the downtown federal courthouse (within a few years they moved into a more luxurious home in Mission Hills, Kansas).[24] Not long after they arrived in Kansas City the *Kansas City Times* reported that Whittaker was eager to sit on one of the courts of appeal when the new term resumed in September and that he had already received several inquiries from various federal appeals judges regarding his availability for special cases.[25] The only consideration potentially limiting Whittaker's ability to judge again was his health. Having suffered a nervous breakdown leading to his hospitalization did not necessarily preclude Whittaker from further judicial service—Justice Burton, after all, retired at age seventy suffering from Parkinson's disease but judged on the U. S. Court of Appeals for four terms before his condition worsened. During that time, Burton's disease was "apparently under reasonable control."[26] By contrast, Whittaker was still relatively young at age sixty-one, but his prognosis was unclear. In July he wrote to his friend and former Court colleague, Tom Clark, "I am making steady, if somewhat slow, progress toward regaining my strength, and have, tentatively, agreed to sit on the Eighth Circuit beginning September 13. I expect, and certainly hope, to be able to resume work at that time."[27] By late August Whittaker's plans to join the Eighth Circuit, as well as an improved outlook, became more definite. He wrote Justice Felix Frankfurter just after Frankfurter's retirement, "As for me, I am at work in preparation for the hearing of arguments to be presented to the Eighth Circuit at St. Louis where I will be sitting for the period of September 10th through September 21st. I am steadily feeling better day by day, thank God, and am hopeful that I may soon be restored to my old vigor and enthusiasm."[28]

There was no evidence, however, that Whittaker served on the Eighth Circuit in the fall of 1962 or on any other court of appeal. When Whittaker resigned his judicial commission in October 1965, giving up forever the possibility of judging again in the federal courts, he had yet to serve on temporary assignment in retired status. For three and a half years Whittaker waited for a judicial assignment. Press reports of Whittaker's leaving the federal judiciary suggested that he had not served on temporary assignment because he chose not to or because his health would not permit it.[29] Whittaker's letters indicated, however, that he both desired and was prepared for temporary duty. At the end of his first year of retirement, Whittaker wrote to a friend, "I expect to start sitting next September [1963] on various ones of the Courts of Appeals. In all, there is a silver lining in the clouds again."[30] One year later the *Kansas City Star* confirmed that Whittaker was still eligible to sit on any lower federal court and that he had received numerous requests for assistance from different courts of appeal, but, the *Star* reported, he had not accepted any of them. According to the *Star*, "In the future, he says, he may accept assignments to serve as needed on one or another of the appellate courts."[31]

What happened to quash Whittaker's enthusiasm to judge again? In the fall of 1962, still in his first year of retirement, Whittaker continued to receive requests from courts of appeals for assistance. His plans to join the Eighth Circuit in September had fallen through, but later that same month one of his former clerks wrote him, "Incidentally, Judge [Elbert] Tuttle was in our office the other day, and told me he had been in touch with you regarding the possibility of your sitting with the Fifth Circuit in the near future."[32] In order to judge again, Whittaker needed the chief judge of a judicial circuit to assign him to a case, and in December 1962 Whittaker wrote Alfred Murrah, chief judge of the Tenth Circuit, "My strength and health continue to improve and I am anxious, perhaps over-anxious, to get back into a judicial routine."[33]

Whittaker's expectations of judging again were dashed by the one man who controlled his fate as a retired justice, the chief justice of the United States, Earl Warren. Convinced that Whittaker would continue to suffer making decisions and not wanting to aggravate Whittaker's depression further, Warren never consented to further judicial duty, reportedly saying, "I never could get him to make up his mind.... So the answer is no."[34] To lend credence to Warren's personal misgivings about Whittaker's abilities, according to Whittaker's own records, Warren "required" Whittaker to return to Washington in March 1963 for an examination by a "board of doctors at Walter Reed General Hospital ... to determine [his] fitness for resumption of judicial service."[35] Whether it was based on the doctors' recommendations or Warren's own reluctance, Whittaker never received Warren's permission to judge again in federal courts.[36]

Not content to wait idly through his retirement for judicial service, Whittaker became active in other civic, legal, and community affairs. In Kansas City he took an interest in the merger of the University of Kansas City with the University of Missouri, and he participated in promoting the construction of a new Children's Mercy Hospital. On the national level Whittaker became active in the AMA's Citizen's Committee on Graduate Medical Education, which made an in-depth study of postgraduate medical education, and he served several years on a committee headed by Dr. John S. Millis, which was established to promote general practice in medicine. In July 1963 the ABA's Section of Judicial Administration had him chair a Sectional Committee on Advocacy in response to the Supreme Court's decision in *Gideon v. Wainwright,* which required that counsel be appointed to all indigent defendants charged with a serious offense in state criminal trials.[37] About this same time Whittaker was also asked to serve as arbitrator to settle a labor dispute between Jay Bee Toy Creations and one of its laid off employees. Both sides in the dispute initially agreed to arbitration, and Whittaker accepted the appointment seeing no conflict of interests. One side, however, later objected and the hearing never took place, causing the lawyer who arranged to have Whittaker serve as arbitrator to jokingly bemoan how he had always wanted to argue before the Supreme Court, either individually or collectively.[38] By mid 1964 Whittaker had appeared several times as a guest speaker before bar association audiences and had written several articles for legal journals. As a result of all these extrajudicial activities, two years into his retirement Whittaker appeared less anxious that he was not judging again. He wrote to a friend, "Technically I am 'retired,' but the word 'retreaded' would more nearly describe my status.... I am eligible to serve on any Federal Court except the Supreme Court, but because I have become so busy in numerous *pro bono publico* [for the good of the people] matters ... I do not have the time nor, indeed, the inclination to accept any judicial assignments."[39]

The pleasure Whittaker once derived from arguing cases or conducting trials he now obtained from making speeches and writing articles. He found, too, that as a retired justice his views and his appearances, particularly among the legal community, received greater attention than he might otherwise have received on his own. Had he confined his rhetoric to strictly legal matters—those concerns of the bench and bar that were the exclusive focus of his early writings—then Whittaker might have escaped public notice altogether.[40] As it was, beginning in February 1964 Whittaker captured both headlines and the public's attention with his comments related to one of the most critical issues confronting the nation—race relations and the passage of a new Civil Rights Act. As conditions in many cities around the country degenerated into violent confrontations and retaliatory action, Whittaker boldly stepped up and spoke out on the issue.[41]

Unfortunately for Whittaker, when read in the light of the great gains made by African Americans at the time only at great risks to their own personal safety, his remarks on civil rights and social protests by comparison seemed shallow and ill-conceived. While his intentions were good—calling for mutual respect, calm and responsible dialogue, and obedience to laws as the only practicable means of resolving disputes—his message oftentimes came across as paternalistic and hopelessly out of touch with the aims of civil rights protesters. At the same time, however, his message struck a chord with many Americans who were fearful of the rising tide of racial unrest and uncertain where it would lead. Like many who shared his conservative ideals, Whittaker believed that those involved in civil rights protests were moving too fast, were behaving with unwarranted and irresponsible impatience, and were forcing their demands on the federal government, the states, and cities without the proper authoritative right to do so. Because his credibility as a justice had not been questioned while he served on the Supreme Court, now that he was a retired justice his credibility to speak out on important social issues was equally above suspicion. Like the riots that followed the March 23, 1963, shooting of an African American woman in Jacksonville, Florida, Whittaker was about to make headlines across the country.

By the time Whittaker made his first public pronouncements on civil rights protests and racial unrest, the movement for racial equality had undergone dramatic shifts in direction, leadership, and effects as new methods were employed and new associations formed. Moving away from the legal based activities of the National Association for the Advancement of Colored People (NAACP) to end racial segregation, protests took the form of direct action, as exemplified by the Montgomery bus boycott of 1956. From the success of that effort a new association, the Southern Christian Leadership Conference (SCLC) and its leader, Dr. Martin Luther King, Jr., emerged to challenge the predominance of the NAACP and groups like the Congress of Racial Equality, which had battled racial discrimination for decades. The youth movement, initiated in February 1960 when four college students sought to integrate a Woolworth's lunch counter in Greensboro, North Carolina, led to the creation of the Student Nonviolent Coordinating Committee. These different groups, all striving towards the same ends, at times competed for resources and recognition. To think that the Civil Rights movement was conducted under one banner, using similar tactics at all times throughout the country, was to oversimplify the wide range of interests and methods employed. Dr. King's message of nonviolent passive resistance and the militant separatism advocated by Black Nationalist leader Malcolm X came to define the polar positions within the movement. Whether it was white molestation of peaceful protesters or angry African American youths engaged in riotous looting, violence seemed always to linger just below the movement's activities, ready to erupt at a moment's notice and engulf whole communities.[42]

The graphic use of violence to thwart racial integration became abundantly clear during the Freedom Rides of May 1961, as interstate bus passengers traveling through states of the deep south were routinely and brutally beaten along the way. Local law enforcement turned aside as vigilante groups like the Ku Klux Klan assaulted the freedom riders, and when the Kennedy administration sought to intervene by sending federal marshals in for protection (too little, too late by some accounts as the F.B.I. had adequate warning that the riders were going to be ambushed), the governor of Alabama, John Patterson, decried the use of federal force. The charge leveled by many, including Patterson, was that by invading southern states from outside and agitating the local populations, the freedom riders were, in fact, responsible for the violence that greeted them.

Two years later in Birmingham, Alabama, a new strategy of massive marches, which included school-age children, had a pronounced effect. The nation witnessed through media coverage the brutal tactics of city police commissioner Eugene "Bull" Connor as he let loose attack dogs and high pressure fire hoses on the throngs of peaceful marchers. As expected, violence followed once a settlement was reached in Birmingham respecting the gradual desegregation of certain public accommodations; bombings in the city directed against African Americans led to riots and armed conflict between the two sides. As a result of the violence in Birmingham, in June 1963 President Kennedy sent to Congress a comprehensive Civil Rights bill, which covered public accommodations, schools, voting rights, and equal employment. The stage was now set for a political showdown over civil rights as city after city in both the south and the north experienced intermittent violence.

Many Americans were confused and alarmed by the seemingly sudden, widespread reports of violence related to civil rights protests. Especially alarming was the perceived militancy of the movement following Birmingham. Retaliatory action frequently followed assaults on African Americans, and fear became the prevailing mood for many who were unused to their daily complacency being threatened. These were the conditions Whittaker witnessed as he formulated his ideas on civil rights and the drive for social equality. Much of the information he gathered and the inspiration he received came from *U.S. News & World Report* magazine, whose editor, David Lawrence, shared similar conservative views.[43] Lawrence believed the protesters themselves provoked the violence that always seemed to accompany civil rights protests, whether or not they initiated or perpetrated the violence. He saw the protests taking place all around the country as organized pressure, forcing the courts and the president into acquiescing to the demands of the protesters. Rather than submitting to the threats and demands of civil rights protesters, Lawrence considered constitutional amendment the only legitimate means for achieving the ends they sought.

In his first public address on civil rights Whittaker chose not to express an opinion on the pending Civil Rights bill before Congress or how it might stand up to a court challenge, but he clearly had misgivings about the constitutionality of its public accommodations section. He reminded his audiences that the Supreme Court in 1883 had declared a similar provision of the 1875 Civil Rights Act unconstitutional. Relying on a rigid, simplistic interpretation, Whittaker cautioned his audiences against ascribing to words like "public" and "private" meanings that, he felt, carried the words beyond their true definitions. Without using accusatory language or inflammatory rhetoric, Whittaker then ascribed much of the tension created by social protests to the use, intentional or otherwise, of what he considered "catchwords" and "clichés." The best way to defuse the passions and prejudices generated by these "clichés" was through the use of calm, responsible, and cooperative reasoning.[44]

Whittaker's charges against civil rights protests were both applauded and reproduced in *U. S. News & World Report* and the *Wall Street Journal*.[45] His sentiments questioning the "public accommodations" section of the proposed Civil Rights bill before Congress and the constitutional justifications for "integration" (which he could find none) became so popular that he was asked to reproduce them in a speech before the State Bar of Texas in the summer of 1964. While his speech before the Texas Bar repeated many of his earlier claims regarding "catchwords" and "clichés," it also reflected his growing concern for recent developments. In Atlanta, Georgia, youths were arrested after lying down and blocking the entries of hotels and restaurants, and in Maryland a race riot erupted when protesters attempted to march into an all white residential area. Concern grew over new nonviolent tactics, like stalling cars on motorways, wasting a city's water supply, or engaging in rent strikes. Press predictions of another violent summer of racial clashes persisted as Malcolm X decided to meet violence with violence, forming his own Black Nationalist Party and encouraging his followers to defend themselves with force. With the Civil Rights bill stalled in the Senate because of a southern-mounted filibuster, civil rights leaders declared they had no intentions of relieving pressure or halting demonstrations. In Jacksonville, Florida, impatience with nonviolence led gangs of youths to employ guns, knives, and "Molotov cocktails" as they rioted, attacking whites and damaging or looting stores. Fear gripped the nation as many prepared for more retaliatory action. One Mississippi official was quoted as saying, "We are more concerned about what the whites will do this summer than we are about what the Negroes will do."[46] Part of that concern centered on the voter registration campaign taking place in Mississippi as hundreds of white college students traveled to (or invaded, depending on one's perspective) the state. The fears of many northern whites were realized when three civil rights workers, two of them young white men from New York, turned up missing.[47]

In this atmosphere of racial unrest and heightened anxiety across much of the nation, Whittaker prepared, reluctantly, to deliver his new speech, entitled "Immutable Moral Values," to the Texas Bar on July 3, 1964, the day after President Johnson signed into law the new Civil Rights Act. Much of the speech remained unchanged from his earlier pronouncements, but, because of recent violent clashes between whites and African Americans and threats of more to come, Whittaker added stronger language to the opening section, indicting not only those who perpetrated violent actions but also those who led demonstrations regardless of their intentions. He did this, he explained, because "I feel a duty to my country, to my fellow men—to the involved minorities no less than others—to speak out in protest, and also to plead, I hope both temperately and seemly, for the preservation of peace and good order of our land, and of the majesty and dominance of its laws, by the prompt, impartial and vigorous prosecution and punishment, under those laws, of all conduct that violates those laws."[48] Now Whittaker took aim directly at Dr. Martin Luther King, Jr., (without actually naming King) for prompting the demonstrations that inevitably led to violent clashes, blaming King for inciting his followers to conduct mass demonstrations on private property and then excusing himself from responsibility once violence ensued. Whittaker also leveled charges against federal authorities or those in "high places" who approved of King's activities and who failed to prosecute King's followers for what Whittaker considered common trespass and disturbance of the peace. In a passage whose theme would be repeated many times over in future speeches, Whittaker said, "Whatever may have been, or may be, the provocations, neither men, nor races of men, can be permitted in a government of laws, to take the law, or what they may think is, or ought to be, the law, into their own hands, either in initial or in retaliatory actions, for that is anarchy and sure to result in chaos."[49]

Seeing many of the sit-in and lie-down demonstrations of civil rights protesters as violations of criminal trespass laws, Whittaker relied on the dissenting opinion of Justice Hugo Black in *Bell v. Maryland* to support his views. Although Black had been a leading proponent on the Court in the expansion of civil liberties and personal freedoms, he saw direct physical protests as a threat to maintaining public order.[50] Relying on Black's dissent in *Bell*, Whittaker emphasized his central theme, namely, "[T]he Constitution does not confer upon any group the right to substitute rule by force for the rule of law."[51] Taking aim at the new Civil Rights Act and its public accommodations provision, Whittaker made clear his views on the scope of the Act; he did not construe "public" accommodations to extend to privately owned and operated businesses. According to Whittaker's understanding of the Fourteenth Amendment, as long as neither the state or its agents engaged in discriminatory practices, then no violations could occur. The law could not effect private discrimination in privately run businesses. Whittaker said so in a newspaper interview conducted a few months later: "The Fourteenth Amendment, of course, applies only to action by a state. It does not apply to discriminatory action by individuals."[52] Supporting Black's views in *Bell*, Whittaker went on to note that when privately owned businesses refuse service to customers, no "state action" was involved. As a result, Whittaker argued, privately owned businesses were free to choose their own customers. Neither the new Civil Rights Act nor the Fourteenth Amendment should be allowed to "destroy what has until very recently been universally recognized in this country as the unchallenged right of a man who owns a business to run the business in his own way."[53]

Whittaker's conservative views on the proper scope of the Civil Rights Act and his interpretation of the reach of the Fourteenth Amendment ultimately proved unpersuasive. The Court had since moved to a more activist posture respecting the protection of "discrete and insular minorities."[54] As the momentum of the Civil Rights movement inspired (some would say pressured) Congress and the executive to extend more and more federal protection to African Americans, Whittaker's rationale separating "private" from "public" facilities, based as it was on an outmoded "state action" doctrine, seemed anachronistic. The result of such a mechanical separation would have meant continued segregation of the races in most areas of social intercourse save those strictly limited to state governmental actions. Such a course was no longer possible given the tremendous expansion of federal regulatory power since World War II over so much of what had previously been considered rightful state authority. Whittaker, however, continued to adhere to the antebellum ideal of dual federalism, whereby the states through their reserved powers guaranteed by the Tenth Amendment were placed on an equal footing with the federal government, each supreme within its own sphere. This idea of state sovereignty free from the interposition of federal authority suited the aims of southern segregationists who wanted to forestall the implementation of Court mandated integration for as long as possible.

The new Civil Rights Act did not depend upon the Thirteenth or Fourteenth Amendments for congressional authority to pass legislation directed against incidents of private discrimination. Instead, the Supreme Court sustained the new law on the basis of Congress's power to regulate commerce (Article 1, Section 8, clause 3).[55] With a broad reading of the commerce clause, federal law could affect all areas of business activity, making possible the eventual integration of what were previously considered private establishments. Such a broad interpretation of the commerce power became the subject of Whittaker's next significant speech, one that came to be associated most with Whittaker's dissatisfaction with the Court. Ironically, this one presentation in October 1964 before the Southern Regional Meeting of the ABA, the only presentation Whittaker ever made concerning the commerce clause, became the one speech most often cited in connection with Whittaker's retirement activities; yet, his presentations related to civil disobedience and the breakdown of law and order were more numerous and far more controversial. This speech, "A Confusion of Tongues," when compared to his later invectives against civil rights leaders and their complicity in provoking violent actions, actually was quite tame and did not, as Henry Abraham charged, "criticize not only the Court's sitting members, but the institution itself." In reality, this speech was little more than a history lesson, albeit a heavily slanted one, describing the causes of and changes in interpretation of the commerce clause relative to expanding federal powers.

The new president-elect of the ABA and future Supreme Court justice, Lewis Powell, first contacted Whittaker about speaking for the annual meeting of the ABA in late January 1964, before Whittaker had publicly addressed any of the social concerns touching on civil rights or integration. The topic of the address was to be "The Layman and the Courts," and Powell was anxious to have Whittaker on the program. At first, Whittaker was reluctant to accept the invitation since the conference focused principally on traffic court problems, a topic Whittaker had previously treated and which he felt he had "wrung from it about all I can." Believing an unrelated topic was inappropriate, Whittaker declined. Powell persisted, though, stressing the subject of the address was less important than having Whittaker as the speaker. By mid–February Whittaker agreed to make the trip to Atlanta but only if his travel and accommodations were compensated.[56]

Through the spring and early summer of 1964 Whittaker worked on his speech, and for much of that time it appeared as though his speech would consider the breakdown in race relations and growing civil unrest that he was beginning to address in other forums. Right up until the end of July, in fact, after he had presented numerous speeches on these themes, Whittaker's planned presentation seemed to focus on contemporary concerns. His first title of a working draft, "Peace Through Law," encapsulated essentially what he had said at his Texas Bar presentation.[57] Whether it was his reluctance to repeat his performance before the Texas Bar or, as he said to his Atlanta audience, because he had been asked many times how changes in the meaning of the Constitution were brought about,[58] Whittaker decided to radically alter his speech and instead address changing interpretations of the commerce clause and expansions of federal power. Using hindsight, he probably should have stuck with his first effort, "Peace Through Law," which still appeared as the title on the program in Atlanta. Instead, Whittaker wrote a speech entitled, "Federal Powers Under the Commerce Clause of the Constitution," which he later changed to "A Confusion of Tongues." The change, no doubt, was to shorten his presentation ("A Confusion of Tongues" was over six typed pages shorter), but he also changed substantial material in the speech—material, which, had he left it in the speech, could have lessened the charges that Whittaker was "attacking" the Supreme Court.[59]

Attacks on the Supreme Court were a regular feature in *U.S. News & World Report* through the summer of 1964, and Whittaker could not have overlooked the rising tide of criticisms following recent Court decisions.[60] On the last day of the term, the Court reversed the murder conviction of Danny Escobedo following his police station confession because he was denied a lawyer during questioning and not advised of his right to remain silent.[61] One week earlier the Court rejected a long line of earlier precedents and incorporated the Fifth Amendment's privilege against self-incrimination against the states.[62] Also decided on the Court's last day was whether the secretary of state could deny a passport to anyone in a Communist action organization. Rejecting the State Department's efforts under the Internal Security Act of 1950, the Court ruled that the language of the Act was too broad to sustain such denials.[63] The Court in two unanimous decisions that term gave further encouragement to civil rights advocates, leading to further consternation from recalcitrant segregationists in the South.[64] Most significant, however, the Court that term radically altered the geographic boundaries of state and national legislative districts by ordering, first, that congressional districts be as nearly equal in population as possible and, second, that both houses of a state's legislature depend on equal voting strength throughout the state.[65] These reapportionment decisions, once thought to be a nonjusticiable issue, raised serious concerns for lawmakers, and in both houses of Congress measures were introduced to reverse the Court's decisions. One House bill would have stripped the federal courts of jurisdiction to rule on state reapportionment, and in the Senate a bill was introduced to postpone the Court's decision until a constitutional amendment could be proposed reversing it.[66]

The feeling among Court critics was that it had exceeded its legitimate authority and was reaching out to decide issues that were beyond its purview. Describing the Court's recent decisions as "usurpation," David Lawrence bemoaned how "the rights of the sovereign States are gradually being extinguished" by a "judicial oligarchy." Rather than relying on the amendment process, Lawrence accused the Court of giving new meaning to the Constitution by interpretation that "stretched far beyond their original meaning" the words of that document.[67] Three months later, in his address before the ABA Whittaker attempted to explain how certain changes in constitutional interpretation had occurred. Obviously, when evaluated within the context of the recently enacted Civil Rights Act and criticisms of the Court's reapportionment decisions, Whittaker's explanation appeared intent on fueling the flames of discontent over the expansion of federal (particularly judicial) power, thereby leading to charges he was "attacking" the Court.

In his first draft, "Federal Powers Under the Commerce Clause of the Constitution," Whittaker included language that clarified his intent. Had he retained this original language in his final speech, then the confusion created over his purposes—whether he was explaining changing interpretations or condemning those changes—might have been avoided. For example, in his first draft Whittaker noted how his topic concerned "a few, now rather old, interpretations" of the Constitution. In his revised text, he updated that to include "the present status" of the Constitution, a phrase that indicated disparagement over recent Court decisions. More significant, however, as his change in title indicated, Whittaker dropped all references in his later speech to changing interpretations of the commerce clause specifically, referring instead generally to all changes in interpretation, which by implication meant anything from school segregation to criminal procedure.[68] The one example he used to demonstrate the Court's changing interpretation of the Constitution, *National Relations Board v. Jones & Laughlin Steel*, was a twenty-seven-year-old opinion that did not reflect "the present status" of the Constitution except in reference specifically to the commerce power of Congress. This one example, in turn, was insufficient to indict recent Court decisions since, as William Wiecek observed, "After World War II, the Court seemed to go out of its way to repudiate the entire structure of economic substantive due process decisions, articulating a standard of extreme deference to legislative policy decisions in economic matters."[69] In other words, Whittaker's reference to *Jones & Laughlin* in no way repudiated the Court's recent decisions; for over two decades the Court had purposely stayed out of the business of regulating business.[70]

Jones & Laughlin grew out of the Depression-era efforts of the federal government to rescue the nation's economy. As part of President Roosevelt's New Deal legislation, the National Labor Relations Act guaranteed to workers the right to organize unions and prohibited employers from discriminating because of union membership. The key to economic recovery, the administration believed, was in more business regulation, which required a greater expansion of federal power. The reach of federal authority over labor relations, though, particularly in manufacturing, had been seriously curtailed by the Supreme Court in decisions that supported a liberty of contract doctrine whereby workers had the right to bargain with employers free of government interference.[71] The Court had also held that manufacturing affected interstate commerce only indirectly and, therefore, was beyond the power of Congress to regulate.[72] With these precedents in mind, the government did not expect to win *Jones & Laughlin*. In a split decision that signaled an end to the Court's interference with federal economic regulation and made Roosevelt's "Court-packing plan" no longer necessary, the Court surprised observers and ruled that any activity affecting commerce, whether directly or indirectly, was within constitutionally accepted powers of Congress to regulate. By so doing, the Court made an about-face, repudiating its own earlier decisions and inaugurating a new era of expanding federal power in economic regulation.

Such a decision no longer had practical force or effect in 1964 since economics had been replaced by equal protection as the principal concern of the Court. Expanding federal power in civil rights legislation had become the order of the day, and the Court in 1964 was willing to uphold federal intrusion into what many considered sociological matters just as an earlier Court had sustained such intrusion in economic matters. Whittaker's reference to *Jones & Laughlin* in his speech, coupled with his support of the Tenth Amendment, left his audience with the impression that he not only objected to the Court's decision there but that he by implication objected to recent Court decisions as well. Without a clearer statement of his purposes, his audience was left to draw its own conclusions.

Whittaker did indicate his purpose clearly in his earlier draft, writing, "It is not my purpose to affirm or deny that such expansion of Federal powers were necessary in the depressed conditions of those times, but only to show *how they were brought into existence.*"[73] To illustrate the dramatic change in the Court's own interpretation of the commerce clause, Whittaker included in his first draft a second Court opinion dropped from his later speech. He used *Schechter v. United States* as an example of how the Court just two years before *Jones & Laughlin* had interpreted the commerce clause as foreclosing federal interference in manufacturing and production that did not affect interstate commerce directly. Citing Chief Justice Charles Evans Hughes in *Schechter*, Whittaker quoted, "If the commerce clause were construed to reach all enterprises and transactions which could be said to have an indirect effect upon interstate commerce, the federal authority would embrace practically all the activities of the people, and the authority of the State over its domestic concerns would exist only by sufferance of the federal government."[74] Whittaker's extensive use of *Schechter* in his first draft was necessary, he wrote, because it showed in the words of the Court how *different* two opinions could be in such a short span of time. With *Schechter* included, Whittaker's speech sounded like a history lesson on how changing interpretations led the Court to back down from the constitutional crisis of 1937; without it his speech came across as an exhortation against all expansions of federal power—particularly in the field of civil rights. In order to blunt charges that he was "attacking" the present Court, Whittaker should have left in his speech this from his earlier draft: "Nor is it my purpose to affirm or deny that these expansions of the meaning of the Commerce Clause were good for the nation. Quite obviously, our great national programs regulating business, labor, agriculture, education, social welfare, civil rights and other matters, could not have existed under the pre–1936 conceptions of Congress' power under the Commerce Clause.... [T]hese and other great national programs that rest on the Commerce power have been so long established and are now such integral parts of our government that they cannot, as a practical matter, be eliminated."[75]

Whittaker's speech before the ABA in October 1964 suffered not so much for what he said as it did for what he left out. As his earlier draft made clear, Whittaker sought to explain the circumstances surrounding changing interpretations of the commerce clause, changes that were necessary for the present Congress to enact and the present Court to sustain the public accommodations section of the 1964 Civil Rights Act under the commerce power, and not to condemn those changes. Whatever his personal views, Whittaker's first draft (and to a lesser extent his later version) carried a note of disinterested neutrality. One may suppose that Whittaker favored the "strict constructionist" view, but he did not come out and declare that *Jones & Laughlin* had been wrongly decided. On the contrary, even if one doubted his conclusion—that "[f]ederal power over local activities was left to a vague rule of men rather than to a definite rule of law"—one could not deny that *Jones & Laughlin* was "a sharp break with what had been regarded as fundamental in the past, and that it opened the gates to ... a vast expansion of Federal power over local activities."[76]

As one example of how the federal government reached out to touch local activities, Whittaker described penalties leveled against a farmer for growing wheat on his own farm to be fed on the same farm to his own livestock, remarking, "It would be a little difficult to imagine an activity more completely local than that."[77] Of course, Whittaker was referring to *Wickard v. Filburn*, a unanimous decision sustaining a portion of the Agricultural Adjustment Act. Whittaker well knew the holding in *Wickard*, citing it in his first draft, and his comments on it related to the dramatic changes in definition of what constituted commerce, not necessarily in denouncing those changes.[78] Justice William Douglas, who heard Whittaker's speech in Atlanta where he failed specifically to name the case, wrote him shortly afterwards, reminding him, "The decision you are using as a cudgel to beat the Court is *Wickard v. Filburn*.... It's too bad you left the Court, for up here you would at least have a chance at the proper time to convince a majority of the Court that *Wickard v. Filburn* was wrongly decided. To do so you would have to change your mind. For I note you joined in opinions that cited *Wickard v.*

Filburn with approval."[79] In his autobiography, Douglas later cited *United States v. Haley*, a unanimous *per curiam* decision, as one in which Whittaker had joined the Court to support *Wickard* although, Douglas observed, "he later roundly denounced the Court for going to such extremes."[80]

Douglas in his correspondence with Whittaker was mistaken on several counts, the least of which was that Whittaker was unaware of the holding in *Wickard*. More substantially, Whittaker never indicated that *Wickard* had been wrongly decided but that it had been decided radically differently from previous Court rulings. Besides, even had Whittaker personally objected to *Wickard*, his sense of duty as a justice and propriety as a speaker did not permit him to argue against it as a precedent; it had been authoritatively decided and sustained for almost two decades. As Whittaker explained years later, "Supreme Court opinions, when relevant and decisive of the particular point before me, were, and were regarded by me as being controlling of my decisions, and I endeavored, as best I could, to follow them—not always an easy task."[81]

The point of Whittaker's Atlanta speech, a point lost to many who heard it or who later reported on it, was that the meaning of the Constitution had changed through judicial interpretation. By 1964 this was no longer a contentious point. "Whether these ... changes in the Constitution were ... both necessary and good for the nation may well be doubted," Whittaker said, "[but] it is obvious that they were not made by the people—they were not made by any amendment of the Constitution."[82] This, Whittaker considered, was usurpation, or the seizing of power without constitutional authority. Whether or not Whittaker meant for his address to suggest that Congress's passage of the Civil Rights Act or the Court's reapportionment decisions were usurpation was doubtful, but that was how many understood his speech. Instead of recognizing the historical references to events and decisions of the 1930s, Whittaker was portrayed in one account as a narrow-minded formalistic judge who was out of touch with contemporary issues and who steadfastly embraced an outmoded judicial philosophy.[83]

That Whittaker never repeated this presentation on the changing meaning of the commerce clause was not surprising given the confusion created over his purpose. He could have avoided charges that he was "attacking" the Supreme Court had he not altered so much from his earlier draft to his final presentation or had he used his original proposal, "Peace Through Law," a theme he presented numerous times in the five years following his retirement from the Court. Further complicating matters for Whittaker, the one time his speech was published in full (the January 1965 *ABA Journal*) the wrong speech was reproduced. Whittaker had, in fact, sent his first draft, "Federal Powers," to the *Journal* before he completed revisions for the October meeting. Once he delivered his revised speech, "A Confusion of Tongues," he notified the *Journal* that their copy was inaccurate and needed to be changed.

Apparently concerned by the length of his first draft, the *Journal* proposed using excerpts from it rather than reproducing it in whole. Whittaker objected to such a course, believing excerpts would only distort its meaning. A complete copy could be reproduced or none at all.[84] As it turned out, the *Journal* reproduced Whittaker's first draft in its entirety, but that did not change the public's perception of his speech. Those who heard it reported that Whittaker "*accused* the Court and Congress of 'usurping' the people's constitutional right to govern themselves," under the banner, "When a Former Justice Speaks Out Against the Supreme Court."[85] Given that excerpts were used to support these claims (precisely what Whittaker had hoped to avoid) the impression became fixed that Whittaker was accusing the men with whom he had served of altering the meaning of the Constitution in a way that was impermissible and ultimately dangerous. Failing to make his point with better clarity, Whittaker gave up remarking on the Supreme Court, its history or operation, and turned his attention back to the subject that held strong personal interest for him—the breakdown of law and order in society.

Violence in American cities did not end with the passage of the Civil rights Act of 1964, neither did protests in support of further civil rights aims. The violence that erupted in July 1964 following the shooting of a fifteen-year-old African American boy by an off-duty white police officer in Harlem, New York, was of a different character, though, than earlier clashes between whites and African Americans. This time the violence occurred in a northern city, where African Americans had presumably enjoyed greater equality, and the perpetrators of the violence were not angry white segregationists but frustrated African American youths who needed little provocation to start a riot. After Harlem, violence spread to other northern cities, including Paterson, New Jersey, Dixmoor, Illinois, Philadelphia, Chicago, and Kansas City. By the end of what was considered "the long, hot summer," riots and property damage in northern cities had reached the crisis stage, and there seemed little relief ahead. Five people had been killed, hundreds more were wounded including police, and over 1,000 businesses had been looted or damaged. The rioters (some called them hoodlums) used projectiles and firebombs to attack police and white-owned businesses in ghetto areas. When called upon by the mayor of New York, Robert Wagner, for assistance during the Harlem riot, Martin Luther King, Jr., the recognized leader of the Civil Rights movement at the time, was unable to offer any meaningful assistance. "With the exception of Mississippi," King was quoted as saying, "I am much more hopeful about the South in race relations than I am about many sections of the North.... [W]e are in for some very tragic periods of rioting and violence."[86]

Alarm over the rising trend toward violent confrontations between whites and African Americans captured the nation's attention in 1965, and Whittaker was not the only prominent jurist to express concern over the seeming acquiescence of public officials to grant African Americans license to protest regardless of the outcome or threats involved.[87] Members of the Supreme Court were becoming increasingly impatient as well with the demands of civil rights protesters, although these views were often held to the minority.[88] In his speech before the Tennessee Bar, Whittaker urged his listeners to exercise restraint, tolerance, and vigilance, telling them, "[W]e must always strive to eliminate injustice and discrimination, but we must do so by orderly processes in the legislatures and the courts, and not by defying their processes and actions; nor by taking the laws into our own hands. We must take the laws into our hearts rather than into our hands, and seek redress in the courts rather than in the streets."[89]

Initially, Whittaker was reluctant to speak before the Tennessee Bar in June 1965, and it took requests from the presidents of the Tennessee Bar and the Judicial Conference as well as letters from the governor of Tennessee and the chief justice of the Tennessee Supreme Court to compel him to appear.[90] Whatever hesitation Whittaker might have felt about going to Nashville to speak, his reservations were dispelled in the eight months he had to prepare his presentation. During that time news reports of racial demonstrations ending in violent clashes continued to make headlines. In Selma, Alabama, for example, on what came to be called "Black Sunday" or "Bloody Sunday," March 7, during a voter registration drive over 500 demonstrators who attempted a 50 mile march to Montgomery, the state capital, were met by over a hundred law enforcement officers. As the demonstrators marched east across the Edmund Pettus Bridge they were stopped and given two minutes to disperse. Instead, the demonstrators knelt in prayer, refusing to move. Armed state troopers then assaulted the marchers with tear gas, and members of Sheriff Jim Clark's mounted posse drove the marchers back with clubs and whips. When some African Americans fought back, law enforcement responded with a viscous pursuit that left dozens of demonstrators wounded. In addition, violent racial clashes erupted in northern cities over poor housing conditions and employment opportunities, and news commentators reported on rising crime rates in America generally, indicating anywhere from 40 to 60 percent increases in the most violent crimes since 1958. Much of the blame for rising crime rates centered on recent Supreme Court decisions, and combating crime (which for some meant ending civil rights demonstrations) became highly politicized.[91] Crime and violent disturbances were becoming major issues, and Whittaker was willing to stand up and speak out on them, warning the country of the consequences for complacency even before Watts exploded into one of the worst urban riots of the 1960s or Richard Nixon campaigned on a "law and order" platform.

Whittaker's speech before the Tennessee Bar, "Law and Order," became his most highly publicized presentation during retirement. In it, Whittaker decried the use of the term "civil disobedience" to describe the technique used by King and his followers, preferring instead to call it "criminal" disobedience of the laws prohibiting trespass upon private property and the obstruction of public walks, streets, and highways. By advocating a philosophy of violating laws they considered unjust, Whittaker believed civil rights leaders promoted "mob actions," which, in turn, attracted the covert activities of Communists and "rabble-rousers" who were determined to destroy American society. Once again indicting Martin Luther King, Jr., as responsible for the violence that attended civil rights demonstrations (but still not naming King directly), Whittaker made reference sarcastically to the fact that King was recently granted an honorary degree from Yale University "not in some new political science—*but in law*," and that King received a Nobel Prize "for, of all things, his *contributions to peace.*" And what, Whittaker asked, "has happened to our sense of values?"[92]

Whittaker may have had in mind the fact that when King led some 1,500 supporters on a second "freedom march" across the Edmund Pettus Bridge in Selma on March 9, he did so in defiance of a federal court order forbidding it. King did not defy the barricade of state troopers, instead turning around and marching back into Selma, but violence and tragedy occurred nonetheless. Three white clergymen who heeded King's call to come to Selma to march were attacked and beaten by an angry white mob. One of them, the Reverend James Reeb, died from his injuries. Reeb's was not the only death as a result of the Selma campaign; earlier an African American, Jimmy Lee Jackson, was slain by state troopers in nearby Marion, Alabama, when he participated in a demonstration supporting those arrested in Selma (over 3,000, including King, for unlawful assembly), and following the successful completion of the Selma to Montgomery march later that month a white mother of five, Viola Gregg Liuzzo, who was transporting marchers to and from Montgomery in her car, was murdered by Klansmen. King had said that he "would rather die on the highways of Alabama than make a butchery of my own conscience,"[93] but for many, like Whittaker, that could neither excuse nor explain the intentional violations of law or the consequent violence that always seemed to follow these so-called peaceful demonstrations.

The central message of Whittaker's Tennessee speech was that government has a duty to enforce the law, whatever law, and citizens have a duty to obey it, whether they liked it or not. There was no room for compromising "the impartial, evenhanded, vigorous, swift and certain enforcement of our criminal laws," he said. "The fact that the provocations may have been themselves constitutionally unlawful cannot justify unlawful means for their resolution," Whittaker continued, "All discriminations that violate the Constitution and laws of the United States are readily redressable in our courts which have always been open to all citizens. And no one has any room to doubt that, if he will resort to those courts, and have the patience to await their processes—as we all must do in an ordered society—all his constitutional and legal rights will be vouchsafed to him, whatever his creed or color."[94]

Whittaker had spent the greater part of his life in the study of and administration of the law. For him, these words were not "platitudes," but were "fundamental" and "vital." He had the utmost respect for and confidence in the courts and faith in the propriety of judges, and whether or not one agreed with their judgments one was still obliged to follow them. "The great pity here," he said, "is that these minority groups, in preaching and practicing defiance of the law, are in fact advocating erosion and destruction of the only structure that can ever assure to them, or permanently maintain for them, due process of law and the equal protection of the laws, and that can, thus, protect them from discriminations and abuses by majorities."[95]

Whittaker may have thought that courts were the "only structures" capable of protecting African Americans from "discriminations and abuses," but he had to realize that waiting on courts to vouchsafe the legal rights of African Americans could take an interminably long time. Ever since the Montgomery bus boycott of 1956, civil rights groups had abandoned the legal strategy of the NAACP in the hopes of assuring for themselves equal treatment, and in the ten years since the Supreme Court announced an end to segregated schools in the South (with the exception of Texas and Tennessee) less than one percent of all African American children living there attended schools with whites.[96] It was not until 1968, in fact, after King was assassinated and Whittaker stopped making public appearances that the Court finally made the substantive right first announced in *Brown v. Board of Education* a positive mandate for the South to create "unitary" school systems, which meant integrated, without further delays.[97]

Following his Tennessee speech on "Law and Order" Whittaker began to enjoy a new celebrity status that he had not experienced as a federal judge. Letters poured into his Kansas City office, and copies or excerpts of his speech were reproduced by the millions. Most of the reactions were positive, and Whittaker sensed a renewed interest in his topic. He remarked to the president of the Tennessee Bar afterwards, "I am encouraged to believe that the timeliness, and I would like to think also the content, of the speech has had a part in bringing about the obvious change of attitude of heretofore complacent people that we are now witnessing, and even in stimulating the new presidential program, announced yesterday, to investigate the causes of the current rash of crimes and to recommend remedial action."[98] Whittaker had addressed similar concerns related to civil rights protests on at least a dozen occasions in the last two years, but public reaction had never before been so pronounced. To one supportive letter, Whittaker responded, "[This speech] came at a time when, I think, many more thoughtful persons have been able to see the results of preachments and practices to defy the law and are becoming aroused, and, hence, are more receptive to our warnings."[99]

Of the few critical letters Whittaker received, which he considered "quite irresponsible," Whittaker's response—marginally noted but never sent—was as simple and straightforward as the ideal he presented in his speech. To one note signed by "a worried American father," which stated, "Martin Luther King has a point that a bad law is just as bad as no law at all," Whittaker wrote, "Then repeal it."[100] Such a course, while intellectually feasible, was practically impossible at the time for African Americans living in the South. The legal mechanisms and social recognition that might have allowed them to repeal laws were the very same means denied to them by the force of law. This gave to Whittaker's speech a dissembling quality. He never rejected the aims of civil rights protesters, only their methods; and yet it was those methods that ultimately proved effective in bringing about meaningful changes for African Americans.[101]

In the three years since his retirement from the Supreme Court, Whittaker received more recognition and gained greater notoriety than ever before in his life. He was becoming a nationally recognized public figure (at least, among conservative Republicans) in large part because of the news coverage given to his public speeches. In October 1965 the *New York Times* reported, "In recent years, Justice Whittaker has become an active speaker at legal meetings and occasionally caused raised eyebrows in legal circles by speaking out on current legal or political issues."[102] Whittaker enjoyed his new notoriety and found satisfaction in making public appearances. Privately he considered his chances in a run for a Senate seat, and rumors surfaced of his name being considered for the Commissioner of Major League Baseball.[103] With so many new possibilities before him, by the summer of 1965 Whittaker had lost all interest in resuming judicial service. He was not about to give up the public limelight that he had actively avoided in his former occupations, so when General Motors first contacted him in May 1965 to offer him a position as dealer relations arbitrator he refused. The initial offer was for $20,000 a year compensation, a figure that satisfied former District Court Judge William Coleman of Maryland, who had served the last nine years as arbitrator, but Whittaker's retirement pension was now $19,750 a year. There was no purpose served in accepting this meager increase to his annual income, not at the cost of losing his stature as a retired justice once he resigned his commission. Believing the matter closed, Whittaker recommended his two former colleagues from the district court, Richard Duncan and Albert Ridge, both recently retired, for the position.[104]

The General Motors Dealer Relations Umpire Plan, which settled disputes between local car dealers and General Motors divisional managers, was part of an experiment by the "Big Three" auto companies to settle disputes through mediation rather than litigation. Any decisions reached by the arbitrators were binding on the companies but not on the local dealers.[105] Intent on obtaining his services, General Motors renewed negotiations with Whittaker over the summer of 1965 and offered him $50,000 a year plus the cost of an office and a secretary. Whittaker found this new offer sufficiently interesting to give it consideration. After calculating the tax return on this proposed change in income and the potential economic loss his family might suffer once he surrendered his lifetime judicial pension, Whittaker determined his minimum "break even" point at $75,000 before he could accept the position. Negotiations dragged on through the summer, causing Whittaker to become impatient to have "the matter settled one way or another as soon as possible," as both sides offered proposals and counter-proposals.[106] Anxious to reach an agreement, finally in late September conditions were settled, and Whittaker prepared to send his formal letter of resignation to President Johnson. In the deal with General Motors, Whittaker received $75,000 a year on a ten-year contract, renewable each year thereafter, the cost for all office furnishings, secretary, and travel expenses, a pension of $12,000 a year if he became incapacitated or his contract was not renewed, complete freedom to engage in any activity not incompatible with his duties as arbitrator, and the lease of a new Cadillac car every year he remained with General Motors.[107]

Whittaker had planned to send his resignation to the president by September 28, allowing General Motors time to publicly announce his new position by October 1, 1965, but his contract was not finalized until one week later. He sent his resignation severing his ties to the federal judiciary to both President Johnson and Chief Justice Warren on October 5 and advised General Motors to wait at least until the president publicly acknowledged receipt of the letter before making any announcement.[108] On October 18, Warren announced Whittaker's resignation to the Court, effective September 30. In his letter to the president Whittaker indicated he had regained his health, and, Warren said, "[H]e now wishes to be freed from the occupational restrictions that necessarily inhere in his retired status, so that he may, with propriety, engage in other activities."[109] Nowhere in his letter of resignation or in the press release from General Motors did Whittaker indicate that he was leaving the federal judiciary because he was not permitted for over three years to judge again. Whittaker also did not acknowledge the terms of his employment with General Motors, leaving the press to speculate, rightfully so, that he was making considerably more money. Financial gain, however, was not the only consideration that went into Whittaker's calculations. He also had to consider the long-term economic consequences involved in losing a lifetime federal pension and the incalculable loss of prestige from leaving the federal judiciary. Ironically, the only times Whittaker ever got to judge again were after he left the federal judiciary. In addition to his duties for General Motors, in 1967 Whittaker served briefly on the International Court of Arbitration in Stockholm, Sweden.

One of the benefits to his work with General Motors was that Whittaker remained free to speak out on public issues, and for the first eighteen months of his new position he continued to address his concerns related to increases in violence and rioting among African Americans. During this time America witnessed some of the worst widespread rioting of the last century, resulting in the loss of hundreds of lives, thousands wounded or arrested, and billions of dollars worth of property damage. Beginning with Watts (a section of Los Angeles) in August 1965, where over 30,000 people participated in looting and burning for five days, violence became a regular disturbing feature of the news. By the summer of 1966, thirty-eight separate riots had occurred in African American ghettos across the country. A year later 164 riots broke out during the "long hot summer" of 1967. Following the April 4, 1968, assassination of Martin Luther King, Jr., rioting broke out in almost every major American city and hundreds of smaller cities (in Kansas City the rioting left six dead; it was prompted by the school board's decision not to close schools in honor of King's death). Whittaker made two notable presentations in response to these events, both prior to King's assassination, but after King's death Whittaker stopped speaking out. "These warnings were not heeded and the consequences are now so evident that further warnings seem superfluous," he responded to one request to have his speech, "Law and Order," tape recorded and broadcast from Memphis following King's assassination, "That would put me in the rather undignified position of saying, 'I told you so.'"[110]

Whittaker's two presentations during the race riots of 1966 and 1967 were no more than extensions of his earlier pronouncements in "Immutable Moral Values" and "Law and Order," but he continued to receive invitations to speak because of his position as a former justice, not because of the popularity of his ideas. What made his last two public appearances so notable was the format of his presentations. The first was a seminar commemorating the centennial anniversary of the University of Kansas that included such renowned personalities as psychiatrist Karl Menninger, stage and film director Harold Clurman, and science fiction author Arthur C. Clarke. The second was a public policy debate sponsored by the American Enterprise Institute between Whittaker and the Reverend William Sloane Coffin, Jr., who as chaplain of Yale University became famous for his support of the Civil Rights movement and his protest against U. S. military involvement in Vietnam. In both of these encounters Whittaker's ideas were questioned and his arguments challenged, and in his debate with Coffin not only did Whittaker respond to Coffin's rebuttal, he defended his ideas before questions from newsmen and academicians.

What became clear during these exchanges was that Whittaker's concern for public safety and law enforcement was inextricably linked to his views on race relations. The other participants found these views particularly offensive, given that throughout America's history African Americans had suffered and continued to endure innumerable abuses. Whittaker's single-minded insistence on holding certain "self-appointed Negro leaders who have exhorted and incited others to violate our laws" as responsible for the prevailing waves of violence sweeping the nation seemed to ignore the violence perpetrated against African Americans even as they peaceably petitioned for equal treatment. Whittaker did not back down, though, in the face of criticism. He told Daniel Berman of American University, who questioned Whittaker's doctrine of responsibility and its partisan application, "I have no ax to grind, Mr. Berman. I have no political ambitions of any sort. I have received every honor that comes to one in my profession. I am simply deeply concerned, as an American citizen, with what I believe to be a very real and progressive threat to the existence of our form of government."[111]

One example of the kind of view challenged by the other participants occurred at the Kansas symposium where Whittaker stated, "Social acceptance is a matter of developmental mutual respect and liking, and this cannot be brought about by force. These are matters of the heart, and it cannot be controlled by force. No minority group that has settled in our land has obtained—or likely ever will obtain—general acceptance and amalgamation here until, by long years of exemplary conduct, a majority of its members have earned the respect and liking of the people generally. And when that's done, the process is easy."[112] The chairman of the department of anthropology at Rutgers University, Ashley Montagu, in his evaluation of Whittaker's speech, referred to Whittaker's statement as "the sheerest hypocrisy and nonsense." Calling Whittaker's attention to 350 years of injustice, wrongs, and evil practiced against African Americans, Montagu said, "Let us first do what we ought to do and redress the wrongs we have done against these people in particular.... so that we at any rate can stand before the bars of humanity, as we cannot at this moment, with some sort of decency."[113]

In his debate with the Reverend Coffin, Whittaker for the first time made specific mention of the "self-appointed Negro leaders" he held responsible for inciting much of the violence that led to riots breaking out in city after city. In addition to naming Martin Luther King, Jr., and his Southern Christian Leadership Conference, Whittaker also indicted Stokely Carmichael of the Student Nonviolent Coordinating Committee, Floyd McKissick of the Congress of Racial Equality, Elijah Muhammad of the Black Muslims, and Robert Franklin Williams of the Revolutionary Action Movement. Whittaker then denounced campus demonstrations, initiated at Berkeley in the fall of 1964, and their use as a platform to launch anti-war demonstrations. He censured high ranking federal officials for encouraging these demonstrations and for failing to prosecute those responsible for lawless acts, expressing his disapproval with recent statements made by the secretary of state, the vice president, and the president. This caused Berman to observe sardonically, "It is not easy to frame a question for a speaker who tends to lump in the same category rioters and Martin Luther King and Mr. [Hubert] Humphrey and Mr. [Lyndon] Johnson and Mr. [Dean] Rusk. But I will make a valiant effort to discuss the topic or to ask you about the topic that I felt we were to be discussing tonight." Berman then framed a question on civil disobedience that went to the heart of Whittaker's argument: should all laws be obeyed? "I wonder, sir," Berman asked, "if you cannot really conceive of any circumstances in which you would condone violation of the law. If it is difficult to imagine yourself a Negro, perhaps it is easier to imagine yourself a Jew in Nazi Germany. Would the law, then too, have deserved the unreserved reverence which you have stated this evening?"[114]

Whittaker was undeterred, and he deflected Berman's question by stating, "You seem to imply that I would sanction the lawlessness that went on by whites against Negroes in the south. That is far from anything that I have said or have had in mind. All violations of the criminal laws ought to be uniformly punished with the full force of the law.... A white man's crime is just as bad as a Negro's crime. There isn't any distinction to be made upon the ground that one has a different color than the other. I am talking not about persons but about conduct."[115] Others in the discussion continued to press Whittaker, hoping to get some concession from him that African Americans were justified in conducting demonstrations protesting unequal treatment. Whittaker held firmly to his conviction, though, that once a demonstration turned violent, then those who planned the demonstration, if it could be reasonably assumed that they had cause to foresee the potential for violence, were just as responsible for the resultant violence as those who perpetrated it. What got lost amid all the discussion over rioting, looting, protesting, and what could properly be considered "civil disobedience" was the fact that Whittaker sympathized with the plight of African Americans and wanted to ameliorate their condition. He applauded the efforts of the NAACP and its legal strategy to end discrimination. He acknowledged, "[I]n the past our laws and the imperfect administration of them imposed grievous injustices upon, and many discriminations against, American Negroes." He recognized that the economic and educational needs of African Americans were not being met and that social acceptance by whites was a long way off. He did not think, however, after passage of the Civil Rights Act of 1964 and the Voting Rights Act of 1965, that "*governmental* or *governmentally sanctioned* discriminations against Negroes" were still possible. As long as existing laws were enforced, Whittaker believed, then there was nothing more that government could do, making further demonstrations unnecessary. Otherwise, protests began to infringe on the rights of others leading to greater incidents of violence.[116]

The most damaging statement Whittaker made in his Coffin debate and the one that consigned his reputation to that of segregationist sympathizer, at least, or hopelessly out of touch with the times, was his characterization of African Americans living in the South before the great migrations of them north to industrial centers during World War II. He described the poor, rural sharecroppers living in the South as "a happy lot," despite the oppressive conditions, because, he said, "With their trusted shotgun, dog, and fishing pole they could, and often did, augment their provisions.... With their trusted ax, they were able to get from nearby forests ample firewood, for chopping to heat their homes."[117] Blaming the overcrowded conditions of northern ghettos and the subsequent loss of economic opportunities on the influx of African Americans, Whittaker proposed eliminating the ghettos and, thus, rescuing African Americans from economic deprivation by finding a means to have them move back to the rural areas of the country. Responding to Whittaker's opening presentation in the debate, the Reverend Coffin pulled no punches in his rebuttal and immediately launched into a harsh criticism of Whittaker's description of African American society, stating, "I feel no high school senior in a current relations class could get away with the kind of scholarship represented on those pages." Ridiculing Whittaker's characterization of life in the South, Coffin wondered how African Americans fared without their "trusted right to vote," their "trusted right to get [their] kids into decent public schools," their "trusted right even to own the land that [they have] been working," or their "trusted right to get some job training." Summarizing Whittaker's idyllic image of African Americans as rustic farmers living off the land, Coffin declared, "It's pretty hard to patronize Negroes more than that!"[118]

Whittaker's debate with Coffin in February 1967 was his last public appearance speaking out on the issues of race and violent disturbances. The two men (when they kept to the same topic) were only tangentially at odds with each other. Whittaker, the literalist who judged all actions and their consequences using the legal formalism of an earlier era, allowed for no deviations from the prompt, even-handed enforcement of all criminal laws. Coffin, on the other hand, as a man of divinity, permitted, even encouraged, adherence to a higher law, which superseded man-made laws when the two conflicted. This, then, became their central point of disagreement, but the two oftentimes spoke at cross-purposes from each other. Coffin was more interested in defending the motivations of those who led civil rights demonstrations (as well as those protesting the war in Vietnam), while Whittaker questioned the methods they employed. Supporting the aims of African Americans, Coffin considered the ends sufficient to justify the means, whereas Whittaker focused only on the means and the potential harm that resulted.

Whittaker had just turned sixty-six, and in the last five years since his retirement from the Supreme Court he had said all he had to say about the preservation of law and the protection of private property. Although his contract with General Motors allowed him to continue speaking out on social or legal issues, Whittaker receded from the public spotlight. He became involved instead in political considerations, serving first as consultant counsel to the Senate's Select Committee on Standards and Conduct and then testifying before a Senate subcommittee on the Separation of Powers. Created in July 1965, the Select Committee on Standards and Conduct was the forerunner of the later Select Committee on Ethics, and its chairman at the time, one of the longest serving senators ever, Democrat John Stennis of Mississippi, had written the first code of ethics for the Senate. According to Whittaker, in late March 1966 several senators began imploring him to accept the position as consultant counsel, which involved advising the Committee on constitutional and legal questions that might arise. He would be paid a "consultant's fee" only if his services proved valuable and enduring, and he could conduct his work from his office in Kansas City. Initially, Whittaker demurred, writing, "[P]rincipally because no such arrangement, so far as I know, ever previously existed, and, hence, the perimeters of the need were altogether unmarked, and, therefore, I feared that the volume might become too great and the responsibilities too onerous."[119] Succumbing to senatorial pressure, though, Whittaker accepted the position the following month. At the news of Whittaker's selection, Committee Chairman Stennis remarked, "[B]ecause the creation of the Committee marks the first time in the history of the Senate that a permanent group has been established to consider matters of ethical conduct of members of the Senate ... the members of the Committee realize that their procedures may be setting important precedent. The Committee has therefore considered it prudent to retain an eminent and distinguished lawyer of national prominence and with recognized ability and vast experience in the legal profession. In Justice Whittaker the Committee feels fortunate in having obtained such a man."[120]

Whittaker's first major case for the Select Committee on Standards and Conduct involved charges of financial misconduct against two-term Democratic Senator Thomas Dodd of Connecticut. Dodd, reportedly a close personal friend of President Johnson, became the seventh Senate member censured by his colleagues in the history of that body.[121] Two years later the investigative eye of the Senate and suspicions of financial impropriety were leveled against Justice Abe Fortas, and following his ignoble resignation from the Court the Senate Judiciary Committee asked Whittaker to appear before the subcommittee on the Separation of Powers to give testimony concerning the propriety of two proposed bills placing constraints on the activities of federal judges. In light of recent events, it was difficult to believe, as the chairman of the subcommittee, Democratic Senator Sam Ervin of North Carolina, claimed, that Whittaker's testimony and the purpose of the hearings were "in no way intended to concentrate on past events."[122] The intents of the bills were in every way suited to prevent the kind of debacle that occurred when Fortas was forced off the Court.

The Fortas affair, as it was known, began one year earlier when Chief Justice Warren, intent on President Johnson naming his successor, announced his resignation from the Court. Johnson, however, had rendered his own political leverage nugatory by announcing in March 1968 that he would not seek re-election. When Johnson announced his intention to elevate Fortas,

Johnson's personal advisor, to the chief's position and, to replace Fortas, Johnson nominated another close, personal friend, former Texas Congressman Homer Thornberry, charges of double cronyism were leveled. Republicans began a weeklong filibuster against the Fortas elevation, claiming that Fortas had acted improperly as a justice by accepting large payments for teaching seminars at American University. In the end, Fortas asked that his name be withdrawn for the center chair. That meant that Richard Nixon, the winner in the fall election, got to choose Warren's successor. Political trouble for Fortas was not over, however, because in May the following spring *Life* magazine ran an expose detailing Fortas's relationship with Louis Wolfson, a convicted stock manipulator.[123] Suggestions were heard that Fortas had acted unethically by accepting large payments (which he later returned) from Wolfson's charitable foundation in return for legal advice during the latter's securities investigation. Within ten days of the *Life* story Fortas resigned from the Court. The results were devastating. Nixon, who had pledged in his campaign to undo much of the "Warren Court" rulings, now had two positions to fill on the Court within months of taking office. Democrats became determined to avenge for losing Fortas.

In June 1969 Warren Burger took his place on the Court as the new chief justice, and Whittaker received his invitation to appear along with other former justices before the subcommittee on the Separation of Powers. Because he and Winifred were vacationing in Europe for much of June and the first week of July, Whittaker was unable to attend the sessions scheduled that summer. When hearings resumed in the fall, Whittaker made plans to testify on October 1. The purpose of the hearings, as Ervin described it to Whittaker, was to consider the extrajudicial activities of federal judges, particularly Supreme Court justices, and included, "the rule-making power of the Supreme Court; ... appointments to concurrent official duties, as exemplified by Justice Jackson's position at the Nuremberg Tribunal and Chief Justice Warren's chairmanship of the Commission to report upon the assassination of President John F. Kennedy; unofficial counsel to Presidents; the growing practice of Supreme Court Justices' giving lectures and press conferences on matters of current public concern; and participation in public or private activities, whether or not these activities run a risk of future litigation."[124] Clearly, the purpose behind the hearings was to focus precisely on the kinds of issues raised by Fortas's detractors. The timing of the hearings was precipitous; during the time that Whittaker prepared to make his testimony the Senate considered Fortas's replacement, Clement Haynsworth, a judge from the Fourth Circuit Court of Appeals.

In his statement for the subcommittee on the Separation of Powers, Whittaker considered the constitutionality of two proposed bills submitted for his consideration. The first, S. 1097, briefly stated that no federal judge could engage in or exercise the power of any office or duty already imposed on officers or employees of the legislative and executive branches. Since the bill contained no means of enforcement, it amounted to little more than an admonition and was not, Whittaker believed, constitutionally suspect. The second, S. 2190, however, gave Whittaker serious reservations, and he advised against its adoption. In essence, the bill was divided into two parts. First, it made financial disclosures incumbent upon all federal judges, and failure to do so (or failure to report accurately) constituted grounds for removal from office. Second, it made grounds for removal from office possible if a federal judge participated in a case in which he or any member of his family had a substantial financial interest. Whittaker considered the punitive provisions of the bill confronted the Senate with "grave questions of legislative constitutional power." The Constitution provided only one means for removing federal judges from office, namely, impeachment, and only then if a judge failed to observe "good behavior," a term left undefined. By providing a means to remove a judge from office for failure to disclose financial investments, Congress defined and expanded the meaning of "good behavior" in such a way that Congress imposed some regulation on the courts, thereby blurring the lines separating the division of power. "There have, indeed, been some instances of indiscreet, and even improper, conduct by federal judges," Whittaker observed, "But those instances have been very few and those judges have been even fewer—indeed so rare and unusual as to arouse 'man-bites-dog' excitements.... [M]oral integrity cannot be created by law." The most effective means of securing competent, honorable judges, Whittaker believed, remained the nominating and confirming processes.[125]

One month after Whittaker's scheduled appearance before the Senate subcommittee he made further public remarks about judges' financial interests, this time to offer his support for Clement Haynsworth's nomination to the Supreme Court. Haynsworth had become the victim of a protracted campaign by Democratic senators, led by Birch Bayh of Indiana, to retaliate for Fortas's forced resignation from the bench. Charges leveled against Haynsworth during his confirmation hearings before the Senate Judiciary Committee included questions about his judicial record on civil rights and labor relations as well as ethical concerns about his investments in companies appearing before him in court. In light of the Fortas affair, the ethical question about Haynsworth's investments became the prevailing charge leading to his defeat on November 21 by a vote of 55 to 45. Ten days before Haynsworth's defeat, Whittaker told reporters in Kansas City that he believed Haynsworth's opponents were falsely assaulting Haynsworth's character "because they want a more 'liberal' justice appointed to the Supreme Court." "It seems evident to me," Whittaker continued, "that any proper sense of moral decency requires those who oppose Judge Haynsworth's confirmation to state their real reasons for opposing him rather than to resort to false charges of unethical conduct."[126]

Beginning with Chief Justice Warren's announced retirement from the Court in 1968, for over three years the nation focused attention on the Court as personnel changes brought the number of new justices to four. In addition, controversy over failed nominations and indiscretions renewed interest in Court appointments. Fortas had been forced to resign, Haynsworth and another Nixon nominee, Harold Carswell, both were defeated in the Senate, Justice Douglas was considered for impeachment, and in September 1971 both Justices Black and Harlan announced their retirements. President Nixon fulfilled his pledge to redirect the Court in a more conservative direction by naming Lewis Powell and William Rehnquist to fill the two empty seats. During this time Court commentators wondered about the Court's "direction" and whether the changes wrought by the "Warren Court" would survive. Asked many times since his retirement to comment on Court decisions, Whittaker consistently refused to share his views, particularly since his analysis of the Commerce Clause had been misconstrued as an "attack" upon the present Court.

In January 1970 Whittaker finally broke his silence and consented to be interviewed about the Court and its most recent vacancy, the failure of Haynsworth to be confirmed. He made clear, though, that he would not discuss specific personalities then serving on the Court. Supporting Nixon's aim to place only "strict constructionists" on the Court, Whittaker explained what he meant by that term, saying, "A strict constructionist as I understand the term is one who decides constitutional and legal questions on precisely what the Constitution or the law says—free from any personal predilections of what the rule ought to be and free from any affinity for ideological concepts to either side of the straight line."[127] When asked about the kind of judge he would look for to fill a Court vacancy, Whittaker responded, "I would look for the best real lawyer that I could find who was as free from alignment with either the left or right as I could possibly find. In other words, a man, a lawyer, who would decide the cases on the facts and the law without regard to any extraneous things or philosophies."[128] Three years later Whittaker was even more forthcoming in response to questions about the proper role of judges. He wrote to one inquiring college student, "[I]n my view, the business of any judge is to make sure of the facts and then of the law, and lastly to apply the latter to the former candidly and honestly without regard to his own views of what the law ought to be, as, in my view, it is not the business of any judge to legislate."[129]

Esteem for Whittaker ran high among local lawyers in Kansas City, and in 1967 the Missouri Bar offered to have a portrait of him presented to the Supreme Court. By tradition, all former members of the Supreme Court had portraits on display, and Whittaker felt an obligation to provide one of himself. He also had an artist in mind to complete the portrait, Charles J. Fox of New York, whose impressive list of nationally recognized clients included numerous politicians, businessmen, and former Supreme Court justices. Six years earlier Fox had made a preliminary sketch of Whittaker in his Supreme Court chambers, but a painting was never commissioned. Now Whittaker wished for Fox to complete the painting so the Missouri Bar could present it to the Court.[130] By 1970 the portrait was completed and ready for delivery. Initially the Missouri Bar considered having its members contribute to the cost of the painting, but Whittaker would not allow it. He felt embarrassed by the prospect, and so, instead, paid for the painting himself, including the frame and attached nameplate. When the president of the Missouri Bar, Jack Oliver, proposed to fly representatives of the Missouri Bar to Washington to present the painting to the justices at a special luncheon, Whittaker put a stop to that as well. "This seems to me to be making too much of a show and ceremony out of what I think should be a simple presentation of the portrait to the Court by the Missouri Bar," Whittaker explained, "I simply would like to avoid any unseemly show or time-consuming and expensive ceremony out of what is in fact the simple presentation to the Court by a State Bar of a portrait of one of its members who was formerly a member of the Court."[131] Acquiescing to Whittaker's wishes, Oliver shipped the portrait to the Court in March 1971 with this sentiment: "On behalf of the lawyers of Missouri, we are pleased to present to the Supreme Court of the United States the portrait of Justice Charles Evans Whittaker, a lawyer of whom the Missouri Bar is inordinately proud.... [W]e wanted more dramatically to demonstrate our fondness and respect for him. You should not, therefore, misinterpret this modest way of presentation as a diminution of our respect or interest in Justice Whittaker.... It is our hope that this modest presentation will be regarded as a token of our highest esteem for Justice Charles Evans Whittaker."[132]

Whittaker may have been reluctant to return to Washington in 1971 for the formal presentation of his portrait to the Court, but he was not ashamed of his performance as a justice or of his difficulties leading to retirement. As his son, Kent, later explained, Whittaker was not embarrassed, he simply did not feel that a ceremony was warranted on this occasion. So much had changed since his retirement from the Court that tribute seemed inappropriate. He was no longer a federal judge; he had stopped making public speeches; and as he approached age seventy he had few ambitions and even less regrets. For example, five months after his portrait arrived at the Court the country first learned of Whittaker's classification as a "failure" when *Life* magazine reported the results of Professors Albert Blaustein's and Roy Mersky's poll on Supreme Court greatness. Concerned that his father might take the news hard, Kent went to visit him at his home to get his reaction to it. "To all appearances it did not seem to bother him," Kent has remembered, "I think he was comfortable in his own assessment of his work."[133]

One year after the *Life* article ran, Blaustein and Mersky published their findings in the *ABA Journal*, offering their own analysis of how justices should

Whittaker with his siblings. On the occasion of their forty-fourth wedding anniversary, Charles and Winifred had this family portrait taken with his three siblings and their spouses. *Left to right*: **Elwin Kiehnhoff, Dorothy Whittaker Kiehnhoff, Norman Ruhnke, Hazel Whittaker Ruhnke, Winifred, Charles, Gladys Whittaker, and Samuel Whittaker. Despite his poor rating among political scientists and historians, Whittaker's family continued to regard his achievements with admiration. Sixteen months after this portrait was taken Whittaker died of an abdominal aneurysm. (Photograph courtesy of Gary Whittaker)**

be selected and including the names of those who did the ratings. Once again, Whittaker was confronted with a poor public image, this time reading about it in his professional journal. It seemed that in the last three years, beginning with Leon Friedman's hypercritical biographical sketch in 1969, Whittaker's stature as a jurist was disintegrating before his own eyes. His "failure" rating became his destiny. But what did it matter? As his youngest son, Gary, later speculated, "Out of all the lawyers who ever practiced, how many became judges? Of all those judges, how many went to the Supreme Court? If I were considered the worst of the top 100 jurists in the nation, that's not so bad when compared to all the lawyers and judges who never went to the Supreme Court. So what's the point?"[134] Indeed, relatively few individuals had achieved from such modest beginnings what Charles Whittaker did, and although his federal court service lasted but eight years he continued to regard it with pride. In his 1969 statement before the Senate subcommittee on the Separation of Powers, Whittaker wrote, "[A]sking your leave to speak a personal word, may

I say that my proudest reflections, in my advancing years, are upon the fact that I was once a federal judge—indeed, at different times, a federal judge on all three levels of the federal judiciary. To be made a federal judge is, I think, to be paid the highest compliment that can come to a lawyer."[135]

One of Whittaker's last public appearances was in 1971 at the University of Missouri-Kansas City where he addressed a political science class on "The Court and the Constitution." Professor David Atkinson has remembered how Whittaker reacted confidently to the students' questions and gave a lively presentation. Impressed with Whittaker's performance, one of the students asked him why he was no longer on the Supreme Court. Whittaker frankly admitted that he had had a nervous breakdown and that his doctor advised him he would die if he did not retire.[136] There was no mention of the depression that had afflicted him periodically throughout his life or of his thoughts of suicide. These remained a family secret for the next twenty-five years. In fact, unknown to the public, it was the depression he struggled with that drove Whittaker to the hospital again in November 1973. Earlier that year he had suffered through a protracted case of influenza, causing him to fall behind in his work for General Motors. This distressed him as he worried over his inability to complete his duties. That same year a long-time friend and client of Whittaker's died, and, according to his son, Kent, Whittaker had a great fear of death. Becoming both physically and mentally exhausted and suffering to a lesser extent the same symptoms that forced him off the Court, Whittaker admitted himself to St. Luke's Hospital in Kansas City for recovery. Unaware of Whittaker's condition, the local press reported that Whittaker stayed in the hospital for five days when, in fact, he remained hospitalized for several weeks.[137]

This was not Whittaker's first trip to St. Luke's since his retirement from the Court. In 1967 he spent a month there recovering from a collapsed right lung, and in 1970 his wife, Winifred, suffered a heart attack and remained hospitalized there for one month. This time, though, too many complications prevented Whittaker from recovering. Several doctors treated his depression, and the lithium they prescribed improved his condition. During his final days Whittaker was happy and talkative. He seemed to be recovering well from his depression, but then unexpectedly his kidneys failed and he was placed on dialysis. An undiagnosed abdominal aneurysm had shut off blood flow to his renal arteries causing urinary failure. At 2:00 P.M. on Monday, November 26, 1973, Whittaker died suddenly when his aorta burst. His son, Keith, was at the hospital at the time and rushed to his room where doctors tried to resuscitate Whittaker, but it was too late.[138]

Funeral services for Whittaker were held two days later at the Central United Methodist Church, located one block west of the University of Missouri-Kansas City Law School. Clergymen from both the United Methodist and Roman Catholic faiths participated in the service, which lasted nearly an hour, with over 200 people in attendance. His family had Whittaker buried in his judicial robe at Calvary Cemetery in Kansas City. Buried next to him is his wife, Winifred, who survived him by eighteen years. She continued to reside in their new three-bedroom condominium at 333 West Meyer Boulevard that they moved into just before Whittaker's death. For a time Winifred's two younger sisters, Irene and Norine Pugh, lived with her and kept her company. The Whittakers' grave marker is a simple, flat gray stone, relatively small, engraved with a cross. In one letter of condolence to Whittaker's sister, Hazel, a sympathetic friend offered the best epitaph for Whittaker. He wrote, "Charley was a good man, a faithful husband and attentive father and a generous brother. He brought distinction and honor to the family name. Honesty and integrity were his hallmarks."[139]

Afterword

Locally, Missouri lawyers and judges, particularly in Kansas City, have been immensely proud of Charles Whittaker's achievements. One year after his death several of his former law clerks and law associates met in Washington as members of the Supreme Court Bar to commemorate Whittaker's passing and to honor his memory with words of praise. These dedications were then presented to the Supreme Court for preservation in the public record.[1] The following year the Lawyers Association of Kansas City, of which Whittaker was a founding member, inaugurated the annual presentation of "The Whittaker Award." This honor, expanded in 1996 to include both a local and national recipient, has recognized those in the legal profession who "promote the welfare of the public and of the bar, encourage cordial relations among members of the bar, advance the science of jurisprudence, support the administration of justice, and aid and support the courts in the administration of their rules governing the practice of law."[2]

The most distinguished public recognition for Whittaker came twenty years after his death when the new federal courthouse, located at Ninth and Locust in downtown Kansas City, was named in his honor. The chief judge of the district court for the Western District of Missouri, Joseph E. Stevens, who worked as a research assistant in Whittaker's law office forty years earlier, was principally responsible for promoting the naming, and in 1994 Congress passed and President Bill Clinton signed into law the designation "Charles Evans Whittaker United States Courthouse."[3] This imposing eleven-story structure took three years to build and cost over $90 million. Its unusual crescent-shape design anchors the north end of the Ilus Davis (former mayor) Civic Mall with Kansas City's City Hall at the south end. Located one block

The Charles Evans Whittaker United States Courthouse. Completed in 1998 at a cost of over $20 million, the new federal courthouse in Kansas City has a unique circular design. Built on the site of Kansas City's first YMCA building, the courthouse sits one block north of the site where once stood Whittaker's first Kansas City residence (the second YMCA building) and overlooks the new civic mall extending south to city hall. (Photograph courtesy of General Services Administration)

north of the former YMCA building, the new courthouse overlooks the place where once Charles Whittaker studied in his first two years at law school. At the building's dedication, Supreme Court Justice Clarence Thomas praised Whittaker's "virtues of hard work and integrity,"[4] and Whittaker's family presented a commemorative display consisting of Whittaker's portrait and all three of his judicial commissions signed by President Eisenhower. When asked about the building naming, Whittaker's son, Kent, a lawyer in Kansas City, said, "You could name all the fountains or avenues in Kansas City after him and it wouldn't make any difference. At one time [1979] consideration was given to naming the new [University of Missouri-Kansas City] law school after him. But I know nothing would have meant as much to him as having the courthouse named after him."[5]

Appendix A:
Whittaker's Scheduled Classes for Law School[1]

Freshman Year, 1920-21

Blackstone's Commentaries. . . . . 11 weeks
Contracts . . . . 16 weeks
Torts . . . . 17 weeks
Criminal law . . . . 12 weeks
Kent's Commentaries . . . . 13 weeks
Sales. . . . . 10 weeks
Agency . . . . 15 weeks
Domestic Relations . . . . 10 weeks
Moot Court

Sophomore Year, 1921-22

Common Law Pleading . . . . 9 weeks
Statutory Rights & Remedies . . . . 10 weeks
Equity. . . . . 10 weeks
Bailments. . . . . 13 weeks
Workmen's Comp. Law . . . . 10 weeks
Code Pleading . . . . 24 weeks
Bankruptcy & Fraudulent Conveyances . . . . 9 weeks

Damages . . . . 10 weeks
Roman Law . . . . 5 weeks

Junior Year, 1922-23

Corporations . . . . 10 weeks
Real Property . . . . 12 weeks
Partnership . . . . 10 weeks
Wills & Administration of Estates . . . . 14 weeks
Equity Jurisprudence . . . . 8 weeks
Negotiable Instruments . . . . 10 weeks
Evidence . . . . 19 weeks
Insurance . . . . 13 weeks
Mines and Mining was dropped

Senior Year, 1923-24

Conflict of Laws . . . . 8 weeks
Corporations . . . . 7 weeks
Real Property . . . . 15 weeks
Municipal Corporations . . . . 10 weeks
Extraordinary Remedies . . . . 10 weeks
International Law . . . . 6 weeks
Guaranty and Suretyship . . . . 13 weeks
Constitutional Law . . . . 10 weeks
Pleading & Practice Under Missouri
   Statutes & Legal Ethics . . . . 7 weeks

Appendix B:
Growth of Large Law Firms
in Kansas City

1924	*Members*
1. Lathrop, Morrow, Fox and Moore	15
2. Miller, Camack, Winger and Reeder	12
3. Krauthoff, McClintock and Quant	9
4. Haff, Mersevey, German and Michaels	8
5. Morrison, Gossett, Ellis, Dietrich and Tyler	8
6. Nugent, Wylder and Berger	7
7. Scarritt, Jones, Seddon and North	7
8. Cooper, Neel and Wright	7
9. Watson, Gage and Ess	5

Source: *Martindale's American Law Directory*, 1924.

1932	*Members*
1. Lathrop, Crane, Reynolds, Sawyer and Mersereau	16
2. Morrison, Nugent, Wylder and Berger	12
3. Watson, Ess, Groner, Barnett and Whittaker	11
4. Mersevey, Michaels, Blackmar, Newkirk and Eager	10
5. Ryland, Stinson, Mag and Thomson	9

Source: *Martindale-Hubbell Law Directory*, 1932.

1943	*Members*
1. Watson, Ess, Groner, Barnett and Whittaker	18
2. Ryland, Stinson, Mag and Thomson	18
3. Lathrop, Crane, Reynolds, Sawyer and Mersereau	16
4. Morrison, Nugent, Berger, Byers and Johns	13
5. Michaels, Blackmar, Newkirk, Eager and Swanson	11

Source: *Martindale-Hubbell Law Directory*, 1943.

1953	*Members*
1. Stinson, Mag, Thomson, McEvers and Fizzell	30
2. Watson, Ess, Whittaker, Marshall and Enggas	25
3. Morrison, Hecker, Buck, Cozad and Rogers	23
4. Spencer, Fane, Britt and Browne	15
5. Lathrop, Woodson, Righter, Blackwell and Parker	13
6. Blackmar, Newkirk, Eager, Swanson and Midgley	12

Source: *Martindale-Hubbell Law Directory*, 1953.

Appendix C:
Changing Names of
the Watson Law Firm

1887	Beebe, Randolph and Watson
1892	Beebe and Watson
1905	Douglass and Watson
1913	Watson and Watson
1914	Watson, Watson and Alford
1915	Watson, Gage and Watson
1919	Watson, Gage and Ess
1930	Watson, Gage, Ess, Groner, and Barnett
1932	Watson, Ess, Groner, Barnett and Whittaker
1946	Watson, Ess, Barnett, Whittaker and Marshall
1949	Watson, Ess, Whittaker, Marshall, and Enggas
1954	Watson, Ess, Marshall and Enggas
1994	Watson and Marshall (until 1996)

Source: *Truffles: The Watson, Ess, Marshall and Enggas Newsletter* (January-February, 1987).

Appendix D:
Clients of the
Watson Law Firm

1920s

Union Pacific Railroad, Kansas City Livestock Exchange, Traders National Bank, Produce Exchange Bank, Broadway Bank, *Kansas City Star*, Constitution Indemnity, Postal Telegraph Cable, Wilson and Company, and Witte Engine Works.

1930s (additional clients)

Dierks Lumber and Coal, Barrick Publishing, Chicago Northwestern Railway, Southern Pacific, Kansas City Public Service, Mid-continent Air Transport, Interstate Transit Lines, Kansas City Hay Dealers Association, Kansas City Testing Laboratories, Jensen-Salsberry Laboratories, Silica Products, Seidlitz Paint and Varnish, Columbian Electric, R. V. Aycock, Postal Life and Casualty Insurance, Union Indemnity, Public Indemnity, and Yellow Cab.

1940s (additional clients)

Pickering Lumber, Sutherland Lumber, Phoenix Indemnity, London Guarantee and Accident, Eagle Indemnity, Royal Indemnity, American Surety, New York Casualty, Manufacturers Casualty, Sun Indemnity, Standard Surety and Casualty, Traders and General Insurance, City National

Bank & Trust, Toplis and Harding, Joyce and Company, Minneapolis-Moline Power Implement, George Muehlbach Brewing, Burroughs Adding Machine, and Montgomery Ward.

1950s (additional clients)

Armour and Company, Safeway Stores, Overland Greyhound Lines, Corn Products Corporation, J. I. Case Company, Cook Chemical, Falls Spring Corporation, The Borden Company, and Robinson Shoe Stores.

Source: *Martindale-Hubbell Law Directory.*

Appendix E:
Opinions Rendered by Charles E. Whittaker While Serving on the Lower Federal Courts

Opinions Rendered by Judge Charles E. Whittaker
while serving on the United States District Court,
Western District of Missouri[1]

(Listed alphabetically by date)

Baker v. Dale, 123 F. Supp. 364 (W. D. Mo. 1954)
Brent v. Westerman, 123 F. Supp. 835 (W. D. Mo. 1954)
C. S. Foreman Co. v H. B. Zachry Co., 122 F. Supp. 859 (W. D. Mo. 1954)
Cooke v. Ford Motor Co., 122 F. Supp. 645 (W. D. Mo. 1954)
Cowley v. Auto Transports, Inc., 122 F. Supp. 689 (W. D. Mo. 1954)
Hart v. Leihy, 122 F. Supp. 510 (W. D. Mo. 1954)
In re Market Basket, 122 F. Supp. 321 (W. D. Mo. 1954)
Lane v. Singer Sewing Machine Co., 122 F. Supp. 694 (W. D. Mo. 1954)
Miller v. United States, 124 F. Supp. 203 (W. D. Mo. 1954)
Smith v. Christian, 124 F. Supp. 201 (W. D. Mo. 1954)
United States v. Hackett, 123 F. Supp. 104 (W. D. Mo. 1954)

United States v. Hackett, 123 F. Supp. 106 (W. D. Mo. 1954)
Weldon v. Steele, 125 F. Supp. 667 (W. D. Mo. 1954)
Wright v. Steele, 125 F. Supp. 1 (W. D. Mo. 1954)
C. S. Foreman Co. v. H. B. Zachry Co., 127 F. Supp. 901 (W. D. Mo. 1955)
Collins v. Public Service Commission of Missouri, 129 F. Supp. 722 (W. D. Mo. 1955)
Davis v. University of Kansas City, 129 F. Supp. 716 (W. D. Mo. 1955)
Exhibitors Service v. Abbey Rents, 135 F. Supp. 112 (W. D. Mo. 1955)
General Elec. Co. v. Central Transit Warehouse Co., 127 F. Supp. 817 (W. D. Mo. 1955)
Pucci v. Blatz Brewing Co., 127 F. Supp. 747 (W. D. Mo. 1955)
Rosenfeld v. Continental Building Operating Co., 135 F. Supp. 465 (W. D. Mo. 1955)
Southern Kansas Greyhound Lines v. United States, 134 F. Supp. 502 (W. D. Mo. 1955)
Stamm v. American Telephone & Telegraph, 129 F. Supp. 719 (W. D. Mo. 1955)
United States v. Columbia Erection Corp., 134 F. Supp. 305 (W. D. Mo. 1955)
United States v. Harris, 133 F. Supp. 796 (W. D. Mo. 1955)
United States v. One 1954 Cadillac & Weston and General Motors Acceptance Corp., 135 F. Supp. 1 (W. D. Mo. 1955)
United States v. Sweet, 133 F. Supp. 3 (W. D. Mo. 1955)
Wessing v. Am. Indemnity Co. of Galveston, Tex., 127 F. Supp. 775 (W. D. Mo. 1955)
Western Newspaper Union v. Woodward, 133 F. Supp. 17 (W. D. Mo. 1955)
Wiles v. Union Wire Rope Corporation, 134 F. Supp. 299 (W. D. Mo. 1955)
Farm Bureau Corp. Mill & Sup. v. Blue Star Foods, 137 F. Supp. 486 (W. D. Mo. 1956)
Henley v. Panhandle Eastern Pipeline Co., 138 F. Supp. 768 (W. D. Mo. 1956)
In re McKinley, 138 F. Supp. 4 (W. D. Mo. 1956)
In re Patterson, 139 F. Supp. 830 (W. D. Mo. 1956)
Jerrolds-Stephens Co. v. Gustaveson, Inc., 138 F. Supp. 11 (W. D. Mo. 1956)
Miller v. Connell, 141 F. Supp. 361 (W. D. Mo. 1956)
St. Paul Fire and Marine Ins. v. Continental Building, 137 F. Supp. 493 (W. D. Mo. 1956)

Federal Rules Decisions

Cole v. Riss & Co., 16 F. R. D. 116 (W. D. Mo. 1954)
Cole v. Riss & Co., 16 F. R. D. 263 (W. D. Mo. 1954)
Colin v. Thompson, 16 F. R. D. 194 (W. D. Mo. 1954)
Federal Enterprises, Inc. v. Frank Allbritten Motors, 16 F. R. D. 109 (W. D. Mo. 1954)

Helverson v. J. J. Newberry Co., 16 F. R. D. 330 (W. D. Mo. 1954)
Soetaert v. Kansas City Coca Cola Bottling Co., 16 F. R. D. 1 (W. D. Mo. 1954)
United States v. Smith, 16 F. R. D. 372 (W. D. Mo. 1954)
Jenkins v. Westinghouse Electric Co., 18 F. R. D. 267 (W. D. Mo. 1955)
Perry v. Edwards, 16 F. R. D. 131 (W. D. Mo. 1955)
Robinson v. Tracy, 16 F. R. D. 113 (W. D. Mo. 1955)
United States v. Bearing Distributors Co., 18 F. R. D. 228 (W. D. Mo. 1955)

Opinions Rendered by Judge Charles E. Whittaker while serving on the United States Court of Appeals Eighth Circuit[2]

Arkansas Public Service Comm. v. United States, 147 F. Supp. 454 (E. D. Ark. 1956)*
Carpenter v. Borden Co., 147 F. Supp. 445 (S. D. Iowa 1956)*
Hartman v. Lauchli, 238 F. 2d 881 (1956)
Jones Truck Lines v. United States, 146 F. Supp. 697 (W. D. Ark. 1956)*
Mitchell v. Burgess, 239 F. 2d 484 (1956)
Moog Industries v. Federal Trade Commission, 238 F. 2d 43 (1956)
Schmidt v. United States, 237 F. 2d 542 (1956)
Schneider v. Kelm, 237 F. 2d 721 (1956)
Soso v. Atlas Powder Co., 238 F. 2d 388 (1956)
United States v. Mills, 237 F. 2d 401 (1956)
Fitts' Estate v. Commissioner of Internal Revenue, 237 F. 2d 729 (1956) (dissent)
Apperwhite v. Illinois Central Railroad Co., 239 F. 2d 306 (1957)
Kleven v. United States, 240 F. 2d 270 (1957)
Mesirow v. Duggan, 240 F. 2d 751 (1957)
Raffety v. Parker, 241 F. 2d 594 (1957)

These cases were each decided in different federal district courts while Whittaker served as an appellate court judge. Chief Judge Gardner of the Eighth Circuit asked Whittaker to assist in clearing up lower court dockets, and Whittaker gladly obliged.

Appendix F:
Justices Who Served
with Justice Whittaker

Listed in order of appointment to the Supreme Court

Justice (State) — Appointed by*	Replaced	Term	Life Span
Hugo L. Black (Ala.) — FDR	VanDevanter	8/37–9/71	1886–1971
Felix Frankfurter (Mass.) — FDR	Cardozo	1/39–8/62	1882–1965
William O. Douglas (Conn.) — FDR	Brandeis	4/39–11/75	1898–1980
Harold H. Burton (Ohio) — HST	Roberts	10/45–10/58	1888–1964
Tom C. Clark (Tex.) — HST	Murphy	8/49–6/67	1899–1977
Earl Warren (Chief) (Cal.) — DDE	Vinson	10/53–6/69	1891–1978
John M. Harlan (N.Y.) — DDE	Jackson	3/55–9/71	1899–1971
William J. Brennan (N.J.) — DDE	Minton	10/56–7/90	1906–1997
Charles E. Whittaker (Mo.) — DDE	Reed	3/57–3/62	1901–1973
Potter Stewart (Ohio) — DDE	Burton	10/58–7/81	1915–1985

*FDR=Franklin D. Roosevelt; HST=Harry S Truman; DDE=Dwight D. Eisenhower

Appendix G:
Clerks Who Served
with Justice Whittaker

From March to August 1957

Manley O. Hudson, Jr.[1]
Harvard Law School

Alan C. Kohn
Washington University

1957 Term

Kenneth W. Dam
University of Chicago

Alan C. Kohn
Washington University

1958 Term

Heywood H. Davis
University of Kansas

William C. Canby, Jr.
University of Minnesota

1959 Term

Patrick F. McCartan
Notre Dame University

Jerome B. Libin
University of Michigan

1960 Term

James M. Edwards
Yale Law School

D. Lawrence Gunnels
Washington University

1961 Term

James N. Adler[2]
University of Michigan

D. Lawrence Gunnels[3]
Washington University

Appendix H:
Opinions Rendered by Justice Whittaker While Serving on the Supreme Court of the United States

Listed by Type of Decision and Date Rendered

Majority Opinions

1956 Term

Fourco Glass Co. v. Transmirra Prod. Corp., 353 U.S. 222 (1957)
Lehmann v. United States ex rel. Carson, 353 U.S. 685 (1957)
Mulcahey v. Catalanotte, 353 U.S. 692 (1957)

1957 Term

Bonetti v. Rogers, 356 U.S. 691 (1958)
Heikkinen v. United States, 355 U.S. 273 (1958)
Lawn v. United States, 355 U.S. 339 (1958)
Payne v. Arkansas, 356 U.S. 560 (1958)
Staub v. City of Baxley, 355 U.S. 313 (1958)
Tacoma v. Taxpayers of Tacoma, 357 U.S. 320 (1958)

United States v. F. & M. Schaefer Brewing Co., 356 U.S. 227 (1958)
United States v. Hvass, 355 U.S. 570 (1958)

1958 Term

Allied Stores of Ohio v. Bowers, 358 U.S. 522 (1959)
Commissioner of Internal Revenue v. Hansen, 360 U.S. 446 (1959)
Draper v. United States, 358 U.S. 307 (1959)
Herd v. Krawill Machinery Corp., 359 U.S. 297 (1959)
Leedom v. Kyne, 358 U.S. 184 (1958)
N. L. R. B. v. Cabot Carbon Co., 360 U.S. 203 (1959)
Parsons v. Smith, 359 U.S. 215 (1959)
Sims v. United States, 359 U.S. 108 (1959)
Williams v. Oklahoma, 358 U.S. 576 (1959)
Youngstown Sheet & Tube Co. v. Bowers, 358 U.S. 534 (1959)

1959 Term

Commissioner of Internal Revenue v. Acker, 361 U.S. 87 (1959)
Federal Power Comm'n v. Tuscarora Indian Nation, 362 U.S. 99 (1960)
Florida Lime & Avocado Growers v. Jacobsen, 362 U.S. 73 (1960)
Hoffman v. Blaski, 363 U.S. 335 (1960)
Minneapolis & St. Louis Ry Co. v. United States, 361 U.S. 173 (1959)
Parr v. United States, 363 U.S. 370 (1960)
United States v. Robinson, 361 U.S. 220 (1960)

1960 Term

Aro Mfg. Co. v. Convertible Top Replacement Co., 365 U.S. 336 (1961)
Bulova Watch Co. v. United States, 365 U.S. 753 (1961)
Chapman v. United States, 365 U.S. 610 (1961)
Lott, et al. v. United States, 367 U.S. 421 (1961)
McNeal, Jr. v. Culver, 365 U.S. 109 (1961)
McPhaul v. United States, 364 U.S. 372 (1960)
Meyer v. United States, 364 U.S. 410 (1960)
Moses Lake Homes, Inc. v. Grant County, 365 U.S. 744 (1961)
Slagle v. Ohio, 366 U.S. 259 (1961)
United States v. Consolidated Edison Co., 366 U.S. 380 (1961)
United States v. Neustadt, 366 U.S. 696 (1961)
Wilson v. Schnettler, 365 U.S. 381 (1961)

1961 Term

Killian v. United States, 368 U.S. 231 (1961)
Turnbow v. Commissioner of Internal Revenue, 368 U.S. 337 (1961)

Concurring Opinions

1957 Term

Byrd v. Blue Ridge Rural Elec. Coop., 356 U.S. 525 (1958)*
NLRB v. Duval Jewelry Co., 357 U.S. 1 (1958)
United States v. Procter & Gamble Co., 356 U.S. 677 (1958)

1958 Term

Frank v. Maryland, 359 U.S. 360 (1959)

1959 Term

Commissioner of Internal Revenue v. Duberstein, 363 U.S. 278 (1960)
Davis v. Virginian Railway Co., 361 U.S. 354 (1960)*
Forman v. United States, 361 U.S. 416 (1960)
Inman v. Baltimore & Ohio R. Co., 361 U.S. 138 (1959)
McElroy v. United States, ex rel. Guagliardo, 361 U.S. 281 (1960)*
Sentilles v. Inter-Caribbean Shipping Corp., 361 U.S. 107 (1959)
United States v. Mersky, 361 U.S. 431 (1960)
United Steelworkers of America v. American Mfg. Co., 363 U.S. 564 (1960)

1960 Term

Carbo v. United States, 364 U.S. 611 (1961)
Gomillion v. Lightfoot, 364 U.S. 339 (1960)
International Assn. of Machinists v. Street, 367 U.S. 740 (1961)*
James v. United States, 366 U.S. 213 (1961)*
Lathrop v. Donohue, 367 U.S. 820 (1961)

Per Curiam

SEC v. Louisiana Public Service Comm'n, 353 U.S. 368 (1957)
Dessalernos v. Savoretti, 356 U.S. 269 (1958)
Harmon v. Brucker, 355 U.S. 579 (1958)
Bushnell v. Ellis, 366 U.S. 418 (1961)
Radiant Burners v. Peoples Gas Light & Coke Co., 364 U.S. 656 (1961)

Dissenting Opinions

1957 Term

Alaska Industrial Bd. v. Chugach Elec. Assn., 356 U.S. 320 (1958)
Denver Union Stock Yd. Co. v. Producers Livestock, 356 U.S. 282 (1958)
Detroit v. Murray Corp., 355 U.S. 489 (1958)
Flora v. United States, 357 U.S. 63 (1958)

Concurring in part and dissenting in part

McAllister v. Magnolia Petroleum Co., 357 U.S. 221 (1958)
Perez v. Brownell, Jr., 356 U.S. 44 (1958)
United States v. R. F. Ball Construction Co., 355 U.S. 587 (1958)
United States v. Detroit, 355 U.S. 466 (1958)
United States v. Township of Muskegon, 355 U.S. 484 (1958)

1958 Term

American Trucking Assns. v. Frisco Trans. Co., 358 U.S. 133 (1958)
Mitchell v. Lublin, McGaughy & Associates, 358 U.S. 207 (1959)
Moore v. Terminal R. Assn. of St. Louis, 358 U.S. 31 (1958)
Northwestern States Portland Cement Co. v. Minnesota, 358 U.S. 450 (1959)
Railway Express Agency v. Virginia, 358 U.S. 434 (1959)
Teamsters Union v. Oliver, 358 U.S. 283 (1959)

1959 Term

Arnold v. Kanowsky, 361 U.S. 388 (1960)
Continental Grain Co. v. Barge FBL-585, 364 U.S. 19 (1960)
Federal Trade Comm'n v. Henry Broch & Co., 363 U.S. 166 (1960)
Flora v. United States, 362 U.S. 145 (1960)
Goett v. Union Carbide Corp., 361 U.S. 340 (1960)
Hess, Jr. v. United States, 361 U.S. 314 (1960)
Local Lodge No. 1424 v. N. L. R. B., 362 U.S. 411 (1960)
Marine Cooks v. Panama S. S. Co., 362 U.S. 365 (1960)
Mitchell v. Robert DeMario Jewelry, Inc., 361 U.S. 288 (1960)
Railroad Telegraphers v. C. & N. W. R. Co., 362 U.S. 330 (1960)
Scripto v. Carson, 362 U.S. 207 (1960)
United States v. Kaiser, 363 U.S. 299 (1960)
United Steelworkers of America v. Enterprise Wheel & Car., 363 U.S. 593 (1960)
United Steelworkers v. Warrior & Gulf Nav. Co., 363 U.S. 574 (1960)

1960 Term

Boynton v. Virginia, 364 U.S. 454 (1960)
Civil Aeronautics Bd. v. Delta Air Lines, 367 U.S. 316 (1961)
Deutch v. United States, 367 U.S. 456 (1961)
Goldberg v. Whitaker House Coop., 366 U.S. 28 (1961)
Kossick v. United Fruit, 365 U.S. 731 (1961)
Local 60, United Brotherhood of Carpenters v. NLRB, 365 U.S. 651 (1961)
Local 357, International Brotherhood of Teamsters v. NLRB, 365 U.S. 667 (1961)
Maynard v. Durham & Southern Ry. Co., 365 U.S. 160 (1961)
Michigan National Bank v. Michigan, 365 U.S. 467 (1961)
United States v. Hougham, 364 U.S. 310 (1960)
United States v. Virginia Elec. & Power Co., 365 U.S. 624 (1961)

1961 Term

Federal Trade Comm'n v. Henry Brock & Co., 368 U.S. 360 (1962)
Still v. Norfolk & Western Ry. Co., 368 U.S. 35 (1961)

Appendix I:
Whittaker Award Recipients
Through 2004

1976   Gordon D. Gee
1977   Arthur Mag
1978   Patrick D. Kelly
1979   Judge William Becker
1980   John R. Gibson
1981   Ilus W. Davis
1982   (no recipient)
1983   Judge Timothy D. O'Leary
1984   Elwood L. Thomas and Harry P. Thomson, Jr.
1985   Judge Floyd Gibson
1986   David B. B. Helfrey and the Kansas City Organized Strike Force
1987   Reed O. Gentry
1988   Stanley P. Weiner
1989   Judge Lewis W. Clymer
1990   William H. Colby
1991   W. H. "Bert" Bates
1992   Edward A. Smith
1993   Frank J. Murphy
1994   Judge Elmo B. Hunter
1995   Judge H. Michael Coburn (posthumously)
1996   Judge Joseph E. Stevens, Jr, and John C. Danforth, Jr.

1997   Judge Russell G. Clark and Judge William H. Webster
1998   David Field Oliver and Morris S. Dees, Jr.
1999   Richard F. Halliburton/Legal Aid of Western Missouri and Judge
         Richard P. Matsch
2000   Linda Gill Taylor and Kenneth W. Dam
2001   Harry Wiggins and Daniel R. Glickman
2002   Linda J. French and Judge Harry T. Edwards
2003   J. Eugene Balloun and Nancy Kassebaum Baker
2004   Heywood "Woody" Davis and Sean O'Brien

Chapter Notes

Preface

1. David N. Atkinson, "Minor Supreme Court Justices: Their Characteristics and Importance," *Florida State University Law Review* 3 (1975): 355.

2. Leon Friedman, "Charles Whittaker," in *The Justices of the United States Supreme Court: Their Lives and Major Opinions*, eds. Leon Friedman and Fred L. Israel, vol. 4 (New York: Chelsea House, 1969), 2903.

3. Bernard Schwartz, *Super Chief: Earl Warren and His Supreme Court—A Judicial Biography* (New York: New York University Press, 1983), 216, and Schwartz, *A Book of Legal Lists: The Best and Worst in American Law* (New York: Oxford University Press, 1997), 30.

4. Victoria S. Woeste, "Charles Evans Whittaker," in *The Supreme Court Justices: A Biographical Dictionary*, ed. Melvin I. Urofsky (New York: Garland Publishing, 1994), 534.

5. See Henry Abraham, *Justices and Presidents: A Political History of Appointments to the Supreme Court*, 3d ed. (New York: Oxford University Press, 1992), 271.

6. "The New Justice," *Time*, March 11, 1957, 17.

7. Albert Blaustein and Roy Mersky, "The Twelve Great Justices of All Time," *Life*, October 15, 1971, 59. See also Blaustein and Mersky, *The First One Hundred Justices: Statistical Studies on the Supreme Court of the United States* (Hamden, Connecticut: Archon Books, 1978), 48.

8. See *Kansas City Star*, February 19, 1954,

and Richard L. Miller, *Whittaker: Struggles of a Supreme Court Justice* (Westport, Connecticut: Greenwood Press, 2002), 5.

9. Russell Baker, interview by author, June 20, 1996. Whittaker was admitted to the Supreme Court bar on October 9, 1944. See Application for Admission, Charles Whittaker, 16952, Record Group 267, Records of the United States Supreme Court, Applications, National Archives, Washington, D.C.

10. Abraham, *Justices and Presidents*, 270, and Robert J. Steamer, *The Supreme Court in Crisis* (Boston: University of Massachusetts Press, 1971), 245. Steamer also mistakenly claimed Arthur Goldberg was President Kennedy's *first* appointment to replace Felix Frankfurter and Byron White was his *second* to replace Whittaker, which was, in fact, just the opposite. Ibid., 262–63.

11. See Alan Kohn, "Supreme Court Law Clerk, 1957–1958 A Reminiscence," *Journal of Supreme Court History* (1998): 40–52. See also Kohn, "Charles E. Whittaker," in *The Supreme Court Justices: Illustrated Biographies, 1789–1995*, ed. Clare Cushman, 2d ed. (Washington, D. C.: Congressional Quarterly, 1995), 451–55.

12. See Judith Cole, "Mr. Justice Charles Evans Whittaker: A Case Study in Judicial Recruitment and Behavior" (M. A. thesis, University of Missouri–Kansas City, 1972).

13. Compare Miller, *Whittaker: Struggles*, and Craig Smith, "Charles Evans Whittaker, Associate Justice of the Supreme Court" (M. A. thesis, University of Missouri–Kansas City, 1997).

1. Leaving the Farm

1. Norma Jean Parrot, interview by author, June 24, 1996. The Native Americans relocated to the Doniphan County area included the Iowa, Sac, Fox, and Kickapoo. Although the *Kansas City Times*, March 4, 1957, reported Whittaker's grandfather moved to Doniphan County in 1854, Richard Miller contended that he moved there illegally in 1853, prior to passage of the Kansas-Nebraska Act, *Whittaker: Struggles of a Supreme Court Justice* (Westport, Connecticut: Greenwood Press, 2002), 1.

2. G. Thomas Vanbebber, interview by author, October 4, 2002. See W. P. King, comp., *A Souvenir: The St. Joseph & Grand Island Railroad: Illustrated* (St. Joseph, Missouri: Lon Hardman Press, 1895), 105, and *Illustrated Doniphan County: 1837–1916*, Supplement to the *Weekly (Troy) Kansas Chief*, April 6, 1916. See also Robert W. Richmond, *Kansas: A Land of Contrasts*, 4th ed. (Wheeling, Illinois: Harlan Davidson, 1999), 29, 60, and 81.

3. Warranty Deeds, November 20, 1891, vol. 30, p. 499, and March 3, 1900, vol. 42, p. 562, and Patent for School Land, March 3, 1900, vol. 43, p. 285, Doniphan County Record of Deeds, Troy, Kansas.

4. District No. 34, Brush Creek, Doniphan County Record of Deeds.

5. *Troy Kansas Chief*, March 7, 1957.

6. Delayed Certificate of Birth, March 1, 1960, Kansas State Board of Health, Charles Whittaker papers, Kansas City, Missouri.

7. Dorothy Kiehnhoff, interview by author, June 24, 1996.

8. Quoted in *Kansas City Times*, March 4, 1957, and *Troy Kansas Chief*, March 7, 1957.

9. Quoted in "Doniphan County Folks Recall Judge's Youth," undated newspaper article, Don Harter papers, Troy, Kansas. Also Kiehnhoff, interview.

10. Quoted in *Kansas City Star*, September 20, 1964.

11. Ibid.

12. See Senate Committee on the Judiciary, *Nomination of Charles E. Whittaker: Hearing before the Committee on the Judiciary*, 85th Cong., 1st sess., March 18, 1957, 32. Discrepancies have been discovered that raise questions about Whittaker's testimony before the Senate Judiciary Committee. County records show him enrolled at Brush Creek School every year from 1906 to 1920, five years longer than he claimed he attended. His sister, Dorothy, recalled that their mother died when Whittaker was eighteen-years-old and already attending the part-time law school in St. Joseph, Missouri, when he returned home for the funeral.

Kiehnhoff, interview. Other family members also reported Whittaker went to law school in St. Joseph for a time. See "Doniphan County Folks Recall Judge's Youth." Records from the YMCA School of Law in St. Joseph no longer exist and any records from the high school in Troy were destroyed by fire shortly after Whittaker arrived in Kansas City.

13. Kiehnhoff, interview.

14. In Kansas the University of Kansas School of Law and Washburn College School of Law both required one year of college course work prior to admission, and in Missouri, the University of Missouri School of Law, Washington University School of Law, and St. Louis University School of Law all required one year of college course work for admission. There were three part-time law schools in St. Louis at the time and one in St. Joseph. Kansas had no part-time law schools. Alfred Z. Reed, *Training for the Public Profession of the Law: Historical Development and Principal Contemporary Problems of Legal Education in the United States* (New York: Carnegie Foundation for the Advancement of Teaching, 1921), 137–38.

15. Quoted in *Kansas City Star*, September 20, 1964.

16. Without noting source material, Miller claimed that Whittaker represented clients in justice of the peace courts while attending law school (it was unclear whether he served as prosecuting or defense counsel), *Whittaker: Struggles*, 2–3. The source for this assertion, the *Kansas City Star*, February 19, 1954, made a similar claim. It was inconceivable with his schedule how Whittaker could have appeared in court as a law student. Besides, as Miller himself noted, the Watson law offices represented corporate elites; it was unlikely they permitted someone from their offices to engage in low-income debt collection.

17. See Wayne K. Hobson, *The American Legal Profession and the Organizational Society, 1890–1930* (New York: Garland Publishing, 1986), 123–24.

18. "The Kansas City School of Law," University of Missouri–Kansas City Archives (UA-KC). See also Lawrence Larsen, *Federal Justice in Western Missouri: The Judges, The Cases, The Times* (Columbia: University of Missouri Press, 1994), 149.

19. Minutes of Annual Meeting of Faculty of Kansas City School of Law (Faculty Minutes, KCSL), June 5, 1920, UA-KC. For a complete list of all subjects Whittaker studied in law school, see Appendix A.

20. In 1918, there were 144 students enrolled at the K. C. School of Law, by 1925 that had climbed to 589, and in 1928 it stood at 719.

Missouri's three full-time law schools, the University of Missouri, Washington University, and St. Louis University, had a combined total attendance in 1928 of only 455 students. See Alfred Z. Reed, "Review of Legal Education in the United States and Canada for the Year 1928," *Annual Review of Legal Education* (1928): 32–33.

21. See Faculty Minutes, KCSL, June 1, 1918, May 81, 1919, June 5, 1920, June 4, 1921, June 3, 1922, May 5, 1923, and May 31, 1924, and Minutes of Meeting of Special Committee of Kansas City School of Law, December 9, 1924, UA-KC.

22. The school initially paid $15,000 for the property. After converting into cash securities $10,000 left in the school's Endowment fund to pay down the balance, the school then planned to pay the remaining $10,000 due on the property within one year to avoid interest charges. See Report of Elmer N. Powell, May 23, 1925, and Faculty Minutes, KCSL, June 4, 1921, and May 5, 1923, UA-KC. The school's many moves became the source of much confusion. For example, C. L. Kelliher claimed the school moved into the Ridge Building in 1910 and then to the fifth floor of the Nonquitt Building in 1924, "Kansas City School of Law Honored by American Bar Association," *Kansas City Bar Bulletin* 13 (December 1936): 4–6; Elmer Powell, on the other hand, claimed the school moved into the Nonquitt building in 1916, "The University of Kansas City School of Law," *Missouri Bar Journal* 14 (February 1943): 60, 79. According to the school's yearbook (*Pandex*, 1926), in 1899 the school moved out of the New York Life building and into the Ridge building, and in 1911 it moved into the Nonquitt building.

23. Faculty Minutes, KCSL, May 31, 1919, and June 3, 1922, UA-KC.

24. Reed, "Review of Legal Education," chart opposite p. 12.

25. Larsen, *Federal Justice*, 149–50.

26. Estimates vary, yet sources agree that part-time law schools increased at a spectacular rate relative to the growth of full-time schools. In 1890 there were fifty-one full-time schools in America; thirty years later there were eighty, an increase of fifty-seven percent. During that same time, part-time law schools went from ten to sixty-two schools, an increase of 520 percent. Jerold Auerbach estimated that by 1905 approximately one in three law students attended a part-time law school, *Unequal Justice: Lawyers and Social Change in Modern America* (New York: Oxford University Press, 1976), 94–97. See also James W. Hurst, *The Growth of American Law: The Law Makers* (Boston: Little, Brown, 1950), 273, and Kermit

L. Hall, *The Magic Mirror: Law in American History*, (New York: Oxford University Press, 1989), 218.

27. See Auerbach, *Unequal Justice*, 95–98, Hall, *The Magic Mirror*, 219, Hobson, *The American Legal Profession*, 118, and Robert B. Stevens, *Law School: Legal Education in America from the 1850s to the 1980s* (Chapel Hill: University of North Carolina Press, 1983), 102.

28. See, for examples, Henry Ballantine, "The Place in Legal Education of Evening and Correspondence Law Schools," *American Law School Review* 4 (February 1919): 369, Maurice Wormser, "The Problem of Evening Law Schools," *American Law School Review* 4 (November 1920): 544, 547, and Orvill C. Snyder, "The Function of the Night Law School," *American Law School Review* 7 (May 1933): 831–33. Charles Scott, the first student editor at the K. C. School of Law, gave his approbation to Snyder's views in "Evening School vs. Day School," *Kansas City Law Review* 1 (January 1933): 3. One year later, Orvill Snyder complained that part-time law schools suffered unwarranted criticism when compared to full-time schools because of a "catholic disregard of the fundamental divergencies of the two types," "The Problem of the Night Law School," *American Bar Association Journal* 20 (January 1934): 109. Paul Martin, the dean at Creighton University Law School, one of only four part-time law schools in 1919 with membership in the AALS, earlier wrote, "Night schools have come to stay, they supply a real need, and it is idle to point the finger of scorn at them merely because their sessions are held at night," in "Night Law Schools" *American Law School Review* 3 (Winter 1914): 455–56.

29. A similar study of medical schools around the turn of the century made a decided impact on the quality of medical education. Dozens of part-time medical schools closed; only "scientific" schools survived. According to Stevens, by 1920 seventy-five medical schools had closed, dropping the total from 160 to 85. During the same time, law schools had increased from 102 to 146. Leading academic and practicing lawyers were galled by this development, seeing the medical profession as "sanitized" while part-time law schools seemed to be thriving. *Law School*, 102–03.

30. See Reed, *Training for the Public Profession*, 56–59 and 398–402.

31. See Afterword. The cornerstone of the original YMCA building, dedicated by President Grover Cleveland on October 13, 1887, is displayed between two stone benches on the southeast corner of the new federal courthouse.

32. Kent Whittaker, interview by author,

April 11, 1996. In 1916 Hughes resigned from the Court after six years to accept the Republican nomination for president. Fourteen years later he returned to the Court as chief justice, where he served another eleven years.

33. Russell W. Gunn, "Remarks of Russell W. Gunn," in *In Memoriam, Honorable Charles Evans Whittaker*, Proceeding of the Bar and Officers of the Supreme Court of the United States and Proceedings Before the Supreme Court of the United States, February 19, 1975, Washington, D.C., 27. 'Man Without a Country,' an intensely patriotic story by Edward Everett Hale, was written as prose, not poetry. In April 1923 the fraternity house at 2506 Independence Avenue burned down and had to be relocated at 3516 Summit Street. See *Pandex* 17 (1921): 84, UA-KC.

34. Mabel Gunn, telephone interview by author, June 8, 1996, and Larsen, *Federal Justice*, 204. School records indicate that Truman was three years behind Whittaker, not one year as Whittaker claimed in Miller, *Whittaker: Struggles*, 4, n.13.

35. William McAdams, interview, October 1971, quoted in Judith Cole, "Mr. Justice Charles Evans Whittaker: A Case Study in Judicial Recruitment and Behavior" (M. A. thesis, University of Missouri–Kansas City, 1972), 15–16, n. 10.

36. Whittaker passed the Missouri bar examination on October 6, 1923, and graduated law school on June 3, 1924. At the time it was not at all unusual for law students to pass the bar examination before they graduated law school, despite Miller's exclamation that Whittaker had done so "*before* graduating at the head of his class," *Whittaker: Struggles*, 4. Miller's emphasis. While Whittaker's grades at law school are not available, school records indicate that he did not graduate *cum laude* or *summa cum laude*. See Faculty Minutes, KCSL, May 31, 1924, UA-KC.

37. Gunn, "Remarks," 27.

38. Walter A. Raymond to Marlin M. Volz, December 20, 1957, in Marlin M. Volz, "Mr. Justice Whittaker," *Notre Dame Lawyer* 33 (March 1958): 165–66.

39. *Pandex* 17 (1921): 84, UA-KC.

40. Faculty Minutes, KCSL, May 31, 1924, UA-KC.

41. *Pandex* 18 (1922): 62, UA-KC.

42. *Pandex* 19 (1923): 120, UA-KC.

43. Ibid.

44. The title of Whittaker's address is all that remains from his speech. Undoubtedly, the title was inspired by one of the poems he enjoyed reciting, Thomas Gray's "Elegy Written in a Country Churchyard," which includes the lines:

The boast of heraldry, the pomp of pow'r,
And all that beauty, all that wealth e'er gave,
Awaits alike th'inevitable hour:
The paths of glory lead but to the grave.

2. Thirty Years at the Bar

1. Charles Thompson, taped interview, 1987, p. 13, Charles Thompson papers, Kansas City, Missouri.

2. Louis Poplinger, interview by author, February 21, 2001.

3. Darrell L. Havener, interview by author, June 11, 1996. See also Kermit L. Hall, *The Magic Mirror: Law in American History* (New York: Oxford University Press, 1989), 212.

4. James W. Hurst, *The Growth of American Law: The Law Makers* (Boston: Little, Brown, 1950), 302–3.

5. See John R. Dos Passos, *The American Lawyer: As He Was—As He Is—As He Can Be* (New York: Banks Law Publishing, 1907), 25–27. According to John Johnson, American legal history in the early twentieth century was marked by a seemingly ubiquitous concern for finding, fashioning, and using new sources of information, what he called an "informational penchant." Fearful of inadequate data, lawyers were consumed by a need to discover, compile, present, or use myriad sources of information. *American Legal Culture, 1908–1940* (Westport, CT: Greenwood Press, 1981), 4–5.

6. Theron G. Strong, *Joseph H. Choate* (New York: Dodd, Mead, 1917), 128. Lawrence Larsen noted how many modern lawyers, especially those who perform specialized legal work in large firms, hardly know the way to the courthouse, *Federal Justice in Western Missouri: The Judges, The Cases, The Times* (Columbia: University of Missouri Press, 1994), 213–14.

7. Larsen, *Federal Justice*, 214.

8. Russell Baker, interview by author, June 20, 1996.

9. Wayne K. Hobson, *The American Legal Profession and the Organizational Society, 1890–1930* (New York: Garland Publishing, 1986), 143, and Hall, *The Magic Mirror*, 213.

10. Russell Baker, interview by author, February 21, 2001. According to Baker, the Watson firm for much of its history had no written partnership agreement. The partners operated under an oral agreement without any formal structure or table of organization. It was not until Watson sought to merge with another firm in 1984 to expand its client base that a formal, written partnership agreement was drafted.

The partners at Gardner, Davis, Kreamer, Norton, Hubbard and Ruzicka of Olathe, Kansas, in fact, were surprised to learn that Watson had no written partnership agreement.

11. For rankings of law firms in Kansas City, see Appendix B.

12. For Watson name changes, see Appendix C.

13. See "Smashing Boss Tom," *Clark County Courier*, February 16, February 23, March 1, March 29, and April 26, 1940, typed manuscript, and Thomas O. Baker, "Short Address to Kansas City Rotary Club," December 21, 1978, Vince Rawson papers, Kansas City, Missouri.

14. Baker, interview, 2001. See also Vernon Kassebaum, taped interview, 1987, pp. 6–7, Thompson papers.

15. Dick Fowler, *Leaders In Our Town* (Kansas City: Burd & Fletcher, n.d.), 139.

16. John Foard, interview by author, February 19, 2001. See also undated article, "Rustler Clue in Tires," John Foard papers, Kansas City, Missouri.

17. Poplinger, interview.

18. Gary Whittaker, interview by author, June 21, 1996. Thirty years after the death of Henry Ess the firm continued to bear his name. In 1994 the firm became simply Watson and Marshall at the insistence of some of its members.

19. Quoted in *Kansas City Star*, September 22, 1963. See also Fowler, *Leaders In Our Town*, 123.

20. Colvin Peterson, interview by author, February 21, 2001. Robert Donnellan, interview by author, February 12, 2001. Charles Thompson, interview by author, March 2, 2001.

21. Poplinger and Peterson, interviews. When Henry Ess died in 1963, Carl Enggas took over control of the firm. Richard Miller overlooked the reactions of Whittaker's colleagues where he noted, "Whittaker got along well with fellow attorneys in the firm," *Whittaker: Struggles of a Supreme Court Justice* (Westport, Connecticut: Greenwood Press, 2002), 27.

22. Peterson, Poplinger, and Thompson, interviews.

23. *Kansas City Star*, July 10, 1930. Also killed in the accident were the president of the Missouri Bar Association, Murat Boyle, the president of the Kansas City Golf Association, Eugene Lynn, a Kansas City builder, R. J. Delano, and the pilot, Gene Gabbert. Another companion, Frederick Dierks, vice president of Dierks Lumber and Coal, was not aboard the plane when it crashed; he had stayed behind to do more fishing.

24. For a comprehensive listing of Watson's growing numbers of clients, see Appendix D.

25. Thompson and Baker, interviews, 2001. James Duncan, interview by author, February 19, 2001.

26. Peterson, Thompson, Duncan, and Donnellan, interviews.

27. Vincent Rawson, interview by author, February 19, 2001.

28. Peterson and Baker, interviews, 2001.

29. Rawson, interview.

30. Keith Whittaker, interview by author, June 3, 1996. By the time of his elevation to the district court, Whittaker belonged to the Kansas City Club, the Mercury Club, and the Boicourt Hunting Club. Whittaker to James P. Jouras, May 11, 1955, University of Missouri–Kansas City Archives [UA-KC].

31. Gary Whittaker, interview.

32. Whittaker was 31 years old in 1932. The associates who were older included Carl Enggas (32), John Moberly (35), and Charles Garnett (42). The other partners were Powell Groner (40), Henry Ess (41), Paul Barnett (44), John Gage (45), and Isaac Watson (73).

33. *Martindale-Hubbell Law Directory*.

34. Kassebaum, taped interview, 2–3.

35. Duncan, interview.

36. In *Kansas City Star v. Julian*, 215 U.S. 589 (1909), the Court dismissed the complaint for lack of jurisdiction. This was the first and only time that Watson lawyers represented the *Star* in oral argument before the Supreme Court.

37. Larsen, *Federal Justice*, 226–28. Considered an authority in libel law, Henry Ess became the principal lawyer for the *Star*, defending it against numerous libel suits. One of the most unusual cases for Watson lawyers involved Dr. John Brinkley, the infamous "Goat Doctor," who sued the *Star* for libel after it revealed that Brinkley's hospital in Milford, Kansas, was a fraud. Offering to restore male sexual vitality by transplanting goat glands, Brinkley created an empire that eventually grew to include a hospital, drug store, bank, and radio station KFKB, the first in Kansas. See Gerald Carson, *The Roguish World of Doctor Brinkley* (New York: Rinehart, 1960), 136–37.

38. *Kansas City Star v. United States*, 240 F.2d 643 (1957), and 354 U.S. 923 (1957).

39. At the district and appeals courts, the rotation of assignments prevented Whittaker's involvement in the case, but at the Supreme Court he had no choice but to recuse himself.

40. Thompson, interview, and Thompson, taped interview, 11.

41. George Haydon, interview by author, February 19, 2001.

42. Baker and Kassebaum, taped interviews, 37–38. James Hurst noted how corporate lawyers' work was "largely ephemeral," writing, "[M]uch of [this] work disappears in the unrecorded words spoken around countless conference tables or in unnumbered, unrecorded hearings; much of it disappears into the scattered files of numerous clients." *The Growth of American Law*, 334.

43. Peterson and Thompson, interviews.

44. Foard and Thompson, interviews. James Hurst discovered that the mean net income in 1947 of lawyers in law firms with nine or more members was more than four and a half times larger than that of lone practitioners. The average annual salary of lawyers in firms the size of Watson, which had between 18 and 20 members, was over $27,000. See Hurst, *The Growth of American Law*, 306.

45. Russell W. Gunn, "Remarks of Russell W. Gunn," in *In Memoriam, Honorable Charles Evans Whittaker*, Proceeding of the Bar and Officers of the Supreme Court of the United States and Proceedings Before the Supreme Court of the United States, February 19, 1975, Washington, D.C., 27.

46. Baker, interview, 1996, and Foard, interview.

47. Thompson, interview.

48. Warranty Deed, May 21, 1941, vol. 184, pp. 13–14, Clinton County Record of Deeds, Plattsburg, Missouri.

49. *Kansas City Star*, February 19, 1954.

50. Dorothy Kiehnhoff, interview by author, June 24, 1996.

51. Keith Whittaker, interview.

52. Kent Whittaker, interview, April 11, 1996. Whittaker listed his two sisters-in-law as dependents on his federal tax returns from 1961 through 1972, Charles Whittaker papers, Kansas City, Missouri.

53. Havener, interview.

54. Kiehnhoff, interview.

55. Marriage License, July 13, 1928, vol. 114, p. 588, Jackson County Recorder of Deeds, Whittaker papers. The Reverend Basil Killoran performed the ceremony.

56. The first, Charles Keith, was born September 4, 1932. Kent arrived March 11, 1936, and Gary was born October 1, 1940. Kent has said that although his parents never spoke openly about it, they were probably disappointed they never had a daughter. Charles had planned to name a daughter Virginia, and in correspondence to friends he sometimes referred to Winifred as "Ginny." Kent Whittaker, interview, April 11, 1996.

57. Keith Whittaker, interview.

58. Mabel Gunn, telephone interview by author, June 8, 1996. The *Kansas City Star* re-ported on February 19, 1954, that Whittaker was a member of the board of trustees and the board of stewards of the Central Methodist Church.

59. Whittaker to Sister Olive Louise, February 14, 1964, Whittaker papers.

60. Kent Whittaker, interview, April 11, 1996. In a letter to his wife that was typical of Whittaker's writing style, he used five pages of type to review the abstract of the title to their new home. There was no personal message of any kind. Charles Whittaker to Mrs. Charles Whittaker, March 17, 1966, Whittaker papers.

61. Keith Whittaker, interview.

62. Hazel Ruhnke, interview by author, June 14, 1996, and Kiehnhoff, interview.

63. Walter A. Raymond to Marlin M. Volz, December 20, 1957, in Marlin M. Volz, "Mr. Justice Whittaker," *Notre Dame Lawyer* 33 (March 1958): 165–66.

64. Lowell L. Knipmeyer, "Charles E. Whittaker, Kansas City Bar Association Man-Of-The-Year, 1962," *The Kansas City Bar Journal* 38 (April 1963): 14.

65. Quoted in Larsen, *Federal Justice*, 230, n. 43.

66. *Kansas City Star*, August 2, 1994.

67. Havener, interview.

68. Alan Kohn, "Supreme Court Law Clerk, 1957-1958 A Reminiscence," *Journal of Supreme Court History* (1998): 42.

69. Keith and Gary Whittaker, interviews.

70. Kent, Keith, and Gary Whittaker, interviews, 1996.

71. Keith Whittaker, interview.

72. Poplinger and Foard, interviews.

73. David Atkinson, *Leaving the Bench: Supreme Court Justices at the End* (Lawrence: University Press of Kansas, 1999), 131.

74. Thompson, interview.

75. Keith Whittaker and Kiehnhoff, interviews.

76. Poplinger, interview, and Baker, interview, 1996.

77. Peterson, interview.

78. Douglas Stripp, interview, October 1971, in Judith Cole, "Mr. Justice Charles Evans Whittaker: A Case Study in Judicial Recruitment and Behavior" (M. A. thesis, University of Missouri–Kansas City, 1972), 19, n. 21.

79. Poplinger, interview.

80. Charles E. Whittaker, "Some Reminiscences," *Nebraska Law Review* 43 (December 1963): 357–58.

81. Kent Whittaker, interview, April 11, 1996.

82. James N. Adler, telephone interview by author, June 26, 1996.

83. Quoted in *Kansas City Star*, September 20, 1964.

84. Ilus W. Davis, interview by author, June 12, 1996.

85. Quoted in *Kansas City Times*, September 25, 1953. Whittaker expressed regret over his parent's deaths in a private letter, Whittaker papers.

86. Knipmeyer, "Charles E. Whittaker," 13–14.

87. Carl E. Enggas, "Remarks of Carl E. Enggas," in *In Memoriam, Honorable Charles Evans Whittaker*, 13. Enggas reminded his audience what Justice Charles Evans Hughes had said, "The highest reward that can come to a lawyer is the esteem of his professional brethren.... It is an esteem commanded solely by integrity of character and by brains and skill in the honorable performance of professional duty." Quoted in Enggas, "Remarks," 16.

88. Poplinger, interview.

89. Enggas, "Remarks," 13–14. The private papers of Charles Whittaker are replete with this remarkable trait.

90. Memo, Vincent Rawson to Susan Parker, September 16, 1991, Rawson papers.

91. Celia J. Barrett, telephone interview by author, June 8, 1996. Barrett served as Whittaker's secretary from 1951 to 1959, when she got married. Always devoted to his support staff, Whittaker officiated at her wedding in Washington, D.C.

92. Baker, interview, 1996. In one of the annual Christmas poems composed for the office party, one of the associates parodied "T'was the Night Before Christmas" with these lines:

> Vice-President Whittaker
> From his farm had come in
> And was dictating a brief,
> With rivaling din.

From "Getting Tight Before Christmas," Rawson papers.

93. Poplinger, interview.

94. Havener, interview.

95. Peterson, interview.

96. Joseph E. Stevens, interview by author, May 17, 1996. Later Whittaker was disappointed that Stevens was not offered a position at the firm.

97. Bruce M. Forrester, "Remarks of Judge Forrester," in *In Memoriam, Honorable Charles Evans Whittaker*, 19.

98. Rawson, interview.

99. Peterson, interview.

100. Havener, interview.

101. Baker, interview.

102. Memo, Rawson to Parker, and Rawson and Thompson, interviews.

103. Havener, interview.

104. Quoted in *Kansas City Star*, May 2, 1954.

105. Quoted in *Kansas City Times*, June 19, 1954.

106. Quoted in Gunn, "Remarks," 29.

107. Foard, interview.

108. Gunn, "Remarks," 28.

3. The Lower Courts

1. The other was Justice Samuel Blatchford, first appointed by Andrew Johnson in 1867 to the District Court for the Southern District of New York, then by Rutherford Hayes in 1878 to the Circuit Court for the Second Circuit, and finally by Chester Arthur in 1882 to the Supreme Court where he served until his death in 1893. The *Kansas City Star*, August 2, 1994, asserted that Whittaker was "the only judge ever to serve at all three levels." Richard Miller claimed that Whittaker was the *first* person to achieve this distinction, *Whittaker: Struggles of a Supreme Court Justice* (Westport, Connecticut: Greenwood Press, 2002), 31, when in fact, he was the *second*.

2. In the first year after Whittaker was appointed to the Supreme Court, Marlin M. Volz tried to determine a "direction" for Whittaker on the Court by analyzing Whittaker's lower court opinions, "Mr. Justice Whittaker," *Notre Dame Lawyer* 33 (March 1958): 159–79. Daniel M. Berman, likewise, tried to characterize Whittaker's Supreme Court jurisprudence by comparing his voting record from his first year on the Court to a small sampling of his lower court decisions, "Mr. Justice Whittaker: A Preliminary Appraisal," *Missouri Law Review* 24 (January 1959): 1–15. Since his appointment to the Supreme Court, no other author has made a systematic evaluation of Whittaker's lower court opinions, contrary to Miller's claim that "for a half century scholars have examined his district and appeals court opinions," *Whittaker: Struggles*, 46.

3. For accurate ratios of Democrats and Republicans then serving in the federal judiciary, see Sheldon Goldman, *Picking Federal Judges: Lower Court Selection From Roosevelt Through Reagan* (New Haven: Yale University Press, 1997), 112, note a. Out of 335 lifetime judgeships, 9 were on the Supreme Court, 68 were circuit court judges, 239 were district court judges, 5 were on the Court of Claims, 9 were on the Customs Court, and 5 were on the Court of Customs and Patent Appeals.

4. Dwight Eisenhower, *Mandate for Change* (New York: Doubleday, 1963), 226.

Eisenhower acknowledged his goal to politically balance the Supreme Court in his diary, February 5, 1957. See Robert H. Ferrell, ed., *The Eisenhower Diaries* (New York: W.W. Norton, 1987), 342.

5. Herbert Brownell, *Advising Ike: The Memoirs of Attorney General Herbert Brownell* (Lawrence: University Press of Kansas, 1993), 183. Quotations from Eisenhower letter, September 30, 1965, in Brownell, *Advising Ike*, 184, n.2.

6. Quoted in Harold Chase, *Federal Judges: The Appointing Process* (Minneapolis: University of Minnesota Press, 1972), 98. Goldman noted that most of Eisenhower's appeals court nominations were primarily partisan-agenda, rather than personal-agenda, appointments, which was consistent with Eisenhower's goal of balancing the federal courts, *Picking Federal Judges*, 130–31.

7. Lawrence Larsen, *Federal Justice in Western Missouri: The Judges, The Cases, The Times* (Columbia: University of Missouri Press, 1994), 219, and Clyde Rayburn, interview by author, June 19, 1996. Reeves continued to serve in senior status another ten years.

8. Russell Baker, interview by author, June 20, 1996.

9. Charles Whittaker, interview, November 1970, quoted in Judith Cole, "Mr. Justice Charles Evans Whittaker: A Case Study in Judicial Recruitment and Behavior" (M. A. thesis, University of Missouri–Kansas City, 1972), 26, n. 42.

10. Charles E. Whittaker, "Some Reminiscences," *Nebraska Law Review* 43 (December 1963): 354.

11. Brownell, *Advising Ike*, 177.

12. Ibid., and Eisenhower letter, September 30, 1965, in Brownell, *Advising Ike*, 184, n. 2. See also William P. Rogers, "Judicial Appointments in the Eisenhower Administration," *Journal of the American Judicature Society* 41 (August 1957): 39–40.

13. Goldman, *Picking Federal Judges*, 115 and 137, and David Alistair Yalof, *Pursuit of Justices: Presidential Politics and the Selection of Supreme Court Nominees* (Chicago: The University of Chicago Press, 1999), 42–43. Joseph Menez emphasized the importance of the ABA's recommendations to Eisenhower: "When President Eisenhower learned from the Bar Association that it had not passed on the nomination of Justice Brennan, he directed that the nomination be held up until the committee could report," "A Brief in Support of the Supreme Court," *Northwestern University Law Review* 54 (1959): 52, n. 136.

14. Eisenhower, *Mandate for Change*, 226.

15. Brownell, *Advising Ike*, 176–77. So

highly regarded was Brownell that Eisenhower twice considered appointing him to the Supreme Court. See Eisenhower's diary, February 5, 1957, in Ferrell, *The Eisenhower Diaries*, and Goldman, *Picking Federal Judges*, 115, note c.

16. Goldman, *Picking Federal Judges*, 111–13, 123, and 131.

17. Brownell, *Advising Ike*, 182.

18. Goldman, *Picking Federal Judges*, 118 and 123. Miller assumed that Eisenhower played a more decisive role in the final selection of federal judges, writing, "His staff may have handled details, but Eisenhower definitely made the final decisions," *Whittaker: Struggles*, 36. This reference was based on Eisenhower's recollections about individuals he had selected while still president, yet Goldman presented persuasive evidence from *during* Eisenhower's presidency that demonstrated Eisenhower's deference to the decisions of the Justice Department. Besides, as Bernard Schwartz noted, Eisenhower could not remember his final appointment, Potter Stewart, often confusing him for Whittaker, *Super Chief: Earl Warren and His Supreme Court—A Judicial Biography* (New York: New York University Press, 1983), 175. Unfortunately, Schwartz, too, was confused where he noted that Stewart was the *second* Republican justice appointed by Eisenhower, when Warren, Harlan, and Whittaker all preceded Stewart.

19. Joel Grossman, *Lawyers and Judges: the ABA and the Politics of Judicial Selection* (New York: John Wiley & Sons, 1965), 42.

20. *Kansas City Star*, February 19, 1954. Interestingly, this was the same article announcing Whittaker's nomination. The article may have focused so much attention on Bennett's failure to receive the nomination in order to divert attention away from the *Star's* considerable support for Whittaker.

21. Rayburn, interview.

22. The salary for district judges went up to $22,500 before Whittaker left for the Eighth Circuit. A circuit court appointment had an annual salary of $25,500 while a Supreme Court justice in 1957 made $35,000 a year. After his nomination was announced, Whittaker told reporters, "My wife is very pleased at the news, but she wonders how I can step down from a job in which my earning power as a lawyer is considerably greater than it would be as a federal judge." Quoted in *Kansas City Star*, May 11, 1954.

23. Gary Whittaker, interview by author, June 21, 1996, and Joseph Stevens, Jr., interview by author, May 17, 1996.

24. Various undated news stories found in the special collections of the Kansas City Pub-

lic Library, including the *Kansas City Times, Kansas City Star, St. Louis Post Dispatch,* and *Time,* December 28, 1959.

25. Eisenhower to Edgar Eisenhower, January 27, 1954, in Louis, Galambos, ed., *The Papers of Dwight David Eisenhower,* vol. 15, *The Presidency: The Middle Way* (Baltimore: The Johns Hopkins University Press, 1996).

26. Eisenhower to Roberts, January 30, 1948, in Galambos, ed., *The Papers of Dwight David Eisenhower,* vol. 9, *The Chief of Staff.*

27. See correspondence between Eisenhower and Roberts in Galambos, ed., *The Papers of Dwight David Eisenhower,* vol. 15, *The Presidency: The Middle Way.*

28. See Yalof, *Pursuit of Justices,* 44–54. Despite Harlan's reluctance, Brownell so wanted his friend on the Supreme Court that he convinced Harlan to serve first on the U.S. Court of Appeals for the Second Circuit to enhance his prospects for promotion to the Supreme Court.

29. Symington and Hennings were not, as Miller suggested, "in a position to halt the nomination if they chose to," *Whittaker: Struggles,* 36. The Senate's rules and traditions that Miller referred to are called Senatorial Courtesy, which, as Chase noted, was usually employed by Senators of the president's party, *Federal Judges,* 6–10. Missouri's two Democratic senators might have received a sympathetic hearing if Democrats controlled the Senate, but Republicans controlled the Senate in the Eighty-third Congress.

30. Goldman, *Picking Federal Judges,* 123, note i. Henry Abraham, among others, claimed that Eisenhower's oldest brother, Arthur, petitioned the president personally on Whittaker's behalf. *Justices and Presidents: A Political History of Appointments to the Supreme Court,* 3d ed. (New York: Oxford University Press, 1992), 270. See also Goldman, *Picking Federal Judges,* 123, and Ed Cray, *Chief Justice: A Biography of Earl Warren* (New York: Simon & Schuster, 1997), 330. Arthur Eisenhower, a director and executive vice president of Commerce Trust Company in Kansas City, certainly knew Whittaker personally and would have supported his nomination, but it was doubtful that President Eisenhower pushed for Whittaker's appointment based solely on familial affection.

31. Charles Whittaker, interview, November 1970, quoted in Cole, "Mr. Justice Charles Evans Whittaker," 29, n. 4.

32. Rayburn, interview.

33. *Kansas City Star,* February 19, 1954.

34. Floyd R. Gibson, interview, quoted in Larsen, *Federal Justice,* 228–29.

35. Harry Darby, interview, October 1971, quoted in Cole, "Mr. Justice Charles Evans Whittaker," 37, n. 19. Darby, who served only eleven months in the Senate, was appointed in 1949 to fill the vacancy created when Republican Clyde M. Reed died. Once Reed's successor, Frank Carlson, was elected in 1950, Darby returned to Kansas. Probably because of support for Whittaker from both Darby and Carlson, Henry Abraham assumed incorrectly that Darby and Carlson were "Kansas's two Republican Senators," *Justices and Presidents,* 270, when, in fact, Carlson and Republican Andrew Schoeppel were the two senators.

36. William Orr, interview, November 1970, quoted in Cole, "Mr. Justice Charles Evans Whittaker," 35, n. 14. Yalof agreed that it was Roberts principally who secured Whittaker's nomination and not Darby, *Pursuit of Justices,* 63, n. 117–18.

37. Interview, quoted in Cole, "Mr. Justice Charles Evans Whittaker," 37, n. 18. Miller failed to account for these other perceptions that seemed to discount Darby's influence, *Whittaker: Struggles,* 36. While both Frank Carlson and Harry Darby of Kansas supported Whittaker's candidacy, neither of them was in a position to insist on a federal judgeship for western Missouri. Roberts, on the other hand, through the *Star* wielded considerable political influence in Kansas City.

38. Brownell to Eisenhower, April 20, 1954, quoted in Cole, "Mr. Justice Charles Evans Whittaker," 48, n. 40.

39. Colvin Peterson, interview by author, February 21, 2001.

40. Quoted in *Kansas City Star,* July 19, 1954.

41. This building, located at 811 Grand Avenue, was the third federal courthouse built in Kansas City. On October 24, 1998, a new federal courthouse, located at 400 E. 9th Street, was dedicated and named in honor of Charles Evans Whittaker. See Afterword.

42. Rayburn, interview. When Whittaker left for the Supreme Court in 1957, he secured a position for Rayburn with a law office in Kansas City. "Next to my parents," Rayburn said, "Judge Whittaker was the most important person in my life. He gave me my start, which then led to my next position that continued until my retirement."

43. Larsen, *Federal Justice,* 195–218.

44. Quoted in *Kansas City Star,* July 19, 1954. Whittaker's youngest son, Gary, who was still living at home at the time, has remarked, "He may have grown tired of working seven days a week as a lawyer, but now he worked seven days a week as a judge." Gary Whittaker, interview.

45. Rayburn, interview.

46. Ibid.

47. Baker, interview, 1996.

48. Daniel J. Kornstein, *Thinking Under Fire: Great Courtroom Lawyers and Their Impact on American History* (New York: Dodd, Mead, 1987), 102.

49. Charles E. Whittaker, "Reflections on Mr. Justice Brandeis," *Saint Louis University Law Journal* 11 (1966): 6. Ironically, Brandeis, like Whittaker, had his middle name changed during his youth. Born Louis David Brandeis, he changed it to Dembitz in honor of his uncle and role model, Lewis Dembitz.

50. Ibid., 7.

51. Whittaker, "Some Reminiscences," 359.

52. Charles E. Whittaker, "Tribute to Judge John B. Sanborn," *Minnesota Law Review* 44 (1959): 199.

53. Ibid., 198.

54. Volz, "Mr. Justice Whittaker," 166.

55. Quoted in *Kansas City Star*, June 12, 1955.

56. Volz, "Mr. Justice Whittaker," 166.

57. Rayburn, interview. See Criminal Case Files (CCFs), 19370–19375, Kansas City, Missouri (KC), U.S. District Courts, Western District of Missouri (USDC-WM), Record Group 21 (RG 21), National Archives, Central Plains Region (NA-CPR).

58. Considering its widespread press coverage in Kansas City and its lasting effect on Whittaker, it is surprising this case has received so little detailed explanation. Larsen succinctly summarized the crime and punishment of Brown, *Federal Justice*, 231; Cole, likewise, in the only case reported during Whittaker's service on the district court, described Brown's crime and punishment and mentioned it affected Whittaker, "Mr. Justice Charles Evans Whittaker," 57–58; and Miller, without providing relevant names or details of the crime, noted how it affected Whittaker, *Whittaker: Struggles*, 38.

59. See Voluntary Statement of Arthur Ross Brown, November 16, 1955, CCF 19376-KC, Precedent Cases (PC), U.S. Attorneys and Marshals, Western District of Missouri (USAM-WM), RG 118, NA-CPR.

60. *Kansas City Star*, August 7, 1955. See also FBI interview with J. David Connell, August 23, 1955, CCF 19376-KC, PC, USAM-WM, RG 118, NA-CPR. Nearly forty years after the crime, the *Kansas City Star*, August 2, 1994, assumed because of her well-to-do status that Allen was a Johnson County, Kansas, resident.

61. *Kansas City Star*, August 5, 1955. See also Handwritten notes of Government Exhibits, *U.S. v. Arthur Ross Brown*, CCF 19376-KC, CCFs (1879–1972), USDC-WM, RG 21, NA-CPR.

62. *Kansas City Times*, August 8, 1955. See also Handwritten notes of Government Witnesses, *U.S. v. Arthur Ross Brown*, CCF 19376-KC, CCFs (1879–1972), USDC-WM, RG 21, and Autopsy Report by Edward B. MacArthur, August 7, 1955, Criminal Case File 19376-KC, PC, USAM-WM, RG 118, NA-CPR.

63. Quoted in *Kansas City Star*, August 8, 1955.

64. *Kansas City Times*, November 10, 1955. Details of Jean Brown's abduction are in FBI Report, January 3, 1956, CCF 19376-KC, PC, USAM-WM, RG 118, NA-CPR.

65. *Kansas City Star*, November 14, 1955. See also FBI Report, January 11, 1956, CCF 19376-KC, PC, USAM-WM, RG 118, NA-CPR.

66. *Kansas City Times*, November 15, 1955. See also FBI Report, November 23, 1955, CCF 19376-KC, PC, USAM-WM, RG 118, and Handwritten notes of Government Witnesses, *U.S. v. Arthur Ross Brown*, CCF 19376-KC, CCFs (1879–1972), USDC-WM, RG 21, NA-CPR.

67. In his initial confession, Brown denied having raped Allen, claiming to have had an involuntary orgasm after shooting her. He later admitted to raping her. See Voluntary Statement of Arthur Ross Brown, November 16 and November 30, 1955, and Amended Statement of Arthur Ross Brown, November 25, 1955, CCF 19376-KC, PC, USAM-WM, RG 118, NA-CPR.

68. See Interview of Mildred Jean Brown, FBI Report, November 18, 1955, FBI Report, November 23 and December 28, 1955, and FBI Report, February 8, 1956, CCF 19376-KC, PC, USAM-WM, RG 118, and Handwritten notes of Government Witnesses, *U.S. v. Arthur Ross Brown*, CCF 19376-KC, CCFs (1879–1972), USDC-WM, RG 21, NA-CPR.

69. *Kansas City Times*, November 29, 1955. See Order Appointing Psychiatrists, December 19, 1955, Letter from Drs. Trowbridge, Robinson, and Young to Whittaker, December 27, 1955, and Indictment and Judgment, *U.S. v. Arthur Ross Brown*, CCF 19376-KC, CCFs (1879–1972), USDC-WM, RG 21, NA-CPR.

70. Quoted in *Kansas City Times*, January 26, 1956.

71. Quoted in *Kansas City Star*, January 25, 1956.

72. See Letter from Percy Wyly, special agent FBI, to Edward L. Scheufler, which included copies of Probation Officer's Report and Recommendation, March 5, 1946, Resume of Psychological Examination, January 7, 1942, and Report on Psychiatric Examination, May 26, 1942, CCF 19376-KC, PC, USAM-WM, RG 118, NA-CPR.

73. *Kansas City Times*, February 24, 1956. See Standard Certificate of Death, CCF 19376-

KC, USDC-WM, RG 21, NA-CPR. Two days prior to his execution Brown confessed to the FBI that he had committed numerous other offenses, including eight robberies and three attempted rapes in the last two years. See FBI Report, April 27, 1956, CCF 19376-KC, PC, USAM-WM, RG 118, NA-CPR.

74. Quoted in *Kansas City Times*, January 26, 1956.

75. Rayburn, interview. Twelve years after Brown's execution the Supreme Court ruled in a six to two decision by Justice Stewart (White and Black dissented, Marshall took no part) that the capital punishment clause of the federal Kidnapping Act violated the Fifth and Sixth Amendments and was therefore unconstitutional, but the Act itself was not invalidated, *United States v. Jackson*, 390 U.S. 570 (1968).

76. George C. Wheeler, Chairman, "Report of the Committee on Academic Freedom and Tenure," *Bulletin of the American Association of University Professors* 43 (1957): 177.

77. Quoted in *Kansas City Times*, June 10, 1953. Whittaker certainly did not, as Miller twice claimed, ignore the issue of Davis's refusal to answer questions of the Senate subcommittee on the grounds that they went beyond the legitimate scope of the subcommittee's investigation, *Whittaker: Struggles*, 82 and 93. While it is true that this issue was presented in *Deutch v. United States*, 367 U.S. 456 (1961), a five to four decision in which Whittaker dissented, at no time during Davis's testimony before the Senate subcommittee did he raise this objection, nor did he present it in his complaint against the university.

78. Quoted in Senate Committee on the Judiciary, *Nomination of Charles E. Whittaker: Hearing before the Committee on the Judiciary*, 85th Cong., 1st sess., March 18, 1957, 9. According to Whittaker's clerk at the district court, who was a student at the university then, law school classmates of his who attended Davis's classes complained that in order to get a good grade "you had to parrot the Communist line." Rayburn, interview.

79. Wheeler, "Academic Freedom and Tenure," 189–90. Emphasis added.

80. Ibid., 179. Since the charges against him did not involve moral turpitude, Davis received a year's severance pay. While the Special Committee on Academic Freedom and Tenure found that the university's dismissal of Davis was grounded "*essentially* on the refusal of Dr. Davis to communicate with the University Administration and faculty," ibid., 184, Miller oversimplified the hearings of early December 1953, declaring the university presented "*no evidence* of communist activity by

Davis," and acted "*solely* on grounds that Davis had refused explicit answers to the three questions put to him," *Whittaker: Struggles*, 85. Emphasis added. The Special Committee on Academic Freedom and Tenure, on which Miller relied, clearly documented how university counsel at those hearings attempted "to prove that Dr. Davis was then a Communist and that he had been a Communist since 1929." See Wheeler, "Academic Freedom and Tenure," 181–82. Whether or not university counsel succeeded in its efforts is, of course, open to interpretation.

81. Wheeler, "Academic Freedom and Tenure," 185–86.

82. *Kansas City Times*, December 18, 1953.

83. Wheeler, "Academic Freedom and Tenure," 185. See Complaint of Horace B. Davis, March 16, 1955, Civil Case Files (Civil), 9667-KC, USDC-WM, RG 21, NA-CPR. In his complaint, Davis specifically cited articles in the *Kansas City Times*, June 11, August 14, September 24, and in the *Star*, September 23, 1953.

84. See Suggestions in Support of Motion to Dismiss, April 4, 1955, Civil, 9667-KC, USDC-WM, RG 21, NA-CPR.

85. Section 241, Title 18 U.S.C.A.

86. Section 1331, Title 28 U.S.C.A. (circa 1955) gave district courts original jurisdiction in all civil actions in excess of $3,000 arising under the Constitution, laws, or treaties of the United States. Without a dollar amount, Davis's complaint could only withstand the jurisdictional requirement if he sought some other type of relief.

87. See Motion for New Trial, April 25, 1955, Civil, 9667-KC, USDC-WM, RG 21, NA-CPR. Farmer appeared in Whittaker's courtroom on one other occasion to subpoena certain copies of former President Truman's private presidential papers. Farmer sought to recover two-thirds of his federal income taxes used to defray the costs of what he considered an "illegal" war waged in Korea, and he wanted to establish that there was no record signed by the president committing the nation to war. Whittaker dismissed his case. See Whittaker's testimony before the Senate Committee on the Judiciary, *Nomination of Charles E. Whittaker*, 33–34.

88. Suggestions in Support of Motion to Dismiss, April 4, 1955, Civil, 9667-KC, USDC-WM, RG 21, NA-CPR. Emphasis added.

89. *McAuliffe v. City of New Bedford*, 155 Mass. 216, 29 N.E. 517 (1892) at 517. Without relying on the university's briefs, David N. Atkinson and Lawrence H. Larsen even remarked how Whittaker's opinion echoed the views of Holmes in *McAuliffe*, "A Case Study in Federal Justice: Leading Bill of Rights Pro-

ceedings in the Western District of Missouri," *Creighton Law Review* 28 (April 1995): 602, n. 42.

90. Kornstein, *Thinking Under Fire*, 10. Considering how much of the university's brief, its language and tenor, found its way into Whittaker's decision, it was not as "perplexing" as Miller believed that Whittaker misdescribed Davis as a public school teacher, *Whittaker: Struggles*, 87. Both Berman, "Mr. Justice Whittaker," 4, n. 10, and Leon Friedman, "Charles Whittaker," in *The Justices of the United States Supreme Court: Their Lives and Major Opinions*, eds. Leon Friedman and Fred L. Israel, vol. 4 (New York: Chelsea House, 1969), 2895, criticized Whittaker's classification of Davis as a "public school teacher" because, they claimed, Whittaker should have known the university was not a public school since he attended it himself. This criticism was irrelevant to Whittaker's ruling in the case, but, more important, it was inaccurate since, strictly speaking, Whittaker attended the Kansas City School of Law, which did not become incorporated into the University of Kansas City until 1938, fourteen years after Whittaker graduated.

91. *Kansas City Star*, April 16, 1955.

92. Miller repeatedly denounced Whittaker's decision for avoiding Davis's conspiracy claim, *Whittaker: Struggles*, 86, 88, and 89. However, in his summary of Davis's complaint, Whittaker noted how the university and Senator Jenner were alleged to be in a conspiracy to deprive Davis of "his usual occupation or calling as a teacher or instructor of economics." As already noted, this was not a right arising from the Constitution or laws of the United States. Therefore, Whittaker did, in fact, address precisely the conspiracy issue when he dismissed Davis's complaint (federal conspiracy charge) for failure to state a claim (constitutional right) upon which relief (injunction or damages) could be granted. Plainer words do not present themselves.

93. Although Miller relied on Farmer's testimony before the Senate Judiciary Committee, which acknowledged that a tenured teacher could be discharged for "just cause" and that it would be within the university's discretion to determine what constituted "just cause," Miller imprudently declared that Davis "could not be fired without proof of incompetence or gross abuse of his position," *Whittaker: Struggles*, 85–86.

94. Wheeler, "Academic Freedom and Tenure," 192–93.

95. See Affidavit of Bias, April 25, 1955, Civil, 9667-KC, USDC-WM, RG 21, NA-CPR.

96. Quoted in *Kansas City Star*, May 18, 1955. Despite their posturing and protesta-

tions, neither Davis nor Farmer ever appealed Whittaker's decision. In June 1955 Davis filed a Notice of Appeal with the Eighth Circuit Court of Appeals, but then in October all the parties in the case, including Farmer, signed a stipulation to dismiss the appeal notice.

97. See Plaintiff's Reply to Defendant's Suggestions, May 10, 1955, Civil, 9667-KC, USDC-WM, RG 21, NA-CPR. Emphasis added.

98. Of those authors who have chosen to address Whittaker's lower court opinions, the only case that every one of them has mentioned has been *Davis*. Volz, "Mr. Justice Whittaker," 167–68, mentioned *Davis* in connection with Whittaker's Supreme Court appointment; in Larsen, *Federal Justice*, 231–33, and Berman, "Mr. Justice Whittaker," 3–5, *Davis* figured most prominently of the few district court opinions considered; Cole, "Mr. Justice Charles Evans Whittaker," 100, n. 59, considered *Davis* "notable"; Friedman, "Charles Whittaker," 2894–95, likewise considered *Davis* "notable," calling it "one of Whittaker's more celebrated opinions"; and Miller, *Whittaker: Struggles*, 77–90, devoted twelve pages to expounding upon *Davis*, oddly enough during Whittaker's Supreme Court years. The over-reliance on this one case as a faithful portrayal of Whittaker's judging has given *Davis* undeserved importance when compared with his other district court decisions.

99. Atkinson and Larsen, "A Case Study in Federal Justice," 602.

100. See Memorandum and Order, April 14, 1955, Civil, 9667-KC, USDC-WM, RG 21, NA-CPR. *The Kansas City Star*, April 15, 1955, using an advance copy of the decision, failed to note these words in its coverage of the decision.

101. Rayburn, interview.

102. Friedman, "Charles Whittaker," 2895. *Davis* has never actually been questioned, criticized, or overruled by any federal appellate decision, and only once was it mentioned in a state case, *Laba v. Newark Board of Education*, 129 A. 2d 273 (1957).

103. *Slochower v. Board of Education*, 350 U.S. 551, 559 (1956). Relying on Friedman, Miller, too, misunderstood the ruling in *Slochower*, concluding that it was "too late to help Davis," when, in fact, it did not even apply to *Davis*. *Whittaker: Struggles*, 90.

104. Friedman, "Charles Whittaker," 2895.

105. Atkinson and Larsen, "A Case Study in Federal Justice," 600 and 602. Emphasis added.

106. Quoted in *Nomination of Charles E. Whittaker*, 33. The fifth case Whittaker cited dealt with the denial of a lawyer's bar application, suggesting that the right to an occupa-

tion was not legally protected. Miller complained that these five cases all dealt with *public* school teachers and were therefore inapplicable to *Davis*, *Whittaker: Struggles*, 87. This failed to account for the fact that these were the *only* cases briefed before Whittaker, so he made his ruling in light of the right asserted, not the institutional setting. For his part, Davis did not offer any precedents contrary to these or more limiting upon the discretion of a private school.

107. Volz, "Mr. Justice Whittaker," 173.

108. His one case appealled to the Supreme Court, *Southern Kansas Greyhound Lines v. United States*, 134 F. Supp. 502 (W. D. Mo. 1955), was affirmed by 351 U.S. 921 (1956). His four district court decisions later appealed to the Eighth Circuit Court of Appeals all arrived there while he served on that court and included *United States v. Sweet*, 133 F. Supp. 3 (W. D. Mo. 1955), later affirmed by 235 F. 2d 801 (1956); *Farm Bureau Cooperative v. Blue Star Foods*, 137 F. Supp. 486, 491 (W. D. Mo. 1956), later affirmed by 238 F. 2d 326 (1956); *In re McKinley*, 138 F. Supp. 4 (W. D. Mo. 1956), later affirmed by *Bostian v. Universal C.I.T. Credit Corporation*, 238 F. 2d 809 (1956); and *United States v. Harris*, 133 F. Supp. 796 (W. D. Mo. 1955), later affirmed by 237 F. 2d 274 (1956). Daniel Berman, "Mr. Justice Whittaker," 6, and Lawrence Larsen, *Federal Justice*, 233, both criticized Whittaker's ruling in *Sweet*, suggesting that it may have been too harsh; twenty-five years after his decision in *Harris*, the Ninth Circuit Court of Appeals reconsidered Whittaker's ruling, and in 1988 the Ninth Circuit specifically denounced Whittaker's ruling, *United States v. Akmakjian*, 647 F. 2d 12 (1981), and *United States v. Caldwell*, 859 F. 2d 805 (1988).

109. Volz was more concerned with the language and style of Whittaker's writing than the actual rulings, "Mr. Justice Whittaker," (1958), and Berman examined only three of Whittaker's district court opinions, "Mr. Justice Whittaker," (1959). Volz and Berman, however, wrote before most of Whittaker's district court opinions were appealed or relied upon by other courts. Friedman and Cole, on the other hand, wrote after much of Whittaker's district court influence was felt, but each of them described only two cases from his district court service. Friedman, "Charles Whittaker," (1969), and Cole, "Mr. Justice Charles Evans Whittaker," (1972). Besides *Davis*, Miller mentioned only four other cases from Whittaker's district court service, relying principally on Volz's analysis for those, *Whittaker: Struggles*, (2002). For a complete list of Whittaker's lower court opinions, see Appendix E.

110. Section 1404 (a), Title 28 U.S.C.A. "For the convenience of the parties and witnesses, in the interest of justice, a district court may transfer any civil action to any other district or division where it might have been brought."

111. *General Electric v. Central Transit Warehouse*, 127 F. Supp. 817, 825–26 (W. D. Mo. 1955). For a complete list of Whittaker's lower court decisions, see Appendix E.

112. *Blaski v. Hoffman*, 260 F. 2d 317, 322 (1958). Also *Goodman v. Columbia Steel and Shafting*, 171 F. Supp. 718 (W. D. Penn. 1959).

113. *Hoffman v. Blaski*, 363 U.S. 335, 342–43 (1960). Several contemporary reviews of Whittaker's opinion were equally divided between those that favored the clarity of the decision and those that found it too limiting.

114. See Frankfurter's dissent in the companion case *Behimer v. Sullivan*, 363 U.S. 335 (1960). Here Frankfurter preferred to favor the majority of district courts that would have allowed a transfer to a district where the defendants may have objected originally but then later consented. In *Hoffman v. Blaski*, Frankfurter dissented because of the way the Court approved of the Seventh Circuit's supersedure of a prior decision of the Fifth Circuit, a coordinate federal court, after the Supreme Court had denied *certiorari* to the appeal from the Fifth Circuit.

115. *United States v. DeBellis*, 649 F. 2d 1 (1981).

116. *Wright v. Steele*, 125 F. Supp. 1, 4 (W.D. Mo. 1954).

117. Ibid. By a remarkable coincidence, the day before Whittaker issued this opinion, the staff at the Springfield facility found the defendant competent for trial; therefore, Whittaker modified his order to send the defendant back to the court of original jurisdiction and, if not there found competent, then released.

118. *Greenwood v. United States*, 219 F. 2d 376 (1955), and 350 U.S. 366 (1956). In this unanimous decision the Supreme Court upheld the constitutionality of holding a mentally incompetent defendant in custody until competent to stand trial.

119. Miller obviously overlooked this and others of Whittaker's district court decisions where he claimed, "None established great legal principles," and, "nothing about either the cases he heard or the way he handled them seems remarkable," *Whittaker: Struggles*, 39 and 41.

120. *United States v. Smith*, 16 F. R. D. 372, 375 (W. D. Mo. 1954).

121. *United States v. Wilson*, 20 F. R. D. 569 (S.D. N.Y. 1957), *United States v. J. M. Huber Corporation*, 179 F. Supp. 570 (S.D. N.Y. 1959), and *United States v. Tucker*, 262 F. Supp. 305

(S.D. N.Y. 1966). In *United States v. J. M. Huber Corporation* the court stated "It must never be forgotten that what is sought by a bill of particulars is not what actually happened but what the opponent *claims* happened."

122. Notes of Advisory Committee to Federal Rules of Criminal Procedure 7 (f), Title 18 U.S.C.A. (as amended July 1, 1966).

123. *Spinelli v. United States*, 382 F. 2d 871, 888 (1967). Also *United States v. Moore*, 57 F. R. D. 640 (N.D. Geo. 1972). Rule 7 (f) has yet to undergo further modification.

124. "The New Justice," *Time*, March 11, 1957, 17.

125. Volz, "Mr. Justice Whittaker," 170.

126. Rayburn, interview.

127. Ibid.

128. Ibid.

129. Ibid.

130. Darrell L. Havener, interview by author, June 11, 1996.

131. In *Pucci v. Blatz Brewing*, 127 F. Supp. 747 (W. D. Mo. 1955), Whittaker sustained the defendant's motion, represented by Douglas Stripp, to quash the return of service of process, but he did not dismiss the suit because it was still possible for the plaintiff to obtain jurisdiction over the defendant. In *Exhibitors Service v. Abbey Rents*, 135 F. Supp. 112 (W. D. Mo. 1955), Whittaker sustained the plaintiff's motion, represented by Carl Enggas, to add additional parties to the suit as defendants.

132. Remarks of Judge Joseph E. Stevens, "Judge Stevens Honors Whittaker in Acceptance Speech," *Advance Sheet, Lawyers Association of Kansas City* 55 (June 1996): 4. Also Stevens, interview. Stevens was appointed to the District Court for the Western District of Missouri in 1981 and served as chief judge there from 1992 to 1995. In 1996 Stevens became the twentieth recipient of the "Whittaker Award."

133. Rayburn, interview.

134. Quoted in *Kansas City Star*, March 16, 1956. See Goldman, *Picking Federal Judges*, 136. The Eighth Circuit comprised Arkansas, Missouri, Iowa, Minnesota, Nebraska, North and South Dakota. Statistics have confirmed Hennings's assessment that Missouri produced the greatest number of cases for the Eighth Circuit.

135. Yalof, *Pursuit of Justices*, 43–44, and Brownell, *Advising Ike*, 184.

136. See Goldman, *Picking Federal Judges*, 136, n. 66, and Yalof, *Pursuit of Justices*, 63.

137. Charles Whittaker, interview, November 1970, quoted in Cole, "Mr. Justice Charles Evans Whittaker," 68, n. 11.

138. Rayburn, interview.

139. Goldman, *Picking Federal Judges*, 115, Yalof, *Pursuit of Justices*, 53, and Eisenhower Diary, February 5, 1957.

140. *Kansas City Star*, May 22, 1956.

141. *Kansas City Star*, June 5, 1956.

142. Quoted in *Kansas City Star*, March 2, 1957.

143. Quoted in *Kansas City Times*, March 5, 1956.

144. Quoted in *Kansas City Star*, June 22, 1956.

145. Kent Whittaker, letter to author, June 27, 2003.

146. In *Daugaard v. Hawkeye Security Insurance*, 239 F. 2d 351 (1956), Judge Johnsen dissented. Whittaker dissented in *Fitts' Estate v. Commissioner of Internal Revenue*, 237 F. 2d 729 (1956), and again in *Milwaukee Insurance Co. v. Kogen*, 240 F. 2d 613 (1957), without opinion. Miller overlooked those cases Whittaker participated in without opinion where he claimed Whittaker only *once* dissented from an opinion written by someone else, and, contrary to Miller's misunderstanding, not once did another judge dissent from a Whittaker opinion, *Whittaker: Struggles*, 43.

147. Theodore J. Fetter, *A History of the United States Court of Appeals for the Eighth Circuit* (Judicial Conference of the United States Bicentennial Committee, 1977), 70. Previously the Court had met in several cities, including St. Louis, Kansas City, St. Paul, and Omaha. In 1969 Judge Harry Blackmum persuaded his colleagues to meet for part of the year in St. Paul, where a new federal courthouse had been built. During Whittaker's term on the court Judge John Sanborn already found the conditions in St. Louis unpleasant. Fetter, *A History of the Eighth Circuit*, 86.

148. Ibid., 51–55 and 62–65. Reflecting the changes taking place at the court, twenty years after Whittaker left the Eighth Circuit there was a marked difference in the average age and length of service of the judges. The average age of Whittaker's colleagues was seventy years and the average length of service was twenty-three and a half years; in 1975 the average age had dropped to fifty-five years and the average length of service to five and a half years.

149. Rayburn, interview.

150. In Iowa Whittaker wrote *Carpenter v. Borden*, 147 F. Supp. 445 (S. D. Iowa 1956), a trademark case, and in Arkansas he wrote for three-judge panels in *Jones Truck Lines v. United States*, 146 F. Supp. 697 (W. D. Ark. 1956), and *Arkansas Public Service Commission v. United States*, 147 F. Supp. 454 (E. D. Ark. 1956), both upholding decisions of the Interstate Commerce Commission.

151. Rayburn, interview.

152. In *Hartman v. Lauchli*, 238 F. 2d 881 (1956), and *Mesirow v. Duggan*, 240 F. 2d 751 (1957), the Supreme Court denied *certiorari*,

353 U.S. 965 (1957) and 355 U.S. 864, (1957), respectively; and in *Arkansas Public Service Commission v. United States*, 147 F. Supp. 454 (E. D. Ark. 1956), and *Moog Industries v. Federal Trade Commission*, 238 F. 2d 43 (1956), the Supreme Court affirmed by *per curiam* opinions, 355 U.S. 4 (1957) and 355 U.S. 411 (1958), respectively.

153. William O. Douglas, *The Court Years, 1939–1975* (New York: Random House, 1980), 250. Whittaker's one district court opinion appealed to the Supreme Court did arrive before him.

154. Volz, "Mr. Justice Whittaker," 170.

155. Charles E. Whittaker, "Some Reminiscences," *American Bar Association Journal* 47 (November 1961): 1090.

4. Arriving at the Supreme Court

1. The three and a half years between Potter Stewart's appointment in October 1958 and Whittaker's departure at the end of March 1962 was the longest period of uninterrupted membership during Warren's tenure. The five years Whittaker served with only one replacement intervening was equaled only by the five years between Arthur Goldberg's appointment in October 1962 and Thurgood Marshall's in October 1967.

2. John D. Fassett, *New Deal Justice: The Life of Stanley Reed of Kentucky* (New York: Vantage Press, 1994), 611.

3. Ibid., 627. David Atkinson relied entirely on Fassett's explanation for Reed's midterm retirement, *Leaving the Bench: Supreme Court Justices at the End* (Lawrence: University Press of Kansas, 1999), 125–26.

4. Cases specifically cited that Fassett claimed Reed hoped to avoid included *Reid v. Covert*, 354 U.S. 1 (reargued February 27), *Watkins v. United States*, 354 U.S. 178 (argued March 7), *Sweezy v. New Hampshire*, 354 U.S. 234 (March 5), and *Service v. Dulles*, 354 U.S. 363 (April 2–3). In addition, Reed made his decision to retire before arguments were heard in *Konigsberg v. State Bar*, 353 U.S. 252 (January 14), and *Schware v. Board of Bar Examiners*, 353 U.S. 232 (January 14–15).

5. Reed began thinking about retirement as early as 1955, just after his seventieth birthday. His delayed decision indicated that he may have been waiting for the right circumstances to announce his retirement. When he interviewed law clerks in the spring of 1955 for the next Court term, one of the applicants,

Roderick Hills, has remembered that Reed mentioned during the interview his intention to retire, but, uncertain of the timing, Reed wanted Hill's assurance that he would continue as Reed's clerk for a second term in case Reed stayed that long. Roderick Hills, telephone interview by author, October 25, 2001. Fassett acknowledged that Reed considered retiring throughout the 1955 term, noting that during Reed's annual meeting with his former law clerks in January 1956 Reed mentioned his retirement, "but stated that while his health and vigor remained good he would continue to sit on the Court," *New Deal Justice*, 612. One year later Reed's health and vigor were still good when he announced his retirement.

6. *New York Times*, February 1, 1957.

7. *New York Times*, April 29, 1937. See also Fassett, *New Deal Justice*, 171–74. Fassett claimed that apart from being informed of the plan during the month preceding its announcement and being present at the meeting where it was decided to go public with it, Reed was not likely a key draftsman of the plan, *New Deal Justice*, 147. William Leuchtenburg, on the other hand, claimed Reed was one of the few in the Justice Department involved in drafting the plan from beginning to end, *The Supreme Court Reborn: The Constitutional Revolution in the Age of Roosevelt* (New York: Oxford University Press, 1995), 130. Morgan Prickett, likewise, contended that Reed was one of the few administration members Roosevelt consulted during the formulation of the plan, "Stanley Forman Reed: Perspectives on a Judicial Epitaph," *Hastings Constitutional Law Quarterly* 8 (1981): 349. Reed himself became demure when discussing his involvement with the plan. "I knew about Roosevelt's intended message to Congress on the Court proposal," he later said, "Yes I had some hand in writing it. I knew what it was and made some suggestions on it. I talked to the attorney general about it. He talked to me about it, and thought that I should not have anything directly to do with it because I was appearing before the Court." Quoted in Fassett, *New Deal Justice*, 148, n. 7.

8. Hills, interview.

9. Ibid.

10. Even some historians considered Reed's retirement "unexpected." See, for examples, Mary Frances Berry, *Stability, Security, and Continuity: Mr. Justice Burton and Decision-Making in the Supreme Court* (Westport, Connecticut: Greenwood Press, 1978), 196, and Ed Cray, *Chief Justice: A Biography of Earl Warren* (New York: Simon & Schuster, 1997), 330.

11. Fassett, *New Deal Justice*, 626.

12. Alan Kohn, telephone interview by au-

thor, June 13, 1996. Also Alan Kohn, "Supreme Court Law Clerk, 1957–1958 A Reminiscence," *Journal of Supreme Court History* (1998): 41–42. Kohn was much more circumspect in his article, claiming Warren "remembered" his application, not that he held on to it for four months planning to give it to Whittaker.

13. *New York Times*, February 1, 1957. Mentioned as potential candidates to fill Reed's seat on the Court were Whittaker, Stewart, and federal Judges Elbert Parr Tuttle and Martin VanOosterhout. Also mentioned were Attorney General Herbert Brownell, Thomas Dewey, and Leonard Hall. The *Times* claimed there was no one on the Court between Cleveland [Justice Burton] and the Pacific Coast [Warren]. Nearly forty years later, the *Kansas City Star*, August 2, 1994, reported that Eisenhower wanted someone on the Court from a state west of Ohio because all of its members were then Easterners. These articles failed to account for the two Southern members of the Court, Justice Black of Alabama and Justice Clark of Texas.

14. Louis Poplinger, interview by author, February 21, 2001.

15. Theodore J. Fetter, *A History of the United States Court of Appeals for the Eighth Circuit* (Judicial Conference of the United States Bicentennial Committee, 1977), 70.

16. *Topeka Journal*, March 2, 1957.

17. David Alistair Yalof, *Pursuit of Justices: Presidential Politics and the Selection of Supreme Court Nominees* (Chicago: The University of Chicago Press, 1999), 44–61.

18. Ibid., 42–43, and Herbert Brownell, *Advising Ike: The Memoirs of Attorney General Herbert Brownell* (Lawrence: University Press of Kansas, 1993), 180–81.

19. Quoted in Harold Chase, *Federal Judges: The Appointing Process* (Minneapolis: University of Minnesota Press, 1972), 92. See also Dwight Eisenhower, *Mandate for Change* (New York: Doubleday, 1963), 230.

20. Brownell, *Advising Ike*, 180.

21. Yalof, *Pursuit of Justices*, 42. Yalof attributed Eisenhower's predilection for judicial promotion to his military training, where one achieved distinction by rising through the ranks, ibid., 45. Justice Frankfurter was especially critical of Eisenhower's policy of judicial promotion, writing, "Apart from meaning that a man had sat on some court for some time, 'judicial service' tells nothing that is relevant about the qualifications for the functions exercised by the Supreme Court.... The Supreme Court is a very special kind of court. 'Judicial service' as such has no significant relation to the kinds of litigation that come before the Supreme Court." "The Supreme Court in the

Mirror of Justices," in *Of Law and Life & Other Things That Matter: Papers and Addresses of Felix Frankfurter, 1956–1963*, ed. Philip Kurland (Cambridge: Harvard University Press, 1965), 82–3.

22. Yalof, *Pursuit of Justices*, 62. The list of candidates included two future Supreme Court justices, Potter Stewart and Warren Burger. Yalof was critical of Eisenhower's insistence that Brownell follow a rigid set of criteria, at least for this nomination, claiming it hampered Brownell's search for more qualified candidates, ibid., 41–44. Calling it a "stilted and inflexible process," Yalof suggested that it was Eisenhower's criteria that yielded such a disappointing choice as Charles Whittaker. The criteria produced a list of mediocre candidates and Whittaker seemed the best of the worst. "Unfortunately, the president's original criteria had narrowed the field considerably," Yalof wrote, "Instead of expanding the search to find an outstanding potential justice, the Eisenhower administration remained wedded to its own pre-determined filters," ibid., 64. This seemed to attribute Whittaker's difficulties on the Court to the selection process itself, an anachronistic conclusion. Both Justices Stewart and Brennan came through the administration's pre-determined filters (Brennan by an even more restrictive set of criteria), yet Yalof did not decry the use of criteria in either of those selections, namely because Stewart and Brennan did not prove to be judicial disappointments like Whittaker.

23. Ibid., 63. Brownell no doubt understated Roberts's considerable influence in the selection, claiming Roberts had "enthusiastically recommended" Whittaker, *Advising Ike*, 181. Both Leon Friedman, "Charles Whittaker," in *The Justices of the United States Supreme Court: Their Lives and Major Opinions*, eds. Leon Friedman and Fred L. Israel, vol. 4 (New York: Chelsea House, 1969), 2896, and Henry Abraham, *Justices and Presidents: A Political History of Appointments to the Supreme Court*, 3d ed. (New York: Oxford University Press, 1992), 271, exaggerated Brownell's support for Whittaker's nomination.

24. Abraham claimed that, according to Whittaker's godson, the president's brother, Arthur, was *the* key figure in Whittaker's Supreme Court nomination, *Justices and Presidents*, 271, n. 55. It should be clear, though, that Eisenhower's deference to Brownell's recommendations and his commitment to follow an objective set of criteria precluded his decision hinging on the word of his brother. Certainly Arthur Eisenhower supported Whittaker's nomination, but such support became pro forma once Roberts contacted the Justice Department.

25. *Topeka Journal*, March 2, 1957, and *New York Times*, March 3, 1957.

26. Patrick F. McCartan, telephone interview by author, June 27, 1996. Also Kent Whittaker, interview by author, April 25, 1996, and Clyde Rayburn, interview by author, June 19, 1996.

27. Quoted in *Kansas City Star*, March 2, 1957.

28. Hills, interview. Although thirty years separated them, Reed and Stewart remained close friends. Stewart was the only Court member in attendance at Reed's funeral twenty-three years later.

29. *Congressional Record*, 85th Cong., 1st sess., 1957, 103, pt. 3: 3055.

30. Quoted in *New York Times*, March 3, 1957.

31. Quoted in *Kansas City Star*, March 3, 1957.

32. Senate Committee on the Judiciary, *Nomination of Charles E. Whittaker: Hearing before the Committee on the Judiciary*, 85th Cong., 1st sess., March 18, 1957, 7 and 11. Beginning in 1955 with the confirmation of Justice John Marshall Harlan, judicial nominees regularly began to appear before the Senate Judicial Committee.

33. Ibid., 22.

34. The hearing lasted from 9:50 to 11:40 A.M. Based on the number of pages involved in their testimonies, it appeared that Committee members questioned Farmer for nearly one and a half hours but Whittaker for only ten minutes.

35. Both the Eighty-fourth Congress that approved his appeals court nomination and the Eighty-fifth Congress that approved his Supreme Court nomination were comprised of ninety-six senators. Only nine new senators were elected in time for his appeals court confirmation, and eight new senators were elected in time for his Supreme Court confirmation, leaving eighty-one senators remaining who approved all three of his federal court appointments.

36. *Cong. Rec.*, 85th Cong., 1st sess., 1957, 103, pt. 3: 2909-10.

37. Laurence Tribe claimed that the Senate rejected a higher proportion of presidential nominations for the Supreme Court than for any other national office. According to Tribe, the myth of the "spineless Senate" has been nurtured by "intermittent periods of relative peace" between the Senate and the White House, *God Save This Honorable Court: How the Choices of Supreme Court Justices Shapes Our History* (New York: Random House, 1985), 78. Twenty-seven years hardly seemed intermittent, though.

38. *Cong. Rec.*, 85th Cong., 1st sess., 1957, 103, pt. 3: 3929.

39. Richard Miller claimed that because Whittaker "recently passed close scrutiny" with his two lower court appointments, his Supreme Court selection was more likely, "given the intense political controversy surrounding the Supreme Court" at the time, *Whittaker: Struggles of a Supreme Court Justice* (Westport, Connecticut: Greenwood Press, 2002), 46. Lucas Powe, however, conclusively demonstrated that Whittaker's appointment *preceded* the controversial decisions of 1957, leading to the "Senate's lack of interest" in his selection, *The Warren Court and American Politics* (Cambridge: Harvard University Press, 2000), 102–03.

40. Quoted in *Kansas City Times*, March 13, 1957.

41. Mabel Gunn, telephone interview by author, June 8, 1996.

42. Quoted in *Kansas City Times*, March 13, 1957.

43. *Kansas City Star*, March 24, 1957, Mabel Gunn, interview, and Gary Whittaker, interview by author, June 21, 1996.

44. Quoted in *Kansas City Star*, March 3, 1957.

45. Poplinger, interview.

46. *Kansas City Times*, May 30, 1957.

47. *Kansas City Times*, June 1, 1957.

48. *Kansas City Star*, March 29, 1962.

49. *Kansas City Star*, March 20, 1960.

50. *Kansas City Star*, March 29, 1962.

51. Gary Whittaker, interview.

52. *Kansas City Times*, August 26, 1958.

53. *Kansas City Star*, January 7, 1959.

54. Kohn, interview. Also Kohn, "Supreme Court Law Clerk," 47.

55. Gary Whittaker, interview.

56. McCartan, interview.

57. Gary Whittaker, interview.

58. Ibid.

59. In *Safeway Stores v. Vance*, 355 U.S. 389 (1958), a Harlan decision with Warren, Black, Douglas, and Brennan dissenting, the Court ruled that Section 3 of the Robinson-Patman Act was not part of "the antitrust laws" of the Untied States, as defined by the Clayton Act, therefore a civil action for treble damages was not available to private litigants.

60. Colvin Peterson, interview by author, February 21, 2001.

61. *Kansas City Star*, March 10, 1957.

62. Rayburn, interview.

63. Quoted in *Kansas City Star*, March 7, 1957.

64. Quoted in *Kansas City Times*, February 23, 1958.

65. Laurance Hyde to Whittaker, June 3,

1960, and Whittaker to Lee Reeder, October 18, 1958, Charles Whittaker papers, Kansas City, Missouri. See also *Kansas City Times*, November 29, 1958, and *Kansas City Star*, November 30, 1958.

66. *Kansas City Star*, March 20, 1960.

67. Quoted in *Kansas City Times*, April 4, 1960.

68. In *Jackson v. Taylor*, 353 U.S. 569 (1957) and its companion *Fowler v. Wilkinson*, 353 U.S. 583 (1957), both Clark decisions, and in *Kingsley Books v. Brown*, 354 U.S. 436 (1957), a Frankfurter decision, the vote was five to four, with Warren, Black, Douglas, and Brennan dissenting.

69. Jon Newman, telephone interview by author, July 31, 2001.

70. The cases held over from Whittaker's first three months as a justice possibly because of a split vote included: *Lambert v. California*, 355 U.S. 225 (1957), *Brown v. United States*, 356 U.S. 148 (1958), *Green v. United States*, 355 U.S. 184 (1957), and *Nishikawa v. Dulles*, 356 U.S. 129 (1958).

71. Shortly after the Philippine Islands were annexed by the United States, the Court decided that not all constitutional guarantees were "applicable" there, particularly when the imposition of those guarantees disrupted locally established customs.

72. Kohn provided a detailed description of the case and the justice's deliberations. "Supreme Court Law Clerk," 44–46. See also Barrett Prettyman, *Death and the Supreme Court* (New York: Harcourt Brace & World, 1961), 85–87.

73. Kohn, interview.

74. Ibid. In his article Kohn failed to mention that Black's first draft included overruling *Trono*, and only after Whittaker threatened to leave the majority did the opinion change, "Supreme Court Law Clerk," 46.

75. Charles Whittaker, interview, April 1971, quoted in Judith Cole, "Mr. Justice Charles Evans Whittaker: A Case Study in Judicial Recruitment and Behavior" (M. A. thesis, University of Missouri–Kansas City, 1972), 141, n. 77.

76. Kohn, "Supreme Court Law Clerk," 47.

77. Burton Diary, June 18, 1957, quoted in David N. Atkinson, "Retirement and Death on the United States Supreme Court: From Van Devanter to Douglas," *University of Missouri Kansas-City Law Review* 45 (Fall 1976): 17, n. 91.

78. Terrance Sandalow, telephone interview by author, August 8, 2001.

79. Whittaker to Hazel Ruhnke, October 7, 1957, Hazel Ruhnke papers, Trimble, Missouri.

80. Whittaker to Robert L. Dominick, November 16, 1957, Whittaker papers.

81. Robert L. Dominick to Whittaker, January 20, 1958, Whittaker papers.

82. William Rogers, interview in Yalof, *Pursuit of Justices*, 64, n. 124. At one point early in his Court service, Whittaker reportedly remarked wryly to Attorney General Herbert Brownell, who had recommended all three of Whittaker's judicial posts, "Herb, I thought you were my friend." Quoted in *Kansas City Star*, March 20, 1960.

83. Whittaker to Rush H. Limbaugh, February 3, 1958, Whittaker papers.

84. George Barrett to Whittaker, August 31, 1959, Whittaker papers.

85. Letter to his physician, October 1957, Whittaker papers. Whittaker's prescriptions included Neurosene, Thorazine, Ultran, and Desbutol, a combination of the drugs Desoxyn and Nembutal.

86. Rayburn, interview.

87. Kenneth Dam, telephone interview by author, July 19, 1996, and Kohn, interview.

88. Poplinger, interview.

89. Norma Jean Parrot, interview by author, June 24, 1996.

90. Prior to Whittaker's appointment, all justices on the Court had been lawyers, but never before had all of them possessed law degrees. Albert Blaustein and Roy Mersky, *The First One Hundred Justices: Statistical Studies on the Supreme Court of the United States* (Hamden, Connecticut: Archon Books, 1978), 20, and David O'Brien, *Storm Center: The Supreme Court in American Politics* (New York: W.W. Norton, 1986), 46. The man Whittaker replaced, Stanley Reed, received two bachelor's degrees, one from Kentucky Weslyan College and another from Yale, and he attended law school at the University of Virginia and Columbia but never received a law degree.

91. Chief Justice Warren received his law degree from the University of California at Berkeley; Justice Clark earned his from the University of Texas at Austin; and Justice Black graduated first in his class from the University of Alabama Law School.

92. Joseph Stevens, interview by author, May 17, 1996. See also Stevens quoted in *Kansas City Star*, August 2, 1994.

93. Quoted in *Kansas City Times*, June 28, 1957.

94. Kent Whittaker, letter to author, June 27, 2003.

95. Jerome Cohen, telephone interview by author, August 8, 2001.

96. Quoted in Cole, "Mr. Justice Charles Evans Whittaker," 115, n. 2.

97. Curtis Reitz, interview, quoted in Cray, *Chief Justice*, 330.

98. Cohen, interview.

99. Quoted in *Kansas City Star*, March 7, 1957.

100. Albert Blaustein and Roy Mersky, "The Twelve Great Justices of All Time," *Life*, October 15, 1971, 53–59, and Blaustein and Mersky, "Rating Supreme Court Justices," *American Bar Association Journal* 58 (November 1972), 1186–7. These survey results were subsequently published in a book, Blaustein and Mersky, *The First One Hundred Justices*, 36–40, and have been continually relied upon to perpetuate Whittaker's classification as a "failure." See, for example, Abraham, *Justices and Presidents*, 412–13.

101. See, for example, "Views of Our Readers," *American Bar Association Journal* 59 (January 1973): 6, and Robert W. Langran, "Why Are Some Supreme Court Justices Rated as 'Failures'?" *Supreme Court Historical Society Yearbook* (1985): 8–14.

102. Michael E. Parrish claimed, "There is now almost a universal consensus that Frankfurter the justice was a failure, a judge who ... left little in the way of an enduring jurisprudential legacy," "Frankfurter, the Progressive Tradition, and the Warren Court," in *The Warren Court in Historical and Political Perspective*, ed. Mark Tushnet (Charlottesville: University Press of Virginia, 1993), 54, and Melvin Urofsky stated, "Frankfurter ranks as one of the great disappointments in modern times," *The Warren Court: Justices, Ruling, and Legacy* (Denver: ABC-CLIO, 2001), 40. In Brennan's defense, Henry Abraham wrote, "There is simply no doubt that [Brennan's] intellectual power, his long tenure, and his extraordinary skill at forging coalitions with his fellow justices rendered him one of the most influential members in the two hundred-year history of the Supreme Court," *Justices and Presidents*, 269. Bernard Schwartz, likewise, elevated Brennan to number five in his list of the "Ten Greatest Justices," *A Book of Legal Lists: The Best and Worst in American Law* (New York: Oxford University Press, 1997).

103. In the history of the Court, only fourteen justices served less time than Whittaker, and six of those ended their service when they died. Of the remaining justices, three retired due to health concerns (Oliver Ellsworth, Alfred Moore, and William Moody), two retired because of disappointment with the position (John Rutledge, who was later rejected by the Senate as chief justice, and Thomas Johnson), two were called on for other service (James Byrnes quit to become director of the Office of Economic Stabilization during World War II and Arthur Goldberg left to become the U.S. ambassador to the United Nations), and one (Abe Fortas) quit amid controversy surrounding his extra-judicial activity.

104. For a list of Whittaker's colleagues at the Court and the order of their appointments, see Appendix F.

105. Kohn, "Supreme Court Law Clerk," 50.

106. Of course, in order to keep Frankfurter with the majority, Douglas had to rely on strictly narrow statutory grounds to rule in favor of Rockwell Kent, who was denied a passport because he was a Communist, without ruling on the constitutionality of the right to travel.

107. A rift formed between Frankfurter and Black fourteen years before Whittaker arrived at the Court with *West Virginia State Board of Education v. Barnette*, 319 U.S. 624 (1943). In that decision the Supreme Court declared unconstitutional a mandatory flag salute law on the grounds that it violated the freedom of speech of Jehovah's Witness children. Frankfurter dissented in *Barnette* primarily because the Court overruled its decision in *Minersville School District v. Gobitis*, 310 U.S. 486 (1940), a decision Frankfurter had authored just three years earlier, which held that mandatory flag salutes for public school children were permissible. In *Gobitis* only Justice Harlan Stone dissented, but by *Barnette* Stone managed to attract five more votes, convincing Justices Black, Douglas, and Frank Murphy to switch sides. Frankfurter felt betrayed by the sudden shift in positions, and he never forgave Black or Douglas.

108. Kohn, "Supreme Court Law Clerk," 50.

109. H. N. Hirsh, *The Enigma of Felix Frankfurter* (New York: Basic Books, 1981), 177.

110. Dan Rezneck, telephone interview by author, August 3, 2001. For examples of Frankfurter's correspondence with Hand, see Bernard Schwartz, *Super Chief: Earl Warren and His Supreme Court— A Judicial Biography* (New York: New York University Press, 1983), 277–78.

111. Paul Bender, telephone interview by author, August 14 and October 1, 2001.

112. Hirsh, *The Enigma of Felix Frankfurter*, 188–89.

113. Bender, interview.

114. Frankfurter to Whittaker, March 5, 1958, quoted in Schwartz, *Super Chief*, 207.

115. Quoted in ibid., 323, n. 105. Frankfurter had first introduced the "shocks the conscience" test five years earlier in *Rochin v. California*, 342 U.S. 165 (1952). There state officials pumped the stomach of an accused drug possessor to obtain evidence used at his trial. While the Court was unanimous to reverse Rochin's conviction, Black wanted to

employ the Fifth Amendment's privilege against self-incrimination as incorporated by the Fourteenth. By using the "shocks the conscience" test, Frankfurter was able to avoid the incorporation debate in favor of a judge-made rule.

116. Roger Newman, *Hugo Black: A Biography* (New York: Pantheon Books, 1994), 482.

117. Quoted in ibid., 481.

118. Guido Calebresi, telephone interview by author, August 22, 2001.

119. Both Newman, *Hugo Black*, 482, and Miller, *Whittaker: Struggles*, 125–26, in reference to *Bartkus*, maintained that Whittaker was the decisive fifth vote; Schwartz, however, argued convincingly that Stewart held the key vote in this and other five to four decisions, *Super Chief*, 322–24.

120. Brennan dissented on separate grounds, claiming the federal government was too involved in the state prosecution.

121. *Benton* overruled *Palko v. Connecticut*, 302 U.S. 319 (1937), on which *Bartkus* had relied as precedent. Ironically, Black joined the majority in *Palko* during his first year on the Court. Thirty years later Black joined the majority in *Benton* to overrule *Palko*.

122. In his autobiography, Douglas asserted, "Though feelings often ran high, there was never a personal vendetta on the Court in my time. As I have explained, though the story was current that Felix Frankfurter and I were enemies, that was not the case. Although we differed greatly on the merits of many cases, we were not enemies," *The Court Years, 1939–1975: The Autobiography of William O. Douglas* (New York: Random House, 1980), 43. One Douglas biographer, James F. Simon, admitted that following the publication of volume one of Douglas's autobiography, *Go East, Young Man*, "Family and long-time friends shrugged at the literary feat, bemusedly debating whether the book should be marketed as fiction or nonfiction," *Independent Journey: The Life of William O. Douglas* (New York: Harper & Row, 1980), 442. Douglas's second book was no more reliable than his first. Phillip Cooper concurred that the personal feud between Frankfurter and Douglas was one of the most vicious and long-standing in the history of the Court and that Douglas's autobiography was more an appeal to history than an accurate portrayal of their relationship, *Battles on the Bench: Conflict Inside the Supreme Court* (Lawrence: University Press of Kansas, 1995), 26–27 and 108–09.

123. See Melvin Urofsky, ed., *The Douglas Letters: Selections from the Private Papers of Justice William O. Douglas* (Bethesda, Maryland: Adler & Adler, 1987), 86–91, particularly the

Memorandum to Conference dated November 21, 1960.

124. Simon, *Independent Journey*, 352–53.

125. Kohn, "Supreme Court Law Clerk," 50.

126. Simon, *Independent Journey*, 353. See also Bernard Schwartz, *A History of the Supreme Court* (New York: Oxford University Press, 1993), 240.

127. Melvin Urofsky credited Douglas's success in obtaining majorities subsequent to writing in dissent to Douglas asking the right questions and then finding the right answers, an admittedly unconventional approach, but one that proved Douglas right more often— that is, if one agreed with the outcome, "Douglas as Common Law Judge," in *The Warren Court in Historical and Political Perspective* (Charlottesville: University Press of Virginia, 1993), 78–81.

128. Simon, *Independent Journey*, 352. In his autobiography Douglas boasted that during Warren's tenure, as the demand for more law clerks increased, he playfully suggested abolishing all law clerks for one year, *The Court Years*, 172. No one took his suggestion seriously.

129. Charles Miller, telephone interview by author, October 17, 2001.

130. Calebresi, interview.

131. William Allen, telephone interview by author, August 6, 2001.

132. Berry, *Stability, Security, and Continuity*, 148–49.

133. Sandalow, interview.

134. Ibid. See also Atkinson, *Leaving the Bench*, 126–27. There has been some discrepancy over when Chief Justice Warren first learned of Burton's plans for retirement, if at all. Berry suggested Burton informed Warren in June following his doctor's advice, *Security, and Continuity*, 225, but Schwartz claimed that Warren knew as early as April 30, *Super Chief*, 319, n. 92. Relying on Burton's diary, Atkinson was silent on the matter, noting how the rest of the Court learned of Burton's plans on September 16.

135. Clerk, letter to author, August 8, 2001.

136. *Youngstown Sheet & Tube v. Sawyer*, 343 U.S. 579 (1952).

137. For quantitative proof, see Stephen Pahl, "A Court Divided: An Analysis of Polarization on the United States Supreme Court in October 1957 Term," *Santa Clara Law Review* 19 (1979): 985, Steven Smith, "Justices Stewart and Clark: Swing Votes on the Warren Court," *Santa Clara Law Review* 19 (1979): 1009, and Barbara Christensen, "Mr. Justice Whittaker: The Man on the Right," *Santa Clara Law Review* 19 (1979): 1061. It was no coincidence that

during the 1957 and 1959 terms, for example, that Clark was assigned the most opinions for the Court and more five to four decisions than any other justice. Stewart bore the responsibility for writing the most five to four decisions in the 1960 term.

138. Mark Tushnet agreed that, with the exception of *Brown*, prior to 1962 "the Warren Court" had not come into being. That did not occur until after Whittaker and Frankfurter left the Court, "The Warren Court as History: An Interpretation," in *The Warren Court in Historical and Political Perspective* (Charlottesville: University Press of Virginia, 1993), 4–7. Urofsky, likewise, stated emphatically, "When we talk about 'the Warren Court' in terms of its great achievements, with the exception of the desegregation cases, all of those decisions took place between 1962 and 1969," *The Warren Court*, 29. See also Powe, *The Warren Court and American Politics*, 497–98. Evidence of the significance of the 1962–1969 period can be found by examining Powe's *Index of Cases*, which lists 38 Warren Court cases decided prior to Whittaker's appointment, 54 decided with Whittaker's participation, but 167 decided after Whittaker's departure.

139. Schwartz rebuffed those who credited Black for the "judicial revolution" that occurred during the later "Warren Court," stressing how although Black's views ultimately prevailed, it was Warren who led the discussion to the results he favored, *A History of the Supreme Court*, 268–69. Powe, likewise, discarded the notion that it was really Brennan's influence that determined the direction of the Court, writing, "The claim that the Warren Court was really the 'Brennan Court' seems largely based on reading Brennan's subsequent career backward or defining a different era.... No one claimed that it was the Brennan Court while Warren sat. Not only had Brennan's career just begun, but he was largely unknown," *The Warren Court and American Politics*, 500.

140. Calebresi, interview. The case was *T.I.M.E. v. United States*, 359 U.S. 464 (1959). Black, Warren, Douglas, and Clark dissented.

141. *Konigsberg v. State Bar*, 353 U.S. 252 (1957), and *Schware v. Board of Bar Examiners*, 353 U.S. 232 (1957).

142. *Jencks v. United States*, 353 U.S. 657 (1957).

143. In *Service v. Dulles*, 354 U.S. 363 (1957), a unanimous Harlan decision, the Court reversed the dismissal of foreign service officer John Service from the State Department. Near the end of 1951 Secretary of State Dean Acheson summarily fired Service, a sixteen-year veteran of Chinese affairs, and Service became the government's scapegoat for the Truman administration allegedly "losing" China to Communism two years earlier. After several loyalty hearings found no evidence of disloyalty, the Review Board in its final audit declared Service a possible security risk, prompting Acheson to fire him.

144. Powe, *The Warren Court and American Politics*, 98.

145. Cray mistakenly concluded, "Whittaker was a possible fifth vote for the liberals as the brethren turned to the four national security cases [*Watkins, Yates, Sweezy*, and *Service*] that remained to be announced by mid–June, 1957," suggesting that Whittaker's vote could have altered the outcome in those cases, *Chief Justice*, 330. Although Cray admitted that Whittaker did not participate in three of those decisions, 332–35, he overlooked the fact that the liberals did not need a fifth vote since those three were all decided by six-person majorities. The unanimous decision in *Service* further blunted Cray's suggestion. Ironically, there was one other decision announced on June 17, or "Red Monday," in which Whittaker did not participate: the Court's refusal to review the conviction of the *Kansas City Star* on charges of monopolizing the dissemination of news and advertising in Kansas City.

146. *New York Times*, July 8 and June 25, 1957.

147. Robert Steamer, *The Supreme Court in Crisis* (Boston: University of Massachusetts Press, 1971), 255. Steamer placed the blame for the Court crisis of 1957–58 not on the Court but on legislatures, governors, and presidents: "The Supreme Court did not seek its role; it was drawn into a vacuum created by irresponsible politics, and it did not shirk its duty." Ibid., 260.

148. "The Supreme Court: The Temple Builder," *Time*, July 1, 1957, 12.

149. Powe, *The Warren Court and American Politics*, 141–42. "What seems inconceivable in retrospect," Powe wrote, "is the extent that the Court's majority held to the religion to which Frankfurter was reborn again in 1958, acting as if domestic communism were too hot an issue to touch. These cases are about as good an example of the dead hand of the past ruling the Court as one gets." Ibid., 154. Friedman was critical of Whittaker's support for many of these five to four decisions, writing, "What is astonishing about so many of the five to four decisions noted above is how few of them lasted after Whittaker's departure from the Court and how out of date they now seem," "Charles Whittaker," 2901. In his assessment, however, Friedman failed to consider the intentional change in direction at the Court. Of the seventeen five to four decisions he "noted

above," nine of them involved suspected Communists. Of course they seemed "out of date" once the Court again reversed directions following Frankfurter's departure.

150. *New York Times*, March 2, 1960. Walter Murphy speculated that the Court may have retreated ostensibly to put the responsibility for protecting civil liberties back on Congress, *Congress and the Court: A Case Study in the American Political Process*, (Chicago: University of Chicago Press, 1962), 267. Given that Whittaker joined in the Court's retreat from further criticisms over its domestic security decisions, Miller assumed that Whittaker possessed a "hostility toward suspected communists" or "anyone with a communist background," amounting to personal bias, *Whittaker: Struggles*, 97 and 105.

151. C. Herman Pritchett, *Congress Versus the Supreme Court, 1957–1960* (Minneapolis: University of Minnesota Press, 1961), 119, and Powe, *The Warren Court and American Politics*, 127–34. Other commentators indicated that, despite the threat to the Court's integrity, the crisis between the Court and Congress was unwarranted, namely because Congress was overreacting to a threat that simply did not exist. See, for example, Joseph Menez, "A Brief in Support of the Supreme Court," *Northwestern University Law Review* 54 (1959): 44, Glen Winters, "Shall We 'Curb' the Supreme Court?" *Journal of the American Judicature Society* 41 (August 1957): 35–36, and Harold W. Chase, "The Warren Court and Congress," *Minnesota Law Review* 44 (1960): 595 and 604.

152. See Powe, chapter 8 in *The Warren Court and American Politics*. See also Tushnet, "The Warren Court as History: An Interpretation," 6–7. Theodore Vestal, noting how this transitional period has been underrated by historians and increasingly neglected as a subject of study, ascribed new value to it with the appellation "Eisenhower Court," preface to *The Eisenhower Court and Civil Liberties* (Westport, Connecticut: Praeger, 2002).

153. Congress created the Seventh Circuit in 1807 to handle the increased judicial activity in the newly formed states of Kentucky, Tennessee, and Ohio. After Hughes, the "seventh seat" was occupied by John Clarke (1916 to 1922), George Sutherland (1922–1938), and Stanley Reed (1938–1957) before Whittaker took his place.

5. Finding a Higher Law

1. Quoted in *Kansas City Star*, March 20, 1960, 1F.

2. Ibid.

3. Charles Miller, telephone interview by author, October 17, 2001.

4. Clerk, correspondence with author, September 7, 2001.

5. Whittaker to A. Scott Mandelup, April 20, 1973, Whittaker papers, Kansas City, Missouri.

6. James Edwards, telephone interview by author, June 17, 1996.

7. Heywood Davis, interview by author, June 11, 1996.

8. Terrance Sandalow, telephone interview by author, August 8, 2001.

9. "The Bright Young Men Behind the Bench," *U.S. News & World Report*, July 12, 1957, 45–48. David Garrow considered an article by future justice William Rehnquist, "Who Writes the Decisions of the Supreme Court?" *U.S. News & World Report*, December 13, 1957, 74, a more likely candidate to prompt Whittaker to want to write all his own decisions, "Mental Decrepitude on the U.S. Supreme Court: The Historical Case for a 28th Amendment," *The University of Chicago Law Review* 67 (2000): 1046, n. 282. Garrow based his conclusion on Whittaker's recollection of the article's content as found in Judith Cole's interview, "Mr. Justice Charles Evans Whittaker: A Case Study in Judicial Recruitment and Behavior" (M. A. thesis, University of Missouri–Kansas City, 1972), 119–20, rather than accepting Alan Kohn's assertion that "Bright Young Men" made this impact, "Supreme Court Law Clerk, 1957–1958 A Reminiscence," *Journal of Supreme Court History* (1998): 43. Rehnquist's article generally indicated that the clerks had no real influence on the justices except for the possibility of unconsciously slanting *certiorari* memoranda, which effected only the justices' vote to hear or deny a case, not the writing of opinions.

10. Richard Miller, among others, assumed that this one article was solely responsible for Whittaker's determination to write his own opinions, an assumption that overlooked the fact that Whittaker had this same determination to act alone throughout his legal career, *Whittaker: Struggles of a Supreme Court Justice* (Westport, Connecticut: Greenwood Press, 2002), 54.

11. Quoted in Cole, "Mr. Justice Charles Evans Whittaker," 128. For a complete list of Whittaker's clerks and their law schools, see Appendix G.

12. William Canby, telephone interview by author, July 17, 1996.

13. Davis, interview.

14. Guido Calebresi, telephone interview by author, August 22, 2001.

15. Kenneth Dam, telephone interview by author, July 19, 1996.

16. Quoted in Kohn, "Supreme Court Law Clerk," 52.

17. Clerk, interview.

18. Alan Kohn, telephone interview by author, June 13, 1996.

19. Ibid., and Celia Barrett, telephone interview by author, June 8, 1996. In his account, Kohn wrote, "At lunch, after the opinion had been distributed, the law clerks had no comments, and I had in print the only paragraph I ever authored for the Justice," "Supreme Court Law Clerk," 52.

20. Paul Bender, telephone interview by author, October 1, 2001.

21. Quoted in *Kansas City Star*, March 20, 1960, 1F.

22. William O. Douglas, *The Court Years, 1939–1975* (New York: Random House, 1980), 250. Douglas also compared Whittaker's views of the world and of law to General Curtis LeMay, who commanded the Strategic Air Command for nearly a decade, was the Air Force chief of staff beginning in 1961, and later unsuccessfully ran as George Wallace's running mate in 1968. This comparison seemed fairly limited, though, since LeMay was far more tactless and ambitious than Whittaker, who had no military experience or political ambition whatever.

23. Thomas Klitgaard, correspondence with author, July 31, 2001.

24. Charles Whittaker, "Some Reminiscences," *Nebraska Law Review* 43 (December 1963): 361.

25. Clerk, interview.

26. Dam, interview.

27. Charles Miller, interview, Bender, interview, and Nathan Lewin, letter to author, August 15, 2001. See also James Clayton, *The Making of Justice: The Supreme Court in Action* (New York: E. P. Dutton, 1964), 84. Comparing Whittaker to Frankfurter, Clayton noted how Frankfurter delivered oral opinions without notes and how they sounded unlike his written opinions, although they usually meant the same.

28. Canby, interview.

29. *Kansas City Star*, March 29, 1962. Clayton observed how Whittaker's attitude in the courtroom was serious, almost somber, yet off the bench he had a delightful sense of humor, *The Making of Justice*, 53.

30. *Texas Law Review* 40 (June 1962): 744, 745, and 747. Leon Friedman expressed skepticism over these comments coming so soon after Whittaker's retirement, observing instead how "[Whittaker's] fellow Justices seemed hard put to say anything complimentary about

his legal ability," "Charles Whittaker," in *The Justices of the United States Supreme Court: Their Lives and Major Opinions*, eds. Leon Friedman and Fred L. Israel, vol. 4 (New York: Chelsea House, 1969), 2903. An editorial in the *Washington Post* appearing just after Justice Harlan's death, December 29, 1971, and honoring his Court service considered Harlan's dedication to Whittaker a better epitaph for Harlan. For Harlan's article, see *Texas Law Review* 40 (June 1962): 748. See also *Washington Post*, January 1, 1972, and Tinsley Yarbrough, *John Marshall Harlan: Great Dissenter of the Warren Court* (New York: Oxford University Press, 1992), 344.

31. Thomas Klitgaard, telephone interview by author, August 15, 2001. Klitgaard explained how he enjoyed watching oral arguments, Douglas wanted his clerk doing research. If he saw his clerk in the courtroom, Douglas sent a note by messenger telling him to get back to work.

32. James Adler, telephone interview by author, June 26, 1996.

33. Jerome Libin, telephone interview by author, June 29, 1996.

34. Bernard Schwartz, *Super Chief: Earl Warren and His Supreme Court—A Judicial Biography* (New York: New York University Press, 1983), 129. Schwartz claimed that in June 1958 "decision Mondays" came to an end and the Court delivered decisions whenever they were ready. Court records indicate, however, that all of Whittaker's opinions were announced on a Monday except for the two times that the Court was not in session on Monday in observance of Washington's birthday and Whittaker announced his decisions on Tuesday, February 24, 1959, and February 23, 1960.

35. Kohn, "Supreme Court Law Clerk," 45. Whittaker destroyed all of his notes after he left the Court.

36. Whittaker himself confirmed the order of voting at conference, Whittaker to Aletha Schultz, January 10, 1963, Whittaker papers, and Charles Whittaker, "The Role of the Supreme Court," *Arkansas Law Review* 17 (Fall 1963): 296. See also Tom C. Clark, "Internal Operation of the U.S. Supreme Court," *Journal of the American Judicature Society* 43 (1959): 45–51, Del Dickson, ed., *The Supreme Court in Conference (1940–1985): The Private Discussions Behind Nearly 300 Supreme Court Decisions* (New York: Oxford University Press, 2001), 107, and Earl Warren, *The Memoirs of Earl Warren* (Garden City, New York: Doubleday, 1977), 282–83. William Rehnquist, on the other hand, noted that when he joined the Court in 1972 the justices had ceased voting in reverse order of seniority because it became

obvious during discussion how the votes would come out, *The Supreme Court: How It Was, How It Is* (New York: William Morrow, 1987), 289.

37. Quoted in David Atkinson, *Leaving the Bench: Supreme Court Justices at the End* (Lawrence: University Press of Kansas, 1999), 128.

38. Jon Newman, telephone interview by author, July 31, 2001.

39. Friedman, "Charles Whittaker," 2899. Friedman failed to name all forty-one instances, citing only seventeen five to four decisions. Despite this inconsistency, Theodore Vestal relied on Friedman's claim, *The Eisenhower Court and Civil Liberties* (Westport, Connecticut: Praeger, 2002), 272. Vestal identified at most thirty-one decisions by a five to four vote where a civil liberty claim was denied and Whittaker was in the majority (not counting three *per curiam* decisions and two close five to three decisions).

40. Warren and Frankfurter did not participate. *Draper* was not Friedman's only mistake. *Chapman v. United States*, 365 U.S. 610 (1961), was an eight to one decision (only Clark dissented), not a six to three decision as Friedman claimed, and *Barenblatt v. United States*, 360 U.S. 109 (1959), was a five to four decision, not a six-man majority, "Charles Whittaker," 2898 and 2900.

41. See Steven Smith, "Justices Stewart and Clark: Swing Votes on the Warren Court," *Santa Clara Law Review* 19 (1979): 1009. Mary Frances Berry, likewise, assigned Clark the role of "swing man on the Court," *Stability, Security, and Continuity: Mr. Justice Burton and Decision-Making in the Supreme Court* (Westport, Connecticut: Greenwood Press, 1978), 213.

42. Schwartz observed how during both the 1959 and 1960 terms Stewart's vote was key in most of the close five to four decisions and how in the 1958 term his vote became decisive in two legislative investigation decisions [*Barenblatt v. United States*, 360 U.S. 109 (1959), and *Uphaus v. Wyman*, 360 U.S. 72 (1959)]. *Super Chief*, 324, 338–39, and 361. Other examples of Stewart's vote being decisive in five to four decisions can be found in Dickson, ed., *The Supreme Court in Conference*. See *Communist Party of the United States v. Subversive Activities Control Board*, 367 U.S. 1 (1961), pp. 294–97, *Shelton v. Tucker*, 364 U.S. 479 (1958), pp. 308–10, and especially *Scales v. United States*, 367 U.S. 203 (1961), pp. 300–07, where Stewart changed his vote. See also Yarbrough, *John Marshall Harlan*, 192. Evidence that Clark or Stewart were principally the swing votes on the Court can also be found in the number of five to four decisions they each were assigned

to author. In the areas of civil rights and civil liberty, Vestal presented thirty-one authored decisions during Whittaker's service where the Court denied a claimed right by a five to four decision, and Clark or Stewart authored more than a third of those. Likewise, in the twelve cases where the Court supported a claimed right by a five to four decision, Clark or Stewart authored almost half of those. *The Eisenhower Court.*

43. Richard Arnold, telephone interview by author, October 25, 2001.

44. Quoted in *Kansas City Star*, March 7, 1957.

45. Kohn, interview.

46. Kent Whittaker, interview by author, April 11, 1996.

47. Quoted in *Time*, March 11, 1957. Emphasis added.

48. Whittaker, "Some Reminiscences," 361.

49. Lewin, letter.

50. Edwards, interview. According to one of Warren's clerks, Whittaker had a difficult relationship with Edwards and afterwards said he would never again hire another Yale graduate. Murry Bring, telephone interview by author, August 16, 2001. One of Whittaker's former clerks has said, "Those bright boys from Yale and Harvard had considerable egos; they thought they could solve the world's problems. None of them were cruel to us [clerks], but some did remark critically about Whittaker." Davis, interview.

51. Carl Enggas, "Remarks of Carl E. Enggas," in *In Memoriam, Honorable Charles Evans Whittaker*, Proceeding of the Bar and Officers of the Supreme Court of the United States and Proceedings Before the Supreme Court of the United States, February 19, 1975, Washington, D.C., 14.

52. Kohn, "Supreme Court Law Clerk," 46. I will continue to use Kohn's appellation of the "Four Framers" to refer to the liberal justices, Black, Douglas, Warren, and Brennan. No derogation should be implied.

53. James Edwards, letter to author, December 19, 1996.

54. Vestal, *The Eisenhower Court*, 271–72.

55. There were examples, what Friedman considered "exceptions" to Whittaker's conservative preference, of Whittaker adopting a liberal position, but these "exceptions" were not as such truly exceptional because many of them were unanimous decisions. These included *Heikkinen v. United States*, 355 U.S. 273 (1958), where Whittaker reversed the conviction of an alien charged with "willful" failure to depart from the United States; *McNeal v. Culver*, 365 U.S. 109 (1961), a precursor to *Gideon v. Wainright*, 372 U.S. 335 (1963),

where Whittaker ruled that the mentally ill defendant was unable to defend himself without the assistance of counsel and therefore deprived of a fair trial; and *Cooper v. Aaron*, 358 U.S. 1 (1958), where the entire Court took the unprecedented step of having all the justices sign the opinion ordering the schools in Little Rock, Arkansas, to desegregate. Friedman, "Charles Whittaker," 2898. Friedman might also have included *Slagle v. Ohio*, 366 U.S. 259 (1961), another unanimous Whittaker decision (Frankfurter did not participate), which reversed the convictions of five defendants who refused to answer questions before the Ohio Un-American activities Committee. These unanimous "exceptions" did not indicate Whittaker had liberal leanings per se, since Clark, whose civil liberty record was even worse than Whittaker's, also joined each of these opinions. Vestal showed that in civil liberty cases Whittaker voted to deny the claimed right in eighty percent of the cases studied whereas Clark did so in ninety-three percent, *The Eisenhower Court.*

56. *Commissioner of Internal Revenue v. Acker*, 361 U.S. 87 (1959).

57. *Hoffman v. Blaski*, 363 U.S. 335 (1960). In his note joining Whittaker's opinion, Douglas wrote, "And I only add that I cannot imagine me changing my mind no matter who writes, no matter how long his dissenting opinion, no matter how many footnotes, etc. In other words, I think you are dead right and I think you have done a fine job." Douglas to Whittaker, May 13, 1960, quoted in Melvin I. Urofsky, ed., *The Douglas Letters: Selections from the Private Papers of Justice William O. Douglas* (Bethesda Maryland: Adler & Adler, 1987), 129.

58. *Parr v. United States*, 363 U.S. 370 (1960).

59. *Aro Manufacturing v. Convertible Top Replacement*, 365 U.S. 336 (1961).

60. *Lott v. United States*, 367 U.S. 421 (1961). For a complete list of Whittaker's Supreme Court opinions, see Appendix H.

61. Schwartz, *Super Chief*, 313–15.

62. Ibid., 316–18. See also Bernard Schwartz, *The Unpublished Opinions of the Warren Court* (New York: Oxford University Press, 1985), 105–07.

63. For example, Lucas Powe noted how "Whittaker switched his votes in the cases three different times," without mention of Brennan's or Harlan's switch, *The Warren Court and American Politics* (Cambridge: Harvard University Press, 2000), 137. Miller, on the other hand, completely overlooked both the companion case to *Perez* and the fact that Whittaker switched his votes in these cases,

preferring instead to focus on those vague and irrelevant arguments Whittaker *might* have raised in his *Perez* dissent, *Whittaker: Struggles*, 72.

64. Douglas, *The Court Years*, 173.

65. Quoted in Schwartz, *Super Chief*, 428.

66. Clark to John D. Randall, June 3, 1965, Tom Clark papers, Box 127, Folder 3, Tarlton Law Library, Austin, Texas.

67. Ed Cray, *Chief Justice: A Biography of Earl Warren* (New York: Simon & Schuster, 1997), 358–59.

68. *Trop v. Dulles*, 356 U.S. 86, 104 (1958).

69. *New York Times*, April 3, 1958. Frankfurter's statement does not appear in his printed opinion. Schwartz described the expatriation cases as the first manifestation of tension between Frankfurter and Warren leading to an irreconcilable break. Unfortunately, Schwartz was unclear as to which statements found their way into the written opinions, "Felix Frankfurter and Earl Warren: A Study of a Deteriorating Relationship," *Supreme Court Review* (1980): 129, n. 93–94, and *Super Chief*, 263, n. 51.

70. *Afroyim v. Rusk*, 387 U.S. 253 (1967). This time Brennan joined Black's five to four decision in *Afroyim*, overturning his previous vote in *Perez*.

71. *Wolf v. Colorado*, 338 U.S. 25, 27 (1949).

72. Schwartz, *Super Chief*, 327–28.

73. Quoted in Melvin Urofsky, *The Warren Court: Justices, Ruling, and Legacy* (Denver: ABC-CLIO, 2001), 47–48. Urofsky considered *Frank* a good example of how Douglas asked the right questions and got the right answers. Douglas's behavior, though, suggested that he preferred a particular result and was willing to ignore precedent to achieve what he thought the law ought to be.

74. Charles Miller, interview. See also Urofsky, *The Warren Court*, 63. Urofsky used *Frank* to characterize both what he admired most in Douglas and what he deplored in Whittaker, describing Whittaker's concurrence in *Frank* as one "that made no sense."

75. In *Camara v. Municipal Court*, 387 U.S. 523 (1967), the dissenters, Clark, Harlan, and Stewart, were all that remained from the original *Frank* majority.

76. *Frank v. Maryland*, 359 U.S. 360, 372 (1959).

77. Ibid., 373–74 (1959). Emphasis added.

78. *Camara v. Municipal Court*, 387 U.S. 523, 539 (1967). Urofsky posited that Douglas's position prevailed in *Camara*, when, as White's qualification makes clear, every civil inspection did not require a search warrant, *The Warren Court*, 47–48.

79. Miller, for example, several times la-

beled Whittaker a "legal technocrat," a term left undefined but suggesting that Whittaker paid far too much attention to the minute legal details of a case rather than looking at the larger social or moral issues raised. See *Whittaker: Struggles*, 46, 57, 74, 107, 131, 132, 134, and 138. Of course, not every case brought to the Court raised larger social or moral issues; in fact, most cases involved the legal construction of statutes, and Whittaker's philosophy of judging considered those minute legal details paramount to the final outcome of a case. Ironically, Miller borrowed the term "legal technocrat" to derogatorily assess Whittaker's abilities as a justice when, strictly speaking, a "technocrat" is a recognized expert specializing in a particular field, such as the law. Victoria Woeste first coined the term "legal technocrat" to describe Whittaker, "Charles Evans Whittaker," in *The Supreme Court Justices: A Biographical Dictionary*, ed., Melvin I. Urofsky, 533–34 (New York: Garland Publishing, 1994), 533.

80. *Alaska Industrial Board. v. Chugach Electric Association*, 356 U.S. 320 (1958).

81. *Peurifoy v. Commissioner of Internal Revenue*, 358 U.S. 59 (1958).

82. *Goldberg v. Whitaker House*, 366 U.S. 28 (1961).

83. *Commissioner of Internal Revenue v. Acker*, 361 U.S. 87, 95 (1959) (dissent).

84. Whittaker to Philip Kirwan, December 7, 1959, Charles Whittaker papers.

85. John McNulty, telephone interview by author, September 5, 2001.

86. Klitgaard, interview.

87. In the second *Reid* decision, Black joined by Warren, Douglas, and Brennan wanted to prohibit military courts martial for any civilian who was not a member of the armed forces. Frankfurter and Harlan concurred in that only courts martial for civilian dependents charged with a capital offense were unconstitutional. Clark, who authored the first *Reid* decision, dissented along with Burton.

88. Friedman criticized Whittaker's concurrence and dissent in *McElroy* and *Kinsella*, charging how they "revealed some of the reasons for his limits as a Justice." Friedman considered Whittaker's rationale in these cases impractical and illogical, "Charles Whittaker," 2902–03. Friedman, however, judged Whittaker's opinion against the rights asserted rather than against the grounds upon which Whittaker rested his opinion, namely, the authority of Congress to make rules for the military.

89. Quoted in Philip Kurland and Gerhard Casper, eds., *Landmark Briefs and Arguments of the Supreme Court of the United States: Constitutional Law*, v. 55 (Arlington, Virginia:

University Publications of America, 1975), 309. The transcript did not indicate which justice was speaking.

90. See Conference notes, October 21, 1960, in Dickson, ed., *The Supreme Court in Conference*, 843–44.

91. Schwartz claimed that Warren and Frankfurter succeeded in persuading Douglas not to issue a separate opinion, *Super Chief*, 378, which they did as far as a full opinion went, but Douglas still concurred in the judgment, reaffirming his support for the dissents in *Colegrove*.

92. *Gomillion v. Lightfoot*, 364 U.S. 339, 346–47 (1960).

93. Ibid., 347.

94. Powe concluded that by relying on the Fourteenth Amendment, Whittaker "ignored the facts" in *Gomillion* and chose the wrong basis for his separate opinion, *The Warren Court*, 177. It was entirely possible that Frankfurter overlooked the Fourteenth Amendment claims in his opinion because that would be the provision used to reconsider *Colegrove* the following term in *Baker v. Carr*, 369 U.S. 186 (1962). During the conference discussion of *Baker*, October 13, 1961, Douglas mistakenly cited *Gomillion* as precedent for resting *Baker* on equal protection grounds, when, in fact, the majority in *Gomillion* had relied on the right to vote for its decision. See Dickson, ed., *The Supreme Court in Conference*, 848. See also Schwartz, *Super Chief*, 416. Schwartz failed to note that *Gomillion* did not rely on equal protection for its decision—only Whittaker's concurrence did.

95. One of Black's clerks at the time has remembered how one of the lawyers representing the Little Rock School Board was so abused by questions from Black and Frankfurter that Warren asked him to come back and try again. Then looking to his right and left Warren said, "*We won't* interrupt you." Calebresi, interview.

96. Vestal, *The Eisenhower Court*, 272, n. 79.

97. Klitgaard, correspondence.

98. Schwartz, *Super Chief*, 299–300, and David O'Brien, *Storm Center: The Supreme Court in American Politics* (New York: W.W. Norton, 1986), 214. O'Brien mentioned the three newest justices for *Cooper* were Brennan, Stewart, and Whittaker, when, in fact, they were Harlan, Brennan, and Whittaker. Stewart did not replace Burton until after *Cooper* was announced.

99. Barrett, interview.

100. Quoted in Phillip Cooper, *Battles on the Bench: Conflict Inside the Supreme Court* (Lawrence: University Press of Kansas, 1995), 22.

101. Schwartz, *Super Chief*, 302–03. Cooper concluded that Frankfurter's efforts, while ostensibly a signal to his former students, were really the product of his overblown ego, *Battles on the Bench*, 22. Although he thought Frankfurter's efforts "slightly better" than the Court's opinion, Powe demonstrated that Frankfurter's separate opinion had little real effect on its intended audience and so became superfluous to the Court's opinion, *The Warren Court*, 161–62.

102. See Conference notes, March 27, 1959, in Dickson, ed., *The Supreme Court in Conference*, 315–16.

103. *Boynton v. Virginia*, 364 U.S. 454, 463 (1960). Miller raised the question following consideration of Whittaker's dissent in *Boynton v. Virginia*, "Does his disregard of facts here express a personal philosophy opposed to desegregation?" *Whittaker: Struggles*. Without answering the question Miller characterized Whittaker's dissent as "the stance of a supreme technocrat" and as having a "scholastic view of jurisprudence," suggesting that Whittaker somehow devised rules of law that allowed him to mask his true intentions, 107–08.

First, Whittaker disregarded no facts in *Boynton*. Miller misconstrued Whittaker's arguments. Whittaker did not, as Miller contended, *concede* that "the bus company's partial ownership of the terminal gave it partial control of the restaurant that leased space there," 108, citing Whittaker's dissent at 466–67. To the contrary, Whittaker definitively stated, "There is not a word of evidence that any carrier had any interest in or control over the lessee or its restaurant.... Indeed, there is not a word of evidence in the record tending to show that any carrier even had any interest in or control over the lessor corporation that owned the building." *Boynton v. Virginia*, 364 U.S. 454, 467 (1960) (dissent).

Second, Whittaker's "scholastic view of jurisprudence" that prevented him from considering documents submitted with the petitioner's briefs because they were not considered by the Virginia courts was not as narrow-minded as Miller presented. Where Whittaker made this pronouncement in a footnote to his dissent, he also acknowledged that had he considered those documents, they, likewise, "do not purport to show that any carrier had any interest in or control over the restaurant involved or in ... the company that owned and operated the restaurant." *Boynton v. Virginia*, 364 U.S. 454, 467, n. 5 (1960) (dissent). By thus misrepresenting the substance of Whittaker's dissent, Miller attributed to Whittaker the kind of policy preferences that might have prompted him

to craft his opinion to achieve a desired outcome. Such was not the case.

104. Powe considered *Boynton* a prelude to later sit-in cases coming before the Court and thought it demonstrated "how solicitous of one side the Court could be when it wanted," *The Warren Court*, 172.

105. 24 Del. Code 1501, in *Burton v. Wilmington Parking Authority*, 365 U.S. 715, 716–17, n. 1 (1960).

106. Powe described Clark's majority opinion as "a real stretch of the 'state action' doctrine, one that was used to transmute private discrimination into government discrimination," suggesting again that the majority reached out for a decision they favored, *The Warren Court*, 172–73. At the conference on *Burton*, Harlan, Whittaker, and Stewart could see no state action involving a question of a Fourteenth Amendment violation. The state had divested itself of surplus land by leasing it to the restaurant owner, they argued, freeing the state from liability for discriminatory acts performed in a private business. See Conference notes, February 24, 1961, in Dickson, ed., *The Supreme Court in Conference*, 707–08.

107. See Conference notes, November 10, 1961, in Dickson, ed., *The Supreme Court in Conference*, 317–18.

108. Whittaker's retirement also changed the outcome in an expatriation case, *Kennedy v. Mendoza-Martinez*, 372 U.S. 144 (1963), when his departure again left the Court split four to four requiring the justices to schedule reargument the following term. Once again, Goldberg's appointment proved decisive to the final outcome. In *Mendoza-Martinez* Goldberg ruled for a five-person majority that a native-born citizen could not be deprived of citizenship after leaving the United States to avoid military service. The Court remained divided over the constitutionality of portions of the Nationality Act, though, which had caused such difficulties in *Perez* and *Trop*.

109. Surprisingly, the *Kansas City Star* at the news of the naming of the new Charles Evans Whittaker federal courthouse in Kansas City noted that he "participated in no landmark cases," August 2, 1994, and Miller has not one word about *Cooper* or *Mapp*, although he mentioned at least a dozen other decisions in which Whittaker participated but wrote no opinion, *Whittaker: Struggles*.

110. Arnold Rice, *The Warren Court, 1953–1969* (New York: Associated Faculty Press, 1987), 249.

111. Henry Abraham, *Justices and Presidents: A Political History of Appointments to the Supreme Court*, 3d ed. (New York: Oxford University Press, 1992), 271. Robert W. Lan-

gran relied on Abraham's assertion, emphasizing how Whittaker "averaged even fewer opinions than had Van Devanter," "Why Are Some Supreme Court Justices Rated as 'Failures'?" *Yearbook Supreme Court Historical Society* (1985): 14. More recently, Miller relied on Abraham's claim that Whittaker composed only eight majority opinions, *Whittaker: Struggles*, 69. What was so remarkable about such a flagrant mistake was that Miller made extensive use of my original research, which showed that Whittaker authored forty-two majority decisions, "Charles Evans Whittaker, Associate Justice of the Supreme Court" (M. A. thesis, University of Missouri–Kansas City, 1997), 121 (table 3) and 181–82 (Appendix C). Far more embarrassing for Miller, however, was that he mentioned in his text, his footnotes, or his index at least a dozen of Whittaker's majority opinions, including *Slagle v. Ohio*, *Bonetti v. Rogers*, *Heikkinen v. United States*, *Lehmann v. Carson*, *Florida Lime & Avocado Growers v. Jacobsen*, *Staub v. City of Baxley*, *Chapman v. United States*, *Draper v. United States*, *Wilson v. Schnettler*, *Payne v. Arkansas*, *McNeal v. Culver*, and *Meyer v. United States*.

112. Schwartz claimed that Warren was fair in his opinion assignments, giving each justice their share of important decisions and assigning them a diverse range of cases, *Super Chief*, 30. Lawrence Baum, on the other hand, relying on statistical research concluded that Warren over-assigned to himself and his ideological allies civil liberty cases but not economic cases, which were presumably less important to them, *The Puzzle of Judicial Behavior* (Ann Arbor: University of Michigan Press, 1997), 110–11.

113. *Aro Manufacturing v. Convertible Top Replacement*, 365 U.S. 336 (1961).

114. *New York University Law Review* 36 (1961): 1399–1400.

115. *Brown v. Maryland*, 25 U.S. (12 Wheat) 419 (1827).

116. *Notre Dame Lawyer* 34 (1958): 593.

117. *Youngstown Sheet & Tube v. Bowers*, 358 U.S. 534, 544 (1959).

118. See, for examples, *Michelin Tire v. Wages*, 423 U.S. 276 (1976), where the Court ruled that a nondiscriminatory *ad valorem* property tax against the inventory of imported goods was not within the prohibition of the Import-Export clause, and *Limbach v. Hooven & Allison*, 466 U.S. 353 (1984), where the Court ruled again that the assessment of a personal property tax on the "original package" did not violate the Import-Export clause.

119. Frankfurter to Harlan, December 9, 1957, in Yarbrough, *John Marshall Harlan*, 127. Two years later Frankfurter was still trying to convince Whittaker of the harms inherent in such a doctrine. See Frankfurter to Harlan, January 12, 1960, in ibid., 128.

120. *Staub v. City of Baxley*, 355 U.S. 313, 321 (1958).

121. *Staub v. City of Baxley*, 355 U.S. 313, 325–26 (1958) (dissent).

122. Vestal, *The Eisenhower Court*, 272.

123. Quoted in *Kansas City Star*, March 20, 1960, 1F.

124. Douglas to Whittaker, May 29, 1958, quoted in Urofsky, ed., *The Douglas Letters*, 129.

125. *Flora v. United States*, 357 U.S. 63, 75 (1958). The principle of "pay first and litigate later" was announced in *Chetham v. United States*, 92 U.S. 85 (1875).

126. *Flora v. United States*, 357 U.S. 63, 69 (1958).

127. Sandalow, interview.

128. *Flora v. United States*, 362 U.S. 145, 178 (1960) (dissent).

129. Ibid., 177–78 (dissent).

130. Ibid., 146–7.

131. Ibid., 197 (dissent).

132. Canby, interview.

133. Bender, interview.

134. Clerk, interviews.

135. *Kansas City Star*, March 20, 1960, 1F.

136. Libin, interview.

137. Whittaker dissented alone in *Arnold v. Kanowsky*, 361 U.S. 388 (1960), *United Steelworkers of America v. Enterprise Wheel*, 363 U.S. 593 (1960), and *United Steelworkers v. Warrior & Gulf*, 363 U.S. 574 (1960).

138. *Commissioner of Internal Revenue v. Duberstein*, 363 U.S. 278 (1960).

139. *United States v. Kaiser*, 363 U.S. 299, 331 (1960) (dissent).

140. *Colwell v. Commissioner of Internal Revenue*, 64 T.C. 584 (1975). Forrester joined the Tax Court in May 1957, just after Whittaker went to the Supreme Court. Soon after this decision Forrester retired but continued to serve in retired status on the Tax Court until 1984.

141. See *Stone v. Commissioner of Internal Revenue*, 50 TCM 1345 (1985).

142. *James v. United States*, 366 U.S. 213, 251 (1961) (dissent).

143. See, for examples, Powe, *The Warren Court*, where only ten percent of the Court's written opinions during Whittaker's service were mentioned by name, and Vestal, *The Eisenhower Court*, which named ninety-four opinions during Whittaker's service (not counting *per curiam* orders) involving civil liberties, still just twenty percent of the Court's written output.

144. Friedman, "Charles Whittaker," 2909. See also Miller, *Whittaker: Struggles*, 52.

145. *Kansas City Star*, March 20, 1960, 1F. Miller relied on this same citation yet maintained that despite this explicit explanation Whittaker never made the adjustment from one court to another, *Whittaker: Struggles*, 58.

146. Friedman, "Charles Whittaker," 2902. In Vestal's study of individual justices' voting records in civil liberty claims, the measure of whether a justice voted for or against a claimed right seemed to be on which side was Douglas. In every one of the fifty-eight cases decided during Whittaker's tenure where the Court ruled *against* a claimed right, Douglas voted in dissent, *The Eisenhower Court*.

147. Quoted in *Kansas City Star*, March 20, 1960, 1F. Relying on this same article Miller ignored Whittaker's change in outlook, succumbing instead to conventional portrayals, *Whittaker: Struggles*, 51–58.

148. Abraham, *Justices and Presidents*, 271. See also Friedman, "Charles Whittaker," 2901. Perpetuating this impression of Whittaker making little contribution to the Court's work, Langran noted how none of Whittaker's opinions were noteworthy, "Why Are Some Supreme Court Justices Rated as 'Failures'?" 14, and Schwartz observed, "There is not one Whittaker opinion that decides an important case or stands out from the humdrum," *A Book of Legal Lists: The Best and Worst in American Law* (New York: Oxford University Press, 1997), 31.

149. See *United States v. Young*, 470 U.S. 1 (1985).

150. *G & T Terminal Packaging v. Hawman*, 870 F.2d 77 (1989). Here the court considered an agency action, whether an amended order of the Secretary of Agriculture was "final" after the original order failed to state the date used for computing interest.

151. *Fiatarudo v. United States*, 8 F.3d 930 (1993).

152. See *Resale Mobile Homes v. Commissioner of Internal Revenue*, 91 T.Ct. 1085 (1988). The Supreme Court in *Thor Power Tool v. Commissioner of Internal Revenue*, 439 U.S. 522 (1979), also supported Whittaker's decision.

153. See *Kozma v. Commissioner of Internal Revenue*, 51 TCM 956 (1986). In one of his first opinions for the Court, *Fourco Glass v. Transmirra Products*, 353 U.S. 222 (1957), Whittaker likewise ruled that a specific statute in patent infringement controlled a more general one. His decision in *Fourco* governed patent law for the next thirty years until Congress amended the general statute.

154. See, for examples, *Somali Development Bank v. United States*, 205 Ct.Cl. 741 (1974),

DeRoo v. United States, 12 Cl.Ct. 356 (1987), and *Reforestacion de Sarapiqui v. United States*, 26 Cl.Ct. 177 (1992).

155. *University of Pennsylvania Law Review* 107 (1959): 1043–44.

156. *Draper v. United States*, 358 U.S. 307, 314 (1959) (dissent).

157. *Hastings Law Journal* 11 (1959): 214–15. Emphasis added. The *Journal of the Bar Association of the State of Kansas* 27 (1958): 78–80, on the other hand, in the year before Whittaker's decision, thought the Tenth Circuit Court of Appeals used sound judgment in its handling of *Draper*, which Whittaker supported.

158. *Tennessee Law Review* 26 (1959): 306–08.

159. Friedman claimed that *Wong Sun v. United States*, 371 U.S. 471 (1963), restricted *Draper*, making *Draper* seem "out of date" because it did not last "after Whittaker's departure from the Court," "Charles Whittaker," 2901. In *Wong Sun*, the Court found that the informer was too untested and his information too vague to establish reasonable grounds for an arrest without a warrant. What distinguished *Draper* from *Wong Sun* and made *Draper* such a leading precedent was the emphasis Whittaker gave to the *reliability* of the informer and the *accuracy* of his descriptions, which the police were able to verify by their own independent observation.

160. In 1991 retired Justice Lewis Powell in *United States v. Miller*, 925 F.2d 695 (4th Circ.) ruled for a three-judge panel that *Draper* still controlled in questions of probable cause, and in 1993 Sam Ervin, chief judge of the Fourth Circuit Court of Appeals, in *United States v. Sinclair*, 983 F.2d 598 (4th Circ.), restated that *Draper* was "the classic case" for deciding these issues.

161. Three justices who joined Whittaker in *Draper*, Clark, Black, and Stewart, found the new standard too rigid.

162. Here the Court reversed the conviction because probable cause was not established. Fortas and Stewart dissented, believing there was a basis for probable cause. Black dissented because he believed the new standard was so inflexible that, in his view, the magistrate's hearing for issuing a search warrant became a full-scale trial.

163. *Spinelli v. United States*, 393 U.S. 410, 416–17 (1969).

164. Ibid., 417–18.

165. Rehnquist, writing for a five-person majority, first referred to *Draper* as "the classic case" on the value of corroborative efforts by police officials. *Illinois v. Gates*, 462 U.S. 213, 242 (1983).

6. Failing Justice

1. Friedman established Whittaker's poor public image, writing, "There was little Whittaker did in his five years on the Court to justify praise as either a judicial thinker or a legal technician.... [H]e was not fitted intellectually or physically for the job. None of his opinions seem to offer any new insight into the problem under analysis. His style and thinking were pedestrian." "Charles Whittaker," in *The Justices of the United States Supreme Court: Their Lives and Major Opinions*, eds., Leon Friedman and Fred L. Israel, vol. 4 (New York: Chelsea House, 1969), 2903. Blaustein and Mersky subsequently relied entirely and unquestioningly on this assessment, "Rating Supreme Court Justices," *American Bar Association Journal* 58 (November 1972): 1183–89. See also Catherine A. Barnes, ed., *Men of the Supreme Court: Profiles of the Justices* (New York: Facts on File, 1978), 168, and Theodore M. Vestal, *The Eisenhower Court and Civil Liberties* (Westport, Connecticut: Praeger, 2002), 273. For over a decade Bernard Schwartz considered Whittaker one of the worst appointments, *Super Chief: Earl Warren and His Supreme Court—A Judicial Biography* (New York: New York University Press, 1983), 216, and *A History of the Supreme Court* (New York: Oxford University Press, 1993), 271. Schwartz since censured Whittaker even more severely, calling him "the dumbest Justice ever appointed," *A Book of Legal Lists: The Best and Worst in American Law* (New York: Oxford University Press, 1997), 30.

2. Dan Rezneck, telephone interview by author, August 3, 2001. One of Justice Harlan's clerks has commented, "Other justices were not remarkably talented, but many of them had enough sense to get through it. Even though Whittaker may not have been smart enough, he did not have enough experience to have the confidence to get through it." Charles Fried, telephone interview by author, August 7, 2001.

3. Friedman considered *Thomas* and *Moore* "almost identical cases," "Charles Whittaker," 2902. Victoria Woeste relied on Friedman's comparison of *Thomas* and *Moore*, concluding, "Whittaker had the most conservative voting record of anyone on the Court during his tenure." "Charles Evans Whittaker," in *The Supreme Court Justices: A Biographical Dictionary*, ed., Melvin I. Urofsky, 533–34 (New York: Garland Publishing, 1994), 533. Richard Miller, likewise, compared *Thomas* to *Moore* and considered the difference between claims based on coerced confession and right to counsel a "technical distinction." *Whittaker:*

Struggles of a Supreme Court Justice (Westport, Connecticut: Greenwood Press, 2002), 134 and 138. For more appropriate comparisons, see Daniel M. Berman, "Mr. Justice Whittaker: A Preliminary Appraisal," *Missouri Law Review* 24 (January 1959): 11–12, Barnes, *Men of the Supreme Court*, 168, n. 5, and Vestal, *The Eisenhower Court*, 271.

4. For a useful explanation of *ratio decidendi*, see Arthur L. Goodhart, "Determining the *Ratio Decidendi* of a Case," *Yale Law Journal* 40 (1930): 161, in Walter Murphy and C. Herman Pritchett, *Courts, Judges, & Politics: An Introduction to the Judicial Process* (New York: McGraw-Hill, 1986), 391–92.

5. Miller accused Whittaker of "originating innovative legal doctrine" in *Crooker*, claiming Whittaker thought "that a defendant's intelligence should be *the determining factor* on whether a defendant accused of a crime was entitled to representation by an attorney." *Whittaker: Struggles*, 134. Emphasis added. Unfortunately, Miller failed to grasp the principal contention of Clark's majority opinion on the question of representation by counsel, namely, "[T]he *sum total* of the circumstances here during the time petitioner was without counsel is a voluntary confession." *Crooker v. California*, 357 U.S. 433 at 440 (1958). Emphasis added.

6. *Thomas v. Arizona*, 356 U.S. 390, 400 (1958). Miller criticized Whittaker for accepting Clark's reliance on "the undisputed facts" of the lower court records, suggesting that his experience as a district court judge should have led Whittaker to consider the disputed facts of the case, *Whittaker: Struggles*, 133. Miller here confused the duties and limits of district court judges and Supreme Court justices.

7. Alan Kohn, "Supreme Court Law Clerk, 1957–1958 A Reminiscence," *Journal of Supreme Court History* (1998): 47–48. Miller, who relied on Kohn's article but failed to mention the compromise made to save Payne's life, expressed gratitude that Whittaker, the supreme legal "technocrat," was not called upon in this case to answer the question, "Would Whittaker let a man die because he did not protest violation of his rights at the bureaucratically appropriate time?" *Whittaker: Struggles*, 131. Certainly Kohn's recollections amply answered that question in the negative.

8. *Payne v. Arkansas*, 356 U.S. 560, 567 (1958).

9. *Watts v. Indiana*, 338 U.S. 49 (1949), quoted in *Payne* at 566.

10. William O. Douglas, *The Court Years, 1939–1975: The Autobiography of William O. Douglas* (New York: Random House, 1980), 173–74. Without mentioning any other aspect

of his life or work, Mark Silverstein used this account to classify Whittaker as one of the "simply wretched" appointments to the Court, *Judicious Choices: The New Politics of Supreme Court Confirmations* (New York: W. W. Norton, 1994), 162, n. 2. Others to use this story to discredit Whittaker included Bob Woodward and Scott Armstrong, *The Brethren: Inside the Supreme Court* (New York: Simon and Schuster, 1979), 63, Woeste "Charles Evans Whittaker," 533–34, Schwartz, *A Book of Legal Lists*, 31, Melvin I. Urofsky, *The Warren Court: Justices, Ruling, and Legacy* (Denver: ABC-CLIO, 2001), 65, Miller, *Whittaker: Struggles*, 73, and Bruce Allen Murphy, *Wild Bill: The Legend and Life of William O. Douglas* (New York: Random House, 2003), 637. Woodward and Armstrong got the story from Douglas even before his autobiography was published, and over a decade later Murphy relied on Douglas's secretary to confirm Douglas's account in his autobiography.

11. See Richard Shenkman and Kurt Reiger, *One Night Stands with American History: Odd, Amusing, and Little-Known Incidents* (New York: William Morrow, 1980), 261. According to James F. Simon, Douglas first met Hamilton in 1955 when her husband clerked for Clark. She began to help Douglas with manuscripts for several of his books beginning in 1962, but she remained anonymous at publication. In fact, when Douglas had Hamilton make arrangements at Random House for the publication of the first volume of his autobiography in 1972, no one there knew who she was. *Independent Journey: The Life of William O. Douglas* (New York: Harper & Row, 1980), 443–46.

12. Quoted in Murphy, *Wild Bill*, 499. According to Simon, following his stroke Douglas repeatedly addressed people at the Court by the wrong name, often uttered *non sequiturs*, or simply stopped speaking altogether. Even after his retirement a year later Douglas insisted on calling himself the tenth justice, expecting to participate in preparing Court decisions. It was in this condition that he worked on revising volume two of his autobiography. *Independent Journey*, 448–54. See also Kim Eisler, *A Justice for All: William J. Brennan, Jr., and the Decisions that Transformed America* (New York: Simon and Schuster, 1993), 257–58. Eisler described how Brennan finally had to convince Douglas that he was no longer a justice, and when he fell ill in 1990 Brennan decided to resign with his mind still intact because he remembered the "undignified and embarrassing exit" of Douglas. Ibid., 280.

13. Quoted in Murphy, *Wild Bill*, 660. Murphy admirably attempted to debunk the Douglas myth. See ibid., 474–75 and 513–14. For

Douglas's paranoia, see Simon, *Independent Journey*, 444, and Murphy, *Wild Bill*, 426.

14. *Meyer v. United States*, 364 U.S. 410, 412–15 (1960).

15. *Meyer v. United States*, 364 U.S. 410, 418–19 (1960) (dissent).

16. See Simon, *Independent Journey*, 352, Murphy, *Wild Bill*, 182, and Woodward and Armstrong, *The Brethren*, 63.

17. James N. Adler, telephone interview by author, June 26, 1996. In a personal interview (1961–63) Douglas claimed he and Whittaker had become close friends. Vestal, *The Eisenhower Court*, 273, n. 88.

18. James M. Edwards, telephone interview by author, June 17, 1996. Douglas's one clerk at the time, likewise, had no recollection of Douglas writing *two* opinions in *Meyer*. Recalling *Meyer*, "which I remember pretty well," this clerk has written, "The Justice [Douglas], as usual, wrote the draft very quickly and I did some work on it; I was not terribly impressed by the draft, but I don't think I improved it much. I may remember the Justice saying it could have gone either way, but that is the best that I can remember and that is not certain." Bernard Jacob, letter to author, June 4, 2003.

19. The tale that provoked such a strong response from his law school classmates was the one where Douglas claimed he had been second in his law school class and was considered for a clerkship at the Supreme Court. Murphy, *Wild Bill*, 474. Regarding Douglas's disregard for thorough, well-supported opinions, Simon wrote, "Douglas appeared to have been interested more in communicating his broad philosophy to the readers of his judicial opinions than in satisfying a scholar's appetite for carefully documented legal arguments. He was not a lawyer's judge or a judge's judge or a scholar's judge. He was a people's judge, promoting his strong equalitarian philosophy regardless of whether or not his views were well supported by precedent." *Independent Journey*, 354. Murphy, likewise, observed, "With his lack of regard for legal jargon in his work, Douglas soon came to see a different audience for his decisions. Rather than writing for the legal community using complicated Latin terms and judicial doctrines, he wrote in plain English for the general public. It was almost as if, rather than writing a judicial opinion, he were drafting a sermon on an issue, much like his father once did, and preparing it for delivery from his high pulpit on decision day." Murphy, *Wild Bill*, 182. Such descriptions of the judicial duty were anathemas to Whittaker.

20. Fried, interview.

21. John McNulty, telephone interview by author, September 5, 2001.

22. Alan Kohn, telephone interview by author, June 13, 1996. See also Kohn, "Supreme Court Law Clerk," 47.

23. When Douglas offered to assist with *Hvass*, Kohn remembered, "I think he was genuinely trying to help; he felt sorry for Whittaker." Kohn, interview. By contrast, Urofsky observed that after assisting with *Meyer*, "Douglas derived some malicious pleasure from recalling this episode." *The Warren Court*, 65. Just *when* Douglas recalled this episode is open to question, but, according to Murphy, Douglas "claimed for years" that he wrote the majority in *Meyer*. *Wild Bill*, 637. Considering the circumstances, Douglas's claims were, at least, doubtful. Ignoring the relevant circumstances of Whittaker's fourth term, Miller considered Whittaker's acceptance of Douglas's assistance in *Meyer* an act of desperation. *Whittaker: Struggles*, 73. More likely, though, Whittaker accepted in *Meyer* the kind of assistance he received in *Hvass*, which included only a few sentences.

24. Quoted in Schwartz, *Super Chief*, 216–17. See also Schwartz, *A Book of Legal Lists*, 31–32. *Times Film Corporation v. City of Chicago*, 355 U.S. 35 (1957), was decided November 12, 1957, by a *per curiam* decision.

25. Schwartz, *A Book of Legal Lists*, 46.

26. See Schwartz, *Super Chief*, 45. Frankfurter also revealed his flair for foreign phrases by writing of Black's dissent in the case, "His roundabout and turgid legal phraseology is a *cri de coeur*." For examples of Frankfurter's "Dialogues" written while Whittaker served, see Schwartz, *Super Chief*, 47 and 346.

27. Whittaker to Roberts, December 10, 1959, Charles Whittaker papers, Kansas City, Missouri.

28. Bernard Schwartz and Stephen Lesher acknowledged that "Whittaker was a staunch admirer of Frankfurter," and that "the former professor alternately flattered and bullied him to make sure of his vote," *Inside the Warren Court* (New York: Doubleday, 1983), 200, and Woodward and Armstrong concluded, "Instead of influencing him, Frankfurter had drawn Whittaker's resentment," *The Brethren*, 176.

29. Whittaker to Frankfurter, August 30, 1962, Whittaker papers.

30. Kent Whittaker, interview by author, April 25, 1996.

31. Guido Calebresi, telephone interview by author, August 22, 2001.

32. Clerk, letter to author, August 8, 2001.

33. Rezneck, interview. The two cases were *Machinists v. Street*, 367 U.S. 740 (1961), and *Lathrop v. Donahue*, 367 U.S. 820 (1960). Widely recognized for his skills in forging majorities,

Brennan was well known for telling his clerks, "Five votes can do anything around here," quoted in Del Dickson, ed., *The Supreme Court in Conference (1940–1985): The Private Discussions Behind Nearly 300 Supreme Court Decisions* (New York: Oxford University Press, 2001), 851. See also Eisler, *A Justice for All*, 178. The justices' efforts to negotiate majorities was not lost on Henry Hart, who wrote following the Court's 1958 term, "The Court gave gratuitous aid and comfort to the most extreme of its critics who say that it twists facts and words at its pleasure in order to reach the results it wants to reach." Hart then concluded pessimistically that this kind of thoughtless decision making would continue as long as the Court was no longer based on law and reason but rather on how many votes a justice could get on his side. "Foreword: The Time Chart of the Justices," *Harvard Law Review* 73 (1959): 110.

34. Schwartz, *Super Chief*, 259.

35. Douglas, *The Court Years*, 173.

36. Michael Parrish, "Frankfurter, the Progressive Tradition, and the Warren Court," in *The Warren Court in Historical and Political Perspective*, ed. Mark Tushnet (Charlottesville: University Press of Virginia, 1993), 54.

37. Quoted in Schwartz, *Super Chief*, 261.

38. Ibid., 35.

39. H. N. Hirsh, *The Enigma of Felix Frankfurter* (New York: Basic Books, 1981), 208. For Frankfurter's relationship with Marion and her difficulties, see ibid., 81–85. Even Warren, the consummate politician, could not cope with the force of Frankfurter's personality. Warren once told a friend, "All Frankfurter does is talk, talk, talk. He drives you crazy." Quoted in Schwartz, *Super Chief*, 257.

40. Frankfurter to Whittaker, March 31, 1958, quoted in Schwartz, *Super Chief*, 260.

41. Frankfurter to Whittaker, March 24, 1960, quoted in Schwartz, *Super Chief*, 260. Arnold Rice, likewise, concluded about Whittaker's service, "In the entire history of the Supreme Court few members labored as intensely as he did and perhaps no one agonized as much as he did over every facet of a pending case." *The Warren Court, 1953–1969*, Publications of the Supreme Court in American Life Series, ed. George J. Lankevich, no. 8 (New York: Associated Faculty Press, 1987), 249.

42. Schwartz, *Super Chief*, 260. Schwartz also included this note from Frankfurter to Whittaker, written on May 5, 1960: "Were I to retire tomorrow, one of the most gratifying memories I would carry with me of my whole judicial life would be your behavior in *Yancy* [*v. United States*, 362 U.S. 389 (1960)]. It was judicial behavior at its finest." Quoted in ibid.

Whittaker's behavior in *Yancy*, other than voting alongside Frankfurter, was unclear since *Yancy* was decided in a *per curiam* order by an equally divided Court (Stewart did not participate). While these notes seemed frivolous enough, they were hardly "ludicrous" to suit Frankfurter's purpose. Besides, there is no evidence that Frankfurter harbored ill feelings toward Whittaker or felt otherwise than these notes indicated. Considering the contempt Frankfurter freely expressed concerning other justices in his correspondence, even against Clark and Stewart, surely if Frankfurter had misgivings about Whittaker's abilities he would have communicated that. See ibid., 278, n. 151.

43. Quoted in Schwartz, *Super Chief*, 259–60.

44. Charles Whittaker, interview, April 1971, quoted in Judith Cole, "Mr. Justice Charles Evans Whittaker: A Case Study in Judicial Recruitment and Behavior" (M. A. thesis, University of Missouri–Kansas City, 1972), 127, n. 34.

45. Nathan Lewin, letter to author, August 15, 2001. Other sources to conclude that consideration of *Baker v. Carr* led to Whittaker's breakdown and retirement included Friedman, "Charles Whittaker," 2903, Eisler, *A Justice for All*, 176, Schwartz, *Super Chief*, 427–28, Vestal, *The Eisenhower Court*, 273, n. 88, and Dickson, *The Supreme Court in Conference*, 851. Relying on my original research, however, David Atkinson and David Garrow concluded that Whittaker's disability lay not with consideration of *Baker*, necessarily, but with a pre-existing medical condition. See Atkinson, *Leaving the Bench: Supreme Court Justices at the End* (Lawrence: University Press of Kansas, 1999), 130, n. 127, citing Smith, "Charles Evans Whittaker, Associate Justice of the Supreme Court" (M. A. thesis, University of Missouri–Kansas City, 1997), 76 and 103, and Garrow, "Mental Decrepitude on the U.S. Supreme Court: The Historical Case for a 28th Amendment," *The University of Chicago Law Review* 67 (2000): 1048, n. 291, citing Smith, "Charles Evans Whittaker," 101 and 106. Miller agreed with more conventional portrayals of Whittaker's disability, writing, "The stress Whittaker felt with this case [*Baker*] has been blamed for his health's catastrophic breakdown," *Whittaker: Struggles*, 150. For support, Miller imprudently cited Atkinson, who, to the contrary, concluded just the opposite.

46. Rezneck, interview.

47. Louis Poplinger, interview by author, February 21, 2001.

48. Quoted in Schwartz, *Super Chief*, 216. See also Schwartz, *A History of the Supreme Court*, 271–72, and Schwartz, *A Book of Legal Lists*, 30–31. Fortunately, Schwartz named Stewart as the source in 1997, otherwise he might have remained anonymous.

49. Schwartz and Lesher, *Inside the Warren Court*, 6.

50. Miller, again, succumbed to conventional portrayals, ascribing Whittaker's feelings of inferiority principally to his law school training. *Whittaker: Struggles*, 4. By the time Whittaker arrived at the Court, though, his thirty years of success at the bar and lower federal court appointments had compensated emotionally for his part-time legal education. One of the clerks Whittaker's first term who observed Whittaker's initial self-assurance before Frankfurter deflated it has said, "I think Whittaker may have come to the Court too haughty. He did not defer to superiors, which may have irked some members of the Court. Whittaker was an enigma." Clerk, interview.

51. Parrish, "Frankfurter, the Progressive Tradition," 53, citing Schwartz, *Super Chief*, 241.

52. Charles Whittaker, "The Role of the Supreme Court," *Arkansas Law Review* 17 (Fall 1963): 296.

53. Phillip Cooper, *Battles on the Bench: Conflict Inside the Supreme Court* (Lawrence: University Press of Kansas, 1995), 9 and 109.

54. Roger Newman, *Hugo Black: A Biography* (New York: Pantheon Books, 1994), 485, n. 10.

55. Cooper, *Battles on the Bench*, 40.

56. See Mary Frances Berry, *Stability, Security, and Continuity: Mr. Justice Burton and Decision-Making in the Supreme Court* (Westport, Connecticut: Greenwood Press, 1978), 216–17.

57. Douglas to the Conference, October 23, 1960, quoted in Melvin Urofsky, ed., *The Douglas Letters: Selections from the Private Papers of Justice William O. Douglas* (Bethesda, Maryland: Adler & Adler, 1987), 90.

58. For an example of exchanges between Frankfurter and Douglas just one month prior to Whittaker's collapse, see Cooper, *Battles on the Bench*, 145–46.

59. Kohn, "Supreme Court Law Clerk," 49.

60. Quoted in Schwartz, *Super Chief*, 254. See also *New York Times*, March 21, 1961.

61. Kohn, "Supreme Court Law Clerk," 49. This incident was quickly defused later the same day. Kohn remembered that all the justices were invited to Whittaker's home for a late afternoon cocktail party. It was the first time Warren and Frankfurter would speak to each other since their courtroom encounter. According to Kohn, when Frankfurter arrived Warren seized the occasion: "He shook Justice Frankfurter's hand energetically, gave him a huge Earl Warren 'Hello, how are you, Felix,'

and then put his big arm around the diminutive Justice. Frankfurter politely returned the hello and smiled." Ibid., 49–50. Future courtroom battles were not so easily smoothed over.

62. *Stewart v. United States*, 366 U.S. 1, 22 (1961) (dissent).

63. Rezneck, interview.

64. Quoted in Schwartz, *Super Chief*, 253. See also *New York Times*, April 25, 1961.

65. Conference notes, December 8, 1961, on *Machibroda v. United States*, 368 U.S. 487 (1962), in Dickson, *The Supreme Court in Conference*, 559–60.

66. Newman, *Hugo Black*, 473. Schwartz, on the other hand, considered Warren the leading advocate for reviewing and reversing on the merits in these cases. *Super Chief*, 268–71.

67. See Frankfurter's dissent in *Rogers v. Missouri Pacific Railroad*, 352 U.S. 500, 524 (1957).

68. In most FELA cases Frankfurter refused to write more, preferring instead to reiterate his dissent in *Rogers* that *certiorari* was improvidently granted.

69. See Harlan's separate opinion in *Rogers* at 559. See also Harlan's memorandum in *Gibson v. Thompson*, 355 U.S. 18, 19 (1957).

70. *Moore v. Terminal Railroad Association of St. Louis*, 358 U.S. 33, 34 (1958) (dissent).

71. Schwartz, *Super Chief*, 271. Miller noted how FELA cases "were often decided by a narrow vote, inflaming the minority justices who lost over and over again." *Whittaker: Struggles*, 139. Of the three FELA cases he mentioned, only one, *Inman v. Baltimore & Ohio Railroad*, 361 U.S. 138 (1959), was decided by a narrow vote (5–4), with the liberal justices dissenting. Otherwise, in every other FELA case the liberal justices comprised part of the majority and the vote was not close (in the only other close case, *Michalic v. Cleveland Tankers*, 364 U.S. 325 [1960], for example, the vote was five to three with Frankfurter refusing to join either side). Since Harlan, Whittaker, Burton, and later Stewart felt compelled to decide these cases on their merits, at times any one of them could concur with the liberal justices, so there was not a consistent liberal minority "who lost over and over again." The only justice who "lost over and over again" was Frankfurter, who steadfastly adhered to his improvidently granted position.

72. Whittaker to Roy Roberts, December 10, 1959, Whittaker papers.

73. Vestal, *The Eisenhower Court*, 272. Vestal also found this opinion to Whittaker's "discredit." Vestal failed, however, to account for the circumstances leading to this opinion or to explain how this opinion "poked fun at the dissent of Justice Douglas." Schwartz failed to

mention that it was Whittaker's concurrence that provoked laughter in the courtroom, and, likewise, neglected to explain how Whittaker's concurrence succeeded in "poking fun" at Douglas's dissent. See Schwartz, *Super Chief*, 271.

74. Whittaker to Roberts, December 10, 1959, Whittaker papers.

75. *Inman v. Baltimore & Ohio Railroad*, 361 U.S. 138, 141–42 (1959).

76. "Supreme Court Justices Disagree on What's Funny," *U.S. News & World Report*, December 28, 1959, 17.

77. *Inman v. Baltimore & Ohio Railroad*, 361 U.S. 138, 142 (1959). According to the *New York Times*, December 15, 1959, Whittaker said, "How this can be though [*sic*] to square with any known concept of 'negligence' *can be devined only in heaven.*" Emphasis added. Considering Whittaker's tendency to read his opinions word for word, it was remarkable for him to alter these at their announcement. Perhaps he got caught up in his own facetiousness. Otherwise, Whittaker was not prone to extemporaneousness.

78. Quoted in *New York Times*, December 15, 1959. See also *Kansas City Times*, December 15, 1959.

79. Jerome Libin, telephone interview by author, June 29, 1996.

80. Despite his over-reliance on my original research, Miller failed to account for Whittaker's letter to Roberts, where Whittaker announced his purpose was for satirical or humorous effect. Such a purpose did not require, as Miller preferred, "citation of law to support his contention." *Whittaker: Struggles*, 141. If *Inman* "touched [Whittaker's] emotions," as Miller claimed, then it was not because of "his sympathy for the railroad," as Miller supposed. Ibid. The emotions triggered by *Inman* were amusement and sardonicism, which stemmed as much from the endless controversy over the worth of deciding FELA cases as the particular facts involved in this case. This case was an exception, in that the railroad prevailed; otherwise the workers usually prevailed, and Douglas's outburst may have been prompted as much by losing a vote as by the laughter in the courtroom.

81. Those relying on the timing of *Baker* as the best explanation for Whittaker's collapse included Friedman, "Charles Whittaker," 2903, Eisler, *A Justice for All*, 176, Schwartz, *Super Chief*, 427–28, Vestal, *The Eisenhower Court*, 273, n. 88, and Dickson, *The Supreme Court in Conference*, 851. Recognizing Whittaker's difficulties working on *Brown Shoe* were Schwartz and Lesher, *Inside the Warren Court*, 201, Schwartz, *Super Chief*, 437, and Lucas Powe,

The Warren Court and American Politics (Cambridge: Harvard University Press, 2000), 205.

82. Whittaker's oldest son, Keith, first shared this revelation in a personal interview with the author, June 3, 1996, and I presented it in "Charles Evans Whittaker," 105–06. Subsequently, Atkinson conducted his own interview, *Leaving the Bench*, 130, n. 128–31.

83. C. Keith Whittaker, interview by author, May 30, 2003.

84. *Colegrove* involved imbalances in Illinois' congressional districts. Of the seven-member Court to decide *Colegrove* (Chief Justice Harlan Fiske Stone had died and Robert Jackson was serving as chief U.S. prosecutor at the Nuremberg trials for Nazi war crimes), only Reed and Burton joined Frankfurter's opinion that the question was nonjusticiable. Justice Wiley Rutledge concurred in the result, but he along with the three dissenting justices comprised a majority that thought the Court had jurisdiction over the issue.

85. *Luther v. Borden* involved the question: which of two competing governments in Rhode Island was legitimate? Taney refused to answer it on the ground that it belonged to the political branches of government, not the judicial. The difficulty applying *Luther* to *Baker* was that *Luther* was brought to the Court under the guarantee clause of Article 4, Section 4 of the Constitution, whereas *Baker* relied on the Equal Protection clause of the Fourteenth Amendment, ratified nineteen years after *Luther* was decided.

86. See Philip B. Kurland and Gerhard Casper, eds., *Landmark Briefs and Arguments of the Supreme Court of the United States: Constitutional Law*, vol. 55 (Arlington, Virginia: University Publications of America, 1975), 595–98. Schwartz agreed that Whittaker was uncharacteristically vigorous in questioning Tennessee's claim that the Court lacked jurisdiction. According to Schwartz, at one point Whittaker interrupted counsel to ask, "If there is a clear constitutional right being violated ... is there not both power and a duty in the courts to enforce the constitutional right?" Quoted in Schwartz, *Super Chief*, 412, n. 67.

87. Conference notes, April 20, 1961, in Dickson, *The Supreme Court in Conference*, 845.

88. Ibid., 846.

89. Ibid., 846–47.

90. Ibid., 847.

91. Conference notes, April 28, 1961, in Dickson, *The Supreme Court in Conference*, 847. Chief Justice Warren, the author of *Brown v. Board of Education*, 347 U.S. 483 (1954), considered *Baker* even more important than *Brown*. Earl Warren, *The Memoirs of Earl War-*

ren (Garden City, New York: Doubleday, 1977), 306–08.

92. Richard Arnold, telephone interview by author, October 25, 2001.

93. Newman, *Hugo Black*, 517, n. 1. See also Schwartz, *Super Chief*, 412.

94. Arnold, interview.

95. Harlan to Whittaker and Stewart, October 11, 1961, quoted in Tinsley Yarbrough, *John Marshall Harlan: Great Dissenter of the Warren Court* (New York: Oxford University Press, 1992), 275–76. See also Schwartz, *Super Chief*, 414–15, n. 75.

96. Conference notes, October 13, 1961, in Dickson, *The Supreme Court in Conference*, 847–48.

97. Ibid., 848.

98. Ibid., 849.

99. Ibid., 848–49.

100. Ibid., 850.

101. Lewin, letter.

102. Conference notes, October 13, 1961, in Dickson, *The Supreme Court in Conference*, 850. Although *Baker* has been credited with establishing the principle of "one person, one vote," see, for example, Miller, *Whittaker: Struggles*, 150, that principle was first articulated one year later in *Gray v. Sanders*, 372 U.S. 368 (1963), which invalidated Georgia's county unit system for conducting primary elections. The following term the Court put into practical effect the "one person, one vote" principle for all congressional elections in *Wesberry v. Sanders*, 376 U.S. 1 (1964), and for all state legislative elections in *Reynolds v. Sims*, 377 U.S. 533 (1964).

103. Lewin, letter.

104. Peter Ehrenhaft, telephone interview by author, August 29, 2001.

105. Ibid.

106. Schwartz, *Super Chief*, 438.

107. Ehrenhaft, interview. One of the problems Whittaker might have encountered was that the son of his old law partner, Henry Ess, assisted in representing the shoe industry. Warren's final opinion in *Brown Shoe* took fifty-two pages with extensive footnotes and appendixes. For a critique of Warren's opinion, see Milton Handler, "Recent Antitrust Developments," *University of Pennsylvania Law Review* 112 (1962): 159–89.

108. Memorandum of Earl Warren, April 25, 1962, Tom Clark papers, Box 124, Folder 4, Tarlton Law Library, Austin, Texas.

109. Ibid.

110. Ibid.

111. See Schwartz, *Super Chief*, 419–20.

112. Memorandum, Vincent Rawson to Susan Parker, September 16, 1991, Rawson papers, Kansas City, Missouri. This was not

Whittaker's first trip to the *Star's* lodge. His sons, Keith and Kent, both remembered accompanying him there while he was still a practicing lawyer.

113. Ibid.

114. Ibid. Also Vincent Rawson, interview by author, February 19, 2001, and John Foard, interview by author, February 19, 2001.

115. Byron Hedges to Whittaker, July 18, 1963, Whittaker papers.

116. James Elliot to Whittaker, May 4, 1964, Whittaker papers.

117. "Ex-Justice Severs Supreme Court Ties," *U.S. News & World Report*, November 1, 1965, 14.

118. C. Keith Whittaker, interview, May 30, 2003. See Inventory and Description of Stocks Issued in the Name of and Owned by Winifred R. Whittaker, February 26, 1962, and Inventory and Description of Stocks and Other Securities issued in the Name of and Owned by Charles E. Whittaker, February 26, 1962, Whittaker papers.

119. *Baker v. Carr*, 369 U.S. 186, 332 (1962) (dissent).

120. Schwartz, *Super Chief*, 421–22. See also Yarbrough, *John Marshall Harlan*, 276.

121. Lewin, letter. Schwartz agreed that Whittaker's vote had never been firm, Schwartz and Lesher, *Inside the Warren Court*, 201, and Schwartz, *Super Chief*, 428, yet he claimed that Whittaker joined Frankfurter's dissent, *Super Chief*, 422 and 428. Ed Cray also noted that Whittaker joined Frankfurter's dissent, *Chief Justice: A Biography of Earl Warren* (New York: Simon & Schuster, 1997), 382.

122. *Baker v. Carr*, 369 U.S. 186, 330–31 (1962) (dissent).

123. George Freeman to John Jeffries, February 26, 1992, in John Jeffries, *Justice Lewis F. Powell, Jr.* (New York: Charles Scribner's Sons, 1994), 638, note. See also Garrow, "Mental Decrepitude on the U.S. Supreme Court," 1048, n. 288.

124. Murry Bring, interview, in Cray, *Chief Justice*, 382–83.

125. Kent Whittaker, interview, in Newman, *Hugo Black*, 518, n. 2.

126. See Schwartz, *Super Chief*, 422–23.

127. Quoted in Yarbrough, *John Marshall Harlan*, 276. See also Schwartz, *Super Chief*, 423.

128. James Adler, interview, in Cray, *Chief Justice*, 383. Cray presented Clark's switch as the sixth vote for the majority and Whittaker's announcement that he would reconsider his position as the seventh, *Chief Justice*, 382. Such an arrangement of events was not possible unless Whittaker announced his decision to reconsider from the hospital.

129. Quoted in *Kansas City Star*, March 29, 1962.

130. Ibid. Henry Abraham characterized Whittaker as "eager" to leave the Court, *Justices and Presidents: A Political History of Appointments to the Supreme Court*, 3d ed. (New York: Oxford University Press, 1992), 271.

131. See *Kansas City Star*, March 29, 1962.

132. Quoted in *New York Times*, March 30, 1962.

133. Quoted in *Kansas City Star*, September 20, 1964.

134. C. Keith Whittaker, interview, May 30, 2003.

135. C. Keith Whittaker, interview, June 3, 1996,

136. Ibid., and C. Keith Whittaker, interview, May 30, 2003. Atkinson noted that Whittaker's doctors prescribed Thioridazine, another phenothiazine, citing C. Keith Whittaker, August 27, 1996. *Leaving the Bench*, 130. Although both drugs were available in 1962, Keith has maintained that Thorazine was given to his father. Whittaker's son, Kent, was also aware that he contemplated suicide. Kent Whittaker, interview, April 25, 1996. Whittaker never mentioned how he planned to commit suicide.

137. Adler, interview by author.

138. Murry Bring, telephone interview by author, August 16, 2001. Bring served with Warren the two terms before Whittaker left the Court.

139. Medical Board Proceedings, March 16, 1962, Earl Warren papers, Box 358, in Garrow, "Mental Decrepitude on the U.S. Supreme Court," 1049, n. 298. See also Dennis Hutchinson, *The Man Who Once Was Whizzer White: A Portrait of Justice Byron R. White* (New York: Free Press, 1998), 312.

140. Clerk, interview. Clark shared this information *circa* 1975.

141. Hutchinson, *The Man Who Once Was Whizzer White*, 312. See also David Alistair Yalof, *Pursuit of Justices: Presidential Politics and the Selection of Supreme Court Nominees* (Chicago: The University of Chicago Press, 1999), 71. Hutchinson argued convincingly that Kennedy had more than three weeks to consider Whittaker's replacement, noting how Attorney General Robert Kennedy met with Justice Douglas on March 5 and probably learned of Whittaker's disability then. *The Man Who Once Was Whizzer White*, 311. Whittaker's son, Keith, who visited Whittaker at Walter Reed in the week before Whittaker informed the president, has remembered how strange it seemed at the time for his mother, Winifred, to receive a phone call from President Kennedy. Rather than a courtesy call, the

president advised Mrs. Whittaker to be careful whom she spoke to in case the phones were bugged. C. Keith Whittaker, interview, May 30, 2003.

142. Others considered for the nomination included Secretary of Labor Arthur Goldberg, who had been promised a seat on the Court, Harvard Law School Professor Paul Freund, and Third Circuit Appeals Court Judge William Hastie, an African American. At the time Goldberg proved too valuable to President Kennedy's cabinet to send to the Supreme Court, but within six months he took Frankfurter's place. While Robert Kennedy preferred a Hastie nomination over Freund, it was viewed as too political and threatened Kennedy's legislative agenda. At the Court, both Warren and Douglas, who were consulted on the nominees, objected to Hastie and Freund, fearing that their views too closely matched Frankfurter's. See Simon, *Independent Journey*, 358–59, Powe, *The Warren Court*, 205, 210–11, Yalof, *Pursuit of Justices*, 72–79, and Hutchinson, *The Man Who Once Was Whizzer White*, 313–15. Hutchinson argued, however, that consideration of other candidates was immaterial; President Kennedy had his mind settled on White from the beginning. *The Man Who Once Was Whizzer White*, 310–11 and 316.

143. C. Keith Whittaker, interview, May 30, 2003. According to his son, Keith, Whittaker's symptoms of akathisia were an unrelenting inability to sit or stand and a severe urge to move about. "[U]nless in retrospect one puts two and two together in facing akathisia," Keith has written, "it may seem that the agitation is due to 'agitated depression' when in fact the behavior is due clearly to the drugs." C. Keith Whittaker to author, November 3, 2003.

144. Friedman assumed that because Whittaker's retirement was announced three days after *Baker* that Whittaker must have still been in the hospital when it was handed down. "Charles Whittaker," 2903. Whittaker's participation in *Baker* would have proved fruitless; only Justices Harlan and Frankfurter dissented. On the majority side, Douglas, Clark, and Stewart wrote separate concurring opinions. Had Whittaker participated in *Baker*, he might have joined the majority (or Stewart's concurrence) to hold reapportionment a justiciable issue, but it was unlikely that had he stayed on the Court he would have joined Black's majority in *Wesberry v. Sanders* to find that "as nearly as is practicable one man's vote in a congressional election is to be worth as much as another's." Following the *Wesberry* decision one of Whittaker's former clerks wrote to him, asking, "What do you think of Justice Black's 'one man, one vote' opinion in

the Georgia redistricting case?" Whittaker penciled in the margin, "No Like." Jerome Libin to Whittaker, March 6, 1964, Whittaker papers.

145. Initially, Robert Kennedy was reluctant to consider his deputy attorney general for Whittaker's replacement because White proved so valuable in his work at the Justice Department. Accusing Robert Kennedy of relying on White, though, turned Kennedy in favor of White's nomination. When pressed to have his name included on the list of potential nominees, White gave an ambiguous answer. Even when Robert Kennedy spoke to White directly on March 27 about his nomination, White seemed unenthusiastic. Hutchinson, *The Man Who Once Was Whizzer White*, 316–17.

146. Quoted in *Kansas City Star*, April 1, 1962.

147. Ibid.

148. William Canby, telephone interview by author, July 17, 1996.

149. Lewin, letter.

150. John French, letter to author, August 13, 2001.

151. Kent Whittaker, interview, April 25, 1996, C. Keith Whittaker, interview, May 30, 2003, and Gary Whittaker, interview by author, June 21, 1996.

152. Kent Whittaker, interview by author, April 11, 1996. Those colleagues who died following Whittaker's departure from the Court included Harold Burton (1964), Felix Frankfurter (1965), Hugo Black (1971), and John Harlan (1971).

153. Darrell Havener, interview by author, June 11, 1996.

154. Kohn, interview.

155. Patrick McCartan, telephone interview by author, June 27, 1996.

156. George Cochran Doub to Whittaker, June 19, 1962, Whittaker papers.

7. Speaking Out

1. *New York Times*, November 27, 1973. In her description of Whittaker's public activities during retirement, Victoria Woeste also noted how Whittaker "became an outspoken critic of the social protest movements waged by civil rights demonstrators and anti-war protesters during the late 1960s." She then cited the *F.B.I. Law Enforcement Bulletin* as "his choice as a forum for his beliefs." "Charles Evans Whittaker," in *The Supreme Court Justices: A Biographical Dictionary*, ed., Melvin I. Urofsky, 533–34 (New York: Garland Publishing, 1994), 534.

2. Olin White to Whittaker, June 21, 1965, and Whittaker to Olin White, August 30, 1965, Charles Whittaker papers, Kansas City, Missouri. For copies of the speech, see, for examples, "Lawlessness in U.S.—Warning from a Top Jurist," *U.S. News & World Report*, July 5, 1965, 60–63, and "Law and Order," *New York State Bar Journal* 37 (October 1965): 397–404.

3. "Planned Lawlessness Threatens to Get Out of Hand," *U.S. News & World Report*, September 19, 1966, 37–43.

4. Kent Whittaker, interview by author, April 11, 1996.

5. See Memorandum of Charles Whittaker, August 6, 1965, p. 2, and General Motors Corporation to Whittaker (contract), September 23, 1965, p. 2, Whittaker papers.

6. Del Dickson, ed., *The Supreme Court in Conference (1940–1985): The Private Discussions Behind Nearly 300 Supreme Court Decisions* (New York: Oxford University Press, 2001), 851.

7. Kim Eisler, *A Justice for All: William J. Brennan, Jr., and the Decisions that Transformed America* (New York: Simon and Schuster, 1993), 176.

8. See, for examples, Robert W. Langran, "Why Are Some Supreme Court Justices Rated as 'Failures'?" *Yearbook Supreme Court Historical Society* (1985): 14, and Theodore M. Vestal, *The Eisenhower Court and Civil Liberties* (Westport, Connecticut: Praeger, 2002), 273.

9. Henry Abraham, *Justices and Presidents: A Political History of Appointments to the Supreme Court*, 3d ed. (New York: Oxford University Press, 1992), 253–54.

10. Vestal, *The Eisenhower Court*, 273. Others to conclude that Whittaker was critical of the Court's decisions included Morgan Prickett, who considered Whittaker's speech a direct attack on the Court, its work, and his former colleagues, "Stanley Forman Reed: Perspectives on a Judicial Epitaph," *Hastings Constitutional Law Quarterly* 8 (1981): 366, n. 110, Gerald Dunne, who claimed that Whittaker "charged his former colleagues with usurping the right of local self-government," *Hugo Black and the Judicial Revolution* (New York: Simon and Shuster, 1977), 387, Dennis Hutchinson, *The Man Who Once Was Whizzer White: A Portrait of Justice Byron R. White* (New York: Free Press, 1998), 312, and Bernard Schwartz, *Super Chief: Earl Warren and His Supreme Court—A Judicial Biography* (New York: New York University Press, 1983), 428, and *A Book of Legal Lists: The Best and Worst in American Law* (New York: Oxford University Press, 1997), 31.

Prickett compared Whittaker's speech to James Byrnes's indictment against the Court in "The Supreme Court Must Be Curbed," *U.S.*

News & World Report, May 18, 1956, 50, yet Byrnes's attack was in response to the desegregation decisions, *Brown v. Board of Education*, 347 U.S. 483 (1954), and *Brown v. Board of Education*, 349 U.S. 294 (1955), and he accused the Court *at that time* of usurping the powers of Congress and the states. Whittaker's 1964 speech to the ABA focused on *National Labor Relations Board v. Jones & Laughlin Steel Company*, 301 U.S. 1 (1937), decided some 27 years earlier. It was impossible for Whittaker to charge his former colleagues with anything in that speech because the longest serving veteran was Justice Black, who joined the Court four months *after* the decision in *Jones & Laughlin*. Schwartz noted how after Whittaker left the Court to accept a highly paid legal post with General Motors, "He then delivered widely reported attacks upon the Court's decisions, notably in a 1964 speech before the American Bar Association," yet Whittaker's 1964 speech to the ABA happened *before* he went to work for General Motors, not afterwards. Hutchinson, who claimed Whittaker "later became an outspoken critic of the Court and of civil disobedience," referred to Whittaker's debate with the Reverend William Sloane Coffin in *Law, Order and Civil Disobedience* (Washington, D.C.: American Enterprise Institute for Public Policy Research, 1967), yet Whittaker's debate with Reverend Coffin focused exclusively on the social upheavals and civil unrest of the 1960s and made no references to the Supreme Court or its decisions.

11. See, for examples, William J. Brennan, Jr., "The Bill of Rights and the States," *New York University Law Review* 36 (April 1961): 773, n. 51–52, where he criticized Whittaker's decision in *McNeal v. Culver*, 365 U.S. 109 (1961), William Douglas, "The Bill of Rights is Not Enough," *New York University Law Review* 38 (1963): 216, where he criticized the majority in *Frank v. Maryland*, 359 U.S. 360 (1959), and Hugo Black, *A Constitutional Faith* (New York: Alfred A. Knopf, 1968), 49–50, where he objected to the majority in *Barenblatt v. United States*, 360 U.S. 109 (1959), *Konigsberg v. State Bar*, 366 U.S. 36 (1961), and *Scales v. United States*, 367 U.S. 203 (1961).

According to Phillip Cooper, Douglas originally made reference to Frankfurter by name in his address but then removed those references in later drafts. So disgusted was Douglas by what he saw as the Court's timidity in the face of important issues that Cooper considered Douglas's speech "nothing less than an indictment of the Court on which he served." *Battles on the Bench: Conflict Inside the Supreme Court* (Lawrence: University Press of Kansas, 1995), 149, n. 100, and 127–28.

12. "Ex-Justice Severs Supreme Court Ties," *U.S. News & World Report*, November 1, 1965, 14. Emphasis added. Following a February 1960 speech on the First Amendment and his belief in "absolutes" contained in the Bill of Rights, Black's views were debated in academic and legal circles, but otherwise there seemed to be little controversy over a sitting justice expressing views on how cases coming before the Court should be decided. See Roger Newman, *Hugo Black: A Biography* (New York: Pantheon Books, 1994), 488–96.

13. Charles E. Whittaker, "A Confusion of Tongues," typed manuscript, address presented at the Southern Regional Meeting of the American Bar Association, Atlanta, Georgia, October 23, 1964, pp. 10–11, Whittaker papers. The only published copy of Whittaker's speech, "A Confusion of Tongues," *American Bar Association Journal* 51 (January 1965): 27–32, was an earlier draft not meant to be published, which did not accurately convey what Whittaker said. Reporters for *U.S. News & World Report* who heard the speech picked up on Whittaker's reference to avoiding recent Court decisions but neglected to include how those recent interpretations might be involved in "current Judicial controversies." See "When a Former Justice Speaks Out Against the Supreme Court," *U.S. News & World Report*, November 9, 1964, 21.

14. Whittaker to Samuel E. Whittaker, October 19, 1964, Whittaker papers. See *Washington Post*, October 24, 1964.

15. Whittaker to Robert J. Wynne, editor, October 26, 1964, Whittaker papers.

16. Donald MacCampbell to Whittaker, December 17, 1964, and Whittaker to MacCampbell, December 22, 1964, Whittaker papers.

17. Quoted in *Kansas City Star*, September 20, 1964.

18. Charles E. Whittaker, "Some Reminiscences," an address before the American Bar Association, August 10, 1961, in St. Louis, *American Bar Association Journal* 47 (November 1961): 1089. Similar stories and sentiments were presented before the Federal Bar Association, September 17, 1960, in Chicago and the Lawyers Association of Kansas City, February 10, 1961. See Charles E. Whittaker, "Judicial Discretion," *Federal Bar News* 7 (December 1960): 367–71, and *Kansas City Times*, February 15, 1961.

19. Ibid., 1087.

20. Ibid., 1091.

21. Charles E. Whittaker, "Some Reminiscences," *Nebraska Law Review* 43 (December 1963): 362.

22. Ibid., 362, referring to *Brown v. Board of Education*, 347 U.S. 483 (1954), *Engel v. Vitale*, 370 U.S. 421 (1962), and *Abington School District v. Schempp*, 374 U.S. 203 (1963). In an Arkansas speech around the same time, Whittaker dropped the reference to "Negroes" and "God," referring instead simply to "emotionally-charged issues," but his defense of Court decisions was just as vigorous. See Charles E. Whittaker, "The Role of the Supreme Court," *Arkansas Law Review* 17 (Fall 1963): 301.

23. Ibid.

24. Like other retired justices, Whittaker maintained an office in the Supreme Court building in Washington, but he never used it. Justice Reed over ten years heard 60 cases while on temporary assignment to the Court of Claims and the Court of Appeals. He wrote 23 opinions on the Court of Claims and 24 opinions on the Court of Appeals. See Fassett, *New Deal Justice*, 634, and Prickett, "Stanley Forman Reed: Perspectives," 366. Justice Burton served temporarily on the Court of Appeals for four terms, hearing over 60 cases and writing ten opinions. See Mary Frances Berry, *Stability, Security, and Continuity: Mr. Justice Burton and Decision-Making in the Supreme Court* (Westport, Connecticut: Greenwood Press, 1978), 228. When Tom Clark retired in 1967 he accepted invitations to serve on federal courts in all the judicial circuits to help with their overburdened caseloads.

25. *Kansas City Times*, April 20, 1962.

26. Berry, *Stability, Security, and Continuity*, 228.

27. Whittaker to Clark, July 18, 1962, Tom Clark papers, Box 127, folder 3, Tarlton Law Library, Austin, Texas.

28. Whittaker to Frankfurter, August 30, 1962, Whittaker papers.

29. See, for examples, "Ex-Justice Severs Supreme Court Ties," 14, and *New York Times*, October 19, 1965.

30. Whittaker to David W. Kendall, June 3, 1963, Whittaker papers.

31. *Kansas City Star*, September 20, 1964.

32. Jerome Libin to Whittaker, September 17, 1962, Whittaker papers.

33. Whittaker to Murrah, December 27, 1962, Whittaker papers.

34. Quoted in Lawrence Larsen, "Observations on One Hundred Years of Federal Judging in Western Missouri District Court," in *Law and the Great Plains: Essays on the Legal History of the Heartland*, ed. John R. Wunder (Westport, Connecticut: Greenwood Press, 1996), 146, n. 35.

35. Memorandum, March 14, 1963, Whittaker papers.

36. Leon Friedman, in his final analysis of Whittaker's judicial abilities, observed, "The

narrowness of Whittaker's vision was confirmed by his activities after his resignation.... All these later activities were what one would expect of a conservative corporate lawyer who had risen high in his legal profession, but hardly of a former Supreme Court justice." "Charles Whittaker," in *The Justices of the United States Supreme Court: Their Lives and Major Opinions*, eds., Leon Friedman and Fred L. Israel, vol. 4 (New York: Chelsea House, 1969), 2903–04. Certainly, had Whittaker been permitted to judge again in retired status, then his other "activities" in retirement would have become unnecessary.

37. The significance of *Gideon* was in the Court's overruling *Betts v. Brady*, 316 U.S. 455 (1942), and incorporating the Sixth Amendment's guarantee of the right to counsel into the Fourteenth as it applied to the states. For more than a decade the rule in *Betts* that state criminal defendants receive appointed counsel only in special circumstances had been greatly eroded. In a note, Whittaker made clear his views on the Supreme Court's ruling in *Gideon*, stating, "It is difficult to believe that any intelligent person, at all familiar with the intricacies of the law and its practice—and surely no lawyer—would deny the good reasons for such a rule." Charles E. Whittaker, "Advocacy—Advance or Adieu?" Kansas Law Review 13 (1964): 233, n. 2. Around this same time in one of his many public appearances Whittaker betrayed his sympathy for certain criminal defendants, especially those without adequate representation. See Whittaker, "Some Reminiscences," *Nebraska Law Review*, 356.

38. Harry L. Brown to Whittaker, July 20, 1963, and Whittaker to Brown, July 12, 1963, Whittaker papers.

39. Whittaker to James R. Elliot, July 9, 1964, Whittaker papers.

40. Two of the pieces he wrote early in his retirement concerned uniquely legal matters; these were also matters on which Whittaker had always held strong personal feelings. The first, greater respect for the law, he presented in an ABA journal article on traffic court improvements. See Charles E. Whittaker, "Lawyers, Laymen and Traffic Courts: Concerted Effort Needed for Improvement," *American Bar Association Journal* 49 (April 1963): 333–36. Throughout his book, Richard Miller relied upon Whittaker's public pronouncements during retirement to describe other times during Whittaker's life, taking these speeches and articles out of context and using them to justify Miller's conclusions. For example, Miller believed that Whittaker in this article was describing justice of the peace courts from forty years earlier, as though Whit-

taker had no idea of the actual conditions in traffic courts during the 1960s. *Whittaker: Struggles of a Supreme Court Justice* (Westport, Connecticut: Greenwood Press, 2002), 3, n. 12. The second legal article Whittaker wrote concerned one of his passions since his days at law school—the art of oral advocacy. See Whittaker, "Advocacy—Advance or Adieu?" 233–45.

41. In the previous year Whittaker had delivered an address to the Kansas Bar Association that touched on labor relations and the growing strength of labor unions in which he accused unions of having "acquired almost dictatorial power over wages." Justice Harlan, who had been a source of encouragement to Whittaker on the Supreme Court, wrote to Whittaker following this presentation, "You have put some simple truths forthrightly and well." Harlan to Whittaker, March 18, 1963, quoted in Tinsley Yarbrough, *John Marshall Harlan: Great Dissenter of the Warren Court* (New York: Oxford University Press, 1992), 139, n. 56.

42. For much of the background on the Civil Rights movement, I relied on Fred Powledge, *Free at Last? The Civil Rights Movement and the People Who Made It* (Boston: Little, Brown, 1991).

43. See, for examples, David Lawrence, "The Only Hope," *U.S. News & World Report*, June 10, 1963, 112, and "What's Become of 'Law and Order'?" *U.S. News & World Report*, August 5, 1963, 104.

44. Charles E. Whittaker, "Can 'Integration' Be Forced by Federal Law?" *U.S. News & World Report*, March 23, 1964, 99, 100. This speech was also delivered to the Kansas City Rotary Club that same month.

45. See David Lawrence, "The Big Change," *U.S. News & World Report*, March 30, 1964, 108, and *Wall Street Journal*, March 30, 1964.

46. Quoted in *U.S. News & World Report*, July 6, 1964, 37.

47. They were James Chaney, an African American, Michael Schwerner, and Andrew Goodman. Six weeks after they were reported missing their bodies were uncovered in an earthen dam. They were shot and killed by the Neshoba County deputy sheriff and members of the Ku Klux Klan.

48. Charles E. Whittaker, "Immutable Moral Values," supplement to *Texas Bar Journal* 27 (August 1964): 2.

49. Ibid., 3. Miller relied upon these presentations to describe Whittaker's courtroom technique from thirty years earlier, although Whittaker was commenting on social conditions of the 1960s. *Whittaker: Struggles*, 6–7, n. 13–14. Miller also used these presentations to

demonstrate how Whittaker evaded account-ability as a lawyer, as though Whittaker's concern over the pending Civil Rights Act had any connection to his trial practice thirty years earlier. *Whittaker: Struggles*, 15, n. 42–44. Finally, Miller confused Whittaker's concern for the social unrest of the 1960s presented in these speeches with his views on race as reflected in his judicial opinions. *Whittaker: Struggles*, 110, n. 120–24.

50. Newman, *Hugo Black*, 542. In *Bell*, sit-in demonstrators who refused to leave a Baltimore restaurant were convicted of violating Maryland's criminal trespass law. Before the case arrived at the Supreme Court, though, Maryland enacted a public accommodations law, making consideration of the constitutional question unnecessary. Even so, Black dissented from the Court's refusal to consider whether the demonstrators' actions constituted criminal trespass in violation of the Fourteenth Amendment. He would have upheld their convictions.

51. Whittaker, "Immutable Moral Values," 3, quoting Black's dissent in *Bell* at 346.

52. Quoted in *Kansas City Star*, September 19, 1964.

53. Whittaker, "Immutable Moral Values," 6, quoting Black's dissent in *Bell* at 343.

54. *United States v. Carolene Products*, 304 U.S. 144 (1938), note 4.

55. *Heart of Atlanta Motel v. United States*, 379 U.S. 241 (1964).

56. Powell to Whittaker, January 30, 1964, Whittaker to Powell, February 6, 1964, Powell to Whittaker February 10, 1964, and Whittaker to Powell, February 13, 1964, Whittaker papers.

57. Whittaker to Robert Ericson, July 31, 1964, Whittaker papers. No draft with this title still exists.

58. See Whittaker, "A Confusion of Tongues," typed manuscript, 10.

59. When referring to different drafts of the speech, I relied on Whittaker's own typed manuscripts, citing either "Federal Powers" or "Confusion of Tongues." This was to avoid further confusion, since the speech reprinted by the ABA, entitled "A Confusion of Tongues," *American Bar Association Journal* 51 (January 1965): 27–32, was, in fact, a reproduction of "Federal Powers" and, therefore, not really what Whittaker said in Atlanta.

60. See, for examples, "High Court: Its Growing Impact," *U.S. News & World Report*, June 29, 1964, 34–37, "How Supreme Court is Reshaping the Country," *U.S. News & World Report*, July 6, 1964, 31–33, and "What the Courts are Ordering States to Do," *U.S. News & World Report*, August 24, 1964, 40–41.

61. *Escobedo v. Illinois*, 378 U.S. 438 (1964).

Earlier that term the Court ruled in *Massiah v. United States*, 377 U.S. 201 (1964), that once adversarial proceedings began against a defendant then the Sixth Amendment right to counsel took effect.

62. *Malloy v. Hogan*, 378 U.S. 1 (1964). Decided the same day, *Murphy v. Waterfront Commission of New York*, 378 U.S. 52 (1964), applied the *Malloy* ruling so that federal officials could not use incriminating statements obtained in state proceedings.

63. *Aptheker v. Secretary of State*, 378 U.S. 500 (1964). The Court had sustained the registration requirement for all Communist action groups three years earlier in *Communist Party v. Subversive Activities Control Board*, 367 U.S. 1 (1961).

64. In *Griffin v. County School Board of Prince Edward County*, 377 U.S. 218 (1964), the Court ordered schools to comply with the desegregation decisions immediately. No more delay would be tolerated. In *New York Times v. Sullivan*, 376 U.S. 254 (1964), a leading First Amendment case on the standards used to determine libel, the Court swept aside efforts to obstruct civil rights activities in the South.

65. *Wesberry v. Sanders*, 376 U.S. 1 (1964), and *Reynolds v. Sims*, 377 U.S. 533 (1964).

66. *U.S. News & World Report*, August 31, 1964. See also Lucas Powe, *The Warren Court and American Politics* (Cambridge: Harvard University Press, 2000), 253. Oddly, Miller made a detailed analysis of Whittaker's speech to describe Whittaker's Supreme Court service, particularly his relations with colleagues, when the circumstances that prompted Whittaker to make this speech (passage of the Civil Rights Act and the reapportionment decisions) did not occur until two years after he left the Court. *Whittaker: Struggles*, 62–66, n. 103–119.

67. David Lawrence, "Our Vanishing Constitution," *U.S. News & World Report*, July 20, 1964, 104.

68. Compare Whittaker, "Federal Powers," 9–10, to Whittaker, "Confusion of Tongues," 9–10.

69. William Wiecek, *Liberty Under Law: The Supreme Court in American Life* (Baltimore: The Johns Hopkins University Press, 1988), 138.

70. In 1963 a unanimous Court declared, "We refuse to sit as a 'super legislature to weigh the wisdom of legislation.' ... Whether the legislature takes for its textbook Adam Smith, Herbert Spencer, Lord Keynes, or some other is no concern of ours. The Kansas debt adjusting statute may be wise or unwise. But relief, if any be needed, lies not with us but with the body constituted to pass laws for the State of Kansas." *Ferguson v. Skrupa*, 372 U.S. 726, 732 (1963).

71. *Lochner v. New York*, 198 U.S. 45 (1905).

72. *United States v. E. C. Knight*, 156 U.S. 1 (1895).

73. Whittaker, "Federal Powers," 23. Emphasis added.

74. *Schechter v. United States*, 295 U.S. 495, 546 (1935), quoted in "Federal Powers," 17. *Schechter* dealt with the constitutionality of the National Industrial Recovery Act, a program that ostensibly was already failing by the time of the Court's decision.

75. Whittaker, "Federal Powers," 24.

76. Whittaker, "Confusion of Tongues," 16.

77. Ibid., 17.

78. Whittaker, "Federal Powers," 22.

79. Douglas to Whittaker, October 30, 1964, quoted in Melvin Urofsky, ed., *The Douglas Letters: Selections from the Private Papers of Justice William O. Douglas* (Bethesda, Maryland: Adler & Adler, 1987), 129.

80. William Douglas, *The Court Years, 1939–1975* (New York: Random House, 1980), 51.

81. Whittaker to A. Scott Mandelup, April 20, 1973, Whittaker papers.

82. Whittaker, "Confusion of Tongues," 17.

83. Friedman, "Charles Whittaker," 2903.

84. Louise Child, editorial assistant, to Whittaker, November 17, 1964, Whittaker to Child, December 2, 1964, and Child to Whittaker, December 7, 1964, Whittaker papers.

85. *U.S. News & World Report*, November 9, 1964, 21.

86. Quoted in *U.S. News & World Report*, August 17, 1964, 34.

87. See, for examples, articles by ABA president and future Supreme Court Justice Lewis F. Powell, "Respect for Law and Due Process—The Foundation of a Free Society," *University of Florida Law Review* 18 (1965): 4–5, which Whittaker quoted in "Law and Order," an address to the 84th Annual Convention of the Tennessee Bar Association, Nashville, June 17, 1965, p. 11; "The State of the Legal Profession," *American Bar Association Journal* 51 (September 1965): 827; and "A Lawyer Looks at Civil Disobedience," *Washington and Lee Law Review* 23 (1966): 205–31.

88. In one peaceful sit-in case Justice Black wrote in dissent, "It is high time to challenge the assumption in which too many people have too long acquiesced, that groups that think they have been mistreated or that have actually been mistreated have a constitutional right to use the public's streets, buildings, and property to protest whatever, wherever, whenever they want, without regard to whom such conduct may disturb." *Brown v. Louisiana*, 383 U.S. 131, 162 (1966) (dissent).

89. Whittaker, "Law and Order" address, p. 12.

90. Whittaker to J. Olin White, president Tennessee Bar, October 16, 1964, Whittaker papers.

91. See David Lawrence, "Bowing to the New Extremists," *U.S. News & World Report*, March 29, 1965, and "The Wrong Way," *U.S. News & World Report*, March 22, 1965.

92. Whittaker, "Law and Order" address, p. 10. Emphasis in original. King also received honorary law degrees from Howard University, Morgan State University, Lincoln University, the University of Bridgeport, Bard College, and the Jewish Theological Seminary before Whittaker's speech, and from Hofstra University and Grinnell College afterwards. Whittaker was not the only commentator to question King's selection for the Nobel Peace Prize. He was undoubtedly influenced by "How Martin Luther King Won the Nobel Peace Prize," *U.S. News & World Report*, February 8, 1965, 76–77.

93. Quoted in *U.S. News & World Report*, March 22, 1965, 33.

94. Whittaker, "Law and Order" address, pp. 10–11.

95. Ibid., 11.

96. Powe, *The Warren Court*, 293.

97. *Green v. County School Board of New Kent County*, 391 U.S. 430 (1968). See also Powe, *The Warren Court*, 295–97.

98. Whittaker to Olin White, July 27, 1965, Whittaker papers. On July 26 President Lyndon Johnson announced the membership of his Commission on Law Enforcement and the Administration of Justice.

99. Whittaker to Arnaud C. Marts, July 2, 1965, Whittaker papers.

100. Unsigned letter postmarked July 7, 1965, Whittaker papers.

101. Within a year of delivering his most famous speech Whittaker and his wife, Winifred, were, ironically, the victims of a burglary. Their home at 6400 Aberdeen Road in Mission Hills, Kansas, was robbed on Whittaker's sixty-fifth birthday while he and Winifred were in Valley Forge, Pennsylvania, for Whittaker to receive the George Washington honor medal from the Freedoms Foundation for his speech, "Law and Order." *Kansas City Times*, February 23, 1966. Of course, the burglary might have been prevented had the same paper that reported it, the *Kansas City Times*, not reported on the morning before the burglary that the Whittakers were in Pennsylvania all that day—including the street address where their vacant home was located. *Kansas City Times*, February 22, 1966.

102. *New York Times*, October 19, 1965.

103. Joseph Stevens, interview by author, May 17, 1996, and Gary Whittaker, interview.

104. Memorandum, July 16, 1965, Whittaker papers. Judge Coleman had served on the district court for 28 years. He resigned his position with General Motors due to failing health. Duncan retired from the district court in late May 1965, and Ridge, who went to the Eighth Circuit Court of Appeals in 1961, retired one month earlier due to health reasons.

105. See Herbert Brownell, *Advising Ike: The Memoirs of Attorney General Herbert Brownell* (Lawrence: University Press of Kansas, 1993), 330. Brownell, who recommended Whittaker to President Eisenhower for all three of his judicial appointments, served as umpire for the Chrysler Corporation from 1966–70.

106. See Memorandums dated August 6 and September 7, 1965, Whittaker papers.

107. See General Motors (GM) Corporation to Whittaker (contract), September 23, 1965, and Whittaker to Louis H. Bridenstine, Director of Legal Staff (GM), September 20, 1965, Whittaker papers.

108. Whittaker to Bridenstine, September 22, 1965, and Whittaker to Aloysius F. Power, Vice President and General Council (GM), October 5, 1965, Whittaker papers.

109. "Resignation of Mr. Justice Whittaker," *Supreme Court Reporter*, vol. 86 (St. Paul: West Publishing, 1967), 14.

110. Whittaker to Robert L. Taylor, April 29, 1968, Whittaker papers.

111. Charles E. Whittaker and William Sloane Coffin, *Law, Order and Civil Disobedience* (Washington, D.C.: American Enterprise Institute for Public Policy Research, 1967), 146.

112. Charles E. Whittaker, "An Appeal to Reason," in *Man and the Future*, edited by James E. Gunn (Lawrence: University Press of Kansas, 1968), 91. This speech was reproduced as "A Former Justice Warns: Return to Law, or Face Anarchy," *U.S. News & World Report*, April 25, 1966, 58–62.

113. Quoted in Gunn, ed., *Man and the Future*, 108.

114. Whittaker and Coffin, *Law, Order and Civil Disobedience*, 83–84.

115. Ibid., 84.

116. Ibid., 7–8. Emphasis in original.

117. Ibid., 19 and 20.

118. Ibid., 49–50. Miller used these exchanges to demonstrate that Whittaker had been "a formidable jury lawyer" thirty years earlier. *Whittaker: Struggles*, 8–11, n. 20–31. Miller also used Coffin's rebuttal to support the contention that Whittaker's Supreme Court opinions were passionless and mechanical, even though Coffin was not responding to one of Whittaker's written opinions. *Whittaker: Struggles*, 69, n. 131. Finally, Miller again confused these descriptions of the social unrest

of the 1960s with Whittaker's views on race as reflected in his written opinions as a justice. *Whittaker: Struggles*, 114–15, n. 136–41.

119. Whittaker to D. M. Smith, Director of Retirement Claims, Railroad Retirement Board, May 31, 1966, Whittaker papers.

120. Quoted in *Kansas City Times*, April 19, 1966.

121. Most recently the Senate had censured Republican Joseph McCarthy of Wisconsin in 1954 by a vote of 67 to 22. In June 1967 by a vote of 92 to 5 the Senate censured Dodd for conduct unbecoming a Senator; he had diverted public funds to his private use.

122. Sam J. Ervin, Jr., to Whittaker, June 12, 1969, Whittaker papers.

123. See "Fortas: A Question of Ethics," *Life*, May 9, 1969, 32–37.

124. Ervin to Whittaker, June 12 1969, Whittaker papers.

125. See Statement of Charles Evans Whittaker to the Subcommittee on Separation of Powers of the Committee on the Judiciary of the United States Senate at Washington on October 1, 1969, Whittaker papers. The hearings scheduled for the fall of 1969 never took place, but Senator Ervin had Whittaker's statement recorded in the published record. Ervin to Whittaker, January 28, 1970, and Whittaker to Ervin, February 9, 1970, Whittaker papers.

126. Quoted in *Kansas City Times*, November 11, 1969. Haynsworth had not, in fact, acted illegally or unethically, but seventeen Republicans joined thirty-eight Democrats to vote against him. Political considerations had led to Haynsworth's defeat (the first such Senate rejection of a Supreme Court nominee in almost forty years). Considered a respectable judge, Haynsworth also had the support of Chief Justice Burger, Attorney General John Mitchell, and several past presidents of the ABA, including future Supreme Court Justice Lewis Powell. Stinging from Haynsworth's defeat, the Nixon administration responded by launching an investigation into possible impeachment charges against Justice Douglas and by nominating for the Supreme Court a man far more objectionable on ethical grounds, Judge Harold Carswell. House minority leader, Republican Gerald Ford of Michigan, who led the investigation of possible impeachment charges against Douglas, later admitted it had been a mistake. Carswell, a judge on the Fifth Circuit Court of Appeals, was defeated in the Senate by a vote of 51 to 45. Considered a racist in outlook, Carswell had one of the highest reversal rates of any federal judge. See Melvin Small, *The Presidency of Richard Nixon* (Lawrence: University Press of Kansas, 1999), 168–71.

127. Quoted in *Kansas City Star*, January 29, 1970.

128. Ibid.

129. Whittaker to A. Scott Mandelup, April 20, 1973, Whittaker papers.

130. Whittaker to Carl Enggas, December 13, 1967, Whittaker papers. Fox had completed portraits already of former Justices Harold Burton, Louis Brandeis, and Harlan Stone.

131. Whittaker to Oliver, December 4, 1970, Whittaker papers.

132. Oliver to Warren Burger, March 22, 1971, Whittaker papers.

133. Kent Whittaker, interviews, April 11 and April 25, 1996. See Albert Blaustein and Roy Mersky "The Twelve Great Justices of All Time," *Life*, October 15, 1971, 53–9.

134. Gary Whittaker, interview. See Albert Blaustein and Roy Mersky, "Rating Supreme Court Justices," *American Bar Association Journal* 58 (November 1972): 1183–89, and Friedman, "Charles Whittaker," 2893–2904.

135. Statement of Charles Whittaker to the Subcommittee on Separation of Powers, October 1, 1969, Whittaker papers.

136. David Atkinson, interview by author, June 10, 1996. See also David Atkinson, *Leaving the Bench: Supreme Court Justices at the End* (Lawrence: University Press of Kansas, 1999), 131.

137. Whittaker to Tom Pugh, July 5, 1973, Whittaker papers, Kent Whittaker, letter to author, December 11, 1996, Kent Whittaker, interview, April 11, 1996, Keith Whittaker, interview by author, June 3, 1996, and *Kansas City Times*, November 27, 1973.

138. Keith Whittaker, interview, June 3, 1996, and May 30, 2003. Keith, himself a physician, believed that for the second time the medical community let his father down, claiming that the doctors attending his father should have discovered the aneurysm once Whittaker's kidneys failed. "The surgery might have killed him," Keith said, "but they should have found it."

139. Kenneth [?] to Hazel Ruhnke, November 29, 1973, Hazel Ruhnke papers, Trimble, Missouri.

Afterword

1. See *In Memoriam, Honorable Charles Evans Whittaker*, Proceeding of the Bar and Officers of the Supreme Court of the United States and Proceedings Before the Supreme Court of the United States, February 19, 1975, Washington, D.C.

2. For a list of award recipients, see Appendix I.

3. Public Law 103–273, July 5, 1994, *U.S. Statutes at Large* 108 (1994): 1402. According to Judge Stevens, Missouri Republican Senator Christopher (Kit) Bond was responsible for moving the bill through the Senate. The bill originated in the House when Missouri Democratic Representative Alan Wheat sought to name the federal office building in Kansas City after Missouri Democratic Representative Richard Bolling. In the Senate, Whittaker's name on the federal courthouse was offered to the bill as an amendment.

4. *Kansas City Star*, October 24, 1998.

5. Kent Whittaker, interview by author, April 25, 1996.

Appendix A

1. Minutes of Annual Meeting of Faculty of Kansas City School of Law, June 4, 1921, June 3, 1922, May 5, 1923, and May 31, 1924, University of Missouri–Kansas City Archives.

Appendix E

1. Adapted from Charles E. Whittaker, *Supreme Court of the United States: Opinions of Mr. Justice Whittaker* (Washington, D.C.: Supreme Court, n.d.), 1:1. This special collection printed especially for the Whittaker family, who, in turn, donated it to the University of Missouri–Kansas City Law School, omitted two cases in which Whittaker wrote opinions. Marlin M. Volz included a list of Whittaker's opinions at both the district and appeals courts but also failed to mention two cases found in the *Federal Supplement*, "Mr. Justice Whittaker," *Notre Dame Lawyer* 33 (March 1958): 178–79.

2. Adapted from Whittaker, *Supreme Court of the United States: Opinions of Mr. Justice Whittaker*, 1:3. Again, one Whittaker opinion was omitted from this collection.

Appendix G

1. Previously clerked for Justice Stanley Reed during 1956 term.

2. Continued to clerk for Chief Justice Earl Warren the remainder of 1961 term.

3. Continued to clerk for Justice Byron White the remainder of 1961 term.

Select Bibliography

Books

Abraham, Henry. *Justices and Presidents: A Political History of Appointments to the Supreme Court.* 3d ed. New York: Oxford University Press, 1992.

Atkinson, David. *Leaving the Bench: Supreme Court Justices at the End.* Lawrence: University Press of Kansas, 1999.

Auerbach, Jerold S. *Unequal Justice: Lawyers and Social Change in Modern America.* New York: Oxford University Press, 1976.

Barnes, Catherine A., ed. *Men of the Supreme Court: Profiles of the Justices.* New York: Facts on File, 1978.

Baum, Lawrence. *The Puzzle of Judicial Behavior.* Ann Arbor: University of Michigan Press, 1997.

Berry, Mary Frances. *Stability, Security, and Continuity: Mr. Justice Burton and Decision-Making in the Supreme Court.* Westport, Connecticut: Greenwood Press, 1978.

Black, Hugo. *A Constitutional Faith.* New York: Alfred A. Knopf, 1968.

Blaustein, Albert and Roy Mersky. *The First One Hundred Justices: Statistical Studies on the Supreme Court of the United States.* Hamden, Connecticut: Archon Books, 1978.

Brownell, Herbert. *Advising Ike: The Memoirs of Attorney General Herbert Brownell.* Lawrence: University Press of Kansas, 1993.

Carson, Gerald. *The Roguish World of Doctor Brinkley.* New York: Rinehart, 1960.

Chase, Harold. *Federal Judges: The Appointing Process.* Minneapolis: University of Minnesota Press, 1972.

Clayton, James E. *The Making of Justice: The Supreme Court in Action.* New York: E. P. Dutton, 1964.

Cole, Judith. "Mr. Justice Charles Evans Whittaker: A Case Study in Judicial Recruitment and Behavior." M. A. thesis, University of Missouri-Kansas City, 1972.

Congressional Record.

Cooper, Phillip J. *Battles on the Bench: Conflict Inside the Supreme Court.* Lawrence: University Press of Kansas, 1995.

Cray, Ed. *Chief Justice: A Biography of Earl Warren.* New York: Simon & Schuster, 1997.

Cushman, Clare, ed. *The Supreme Court Justices: Illustrated Biographies, 1789–1995*. 2d ed. Washington, D. C.: Congressional Quarterly, 1995.

Dickson, Del, ed. *The Supreme Court in Conference (1940–1985): The Private Discussions Behind Nearly 300 Supreme Court Decisions*. New York: Oxford University Press, 2001.

Dos Passos, John R. *The American Lawyer: As He Was—As He Is—As He Can Be*. Littleton, CO: Fred B. Rothman, 1986.

Douglas, William O. *The Court Years, 1939–1975: The Autobiography of William O. Douglas*. New York: Random House, 1980.

Dunne, Gerald. *Hugo Black and the Judicial Revolution*. New York: Simon and Shuster, 1977.

Eisenhower, Dwight. *Mandate for Change*. New York: Doubleday, 1963.

Eisler, Kim I. *A Justice for All: William J. Brennan, Jr., and the Decisions that Transformed America*. New York: Simon and Schuster, 1993.

Fassett, John D. *New Deal Justice: The Life of Stanley Reed of Kentucky*. New York: Vantage Press, 1994.

Ferrell, Robert H., ed. *The Eisenhower Diaries*. New York: W.W. Norton, 1987.

Fetter, Theodore J. *A History of the United States Court of Appeals for the Eighth Circuit*. Judicial Conference of the United States Bicentennial Committee, 1977.

Fowler, Dick. *Leaders In Our Town*. Kansas City: Burd & Fletcher, n.d.

Frankfurter, Felix. "The Supreme Court in the Mirror of Justices." In *Of Law and Life & Other Things That Matter: Papers and Addresses of Felix Frankfurter, 1956–1963*, edited by Kurland, Philip. Cambridge: Harvard University Press, 1965.

Friedman, Leon and Fred L. Israel, eds. *The Justices of the United States Supreme Court: Their Lives and Major Opinions*. Vol. 4. New York: Chelsea House, 1969.

Galambos, Louis, ed. *The Papers of Dwight David Eisenhower*. 21 Vols. Baltimore: The Johns Hopkins University Press, 1996.

Galanter, Marc and Thomas Palay. *Tournament of Lawyers: The Transformation of the Big Law Firm*. Chicago: University of Chicago Press, 1991.

Goldman, Sheldon. *Picking Federal Judges: Lower Court Selection From Roosevelt Through Reagan*. New Haven: Yale University Press, 1997.

Green, George F. *A Condensed History of Kansas City Area: Its Mayors and Some VIPs*. Kansas City: Lowell Press, 1968.

Grossman, Joel. *Lawyers and Judges: the ABA and the Politics of Judicial Selection*. New York: John Wiley & Sons, 1965.

Hall, Kermit L. *The Magic Mirror: Law in American History*. New York: Oxford University Press, 1989.

Hirsh, H. N. *The Enigma of Felix Frankfurter*. New York: Basic Books, 1981.

Hobson, Wayne K. *The American Legal Profession and the Organizational Society, 1890–1930*. New York: Garland Publishing, 1986.

Hurst, James W. *The Growth of American Law: The Law Makers*. Boston: Little, Brown, 1950.

Hutchinson, Dennis. *The Man Who Once Was Whizzer White: A Portrait of Justice Byron R. White*. New York: Free Press, 1998.

In Memoriam, Honorable Charles Evans Whittaker. Proceedings of the Bar and Officers of the Supreme Court of the United States and Proceedings Before the Supreme Court of the United States. Washington, D.C., February 19, 1975.

Jackson, Percival E. *Dissent in the Supreme Court: A Chronology*. Norman: University of Oklahoma Press, 1969.

Jeffries, John C., Jr. *Justice Lewis F. Powell, Jr*. New York: Charles Scribner's Sons, 1994.

Johnson, John W. *American Legal Culture, 1908–1940*. Westport, Connecticut: Greenwood Press, 1981.

King, W. P., comp. *A Souvenir: The St. Joseph & Grand Island Railroad: Illustrated.* St. Joseph, Missouri: Lon Hardman Press, 1895.

Kornstein, Daniel J. *Thinking Under Fire: Great Courtroom Lawyers and Their Impact on American History.* New York: Dodd, Mead, 1987.

Kurland, Philip B. and Gerhard Casper, eds. *Landmark Briefs and Arguments of the Supreme Court of the United States: Constitutional Law.* Vol. 55. Arlington, Virginia: University Publications of America, 1975.

Larsen, Lawrence H. *Federal Justice in Western Missouri: The Judges, The Cases, The Times.* Columbia: University of Missouri Press, 1994.

_____. "Observations on One Hundred Years of Federal Judging in Western Missouri District Court." In *Law and the Great Plains: Essays on the Legal History of the Heartland,* edited by John R. Wunder, 137–50. Westport, Connecticut: Greenwood Press, 1996.

Leuchtenburg, William. *The Supreme Court Reborn: The Constitutional Revolution in the Age of Roosevelt.* New York: Oxford University Press, 1995.

Martindale-Hubbell Law Directory.

Mersky, Roy and J. Myron Jacobstein, eds. *The Supreme Court of the United States: Hearings and Reports on Successful and Unsuccessful Nominations of Supreme Court Justices by the Senate Judiciary Committee, 1916–1975.* Vol. 6. Austin: William S. Hein, 1977.

Miller, Richard L. *Whittaker: Struggles of a Supreme Court Justice.* Westport, Connecticut: Greenwood Press, 2002.

Murphy, Bruce Allen. *Wild Bill: The Legend and Life of William O. Douglas.* New York: Random House, 2003.

Murphy, Walter F. *Congress and the Court: A Case Study in the American Political Process.* Chicago: University of Chicago Press, 1962.

Murphy, Walter F. and C. Herman Pritchett. *Courts, Judges, & Politics: An Introduction to the Judicial Process.* New York: McGraw-Hill, 1986.

Newman, Roger K. *Hugo Black: A Biography.* New York: Pantheon Books, 1994.

O'Brien, David M. *Storm Center: The Supreme Court in American Politics.* New York: W.W. Norton, 1986.

Pound, Roscoe. *The Lawyer from Antiquity to Modern Times.* St. Paul: West Publishing, 1953.

Powe, Lucas A. *The Warren Court and American Politics.* Cambridge: Harvard University Press, 2000.

Powledge, Fred. *Free at Last? The Civil Rights Movement and the People Who Made It.* Boston: Little, Brown, 1991.

Prettyman, Barrett, Jr. *Death and the Supreme Court.* New York: Harcourt Brace & World, 1961.

Pritchett, C. Herman. *Congress Versus the Supreme Court, 1957–1960.* Minneapolis: University of Minnesota Press, 1961.

Reed, Alfred Z. *Training for the Public Profession of the Law: Historical Development and Principal Contemporary Problems of Legal Education in the United States.* New York: Carnegie Foundation for the Advancement of Teaching, 1921.

Rehnquist, William H. *The Supreme Court: How It Was, How It Is.* New York: William Morrow, 1987.

Rice, Arnold. *The Warren Court, 1953–1969.* Publications of the Supreme Court in American Life Series, ed. George J. Lankevich, no. 8. New York: Associated Faculty Press, 1987.

Richmond, Robert W. *Kansas: A Land of Contrasts.* 4th ed. Wheeling, Illinois: Harlan Davidson, 1999.

Schmidhauser, John, R. *The Supreme Court: Its Politics, Personalities, and Procedures.* New York: Holt, Rinehart and Winston, 1964.

Schwartz, Bernard. *A Book of Legal Lists: The Best and Worst in American Law.* New York: Oxford University Press, 1997.

_____. *A History of the Supreme Court.* New York: Oxford University Press, 1993.

_____. *Super Chief: Earl Warren and His Supreme Court—A Judicial Biography.* New York: New York University Press, 1983.

_____. *The Unpublished Opinions of the Warren Court.* New York: Oxford University Press, 1985.

Schwartz, Bernard and Stephen Lesher. *Inside the Warren Court.* New York: Doubleday, 1983.

Shenkman, Richard and Kurt Reiger. *One Night Stands with American History: Odd, Amusing, and Little-Known Incidents.* New York: William Morrow, 1980.

Silverstein, Mark. *Judicious Choices: The New Politics of Supreme Court Confirmations.* New York: W. W. Norton, 1994.

Simon, James F. *Independent Journey: The Life of William O. Douglas.* New York: Harper & Row, 1980.

Small, Melvin. *The Presidency of Richard Nixon.* Lawrence: University Press of Kansas, 1999.

Smith, Craig. "Charles Evans Whittaker, Associate Justice of the Supreme Court." M. A. thesis, University of Missouri-Kansas City, 1997.

Steamer, Robert J. *The Supreme Court in Crisis.* Boston: University of Massachusetts Press, 1971.

Stevens, Robert B. *Law School: Legal Education in America from the 1850s to the 1980s.* Chapel Hill: University of North Carolina Press, 1983.

Strong, Theron G. *Joseph H. Choate.* New York: Dodd, Mead, 1917.

Tribe, Laurence H. *God Save This Honorable Court: How the Choices of Supreme Court Justices Shapes Our History.* New York: Random House, 1985.

Tushnet, Mark, ed. *The Warren Court in Historical and Political Perspective.* Charlottesville: University Press of Virginia, 1993.

Urofsky, Melvin I. *The Warren Court: Justices, Ruling, and Legacy.* Denver: ABC-CLIO, 2001.

Urofsky, Melvin I., ed. *The Douglas Letters: Selections from the Private Papers of Justice William O. Douglas.* Bethesda, Maryland: Adler & Adler, 1987.

U.S. Senate Committee on the Judiciary. *Nomination of Charles E. Whittaker: Hearing before the Committee on the Judiciary.* 85th Cong., 1st sess., 18 March 1957.

Vestal, Theodore M. *The Eisenhower Court and Civil Liberties.* Westport, Connecticut: Praeger, 2002.

Warren, Earl. *The Memoirs of Earl Warren.* Garden City, New York: Doubleday, 1977.

Whittaker, Charles E. "An Appeal to Reason." In *Man and the Future,* edited by James E. Gunn, 85–108. Lawrence: University Press of Kansas, 1968.

_____. *Supreme Court of the United States: Opinions of Mr. Justice Whittaker.* 3 Vols. Washington, D.C.: Supreme Court, n.d.

Whittaker, Charles E. and William Sloane Coffin, Jr. *Law, Order and Civil Disobedience.* Washington, D.C.: American Enterprise Institute for Public Policy Research, 1967.

Whittaker, William A. *The Whittaker and Allied Families.* N.p., 1962.

Wiecek, William. *Liberty Under Law: The Supreme Court in American Life.* Baltimore: The Johns Hopkins University Press, 1988.

Woeste, Victoria S. "Charles Evans Whittaker." In *The Supreme Court Justices: A Biographical Dictionary,* edited by Melvin I. Urofsky, 533–34. New York: Garland Publishing, 1994.

Woodward, Bob and Scott Armstrong. *The Brethren: Inside the Supreme Court.* New York: Simon and Schuster, 1979.

Yalof, David Alistair. *Pursuit of Justices: Presidential Politics and the Selection of Supreme Court Nominees.* Chicago: The University of Chicago Press, 1999.
Yarbrough, Tinsley E. *John Marshall Harlan: Great Dissenter of the Warren Court.* New York: Oxford University Press, 1992.

Journal Articles

Atkinson, David N. "Minor Supreme Court Justices: Their Characteristics and Importance." *Florida State University Law Review* 3 (1975): 348–59.
_____. "Retirement and Death on the United States Supreme Court: From Van Devanter to Douglas." *University of Missouri Kansas-City Law Review* 45 (Fall 1976): 1–28.
Atkinson, David N. and Lawrence H. Larsen. "A Case Study in Federal Justice: Leading Bill of Rights Proceedings in the Western District of Missouri." *Creighton Law Review* 28 (April 1995): 595–610.
Ballantine, Henry Winthrop. "The Place in Legal Education of Evening and Correspondence Law Schools." *American Law School Review* 4 (February 1919): 369–78.
Berman, Daniel M. "Mr. Justice Whittaker: A Preliminary Appraisal." *Missouri Law Review* 24 (January 1959): 1–15.
Bickel, Alexander and Harry Wellington. "Legislative Purpose and the Judicial Process: The Lincoln Mills Case." *Harvard Law Review* 71 (1957): 1–39.
Blaustein, Albert and Roy Mersky. "Rating Supreme Court Justices." *American Bar Association Journal* 58 (November 1972): 1183–89.
Brennan, William J., Jr. "The Bill of Rights and the States." *New York University Law Review* 36 (April 1961): 762–78.
"Charles E. Whittaker, 1901–1973." *Journal of Missouri Bar* 30 (January-February 1974): 61–2.
"Charles Evans Whittaker," *Texas Law Review* 40 (June 1962): 742–750.
"Charles Evans Whittaker, In Memoriam, 1901–1973." *University of Missouri Kansas-City Law Review* 42 (fall 1973): ii–iii.
Chase, Harold W. "The Warren Court and Congress." *Minnesota Law Review* 44 (1960): 595–637.
Christensen, Barbara B. "Mr. Justice Whittaker: The Man on the Right." *Santa Clara Law Review* 19 (1979): 1039–61.
Clark, Tom C. "Internal Operation of the U.S. Supreme Court." *Journal of the American Judicature Society* 43 (1959): 45–51.
Douglas, William. "The Bill of Rights is Not Enough." *New York University Law Review* 38 (1963): 207–42.
Garrow, David J. "Mental Decrepitude on the U.S. Supreme Court: The Historical Case for a 28th Amendment." *The University of Chicago Law Review* 67 (2000): 995–1087.
Hart, Henry M., Jr. "Foreword: The Time Chart of the Justices." *Harvard Law Review* 73 (1959): 84–125.
"The Honorable Charles E. Whittaker Installed as United States District Judge." *Kansas City Bar Journal* 29 (September 1954): 8–9.
Kelliher, C. L. "Kansas City School of Law Honored by American Bar Association." *Kansas City Bar Bulletin* 13 (December 1936): 4–6.
Knipmeyer, Lowell L. "Charles E. Whittaker, Kansas City Bar Association Man-of-the-Year, 1962." *The Kansas City Bar Journal* 38 (April 1963): 13–15.
Kohn, Alan C. "Supreme Court Law Clerk, 1957–1958 A Reminiscence." *Journal of Supreme Court History* (1998): 40–52.

Langran, Robert W. "Why Are Some Supreme Court Justices Rated as 'Failures'?" *Yearbook Supreme Court Historical Society* (1985): 8–14.

Martin, Paul L. "Night Law Schools." *American Law School Review* 3 (Winter 1914): 454–56.

Menez, Joseph. "A Brief in Support of the Supreme Court." *Northwestern University Law Review* 54 (1959): 30–59.

Nagel, Stuart S. "Characteristics of Supreme Court Greatness." *American Bar Association Journal* 56 (October 1970): 957–59.

Pahl, Stephen D. "A Court Divided: An Analysis of Polorization on the United States Supreme Court in October 1957 Term." *Santa Clara Law Review* 19 (1979): 985–1003.

Powell, Elmer N. "The University of Kansas City School of Law." *Missouri Bar Journal* 14 (February 1943): 60, 79.

_____. "Kansas City School of Law Merger." *Missouri Bar Journal* 9 (December 1938): 281.

Powell, Lewis F. "A Lawyer Looks at Civil Disobedience." *Washington and Lee Law Review* 23 (1966): 205–31.

Prickett, Morgan. "Stanley Forman Reed: Perspectives on a Judicial Epitaph." *Hasings Constitutional Law Quarterly* 8 (1981): 343–69.

Reed, Alfred Z. "Raising Standards of Legal Education." *American Bar Association Journal* 7 (January 1921): 571–78.

_____. "Rising Bar Admission Requirements and Evening Law Students." *American Bar Association Journal* 15 (January 1929): 429–31.

_____. "Review of Legal Education in the United States and Canada for the Year 1928." *Annual Review of Legal Education* (1928).

_____. "Social Desirability of Evening or Part Time Law School." *American Law School Review* 7 (May 1931): 198–207.

Rogers, William P. "Judicial Appointments in the Eisenhower Administration." *Journal of the American Judicature Society* 41 (August 1957): 38–42.

Schwartz, Bernard. "Felix Frankfurter and Earl Warren: A Study of a Deteriorating Relationship." *Supreme Court Review* (1980): 115–42.

Smith, Steven. "Justices Stewart and Clark: Swing Votes on the Warren Court." *Santa Clara Law Review* 19 (1979): 1009–28.

Snyder, Orvill C. "The Function of the Night Law School." *American Law School Review* 7 (May 1933): 827–35.

_____. "The Problem of the Night Law School." *American Bar Association Journal* 20 (January 1934): 109–12.

Stevens, Joseph E. Jr. "Judge Stevens Honors Whittaker in Acceptance Speech." *Advance Sheet* 55 (June 1996): 3–4.

Volz, Marlin M. "Mr. Justice Whittaker." *Notre Dame Lawyer* 33 (March 1958): 159–79.

Wheeler, George C. "Report of the Committee on Academic Freedom and Tenure." *Bulletin of the American Association of University Professors* 43 (1957): 177–95.

Whittaker, Charles E. "Advocacy—Advance or Adieu?" *Kansas Law Review* 13 (1964): 233–45.

_____. "A Confusion of Tongues." *American Bar Association Journal* 51 (January 1965): 27–32.

_____. "The General Motors Dealer Relations Umpire Plan." *The Business Lawyer* 28 (January 1973): 623–26.

_____. "Immutable Moral Values." Supplement to *Texas Bar Journal* 27 (August 1964): 1–8.

_____. "Judicial Discretion." *Federal Bar News* 7 (December 1960): 367–71.

_____. "Law and Order." *New York State Bar Journal* 37 (October 1965): 397–404.

_____. "Lawyers, Laymen and Traffic Courts: Concerted Effort Needed for Improvement." *American Bar Association Journal* 49 (April 1963): 333–36.

_____. "Planned Mass Violations of Our Laws: The Causes, and the Effects Upon Public Order." *Vital Speeches of the Day* 33, no. 11 (1967): 322–28.

_____. "Reflections on Mr. Justice Brandeis." *Saint Louis University Law Journal* 11 (1966): 6–8.

_____. "The Role of the Supreme Court." *Arkansas Law Review* 17 (Fall 1963): 292–301.

_____. "Some Reminiscences." *American Bar Association Journal* 47 (November 1961): 1087–91.

_____. "Some Reminiscences." *Nebraska Law Review* 43 (December 1963): 352–62.

_____. "Tribute to Judge John B. Sanborn." *Minnesota Law Review* 44 (1959): 197– 99.

Winters, Glen R. "Shall We 'Curb' the Supreme Court?" *Journal of the American Judicature Society* 41 (August 1957): 35–6.

Wormser, I. Maurice. "The Problem of Evening Law Schools." *American Law School Review* 4 (November 1920): 544–47.

Magazine Articles

Blaustein, Albert and Roy Mersky. "The Twelve Great Justices of All Time." *Life*, October 15, 1971, 53–9.

"The Bright Young Men Behind the Bench." *U.S. News & World Report*, July 12, 1957, 45–48.

Byrnes, James F. "The Supreme Court Must Be Curbed." *U.S. News & World Report*, May 18, 1956, 50–8.

"Court Nominee Revealed." *Life*, March 11, 1957, 40.

"Everyone's in on Girard Act." *Life*, July 1, 1957, 30.

"Ex-Justice Severs Supreme Court Ties." *U.S. News & World Report*, November 1, 1965, 14.

"High Court: Its Growing Impact." *U.S. News & World Report*, June 29, 1964, 34–37.

"How Martin Luther King Won the Nobel Peace Prize." *U.S. News & World Report*, February 8, 1965, 76–77.

"How Supreme Court is Reshaping the Country." *U.S. News & World Report*, July 6, 1964, 31–33.

"Fortas: A Question of Ethics." *Life*, May 9, 1969, 32–37.

Lawrence, David. "The Big Change." *U.S. News & World Report*, March 30, 1964.

_____. "Bowing to the New Extremists." *U.S. News & World Report*, March 29, 1965.

_____. "The Only Hope." *U.S. News & World Report*, June 10, 1963.

_____. "Our Vanishing Constitution." *U.S. News & World Report*, July 20, 1964.

_____. "What's Become of 'Law and Order'?" *U.S. News & World Report*, August 5, 1963.

_____. "The Wrong Way." *U.S. News & World Report*, March 22, 1965.

"The New Justice." *Time*, March 11, 1957, 17.

Rehnquist, William. "Who Writes the Decisions of the Supreme Court?" *U.S. News & World Report*, December 13, 1957.

"Supreme Court Justices Disagree on What's Funny." *U.S. News & World Report*, December 28, 1959, 16–17.

"The Supreme Court: The Temple Builder." *Time*, July 1, 1957, 11–17.

Truffles: The Watson, Ess, Marshall and Enggas Newsletter (January-February, 1987).

"What Congress is Doing to Curb the Supreme Court." *U.S. News & World Report*, July 12, 1957, 50.

"What the Courts are Ordering States to Do." *U.S. News & World Report*, August 24, 1964, 40–41.

"When a Former Justice Speaks Out Against the Supreme Court." *U.S. News & World Report*, November 9, 1964, 21.

Whittaker, Charles E. "Can 'Integration' Be Forced by Federal Law?" *U.S. News & World Report*, March 23, 1964, 99–101.

_____. "Lawlessness in U.S.—Warning from a Top Jurist." *U.S. News & World Report*, July 5, 1965, 60–63.

_____. "A Former Justice Warns: Return to Law, or Face Anarchy." *U.S. News & World Report*, April 25, 1966, 58–62.

_____. "Planned Lawlessness Threatens to Get Out of Hand." *U.S. News & World Report*, September 19, 1966, 37–43.

"Why Supreme Court is Under Fire." *U.S. News & World Report*, June 27, 1958, 44–6.

Newspapers

Illustrated Doniphan County: 1837–1916. Supplement to the *Weekly (Troy) Kansas Chief,* April 6, 1916.

Kansas City Star
Kansas City Times
New York Times
St. Louis Post Dispatch
Topeka Journal
(Troy) Kansas Chief
Washington Post

Speeches

Whittaker, Charles E. "A Confusion of Tongues." Address presented at the Southern Regional Meeting of the American Bar Association, Atlanta, Georgia, October 23, 1964.

_____. "Federal Powers Under the Commerce Clause of the Constitution." Address presented at the Southern Regional Meeting of the American Bar Association, Atlanta, Georgia, October 23, 1964.

_____. "Law and Order." Address presented at the 84th Annual Convention of the Tennessee Bar Association, Nashville, Tennessee, June 17, 1965.

_____. "Some Common and Kindred Problems of the Medical and Legal Professions." Address presented to the American Medical Association and American Bar Association Medicolegal Symposium, Las Vegas, Nevada, March 12, 1965.

_____. "Statement of Charles Evans Whittaker." Paper presented to the Subcommittee on Separation of Powers of the Committee on the Judiciary of the United States Senate, Washington, D. C., October 1, 1969.

Archives

National Archives and Records Administration
Central Plains Region, Kansas City, Missouri

Record Group 21, Records of the United States District Courts
  Missouri, Western District—Criminal Cases
Record Group 118, Records of the United States Attorneys and Marshalls
  Missouri, Western District—Precedent Cases

Manuscript Collections

Clark, Tom C. Papers. Tarlton Law Library, Austin, Texas .
Clinton County Record of Deeds. Plattsburg, Missouri.
Doniphan County Record of Deeds. Troy, Kansas.
Kansas State Historical Society. Topeka, Kansas.
National Archives. Kansas City, Missouri.
University of Missouri-Kansas City Archives. Kansas City, Missouri.
Whittaker, Charles E. Papers. Kansas City, Missouri.

Case Index

Subject Index

district court 272–74; written opinions, Supreme Court 278–82
Whittaker, Gary (son) 91, 93, 96
Whittaker, John H. (grandfather) 5–6
Whittaker, Keith (son) 93, 220
Whittaker, Kent (son) 93
Whittaker (Pugh), Winifred (wife) 34–35, 91–95, 220, 224, 256, 261–62
Whittaker Award 76, 263, 283–84
Wiecek, William 241
Williams, Robert 252

Woeste, Victoria 2
Wolfson, Louis 256
Woodrough, Joseph 79
World War I 10, 22
World War II 6, 36, 117, 119, 122, 222, 238, 241, 253

Yalof, David 300n22
Young Men's Christian Association (YMCA) 14–15, 264, 287n31